I0031405

Allocation, Distribution, and Policy

Allocation, Distribution, and Policy

Notes, Problems, and Solutions in Microeconomics

SAMUEL BOWLES AND WEIKAI CHEN

Open Book Publishers in collaboration with the Santa Fe Institute

OpenBook Publishers

Santa Fe Institute

https://www.openbookpublishers.com

©2025 Samuel Bowles and Weikai Chen

This work is licensed under the Creative Commons Attribution-NonCommercial 4.0 International (CC BY-NC 4.0). This license allows you to share, copy, distribute and transmit the text; to adapt the text for non-commercial purposes of the text providing attribution is made to the authors (but not in any way that suggests that they endorse you or your use of the work). Attribution should include the following information:

Samuel Bowles and Weikai Chen, *Allocation, Distribution, and Policy: Notes, Problems, and Solutions in Microeconomics*. Cambridge, UK: Open Book Publishers, 2025, https://doi.org/10.11647/OBP.0466

Further details about Creative Commons licenses are available at
https://creativecommons.org/licenses/by-nc/4.0/

All external links were active at the time of publication unless otherwise stated and have been archived via the Internet Archive Wayback Machine at https://archive.org/web

Digital material and resources associated with this volume are available at
https://doi.org/10.11647/OBP.0466/resources

Information about any revised edition will be provided at https://doi.org/10.11647/OBP.0466

ISBN Paperback: 978-1-80511-622-6
ISBN PDF: 978-1-80511-623-3

DOI: https://doi.org/10.11647/OBP.0466

Cover image: of ancient rivers and lakes in Western Australia by Leah Kennedy (whose works can be found at leah@leahkennedyphotography.com.au), used with her kind permission.
Cover design: Jeevanjot Kaur Nagpal

Contents

Preface

Many people have contributed this project, including our students over the years: Bridget Diana, Suresh Naidu, Ceren Soylu, Katie Baird, Sung-Ha Hwang, Seung-yun Oh, Shih-Yen Pan, Meghana Prasad Nuthanapati, Jung-Kyoo Choi, Jesus Lara Jauregui, Nicolas Bohme Olivera, and Diogo Martins. Daniele Cassese and Max Greenberg read the entire manuscript, suggesting numerous improvements and new problems. Hong Xu prepared the index with care and attention to detail. Caroline Seigel of the Santa Fe Institute Library has provided invaluable support.

Wendy Carlin, Luka Crnjakovic, and Giacomo Piccoli of the CORE Econ project as well as the Electric Book Works team have given valuable advice. The economics programs at the University of Massachusetts and the University of Siena as well as the Santa Fe Institute have provided ideal scientific environments for the gestation of the ideas presented here. We are also grateful for the support of a generous grant on Emerging Political Economy from the Omidyar Network to the Santa Fe Institute.

Weikai Chen would like to express his gratitude to the School of Economics at Renmin University of China for their support, and to colleagues and mentors at Renmin whose advice and encouragement have been vital to his academic work. He is also grateful to the teachers who have guided him at various stages of his intellectual journey, including Zhang Junshan, Liu Fengyi, Chen Shu-Heng, Juang Wei-Torng, David Kotz, Peter Skott, Deepankar Basu, Naoki Yoshihara, Itai Sher, and many others. Warm thanks go to Qi Hao, Huang Biao, Liang Junshang, and Zhao Junfu for their enduring support. Finally, he is deeply grateful to Sam Bowles — not only for the collaboration on this book, but also for the inspiration he has drawn from Sam's teaching, generosity, and way of engaging with the world as a scholar and a teacher.

We welcome readers' assistance in improving the book; any errors or inconsistencies may be reported through the Errata and Feedback Sheet (https://tinyurl.com/3p27ye53), which will guide interim updates and future editions.

Samuel Bowles, Santa Fe Institute and CORE Econ
Weikai Chen, Renmin University of China
October 2025

Introduction: Doing Post-Walrasian Microeconomics | 1

In 1790 the English royalist Edmund Burke railed against those who had insulted the Queen of France and the French aristocrats who had failed to come to her defence: "[T]he age of chivalry is gone," he lamented, "that of Sophisters, economists, and calculators has succeeded." [37, p. 86] Economics students working on homework late at night have probably also cursed "economists and calculators" namely, their instructors, who assigned the problem sets. That would mean, us.

But we offer no apologies. Learning economics is not simply (or even mostly) about transferring information; it is about skill building, more like learning a language than like filling up a jug with knowledge. Our mantra about pedagogy is: "If you are not doing something you are not learning anything!" Solving problems is something you can do.

[37]: Burke (1955), 'Reflections on the Revolution in France'

1.1 "If you are not doing something, you are not learning anything"

The notes and problems on microeconomic theory that follow were developed in both PhD-level and advanced undergraduate courses at the University of Massachusetts in Amherst, the University of Siena, Bogazici University in Istanbul, and Sciences Po in Paris.

Learning by doing economics is the approach that one of us (SB) adopted as a new assistant professor in the late 1960s when assigned to co-teach the advanced micro-economic theory course in the PhD program at Harvard. We did not give a single lecture; we just asked questions to be discussed based on the readings and set problems to be solved [31]. It appears to have been the first time that problem sets — already routinely used in physics — were made a centerpiece of teaching economic theory.

Our objective in *Allocation, Distribution, and Policy* has been to design problems that illustrate important insights and intuitions about economics without being particularly demanding in terms of mathematics or computation. (This explains why we make such frequent use of simple easy-to-differentiate quasi-linear and quadratic functions.) The problems differ greatly in the level of difficulty: some are quite challenging, others are more like confidence-building warm-up exercises.

Some background for these problems is laid out in Bowles [14] and Bowles and Halliday [29]. At the beginning of each chapter that follows, we indicate the chapters in these two works that you may wish to consult. But most of the problems can be solved without reference to these works and also without reference to problems in other chapters of this book.

We have provided solutions to most of the problems, but you will learn a lot more if you work on the problem until you (and perhaps others who you are working with) get stuck. And then, rather than going to the answers we provide, it will be worth the extra time it takes in additional learning if you make brief presentations to others, give your proposed solutions to the problems (both the analytical logic and the

Figure 1.1: Léon Walras (1834–1910) was a French economist with a passion for social justice and mathematics. He advocated public ownership of land and cooperatives as a form of business organization. Notable among his contributions to economics was the refinement of the idea of marginal utility and the general equilibrium analysis of a multi-market economy. Along with Alfred Marshall, Walras is considered the founder of the "neoclassical school" of economics that in most countries was the predominant approach to microeconomics during the 20th century. Wikimedia Commons, public domain, https://commons.wikimedia.org/wiki/File:L%C3%A9on_Walras.jpg.

[31]: Bowles and Kendrick (1970), *Notes and Problems in Microeconomic Theory*
You may be interested in a similar book by John Harte [57] teaching ecology and environmental sciences through problem solving.

[57]: Harte (1988), *Consider a Spherical Cow*

[14]: Bowles (2004), *Microeconomics*

[29]: Bowles and Halliday (2022), *Microeconomics*

©2025 Samuel Bowles and Weikai Chen, CC BY-NC 4.0

https://doi.org/10.11647/OBP.0466.01

The Bowles and Halliday [29] book is available as a free pdf here. Closely related in approach is the free introductory-level course (with a calculus option) by the CORE Project titled *The Economy 2.0*, available as a free interactive e-text or a conventional book at www.core-econ.org. CORE Econ is a global team of economic researchers and teachers who create open-access economics courses and other free materials for learning economics.

The word of warning from [31] continued: "By viewing economic behavior broadly as part of a complex system of social relationships, theorists such as Schumpeter, Bohm-Bawerk, Marx and many of the classic writers have vastly enriched [economics]. But to capture the full contribution of any of these writers in a simply manipulated mathematical problem is virtually impossible."

Figure 1.2: John von Neumann (1903–1957) was a Hungarian-American mathematician, computer scientist, and physicist who is regarded as the father of game theory, which he hoped would allow us to better understand the anti-Semitism and fascist political upheavals that he had witnessed in the early 20th century and provide the basis for understanding how groups interact. Wikimedia Commons, public domain, https://commons.wikimedia.org/wiki/File:HD.3F.191_(11239892036).jpg

[14]: Bowles (2004), *Microeconomics*
[74]: Mas-Colell, Green, et al. (1995), *Microeconomic Theory*
[29]: Bowles and Halliday (2022), *Microeconomics*
[42]: CORE (2023), *The Economy 2.0*

Game theory

Game theory is a branch of applied mathematics that studies strategic interactions with important applications in economics, the other social sciences, biology, and computer science.

computations), and explain where you are having difficulty. We have not provided "answers" to a few of the more open ended questions (in the final chapter) that we have found work well for projects that groups of 2-3 students work on and present to an entire class.

In part thanks to the work of Léon Walras (along with Alfred Marshall and others who followed their lead), we are now able to express many important questions and some of the answers in mathematical terms. So learning how to do this through practice with problem sets is essential to doing economics.

An important part of doing economics (not just learning it) is developing the capacity to mathematically model the problems you have set for yourself, and learning how to manipulate these models to provide new insights and pose further questions. But there is much more to doing economics than solving problem sets, including learning econometric, experimental, computational, and other methods, studying society and its history so as to have a better sense of what are interesting questions, and being able to pose and evaluate arguments that cannot be adequately tested experimentally or expressed as mathematical propositions (or at least not yet).

A word of warning from the introduction to a book of problem sets based on the Harvard course is therefore worth repeating: the problem set method of teaching "itself tends to bias the choice of subject matter. By concentrating on solvable problems and confining ourselves to exercises which can be posed and solved mathematically we have diverted attention away from those areas in which there are no simple answers and where the present state of the theory does not admit precise mathematical formulation." [31, p. vi]

1.2 Post-Walrasian microeconomics: A new set of benchmark models

Reflecting the state of economic theory at the time, the problem sets introduced to Harvard PhD candidates in the late 1960s were focused on a rather limited skill: learning how the price-taking owners of firms or consumers could do constrained optimization in a variety of settings, all based on highly unrealistic institutional, technological, and behavioral assumptions. This brings us to *post-Walrasian microeconomics*.

This is the term we give to the main body of micro-economic theory that research economists today use and is taught to doctoral students [14, 74], and increasingly to undergraduates as well [29, 42]. Its central ideas are based on advances in economic theory made during the last century and continuing today, including the economics of limited and asymmetric information, strategic interaction and game theory, contract theory, behavioral economics, evolutionary dynamics, and mechanism design.

We treat the model of perfectly competitive equilibrium among price-taking economic actors pioneered by Walras as a special case of limited empirical applicability or pedagogical value. But the main difference between post-Walrasian and Walrasian (also termed "neoclassical") approaches is not about the degree of competition. It is about more fundamental questions, namely what the economy is and what we want to know about it: who are the actors? How do they interact with each other and with our natural environment? How do we characterize the economic outcomes that form the basis of our predictions? And what are the important questions that we strive to answer?

Table 1.1 presents our view of the contrasting "default settings" of the conventional Walrasian model and a post-Walrasian alternative. A comparison of these two benchmarks in greater detail is in Bowles and Carlin [18] and Bowles and Gintis [24].

Post-Walrasian economics can be thought of as a new set of default settings or benchmark models that shape the way an economist will frame problems and the assumptions about the way the world works that come naturally to a researcher or policy analyst. The Walrasian default settings make up a benchmark model that has constituted the primary content of the required courses for economics majors since the middle of the last century.

The Walrasian benchmark is found, for example, in the content of two second-year microeconomics textbooks written during the Second World War: George Stigler's *The Theory of Price*, and Abba Lerner's *The Economics of Control*, and in the subsequent intermediate microeconomics textbooks that dominated undergraduate instruction for the rest of the 20th century.

Over the same time period, the conceptual contributions that would make up the post-Walrasian benchmark emerged piecemeal and for very different reasons. John von Neumann wanted game theory to illuminate the hostilities that in the 1930s and '40s had riven his native Hungary and the rest of Europe. The models of credit and labor markets that do not clear in competitive equilibrium developed by Joseph Stiglitz, George Akerlof, and others were initially considered to be contributions to macroeconomics — providing some missing pieces in the Keynesian model — rather than building blocks for a new benchmark in microeconomics.

Friedrich Hayek's contribution to the post-Walrasian benchmark — his observation that information is incomplete and local [58] — is now the foundation of modern contract theory, explaining why complete contracts are an exception rather than the rule. But it originated as the key point in Hayek's critique of centralized planning, at the time being practiced (with considerable success) in the Soviet Union.

In a few cases we provide what we call M-Notes, that look like this, to clarify the mathematical reasoning or derivation in the main text. With very few exceptions, the methods required to work these problems will be familiar to anyone who has fulfilled the mathematics requirements for a typical undergraduate economics major.

[18]: Bowles and Carlin (2020), 'What Students Learn in Economics 101'
[24]: Bowles and Gintis (2000), 'Walrasian Economics In Retrospect'

The fact that Lerner, a democratic socialist, and Stigler, a leading figure in the famously conservative University of Chicago Department of Economics, could agree on the microeconomic theory that most undergraduates should know suggests the dominance of the Walrasian benchmark.

[58]: Hayek (1945), 'The Use of Knowledge in Society'

Figure 1.3: Friedrich Hayek (1899–1992) was an Austrian-born philosopher and economist. Hayek was a critic of the centrally planned economy and an advocate of limited government. But he had little time for the models of perfectly competitive equilibrium often deployed in opposition to government interventions in the economy. He won a Nobel Prize in economics for his work demonstrating (in the words of the prize committee) "how prices as such are the carriers of essential information on cost and demand conditions, how the price system is a mechanism for communication of [. . .] information." Source: PA Images via Alamy.

Table 1.1: Benchmark representations of the economy: Walrasian and post-Walrasian microeconomics

Subject	Walrasian benchmark	A post-Walrasian benchmark
People...	... resemble *Homo economicus*, who is far-sighted and self-interested.	... are also cognitively limited and have social preferences and norms of fairness, reciprocity and "us" versus "them".
Social interactions...	... are, for the most part, limited to buying and selling as price takers.	... also include price-making and non-market strategic interactions, including collective action.
Information...	... is complete and verifiable.	... is often incomplete, asymmetric, and non-verifiable.
Contracts...	... are complete and enforceable at zero cost to the exchanging parties.	... are incomplete in labor, credit and other markets; there are also missing markets (traffic congestion, knowledge).
Institutions...	... include markets, private property, and government, and are exogenous.	... are modeled generically as "rules of the game," including informal rules (norms), and are endogenous.
Technology...	... is exogenous, with constant or decreasing returns.	... is also endogenous with constant or increasing returns.
Competition...	... is mostly "perfect" among price-taking agents.	... is typically monopolistic or monopsonistic among price-making firms, often with winner-take-all outcomes.
Heterogeneity among actors...	... is due to differences in preferences and budget constraints among buyers and sellers.	... also includes asymmetric positions, e.g. as employers or employees, lenders or borrowers.
Power...	... is exercised in non-competitive markets and by government; exogenous.	... includes also a principal's power over an agent in labor, credit, and other markets; endogenous.
Economic rents...	... are inefficient and originate in mistaken public policy or limited competition.	... also create incentives to innovate, to work hard, to use borrowed funds prudently and to equilibrate markets.
Stability...	It is typically assumed that we will observe a unique stable equilibrium.	Stability and instability (along with tipping points between multiple equilibria) are both characteristics of the economy and our relationship with the biosphere.
Policy...	... is directed by a Pigou-Marshall-style beneficent, impartial social planner to correct market failures.	... also includes systemic state failures due to information limitations on policy design and implementation and rent-seeking by states' elites.
Evaluation...	... is confined to the presence of unexploited mutual gains (Pareto-inefficiency).	... also includes procedural and substantive fairness, as well as environmental sustainability.
20th-century provenance...	Marshall, Walras...	... also Hayek, Robinson, Nash, von Neumann, Schumpeter, Coase, Ostrom.

1.3 What should economics be *about*?

We have provided this set of problems based on the post-Walrasian benchmark (rather than the Walrasian one) because we think that the new approach provides a more adequate theoretical framework for posing and addressing some of the key societal challenges today, especially the problems of unjust inequality and climate change.

We are not atypical in thinking that learning tools to better understand these challenges should be a top priority for those learning economics. The CORE Team posed the following question to students around the world on the first day of their introductory classes: "What is the most pressing problem economists today should be addressing?" The results from a total of 12,261 students from 67 universities in 25 countries over the years 2016–2023 are summarized in the word cloud in Figure 1.4.

Figure 1.4: **Student replies (2016–2023) to the question "What is the most pressing problem economists should be addressing?"** Image by the CORE Team. The size of the font in the figure is proportional to the frequency with which subjects mentioned the word or term. The students responding are from Australia, Canada, Chile, China, Colombia, France, Germany, Hong Kong, India, Indonesia, Italy, Mexico, Netherlands, New Zealand, Pakistan, Peru, the Philippines, Portugal, Reunion Island, South Africa, Spain, Switzerland, Turkey, the United Kingdom, and the United States. The less frequently mentioned — smaller font — topics are more readable in the individual word clouds from each of the samples of students that you can access at https://tinyco.re/6235473.

As expected, "COVID-19" was big during 2020–2022, as was "inflation" in the years following. But the themes are remarkably consistent across countries and over time. Unemployment and inflation, important topics in most macroeconomics courses, are on the minds of students. But "inequality" (along with "poverty") is the overwhelmingly dominant issue, with environmental problems ("climate change," "sustainability," and "environment") a close second.

The microeconomic theory that you will learn how to use by solving the problems in this book has a lot to say about these issues. Included are tried-and-true workhorse concepts that you may have already encountered, such as opportunity costs, mutual gains from exchange, constrained optimization, and trade-offs. Also essential in understanding issues like those in the word cloud, however, are concepts that have more recently risen to prominence in economics but are given less attention in economics courses, especially at the undergraduate level.

Examples include: modeling institutions as a set of "rules of the game"; the importance of cooperation as well as competition; social motivations in addition to individualistic self-interest; incomplete contracts and markets that do not clear in competitive equilibrium; price setting (not just price taking) and other strategic aspects of interactions among economic actors; settings in which positive feedbacks (due for example

Complete contract

A contract is complete if it (a) covers all of the aspects of the exchange in which anyone affected by the exchange has an interest, and (b) is enforceable (by the courts) at close to zero cost to the parties.

Institutions

Institutions are the laws, informal rules, and mutual expectations which regulate social interactions among people and between people and the biosphere.

to strategic complementarities) lead to a multiplicity of path-dependent equilibria, so that history matters; and conflicts over the distribution of mutual gains from exchange, including the exercise of power by private economic actors (employers over workers, for example).

1.4 By necessity, post-Walrasian microeconomics is dynamic, multi-disciplinary, and pluralist

As these examples suggest, post-Walrasian microeconomics by necessity goes beyond the usual comparative static analysis and draws upon the insights of many scholarly disciplines beyond economics and upon ideas from many schools of thought. The societal problems motivating the new approach — suggested by Figure 1.4 — are part of the reason for this. But the new conceptual content, itself, requires a broader and more dynamic approach.

Here is an example. If positive feedbacks are common, then there will often be a multiplicity of path-dependent equilibria, some of them unstable, so that predicting outcomes or designing public policy will require an assessment of which of the equilibria is most likely to be observed. This is termed equilibrium selection, often accomplished by means of explicit analysis of out-of-equilibrium dynamics, history, or computational methods.

Here is another example. The post-Walrasian model of the firm and the labor market start from the observation that employer and employee have conflicting interests about the workers' level of effort on the job. The idea that the labor contract cannot ensure that the employee works hard is a common illustration of the modern microeconomics of incomplete contracts. But its provenance is Karl Marx, not Walras or Marshall.

The reason why the labor contract is incomplete is that information is both local and scarce, the cornerstone of the economics of Friedrich Hayek, although subsequently developed in very different ways by contributions to principal-agent modeling over the past three decades. The employer cannot possibly have the information needed to legally enforce the many dimensions of work effort.

We then learn from Ronald Coase that "the distinguishing mark of the firm is the suppression of the price mechanism" in favor of a system of authority in which the worker, "for a certain remuneration agrees to obey the directions of the entrepreneur." This, too, sounds more like Marx than the University of Chicago where Coase taught.

Wages and the amount of work done thus are determined in part by the exercise of power by the employer and the work ethic or other social norms that affect employees' willingness to work hard, not simply by market competition. The importance of social norms and the exercise of power by employers over their employees [43] make sociology, psychology, political science, and law all integral to understanding how the firm and the labor market work. Moving on to modeling these processes, we find that Herbert Simon — an economist and computer scientist whose degree was in political science — provided the first mathematical model of this process in the middle of the last century [91].

Economic analysis of what are termed complex systems and spontaneous order shares many features with the post-Walrasian approach used here, including multiple equilibria, attention to dynamics, and interdisciplinarity. Herbert Simon defined a complex system as "made up of a large number of parts that interact in a non-simple way. In such systems, the whole is more than the sum of the parts [...] given the properties of the parts and the laws of their interactions, it is not a trivial matter to infer the properties of the whole." [92, pp. 183–184] The earliest example in economics is Adam Smith's surprising claim that under the right rules of the game, interactions of entirely self-interested individuals might by means of "an invisible hand" result in a socially beneficial allocation of society's resources. On complex systems and spontaneous order in economics, see for example, Arthur [4], Kirman [68], Miller [77], and Sugden [100].

[92]: Simon (1996), *The Sciences of the Artificial*

[4]: Arthur (1999), 'Complexity and the Economy'
[68]: Kirman (2010), *Complex Economics*
[77]: Miller (2016), *A Crude Look at the Whole*
[100]: Sugden (1989), 'Spontaneous Order'

[43]: Dahl (1977), 'On Removing Certain Impediments to Democracy in the United States'

[91]: Simon (1951), 'A Formal Theory of the Employment Relationship'

Pluralism is therefore not just an option but a necessity in the new benchmark model. Imagine that, instead of the above model based on incomplete contracts, the labor market and the firm were represented as in the standard supply and demand market-clearing model. The firm is supposed to purchase labor (that is, work) from the worker in a transaction with a complete contract no different from the firm's purchase of kilowatt-hours of electricity or any other input. The implications are profound. There would be no unemployment in the equilibrium of the labor market, no conflicts of interest over work, no exercise of power by the employer, and no role for social norms to play.

Similar reasoning applies to the entire economy: if the benchmark model is based on a selfish economic man in a world of complete information, complete contracts, and clearing markets, then pluralism seems a distraction. The conventional benchmark thus depicts a world in which key ideas of Coase, Hayek, Marx, Simon, and Schumpeter would be of little value.

Because we think that the ideas of these economists provide essential insights for understanding the economy of today and the future, in the pages that follow we consider models based on the view of the economy and people as economic actors in the second "post-Walrasian" column of the above table.

Strategic Interactions | 2

Because economics is about social interactions and how these are governed by institutions, we begin with some exercises on game theory rather than (as is conventional in microeconomics) with isolated individuals and their preferences. Most of the interactions making up the economy involve strategic behavior: the actors recognize that the benefits and costs that they will experience depend on their own actions and how others respond to their actions.

To capture this "mutual dependence recognized" aspect of our relationships with others, we represent interactions as games, and the institutions governing our interactions as the rules of the game. When we study the evolution of institutions (in Chapter 14), we also represent institutions as equilibria of some underlying game that governs how the rules may change.

In this and later chapters we often use two-person games to represent interactions in a larger society that are non-cooperative, meaning that the players do not have the option of agreeing on a common course of action. It seems counter-intuitive to represent a two-person game as non-cooperative. David Hume, the 18th-century English philosopher-economist, justified his own use of two-person examples of non cooperative action as follows: "Two neighbors may agree to drain a meadow which they possess in common... but 'tis very difficult and indeed impossible that a thousand persons shou'd agree to such an action." [63, p. 304] Keep in mind that our 2 × 2 non-cooperative games are meant to represent much larger numbers of people who, as Hume says, often cannot find ways to jointly commit to a common strategy.

In the sections that follow, we first introduce a variety of games to underline the diversity of institutions governing our interactions, hoping that this will plant in your mind the question: why are they playing this particular game rather than some other, and how might they change the structure of the game they are playing? We then introduce a game (Plant or Steal) demonstrating how conflicts of interest that are resolved non-cooperatively often result in Pareto-inefficient outcomes, then an employer monitoring a worker's level of on the job effort (a rare example of a situation in which a mixed strategy equilibrium might have some empirical relevance), then a game illustrating the limitations of the Nash equilibrium concept ("too individualistic"), and finally a game suggesting the versatility of the Nash equilibrium concept by showing its application to a question concerning residential segregation.

Some background for the problems in this chapter is found in Chapter 1 of Bowles [14], and Chapters 1 and 4 of Bowles and Halliday [29].

Figure 2.1: John F. Nash (1928–2015) was an American mathematician who contributed to the theory of bargaining and to the concept of equilibrium that bears his name. He won the Nobel Prize in Economics in 1994. His life was documented in the book and movie *A Beautiful Mind*. Wikimedia Commons, CC BY-SA 3.0, https://commons. wikimedia.org/wiki/File:John_Forbes_Nash,_Jr._by_Peter_Badge.jpg

[63]: Hume (1964), *The Philosophical Works*

Non-cooperative game

A non-cooperative game is a strategic interaction in which the players' choice of a strategy is not subject to a binding (enforceable) agreement.

[14]: Bowles (2004), *Microeconomics*

[29]: Bowles and Halliday (2022), *Microeconomics*

©2025 Samuel Bowles and Weikai Chen, CC BY-NC 4.0

2.1 The language of game theory

1. Suppose Table 2.1 is the payoff matrix for the row player in a two-person symmetrical non-cooperative game. Indicate the restrictions on the values of the payoffs a, b, c, and d which are necessary and sufficient in each case for the game to be properly defined as a Hawk Dove Game, an Assurance Game, and a Prisoners' Dilemma Game.

2. North and South are selecting environmental policies. The well-being of each is interdependent, in part due to global environmental effects. Each has a choice of two strategies: Emit or Restrict Emissions. Suppose this is just a two-person game. It may clarify things to let the representative citizen in each region have a reduced form utility function $u^i = u^i(e^i, e^j)$, where e is the level of emissions (0 or 1) and the superscripts i and j refer to North and South. (It is a reduced form because the citizens' well-being is proximately affected not by emissions per se but by the things with which emissions are associated positively, such as consumption, or negatively, such as health status.) Some have modeled this problem as a Prisoners' Dilemma, while others have proposed the Assurance Game or even the Chicken (Hawk Dove) Game [101]. Illustrate each of these possibilities with a payoff matrix.

Suppose North's utility function has the form

$$u^i = \alpha e^i + \beta e^j + \gamma e^j e^i \tag{2.1}$$

and South's is identical (with appropriate substitution of superscripts). What values of the parameters of these utility functions would make each of these three games the appropriate model of the North-South Emissions Game? (Be sure you could explain the reasoning — from economics, politics, climate science — that would motivate the three sets of parameters.)

Strategy sets

A list for each player of every course of action available to them at each point where they must make a choice (including actions that depend on the actions taken by other players, or on chance events). The strategies selected by each of the players — the outcome of the game — is called the strategy profile.

Hawk Dove Game

In a 2×2 Hawk Dove Game neither Hawk nor Dove is a best response to itself and the two asymmetrical strategy profiles are Nash equilibria in which the Hawk player's payoffs exceed the Dove's.

[101]: Taylor (1987), *The Possibility of Cooperation*

Prisoner's Dilemma Game

A Prisoners' Dilemma is a 2×2 social interaction in which there is a unique Nash equilibrium (that is also a dominant strategy equilibrium), but there is another outcome that gives a higher payoff to both players (and also a higher total sum of payoffs than any other outcome), so that the Nash equilibrium is not Pareto-efficient.

Assurance Game

An Assurance Game is a 2-person, symmetric, strategic interaction with two strict Nash equilibria, one of which is Pareto-superior to the other.

Table 2.1: Payoffs in the symmetrical games. Symmetrical Hawk Dove Game, Assurance Game, and the Prisoners' Dilemma Game (row player's payoff)

Answers.

1. a) Hawk Dove Game, when $a > b > d > c$. Note that we usually assume $c < 0$ in the Hawk Dove Game.

   b) Assurance Game, when $b > a$, $b > c > d$.

   c) Prisoner's Dilemma, when $a > b > c > d$. Note that we may also require that $2b > a + d$ so that mutual cooperation maximizes total payoffs in order to exclude the case (in a repeated Prisoners' Dilemma) that playing Cooperate and Defect alternatively (with average payoffs $(a + d)/2$) is better than both playing Cooperate.

	Cooperate (Dove)	Defect (Hawk)
Cooperate (Dove)	b	d
Defect (Hawk)	a	c

2. By the utility function (2.1), we have the payoff matrix as shown in Table 2.2. Then we have:

	Emit	Restrict
Emit	$\alpha + \beta + \gamma$	α
Restrict	β	0

Table 2.2: The Environmental Policies Game: Row player's payoffs

a) Prisoner's Dilemma, when $\alpha > 0 > \alpha + \beta + \gamma > \beta$ and $\alpha + \beta < 0$.

b) Assurance Game, when $\beta < \alpha < \alpha + \beta + \gamma < 0$.

c) Chicken (Hawk Dove) Game, when $\alpha > 0 > \beta > \alpha + \beta + \gamma$.

2.2 Risk dominance in the Plant or Steal Game

The question — plant or steal? — is more than a game. "The balance between [...][two] modes of economic activity — the one leading to greater aggregate wealth, the other to conflict over who gets the wealth — provides the main story line of human history." This is how Jack Hirshleifer posed the problem in his Presidential Address to the Western Economic Association [61].

Here is the Plant or Steal Game. Two farmers may adopt one of two strategies, planting a crop (Plant) or not planting and attempting to steal the other's crop at harvest time (Steal). Consider the non-cooperative game described by this payoff matrix, Table 2.3, where the first entry in each cell denotes the row player's payoff and the second entry the column player's payoff.

Best response

A strategy is a player's best response (also termed best reply) to the strategies adopted by others if no other strategy available would result in higher expected payoffs. A weak best response is a strategy for which there exists at least one other strategy with equal payoffs (so it is not a strict best response).

[61]: Hirshleifer (1994), 'The Dark Side of the Force'

	Plant	Steal
Plant	$1, 1$	$-1, 0.5$
Steal	$0.5, -1$	$0, 0$

Table 2.3: Non-cooperative Plant or Steal Game

1. Suppose you were the row player and that you assign some probability, p, to the likelihood that the column player will play Plant (and so you believe they will play Steal with probability $1 - p$). What is the minimum value of p that would induce you to plant?

2. Do the players have a *risk-dominant strategy*?

3. Which (if either) of the equilibria is risk dominant?

Nash equilibrium

A Nash equilibrium is a profile of strategies — one strategy for each player — each of which is a best response to the strategies of the other players.

Risk-dominant strategy

The risk-dominant strategy in a 2×2 game is the strategy that would maximize the player's expected payoffs if the other's strategy choices were equally likely.

Figure 2.2: Risk dominant equilibrium. $\pi_p(p)$ and $\pi_s(p)$ are the expected payoffs of playing plant and steal, respectively. From
$$\pi_p(p) = \pi_s(p),$$
we have $p^* = 2/3$. To find the risk-dominant equilibrium, we assume that the other player will randomize their choice with equal probabilities, i.e., $p = 1/2 < p^*$. Since
$$0 = \pi_p(1/2) < \pi_s(1/2) = \frac{1}{4},$$
Steal is the risk-dominant strategy. Therefore, (Steal, Steal) is a risk-dominant equilibrium.

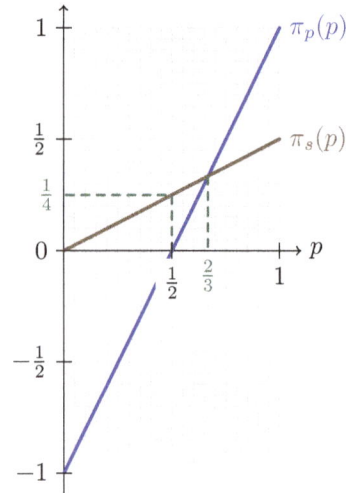

Answers.

1. For the row player, the expected utility of playing Plant is

$$\pi_P(p) = p - (1 - p) = 2p - 1,$$

and that of playing Steal is

$$\pi_S(p) = \frac{p}{2}.$$

Dominant strategy

A strategy is dominant if it yields the highest payoff for a player for any strategy chosen by the other players. Weak dominance refers to the case where there are one or more other strategies yielding the same payoff.

The row player would Plant if and only if

$$\pi_P(p) \geq \pi_S(p) \Rightarrow 2p - 1 \geq \frac{p}{2} \Rightarrow p \geq \frac{2}{3}.$$

Thus, the minimum value of p that would induce you to plant is $2/3$.

2. Steal is risk dominant for both players.

3. And so (Steal, Steal) is a risk-dominant equilibrium, as shown in Figure 2.2.

2.3 Monitoring, working, and mixed strategies

Empirical examples of mixed strategies are not very common, but randomizing one's actions — that is, adopting a mixed strategy — often makes sense in situations in which one party is monitoring the work effort, legal compliance, emissions reductions, or arms limitations of another.

Mixed-strategy Nash equilibrium

A mixed strategy is a probability distribution over the set of actions. A mixed-strategy Nash equilibrium is a mixed-strategy action profile in which all players maximize their expected payoff given others' mixed strategy.

Here is an example. An employer agrees to pay a wage, w, to a worker who may then either Not Work (at no cost to the worker) or Work, expending a subjective cost of effort, e, with the payment of the wage being conditional on whether the worker has been detected as Not Working (Table 2.4). The employer can determine if the worker Worked by paying an inspection cost of c and can decide whether to Monitor (that is, inspect) or Not Monitor. If the worker Works, the employer gets revenue y, and the payoff to the employer is $y - w - c$ if the employer chooses to Monitor; otherwise it is $y - w$. Suppose the worker randomizes their actions, choosing the mixed strategy: Not Work with probability σ, otherwise Work. Likewise suppose the employer chooses the strategy Monitor with probability μ, otherwise, Not Monitor. The mixed-strategy Nash equilibrium is a pair (σ^*, μ^*) such that neither employer nor worker could gain higher expected payoffs by adopting a different strategy.

Worker	Employer	
	Monitor	Not Monitor
Not Work	$0, -c$	$w, -w$
Work	$w - e, y - w - c$	$w - e, y - w$

Table 2.4: Payoffs in the Monitor and Work Game

1. Show that the mixed-strategy Nash equilibrium for this game is $\sigma^* = c/w$ and $\mu^* = e/w$.

2. Explain why the equilibrium probability of Not Working varies inversely with the wage and why the equilibrium probability of Monitoring varies with the subjective cost of effort.

Strict Nash equilibrium

A Nash equilibrium is strict if a player deviating from it would have strictly lower payoffs, thereby excluding a weak mutual best response as a non-strict Nash equilibrium.

3. Show that (σ^*, μ^*) cannot be a strict Nash equilibrium. Show that the worker would do equally well by adopting any strategy, that is, choosing σ over $[0, 1]$, as long as the employer played the Nash equilibrium mixed strategy, and that the analogous statement is true of the employer.

Answers.

1. For the worker, the expected payoffs are

$$E[\text{Not Work}|\mu] = 0 + w(1 - \mu) = w(1 - \mu)$$
$$E[\text{Work}|\mu] = (w - e)\mu + (w - e)(1 - \mu) = w - e$$

When $\mu < e/w$, the expected payoff of Not Working is greater than that of Working and the worker will choose to Not Work for sure, that is $\sigma = 1$. Similar logic applies to other cases and we have the best response of the worker

$$\sigma(\mu) = \begin{cases} 1 & \mu < e/w \\ [0, 1] & \mu = e/w \\ 0 & \mu > e/w \end{cases}$$

The top inequality can be rewritten $\mu w < e$, meaning that the expected cost of Not Working (the probability that the worker will be Monitored (μ) times the wage (w) they will lose if Monitored while Not Working) is less than the cost of Working, e. Similarly, we have

$$E[\text{Monitor}|\sigma] = (-c)\sigma + (y - w - c)(1 - \sigma)$$
$$E[\text{Not Monitor}|\sigma] = -w\sigma + (y - w)(1 - \sigma)$$

and so the best response of the employer is

$$\mu(\sigma) = \begin{cases} 1 & \sigma > \frac{c}{w} \\ [0, 1] & \sigma = \frac{c}{w} \\ 0 & \sigma < \frac{c}{w} \end{cases}$$

Similar to the worker's best response, the top equation (here rewritten as $\sigma w > c$) says the employer should Monitor if the expected gain (not having to pay the wage if the Monitored worker is Not Working) exceeds c the cost of Monitoring. At equilibrium (σ^*, μ^*), we should have $\sigma^* = \sigma(\mu^*)$ and $\mu^* = \mu(\sigma^*)$. Thus, $\sigma^* = c/w$ and $\mu^* = e/w$. (See Figure 2.3)

2. Higher wages lead to increased Monitoring by the employer (the payoff to Monitoring — not having to pay the wage if the worker is not working — is greater). This, in turn, decreases the likelihood of the worker choosing to Not Work. On the other hand, if the subjective cost of effort increases for the worker, the likelihood of Not Working increases, prompting the employer to Monitor the worker more frequently.

3. The pair (σ^*, μ^*) is a strict Nash equilibrium if and only if, for any (σ, μ) such that $\sigma \in [0, 1]$, $\mu \in [0, 1]$, $\sigma \neq \sigma^*$, and $\mu \neq \mu^*$, we have

$$E_w(\sigma, \mu^*) < E_w(\sigma^*, \mu^*)$$

and

$$E_e(\sigma^*, \mu) < E_e(\sigma^*, \mu^*)$$

where E_w and E_e are the expected payoff of the worker and the employer respectively.

Since $E[\text{Not Work}|\mu^*] = E[\text{Work}|\mu^*]$ for the worker for any $\sigma \in [0, 1]$,

$$\begin{aligned} E_w(\sigma, \mu^*) &= \sigma E[\text{Not Work}|\mu^*] + (1 - \sigma)E[\text{Work}|\mu^*] \\ &= \sigma^* E[\text{Not Work}|\mu^*] + (1 - \sigma^*)E[\text{Work}|\mu^*] \\ &= E_w(\sigma^*, \mu^*) \end{aligned}$$

Therefore, σ^* is only a weak best response by the worker to the employer's μ^*, and similar reasoning shows the μ^* is a weak best response by the employer to the worker's σ^*, so (σ^*, μ^*) is not a strict Nash equilibrium (Figure 2.3).

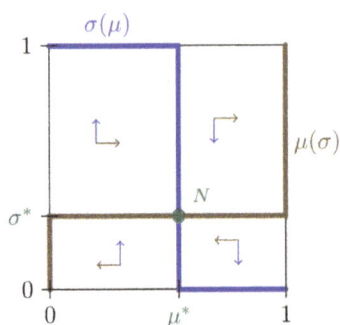

Figure 2.3: Mixed strategy Nash equilibrium. The colored step functions, $\sigma(\mu)$ and $\mu(\sigma)$ are the best response functions of the worker and the employer, respectively. The arrows indicate the direction of change based on the best response of the worker and employer for each of the regions in the set of joint strategies. The Nash equilibrium is the intersection of the best response functions, i.e, (μ^*, σ^*) where

$$\mu^* = \frac{e}{w}, \sigma^* = \frac{c}{w}$$

At equilibrium, the employer's response $\mu(\sigma^*)$ is a horizontal line, and the worker's best response $\sigma(\mu^*)$ is a vertical line. Therefore, the Nash equilibrium is not *strict*.

In general, one could show that strict Nash equilibria only exist in pure strategies by the same reasoning.

2.4 Nash's "American Way," collective action, and alternative equilibrium concepts

It seemed to von Neumann that as a solution concept Nash's equilibrium was "too individualistic" as it considers only the potential gains that are to be had by deviating from a strategy profile singly, ignoring the possibility that more than one individual might deviate collectively (for example when workers of a given employer jointly go on strike). When von Neumann shared this criticism with Nash, he responded that "it's the American way." [1]

1: We have this from Martin Shubik (1926-2016), who was a student of von Neumann's coauthor and friend, Oskar Morgenstern.

But if deviations by more than one individual are possible, why not everyone at once (and then we would have a cooperative game, and Pareto-inferior equilibria would be impossible)? Or why not some set of feasible deviations from a status quo strategy profile intermediate between the fully cooperative game and Nash's "American way" in which only solo deviations are considered in defining equilibrium?

If we know the social relationships among the individuals then we may be able to say plausibly who might have the capacity to act collectively to disrupt a status quo strategy profile. For example, the individuals making up a family might find it easy to coordinate a deviation, or members of trade union who are brought together daily in their employment. Network theory and data can help us answer this question [64, 67].

[64]: Jackson (2008), *Social and Economic Networks*
[67]: Kets, Iyengar, et al. (2011), 'Inequality and Network Structure'

To see how a network of these relationships might help determine if a particular strategy profile is an equilibrium, let's consider the social network represented by what is termed an adjacency matrix

$$G = \begin{bmatrix} 0 & 1 & 0 & 0 & 0 \\ 1 & 0 & 1 & 0 & 0 \\ 0 & 1 & 0 & 1 & 1 \\ 0 & 0 & 1 & 0 & 1 \\ 0 & 0 & 1 & 1 & 0 \end{bmatrix}$$

The matrix G describes the social relationships among 5 people (called nodes of the network) where the entries $g_{ij} = 1$ if individual i and j are connected by an edge and $g_{ij} = 0$ otherwise.

Degree

The degree of a node is the number of edges that are connected to that node.

The degree of a node i can be computed summing the i-th row of the adjacency matrix.

1. Draw the social network represented by G, with an edge depicted as a line between the points representing the nodes.

Now consider the following game called Planting in Palanpur, described in Bowles [14], based on a village in India. The coordination problem faced by the villagers, they explained to a visitor (SB), is that their crops would grow better if they all planted earlier, but if just one or a few were to shift to planting early, birds would concentrate on the few first-planted fields and eat all of the seeds [60, 69].

Figure 2.4: Palanpur farmers threshing and winnowing grain (separating grain from chaff). Photo courtesy of Nicholas Stern.

A related problem of collective action on social networks is presented in Section 13.3.

[60]: Himanshu, Lanjouw, and Stern (2018), *How Lives Change*
[69]: Lanjouw and Stern (1998), *Economic Development in Palanpur over Five Decades*

The players' social relationships are represented by G and each player has two strategies, Plant Early (E) and Plant Late (L). Suppose that the payoffs to adopting strategy $s_i \in \{E, L\}$ depend on how many others are planting early. So, where n_i is the number of *others* adopting E, the payoffs of each strategy are given by

$$u_i(s_i, n_i) = \begin{cases} 2 + 0.25n_i & s_i = L \\ n_i & s_i = E \end{cases} \qquad (2.2)$$

Note that payoffs are independent of the structure of the network — they depend only on how many others are planting early or late.

2. Identify any pure strategy Nash equilibria of this game.

Now define an *m*-equilibrium as a strategy profile such that no person can do better by deviating (that is, adopting a different strategy), when the individuals making up a feasible deviation group must be all within distance *m* between each other. That is, players can deviate together as a group composed of nodes in the network as long as there are at most *m* edges between each two of them. This definition includes Nash equilibria as a special case with $m = 0$.

3. Is all planting late a 1-equilibrium of the game? Explain your reasoning.

4. What is the least value of *m* such that all planting early is the unique *m*-equilibrium of this game?

5. Denote the set of *m*-equilibria by $\mathcal{N}(m)$. What is the relationship between the two sets $\mathcal{N}(m)$ and $\mathcal{N}(m - 1)$ in general? Is $\mathcal{N}(m)$ a subset of $\mathcal{N}(m - 1)$? Explain your reasoning.

Answers.

1. The social network represented by G is shown in Figure 2.5.

2. Denote the total number of players playing E by N, $N = 0, 1, \ldots, 5$, and correspondingly the number of *other* players planting early as $n = 0, 1, \ldots, 4$. Then all planting late and all planting early are the two pure Nash equilibria as discussed below and shown in Figure 2.6.

   a) For $N = 0$, i.e., all players play L. For any player i, we have $n_i = 0$ and

   $$u_i(L, 0) = 2 > u_i(E, 0) = 0$$

   which means no one has incentive to deviate. Therefore, all players playing L is a Nash equilibrium.

   b) For $N = 1$, i.e., all but one play L. For the one playing E, we have $u_i = 0$. Because

   $$u_i(E, 0) = 0 < u_i(L, 0) = 2$$

   the early planter has an incentive to deviate. Therefore, $N = 1$ is not a Nash equilibrium. By similar reasoning we find that $N = 2, 3, 4$ are not Nash equilibria.

Path

A path is a sequence of edges that connect a sequence of nodes, such that all nodes are distinct.

Distance

The distance between two nodes in a network is the number of edges on the shortest path between the two nodes.

The *m*-equilibrium solution concept is described in [67].

The visitor to the village asked a farmer why he and the other the Palanpur villagers did not simply agree to all plant early. The farmer replied: "If we knew how to do that we would not be poor."

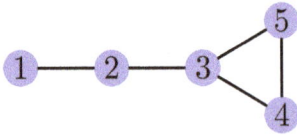

Figure 2.5: The social network in Palanpur. The social network represented by the adjacency matrix

$$G = \begin{bmatrix} 0 & 1 & 0 & 0 & 0 \\ 1 & 0 & 1 & 0 & 0 \\ 0 & 1 & 0 & 1 & 1 \\ 0 & 0 & 1 & 0 & 1 \\ 0 & 0 & 1 & 1 & 0 \end{bmatrix}$$

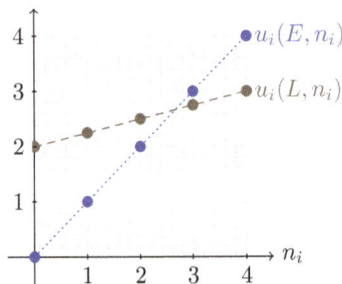

Figure 2.6: The payoff functions in the game "Plant in Palanpur."

$$u_i(E, n_i) = n_i$$
$$u_i(L, n_i) = 2 + 0.25n_i$$

where n_i is the number of *others* adopting N. Note that for any player i, n_i remains the same when she deviates *alone*.

c) For $N = 5$, i.e., all players play E. For any player, we have $n_i = 4$. Because

$$u_i(E, 4) = 4 > u_i(L, 4) = 3$$

no one has incentive to deviate. Therefore, all players playing E is a Nash equilibrium.

3. When $m = 1$, the largest deviation group is $\{3, 4, 5\}$ as shown in Figure 2.7. Consider the case that $N = 0$, i.e., everyone plays L. We can show that the group $\{3, 4, 5\}$ has no incentive to deviate, since for any $i \in \{3, 4, 5\}$, the payoff to deviate together is

$$u_i(E, 2) = 2$$

which is not greater than $u_i(L, 0) = 2$. Therefore, all planting late is a (weak) 1-equilibrium.

4. When $m = 2$, the largest deviation group is $\{2, 3, 4, 5\}$, as shown in Figure 2.8. When all plant late, the payoff to each player in this group is $u_i(L, 0) = 2$. However, if they deviate together, then for any $i \in \{2, 3, 4, 5\}$, we have $n_i = 3$ and

$$u_i(E, 3) = 3 > u_i(L, 0) = 2$$

That is, each member of the group $\{2, 3, 4, 5\}$ has an incentive to deviate together. Therefore, planting late is not a 2-equilibrium.

Next we check that everyone planting early is a 2-equilibrium. For any player in any feasible deviation group, the payoff after deviating is

$$u_i(L, n_i) = 2 + 0.25 n_i \leq 3 < u_i(E, 4) = 4$$

since $n_i \leq 4$. Therefore, no one has the incentive to deviate within any possible deviation group. In sum, $m = 2$ is the least value such that planting early is the unique equilibrium of this game.

5. Any feasible deviation group for an $(m - 1)$-equilibrium, with all members connected by at most $m - 1$ edges, is also a feasible deviation group for an m-equilibrium. Hence, any m-equilibrium must survive the deviation tests for the $(m - 1)$-equilibrium. Therefore,

$$\mathcal{N}(m) \subseteq \mathcal{N}(m - 1)$$

In other words, a larger m may destabilize the equilibrium. From this observation you may consider m to be an indicator of the ease with which people can coordinate their actions with others, and so, by means of collective action, avoid getting trapped (like the people of Palanpur) in a Pareto-inferior equilibrium.

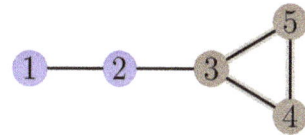

Figure 2.7: Deviation group when $m = 1$. The largest deviation group when $m = 1$, in which one could reach another by at most 1 edge, is $\{3, 4, 5\}$. The possible deviation groups with 2 members include $\{1, 2\}$, $\{2, 3\}$, $\{3, 4\}$, $\{3, 5\}$ and $\{4, 5\}$. All singletons are deviation groups with 1 member.

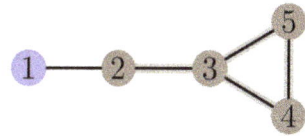

Figure 2.8: Deviation group when $m = 2$. The largest deviation group when $m = 2$, in which one could reach another by at most 2 edges, is $\{2, 3, 4, 5\}$. The possible deviation groups with 3 members include $\{1, 2, 3\}$, $\{2, 3, 4\}$, $\{2, 3, 5\}$ and $\{3, 4, 5\}$.

For example in the network G, $\mathcal{N}(1) = \{$all E, all $L\}$ and $\mathcal{N}(2) = \{$all $E\}$. Thus we have

$$\mathcal{N}(2) \subseteq \mathcal{N}(1)$$

2.5 Residential segregation and integration as Nash equilibria

Figure 2.9: Residential segregation in Manhattan. Segregation in Manhattan, the central borough of New York City, in 2018. The rectangle without shading is Central Park. Source: Sethi and Somanathan [89] using updated 2018 block data from the American Community Survey, 2018.

[89]: Sethi and Somanathan (2009), 'Racial Inequality and Segregation Measures'

Other problems that use social networks can be found in Sections 13.3.

[29]: Bowles and Halliday (2022), *Microeconomics*

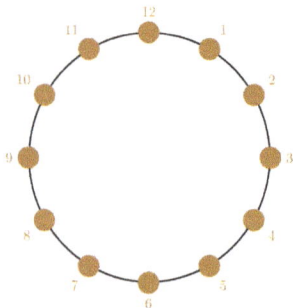

Figure 2.10: The "geography" of the neighborhood, showing that, for example, the citizen at position 2 on the circle has two immediate neighbors, the people at positions 1 and 3.

The example of residential segregation is further analyzed in Section 5.4.

Segregated communities — whether on grounds of ethnicity, race, religion, or class — often cultivate inter-group prejudice and hostility and are the basis for the systematic denial of equal dignity to all citizens. The correlates of segregation typically include systematic deprivation of adequate schooling, health facilities, personal security, and other necessities of life to a politically subordinate demographic group.

Racial segregation in Manhattan, part of New York City, is illustrated in Figure 2.9.

Segregation often results from deliberate policies of discrimination by governments, banks, and home owners. Examples are the apartheid system of enforced racial separation in South Africa that persisted until 1994 and legally mandated housing segregation in the U.S. — the so-called racial covenants that were finally outlawed in 1968. Deliberate attempts to sustain segregated communities continue to the present; in the U.S. for example by state laws — "single family zoning" — that effectively make it impossible to build inexpensive housing in high-income neighborhoods.

But segregation can also result from the uncoordinated decisions of people who would actually prefer to live in integrated communities. This counterintuitive result illustrates the use of the Nash equilibrium concept.

The example of segregation underlines the lesson already learned from the interaction among the Palanpur farmers modeled in Section 2.4. This is that there may be more than one Nash equilibrium — one Pareto-superior to the other — and a society can find it difficult to escape the inferior equilibrium. The example of segregation is also a reminder — like the case of planting in Palanpur — of the fact that just because an outcome is a Nash equilibrium, it does *not* mean that it is something that the players would choose if they could coordinate and decide jointly on the outcome.

A model of a residential community made up of people from two different groups — called "Blues" and "Greens" — appears in Section 1.15 of Bowles and Halliday [29]. Suppose that there are 6 Greens and 6 Blues occupying alternating positions in the 12 "houses" at the locations on the circle that are numbered as on a clock as shown in Figure 2.10. The twelve homes on the circle are "the neighborhood." Greens and Blues have identical preferences and they care only about the group identity of their two immediate neighbors.

All people in the neighborhood would prefer to have one neighbor of each group. But they are "satisfied" as long as they either have an immediate neighbor of each group or if both are of their own group. In other words, the ideal "neighborhood" of both Greens and Blues is to have one next-door neighbor of each type, so people prefer an integrated neighborhood.

People are "dissatisfied" if both immediate neighbors are of the other group. Then there are two strategies: "Do Nothing" or "Signal Dissatisfaction." Signaling dissatisfaction means being willing to switch positions with another person — anywhere in the neighborhood — who has also signaled dissatisfaction. People are willing to switch only if they prefer the new location to their old location.

A Nash equilibrium in this setting is a stationary state that will not be changed by any pair of persons who are willing to switch with each other.

1. Show that a maximally integrated neighborhood — Greens and Blues alternating around a circle of adjacent homes as shown in Figure 2.11 — is not a Nash equilibrium.

2. Represent (in a figure) a maximally segregated neighborhood and show that it is a Nash equilibrium.

3. Show that there exists an integrated neighborhood that exactly matches the allocation preferred by both Greens and Blues and that it is a Nash equilibrium.

4. Give an example of a step-by-step process — a succession of bilateral "switching places" — by which the neighborhood could go from the maximally integrated (not Nash) neighborhood to the ideal integrated (Nash equilibrium) neighborhood.

5. Show that the ideal integrated neighborhood is Pareto-superior to the completely segregated neighborhood.

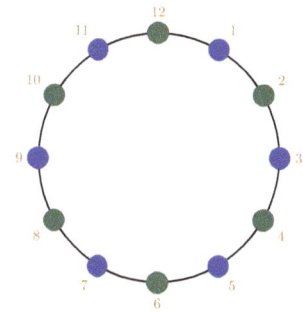

Figure 2.11: A maximally integrated neighborhood: the two immediate neighbors of each citizen are of the other type.

Now consider two changes in the rules of the game. First, suppose that, instead of bilateral switches by single households, two neighbors (living in adjacent houses) may jointly signal dissatisfaction and trade places with another pair (also living in adjacent houses) that signaled dissatisfaction. Second, individuals may signal dissatisfaction even if both of their immediate neighbors are of the same group as them because there is some different composition of neighbors that they would prefer (namely one neighbor of each type).

6. For this new game, explain, by means of an example, why the completely segregated neighborhood would not be an equilibrium. Notice this new setup is equivalent to showing (using the terms of Section 2.4) that the segregated neighborhood is a 0-equilibrium (that is, Nash) but not a 1-equilibrium.

Answers.

1. In the maximally integrated neighborhood, all Blues have Greens as their immediate neighbors and vice versa, as shown in Figure 2.11. Given the strategies and preferences, we know that every individual in the maximally integrated neighborhood will signal dissatisfaction as their neighbors on both sides are members of the other group; they are therefore willing to swap with any member of

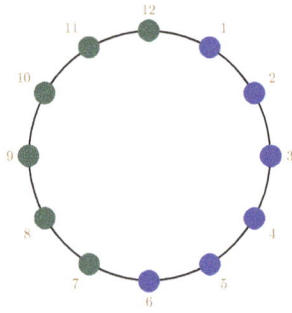

Figure 2.12: The figure illustrates a maximally segregated neighborhood that is also a Nash equilibrium.

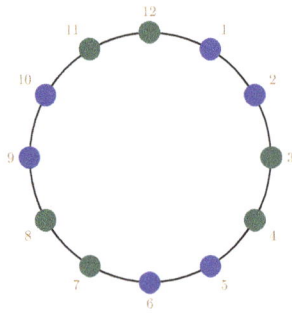

Figure 2.13: This is an ideal neighborhood where every individual is surrounded by one person from their own group on one side and by another person from the other group on the other side.

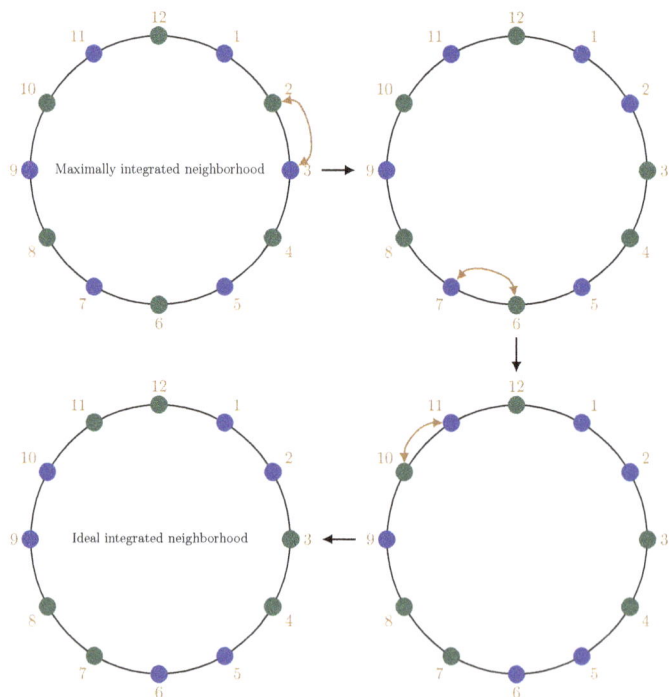

Figure 2.14: The step-by-step switches from the maximally integrated neighborhood to the ideal integrated neighborhood.

the other group. Therefore, the maximally integrated neighborhood is not a Nash equilibrium.

2. Figure 2.12 shows an an example of a maximally segregated neighborhood with Blues on one side and Greens on another. This is a Nash equilibrium since no player will signal dissatisfaction because none have both neighbors of the "other" type.

3. Figure 2.13 shows an integrated allocation in which both Greens and Blues have one neighbor from each group. This is a Nash equilibrium since no individual will signal dissatisfaction (i.e., has an incentive to move) as this is the ideal neighborhood where every individual's immediate neighbors are a person from each group on either side.

4. The neighborhood could go from being maximally integrated to the ideal neighborhood as shown in Figure 2.14.

   a) the Green in position 2 and the Blue in position 3 will signal being dissatisfied and switch positions;

   b) subsequently, the Green in position 6 and the Blue in position 7 will signal being dissatisfied and switch positions;

   c) finally, the Green in position 10 and the Blue in position 11 signal being dissatisfied and switch.

5. By moving to the ideal integrated neighborhood as shown in Figure 2.13, the Blues in position 2, 3, 4, 5 and the Greens in position 8, 9, 10, and 11 in the completely segregated neighborhood in Figure 2.12 will be better off, while the persons in position 1,

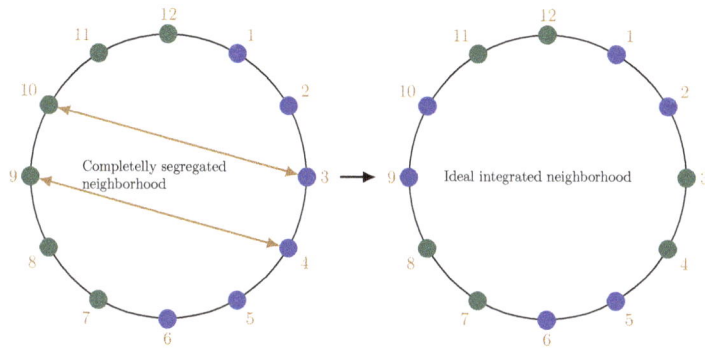

Figure 2.15: How collective action — two neighbors jointly agreeing to switch with another pair of neighbors — destabilizes segregation. The Blues at position 3 and 4 swap with the Greens at position 9 and 10.

6, 7, 12 would be equally well-off. Therefore, the ideal integrated neighborhood is Pareto-superior to the completely segregated neighborhood.

6. Starting from the completely segregated neighborhood in the left panel in Figure 2.15, the Greens at position 3 and 4 would like to swap with the Blues at position 9 and 10 since these individuals would be better off to achieve their ideal situation, i.e., to have immediate neighbors from each group. Therefore, the maximally segregated neighborhood is not an equilibrium (meaning it will not persist) when two neighbors can trade places with another pair, even though it is a Nash equilibrium.

The fact that the change in the rules of the game resulted in a very different equilibrium is a reminder that, while a valuable analytical tool, the Nash equilibrium concept is limited to situations in which individuals act without coordinating their actions with others. Here neighbors acted collectively: a pair of neighbors agreeing to switch with another pair.

Preferences, Beliefs, and Behavior | 3

In the preferences, beliefs, and constraints approach to decision-making, preferences are evaluations of states that may result from the actions one takes. Until recently economists have in practice treated preferences as self-regarding, that is, evaluations of states that the actor themself will experience. Here we take up other-regarding preferences, that is, preferences that also take account of states experienced by others as a result of one's own actions. Included are altruism and inequality aversion, preferences widely thought to be admirable, but also negative sentiments towards others such as envy, spite, and hostility toward members of other groups.

We also consider reciprocal preferences, according to which the valuation that one places on the payoffs of others depends on one's assessment of the type of the others (generous, for example, as opposed to self-regarding). We also take up the case in which the preferences guiding an individual's behavior are not exogenously given but instead depend on the situation, in this case on the nature of material incentives that are provided for the actions in question.

Finally, we consider cases in which we have preferences not just about states — a particular allocation, for example — but also about how the state came about, for example, as a result of one's own self-determined choice, or by imposition by another person. We consider a problem concerning *control aversion* — the value we place on self-determination — as an illustration of such "process-regarding preferences."

Working through these problems, you will see that taking this more empirically based approach to preferences — especially concerning altruism and inequality aversion — does not require a fundamentally new set of analytical methods. Reciprocity is an exception because in an ongoing interaction, the value that one places on the payoffs of the other will evolve over time in response to the actions of the other, which themselves will evolve in response to the behavior of the initial actors. Taking account of these reciprocal effects requires an explicit treatment of preference dynamics, and admitting to the possibility of multiple equilibria, even in very simple interactions among just two individuals.

Taking account of other-regarding preferences expands the domains of economic problems, public policy analysis, and institutional design that economics can address. Included are the facts that people often act cooperatively, and respond to the incentives and constraints of policies and institutions differently than would entirely self-regarding actors.

Some background for the problems in this chapter is found in Chapter 3 in Bowles [14] and Chapter 2 in Bowles and Halliday [29].

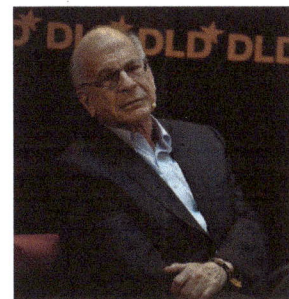

Figure 3.1: Daniel Kahneman (1934–2024), a psychologist was awarded an economics Nobel Laureate in 2002 for integrating psychological research into economics. His prospect theory demonstrated how behavior is influenced by cognitive biases, and in his paper 'New Challenges to the Rationality Assumption' he challenged the standard assumption that behavior can be understood as the result of individuals' maximizing expected utility. Kahneman titled another of his papers 'Back to Bentham?' to pay homage to the early 19th-century philosopher-economist Jeremy Bentham's utilitarian theory. Wikimedia Commons, CC BY-SA 2.0, https://commons.wikimedia.org/wiki/File:Daniel_Kahneman_(3283955327)_(cropped).jpg

[14]: Bowles (2004), *Microeconomics*

[29]: Bowles and Halliday (2022), *Microeconomics*

©2025 Samuel Bowles and Weikai Chen, CC BY-NC 4.0

https://doi.org/10.11647/OBP.0466.03

3.1 An offer you *can* refuse: Inequality aversion

Preferences

Preferences are evaluations of outcomes of one's actions that provide reasons for taking one course of action over another.

Two players i and j are playing the Ultimatum Game dividing one unit between the proposer and the responder. The proposer offers a certain portion to the responder. If the responder accepts, the responder gets the proposed portion and the proposer keeps the rest. If the responder rejects the offer, both get nothing. Now suppose that individual i's preferences are given by

$$u_i = \pi_i - \delta_i \max(\pi_j - \pi_i, 0) - \alpha_i \max(\pi_i - \pi_j, 0) \qquad (3.1)$$

[51]: Fehr and Schmidt (1999), 'A Theory of Fairness, Competition, and Cooperation'

with $\alpha_i = 1/2$ and $\delta_i = 3/4$, where π_j and π_i are the material payoffs to the two individuals [51].

Inequality aversion

A preference for more equal outcomes and a dislike for both disadvantageous inequality that occurs when others have more than the actor and advantageous inequality that occurs when the actor has more than others.

1. Were i the respondent in an Ultimatum Game, what is the smallest offer they would accept?

2. If i was the proposer and knew that the respondent had identical preferences to theirs, can you say what they would offer?

Answers.

1. Suppose $\pi_i \leq \pi_j$, with $\alpha = 1/2$ and $\delta = 3/4$. We have

$$u_i = \pi_i - \frac{3}{4}(\pi_j - \pi_i) = \pi_i - \frac{3}{4}(1 - 2\pi_i) = \frac{5}{2}\pi_i - \frac{3}{4}$$

Letting $u_i \geq 0$, we have $\pi_i \geq 0.3$ as shown in Figure 3.2.

Figure 3.2: The utility function for the inequality aversion preference. Given the parameters $\alpha = 1/2$, $\delta = 3/4$, and $\pi_j = 1 - \pi_i$ we have

$$u_i(\pi_i) = \begin{cases} \frac{5}{2}\pi_i - \frac{3}{4}, & 0 \leq \pi_i \leq \frac{1}{2} \\ \frac{1}{2}, & \frac{1}{2} < \pi_i \leq 1 \end{cases}$$

If i is the respondent, then $\pi_i^{min} = 0.3$ is the smallest offer they would accept to make sure $u_i \geq 0$. Suppose i is the proposer and the respondent has same utility, then to make sure that j would accept the offer, we have $\pi_i^{max} = 0.7$. Therefore, they would set

$$0.5 \leq \pi_i \leq 0.7$$

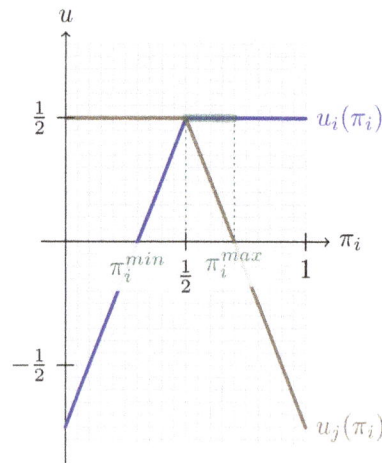

2. Since j has the same preferences as i, the smallest offer j would accept is $\pi_j^{min} = 0.3$. For $\pi_i > \pi_j$, we have

$$u_i = \pi_i - \frac{1}{2}(\pi_i - \pi_j) = \frac{1}{2}$$

That is, i is indifferent among any payoffs $\pi_i \geq 0.5$. Therefore, they would offer $\pi_j \in [0.3, 0.5]$ as shown in Figure 3.2.

3.2 Reciprocity and Bayesian Nash equilibrium

Where individuals have social preferences there may be a large number of equilibria even in simple interactions. This is particularly the case if preferences are endogenous or if reciprocity is a strong motive. Here is an example concerning reciprocity. Two individuals are considering contributing effort e_i and e_j, both in $[0, 1]$, to a common project, the output of which, $e_i + e_j$, will be shared equally between the two. The two have preferences as described below.

$$u_i = \pi_i + \beta_{ij}\pi_j \qquad (3.2)$$

where

$$\beta_{ij} = \frac{b_i + \lambda_i a_j}{1 + \lambda_i} \qquad (3.3)$$

The parameter $b_i \in [-1, 1]$ is i's level of unconditional good will or ill will (altruism or spite) toward others, and $a_j \in [-1, 1]$ is i's belief about j's good will, while $\lambda_i \geq 0$ indicates the extent to which i conditions his evaluations of others' payoffs on (beliefs about) the other's type.

Suppose the subjective cost of effort is

$$c(e) = \frac{3}{4}e$$

and

$$b = \lambda = \frac{1}{2}$$

for each person. The belief about the goodwill of the other is simply the amount that each believes the other will contribute to the project (so, for example, if i believes that j will contribute 1 to the project, then $a_j = 1$).

1. Identify the three pure strategy Bayesian equilibria of this game.

2. Indicate which are stable, and give the critical values of the initial beliefs a_i and a_j, such that the Pareto-superior outcome can be sustained as a Bayesian Nash equilibrium.

Answers.

1. The material payoff is

$$\pi_i = \frac{e_i + e_j}{2} - \frac{3}{4}e_i = \frac{1}{2}e_j - \frac{1}{4}e_i$$
$$\pi_j = \frac{e_i + e_j}{2} - \frac{3}{4}e_j = \frac{1}{2}e_i - \frac{1}{4}e_j$$

Given the parameters $b = \lambda = 1/2$ we have

$$\beta_{ij} = \frac{0.5 + 0.5a_j}{1 + 0.5} = \frac{1 + a_j}{3}$$

Utility functions based on reciprocal preferences were first proposed by Rabin [84] and Levine [72].

[84]: Rabin (1993), 'Incorporating Fairness into Game Theory and Economics'

[72]: Levine (1998), 'Modeling Altruism and Spitefulness in Experiments'

Reciprocal preferences

A person with reciprocal preferences places a positive value on the payoffs of others who they believe to be generous or to have upheld other social norms, and a negative value on the payoffs of those who they believe to have treated others badly. A person with reciprocal preferences, as a result, may help others who uphold social norms and punish those who violate norms, even at a cost to themselves.

Bayesian Nash equilibrium

A Bayesian Nash equilibrium is a strategy profile that is a mutual best response among all players given their beliefs about the other players' types.

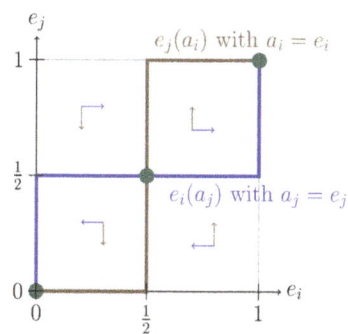

Figure 3.3: **The best reply with consistent belief.** Any point (e_i, e_j) in the region $[0, 1] \times [0, 1]$ can be supported as a Nash equilibrium by some belief system (a_i, a_j). With consistent belief $a_j = e_j$ and $a_i = e_i$, $e_i(e_j)$ and $e_j(e_i)$ are the best reply for i and j. There are three (Bayesian) Nash equilibria:

$$(0, 0), (1, 1), (\tfrac{1}{2}, \tfrac{1}{2})$$

The colored arrows represent the out-of-equilibrium direction of best responses at each of the strategy profiles in the four non-equilibrium regions of the figure. They show that $(0, 0), (1, 1)$ are stable while $(1/2, 1/2)$ is not.

then

$$u_i = \pi_i + \beta_{ij}\pi_j = \frac{2a_j - 1}{12}e_i + \frac{5 - a_j}{12}e_j \implies \frac{du_i}{de_i} = \frac{1}{6}(a_j - \frac{1}{2})$$

Therefore, we have

$$e_i^* = \begin{cases} 1 & a_j > \frac{1}{2}, \\ [0,1] & a_j = \frac{1}{2}, \\ 0 & a_j < \frac{1}{2}. \end{cases}$$

At any Bayesian equilibrium, the belief a_j should be consistent with the behavior of j. Therefore, the three pure Bayesian Nash equilibria are $e_i = e_j = a_i = a_j = 1$, $e_i = e_j = a_i = a_j = 0$ and $e_i = e_j = a_i = a_j = 1/2$, as shown in Figure 3.3.

2. Both $e_i = e_j = a_i = a_j = 1$ and $e_i = e_j = a_i = a_j = 0$ are stable in the sense that a small disturbances in the beliefs would bring the system back to the equilibrium. The third equilibrium, $e_i = e_j = a_i = a_j = 1/2$, is not stable as can be inferred from the vectors (arrows) representing the direction of best response in the four regions of effort choices of the two. The Pareto-superior outcome is $e_i = e_j = 1$, which is supported as an equilibrium when a_i and a_j are greater than $1/2$.

Figure 3.4: Gary Becker (1930-2014), was a professor of economics and sociology at the University of Chicago for four decades. In 1977 he coauthored an article "De Gustibus Non Est Disputandum," a Latin expression usually translated in English as "there's no accounting for tastes," in which he and his coauthor George Stigler analogized preferences to "the Rocky Mountains — both are there, will be there next year too, and are the same to all men." The book he published two decades later was *Accounting for Tastes*, in which he analyzed how preferences change. He was awarded the Nobel Prize in economics for contributions to our understanding of marriage, crime, politics, discrimination, and other aspects of social interactions. Source: Ullstein Bild via Getty Images

3.3 Other-regarding preferences: Altruism and reciprocity

Two individuals i and j are to play a Prisoners' Dilemma Game with material payoffs π_i and π_j as indicated in Table 3.1.

Table 3.1: Payoffs in a Prisoners' Dilemma Game. We adopt the convention that the first entry in a cell is the payoff to the row player, the second is the payoff to the column player

	Cooperate	Defect
Cooperate	4, 4	1, 5
Defect	5, 1	2, 2

Other-regarding preferences

In choosing which action to take, a person with other-regarding preferences (including altruism and inequality aversion as well as envy, spite, and hostility towards others) takes account of the effect of their choice on the states experienced by others as well as themselves.

Altruistic preferences

Altruistic preferences motivate a person to help others even at a cost to themselves.

They have the following utility functions

$$u_i = \pi_i + \pi_j(b_i + \lambda_i a_j)$$
$$u_j = \pi_j + \pi_i(b_j + \lambda_j a_i) \tag{3.4}$$

where a_j takes the value of 1 if i believes that j is a cooperator and -1 otherwise, and a_i takes the value of 1 if j believes that i is a cooperator and -1 otherwise. More generally we can say that the parameter b_i is i's level of unconditional good will or ill will (altruism or spite) toward others, and λ_i indicates the extent to which i conditions their evaluations of others' payoffs on (beliefs about) the other's type. If both a_i and λ_i are positive, for example, then i is an altruistic reciprocator.

1. Suppose $b_i = b_j = 0$ and $\lambda_i = \lambda_j = 1/2$.

a) Identify any (Bayesian) Nash equilibria in this game.

b) What is the least probability one would have to assign to the likelihood that the other chooses Cooperate in order to choose Cooperate oneself?

c) Identify any risk-dominant equilibria that may (or not) exist in this game.

2. Suppose now that $b_i = b_j = 0$, $\lambda_i = 1/2$, and $\lambda_j = 0$. Prior to any actions being taken, j knows i's utility function, but i knows nothing about j's preferences or past behaviors. The game is played sequentially (one person chooses an action, which is then revealed to the other, who then takes an action). If j is the first mover, how will it be played? Explain your answer (show the calculations that gave you the answer).

First mover

A player who can commit to a strategy in a game before other players have acted is a first mover.

Answers.

1. Considering Bayesian Nash equilibria with consistent beliefs, we have

$$u_i(C, C) = 4 + \frac{1}{2} \times 4 = 6$$

and so on. Therefore, we have a new matrix with the utilities as in Table 3.2.

	Cooperate	Defect
Cooperate	6, 6	−1.5, 5.5
Defect	5.5, −1.5	1, 1

Table 3.2: Prisoners' Dilemma Game with social preference: $b_i = b_j = 0$ and $\lambda_i = \lambda_j = 1/2$

a) There are two (Bayesian) Nash equilibria, both Cooperate and both Defect.

b) For player i, the expected utility of playing Cooperate is

$$v_i(p, C) = 6p - 1.5(1 - p) = 7.5p - 1.5,$$

and that of playing Defect is

$$v_i(p, D) = 5.5p + (1 - p) = 4.5p + 1,$$

where p is the probability that they assign to the likelihood that the other chooses Cooperate. They would choose Cooperate if and only if

$$v_i(p, C) \geq v_i(p, D) \Rightarrow 7.5p - 1.5 \geq 4.5p + 1 \Rightarrow p \geq \frac{5}{6}.$$

Thus, the least p that would induce one to choose Cooperate is 5/6 as show in Figure 3.5.

c) The risk-dominant equilibrium is both choosing Defect since Defect is the risk-dominant strategy as shown in Figure 3.5.

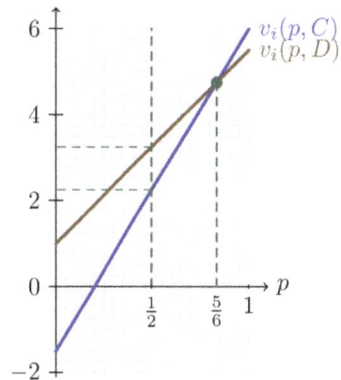

Figure 3.5: Risk-dominant equilibrium in the Prisoners' Dilemma game with social preference. $v_i(p, C)$ and $v_i(p, D)$ are the expected payoffs of playing Cooperate and Defect, respectively when one believes that the other player will play Cooperate with probability p. From

$$v_i(p, C) = v_i(p, D),$$

we have $p^* = 5/6$. Since

$$v_i(\tfrac{1}{2}, C) < v_i(\tfrac{1}{2}, D),$$

Defect is the risk-dominant strategy and (Defect, Defect) is a risk-dominant equilibrium.

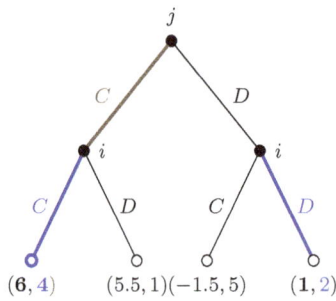

Figure 3.6: The game tree of Prisoners' Dilemma with social preference. When *j* is the first mover, *i* will choose C when *j* chose C, and D when *j* chose D. Knowing this, *j* will choose C as a first mover. The first number in the parenthesis in each case is i's payoff and the second is j's.

2. Given the parameters $b_i = b_j = 0$, $\lambda_i = 1/2$, and $\lambda_j = 0$, we have

$$u_i(C,C) = 4 + \frac{1}{2} \times 4 = 6$$

$$u_j(C,C) = 4$$

and so on. Since *j* is the first mover, the game can be represented as a game tree shown in Figure 3.6. As the first mover, *j* knows that if they choose Cooperate then *i*, who has reciprocal preferences, will choose Cooperate, so their utility $u_j(C,C) = 4$. Likewise, if they choose Defect, then *i* will also choose Defect, so they will get $u_j(D,D) = 2 < 4$. Therefore, *j* will play Cooperate.

3.4 Incentives may crowd out ethical and other-regarding preferences

This problem considers the case of state-dependent preferences, in which the state varies with the absence or presence (and magnitude) of a material incentive to contribute to a public good. The set up of the problem is laid out in Figure 3.7.

Figure 3.7: The problem of non-separability and crowding out. Arrows are positive or negative causal effects showing that the citizen will contribute to the public good if they value doing so more than the net cost of contributing. Crowding out occurs when there is a negative effect (−) from "Incentive" to "Experienced values," so that the total effect of the incentive on contributions to the public good is less than the direct effect operating (as intended by the policy maker) by reducing the net cost of contributing to the public good.

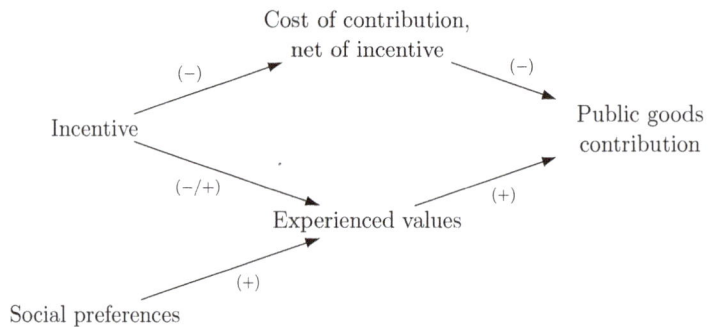

Social planner

The social planner is a fictive individual who designs incentives, constraints, and other ways of affecting people's behavior such that their non-cooperative interactions will result in some socially desirable property, such as an allocation that is Pareto-efficient or that maximizes the sum of individuals' welfare.

Consider an individual who may bear a cost to take an action that confers benefits on others (contributing to the provision of a public good, for example), which may be rewarded by a subsidy implemented by a social planner. Citizens also have values that may motivate such pro-social actions even in the absence of the subsidy. We study a single member of a community of identical citizens who may contribute to a public project by taking an action *a* at a cost $g(a)$ that is increasing and convex in its argument, and that may be offset partially by a subsidy *s* which is proportional to the individual's level of contribution. The output of the project is available in equal measure to all, and it varies positively and linearly with *A*, the sum of the *n* members' contributions, according to ϕA where ϕ is a positive constant.

We express the individual's social preferences as *v* — the effect of an increase in their contribution level on the individual's utility that is unrelated to material payoffs. Thus we have the individual's utility

$$u = \phi A - g(a) + as + av \qquad (3.5)$$

We make explicit the value function for the individual's social preferences as

$$v(s; \lambda_o; \lambda_c, \lambda_m) = \lambda_0(1 + \mathbf{1}_{\{s>0\}}\lambda_c + s\lambda_m) \tag{3.6}$$

where the indicator $\mathbf{1}_{\{s>0\}} = 1$ if $s > 0$ and zero otherwise. In equation (3.6) $\lambda_0 \geq 0$ measures the citizen's baseline social preferences (namely the citizen's values in the absence of a subsidy, $v(s; 0)$), λ_c measures the categorical effect of the presence of an incentive, and λ_m measures the marginal effect of variations in s on values for $s > 0$. The possible crowding effects are represented by λ_c and λ_m.

1. Suppose (here and below) that $g(a) = \frac{1}{2}a^2$. What is the individual's best response function?

Let θ be the marginal benefits of contributing, i.e., the returns from the public good plus the subsidy plus the effect on the individual's values

$$\theta = \phi + s + v(s; \lambda_o; \lambda_c, \lambda_m) \tag{3.7}$$

2. Consider the case in which there initially is no incentive. Find the effect of an incentive on θ, i.e. $\Delta\theta/\Delta s$, at $s = 0$.

We say that a particular change in incentive Δs has crowded out social preferences if $\Delta\theta/\Delta s < 1$, that is, if the total effect of the incentive is less than the direct effect, and conversely for the case of crowding in. What we term strong crowding out holds if $\Delta\theta/\Delta s < 0$.

3. If baseline social preferences are $\lambda_0 = 1$, and $\Delta s = 1$, what are the values of the two crowding parameters λ_c and λ_m such that strong crowding out occurs?

The planner wishes to maximize the citizens' benefits of the public good project, net of the cost of their contribution and the administrative cost of the subsidy $c(s)$. Because citizens are identical we can just let the planner consider a single individual, and assume the planner's objective function

$$\omega(a, s) = \phi A - g(a) - c(s) \tag{3.8}$$

where $c(s) = \frac{1}{2}s^2$. The planner, whom we call "sophisticated," knows that explicit economic incentives may crowd out social preferences, while a new actor, a "naive planner," is unaware of the crowding out problem. In other words, the sophisticated planner knows the true value of λ_m and λ_c, while the naive planner does not and takes them as zeros.

4. If $\lambda_0 = 1, \lambda_m = -0.5, \lambda_c = 0, n = 15$, and $\phi = 0.1$, what levels of s will be selected by the sophisticated and naive planner respectively? Why does the sophisticated planner implement a lesser subsidy than the naive planner?

Empirical evidence, models, and public policy applications concerning state dependent preferences and the possibility that incentives may crowd out ethical or other regarding preferences can be found in Bowles and Polania-Reyes [33] and Bowles [15].

[33]: Bowles and Polania-Reyes (2012), 'Economic Incentives and Social Preferences: Substitutes or Complements?'

[15]: Bowles (2016), *The Moral Economy*

Recall that the average rate of change of a function $f(x)$ over a finite interval h is given by

$$\frac{f(x + \Delta x) - f(x)}{\Delta x}$$

also called difference quotient. The limit of the difference quotient as $\Delta x \to 0$ is the derivative of the function.

Answers.

1. The utility function for individual i is

$$u_i = \phi \sum a_i - g(a_i) + a_i[s + \lambda_0(1 + \mathbf{1}_{\{s>0\}}\lambda_c + s\lambda_m)] \qquad (3.9)$$

Then the first order condition of a_i to maximize u_i is

$$\phi - g'(a_i) + [s + \lambda_0(1 + \mathbf{1}_{\{s>0\}}\lambda_c + s\lambda_m)] = 0$$

That is (using the quadratic cost of contributing function)

$$a_i = \phi + s + \lambda_0(1 + \mathbf{1}_{\{s>0\}}\lambda_c + s\lambda_m) \qquad (3.10)$$

which is the best response function of the citizen.

2. From the utility function (3.9), we have the marginal benefit

$$\theta = \phi + s + \lambda_0(1 + \mathbf{1}_{\{s>0\}}\lambda_c + s\lambda_m)$$

and thus

$$\frac{\Delta\theta}{\Delta s} = 1 + \lambda_0\left(\frac{\lambda_c}{\Delta s} + \lambda_m\right) \qquad (3.11)$$

3. The condition of strong crowding out is

$$\frac{\Delta\theta}{\Delta s} = 1 + \lambda_0\left(\frac{\lambda_c}{\Delta s} + \lambda_m\right) = 1 + \lambda_c + \lambda_m < 0$$

4. The social planner would maximize the objective function subject to the implementation technology given by the individual's best response function. Therefore, for the sophisticated planner, the problem is

$$\max_s \quad \omega(a, s) = \phi A - g(a) - c(s)$$
$$\text{subject to} \quad a = \phi + s + \lambda_0(1 + \mathbf{1}_{\{s>0\}}\lambda_c + s\lambda_m) \qquad (3.12)$$

The first order condition requires equating the marginal rate of substitution (MRS) to the marginal rate of transformation of the subsidy into action (MRT), i.e.,

$$MRT = \frac{1 + \lambda_0\lambda_m}{g''(a)} = \frac{c'(s)}{n\phi - g'(a)} = MRS \qquad (3.13)$$

That is

$$1 + \lambda_0\lambda_m = \frac{s}{n\phi - [\phi + s + \lambda_0(1 + \mathbf{1}_{\{s>0\}}\lambda_c + s\lambda_m)]}$$

Given the parameters $\lambda_0 = 1, \lambda_m = -0.5, \lambda_c = 0, n = 15$, and $\phi = 0.1$, we have

$$1 - 0.5 = \frac{s}{15 \cdot 0.1 - (0.1 + s + 1 - 0.5s)} \Rightarrow s = 0.16$$

For the naive planner who does not consider the crowding out effect and takes $\lambda_c = \lambda_m = 0$, we have

$$1 = \frac{s}{15 * 0.1 - (0.1 + s + 1)} \Rightarrow s = 0.2$$

The sophisticated planner implements a lesser subsidy than the naive planner ($0.16 < 0.2$). This is because the naive planner overestimates the marginal rate of transformation of the subsidy into action, without considering the crowding out effect.

3.5 Inferring control-averse preferences from experiments

The common desire for individual autonomy and self determination — called control aversion in economics — is evident in behavioral experiments. In one, designed by Falk and Kosfeld [49], an agent chooses how much "effort" to provide to a project valued by the principal, who may (prior to the agent's choice of an effort level) impose a lower limit on how much effort the agent is allowed to provide.

Effort is costly for the agent to provide and beneficial to the principal. The agent's chosen level of effort (possibly constrained by the lower bound) determines the distribution of payoffs between the two.

In this experiment, it is common for agents to provide a substantial amount of effort for the principal, in many cases resulting in a 50-50 split of payoffs between the two (plausibly placing a value on fairness, including a negative value on advantageous inequality). The imposition of control by the principal typically reduces the amount of effort provided by these generous or fair-minded agents.

Here we propose a control-averse individual utility function and illustrate how behavior in the Falk-Kosfeld experiment may allow us to estimate the effect of control on the parameters of this utility function.

To clarify what we can say about control-averse preferences (as distinct from behavior), suppose the agent interacting with a principal has the following utility function:

$$u = W - \frac{e^2}{2} + (\alpha + \lambda\beta)e \tag{3.14}$$

where W is the amount provided to the agent by the experimenter as an "endowment" (their payoff if they contribute no effort) and e is the agent's effort provided to the principal. The second term on the right is the (convex, increasing) cost of effort to the agent. The term $(\alpha + \lambda\beta)$ captures how contributing affects the agent's utility due to how they value (positively or negatively) the payoffs of the principal. Thus λ is the agent's degree of reciprocity, and β is the agent's belief about the principal's type with $\beta = -1$ if the principal has imposed a control and $+1$ otherwise. The agent's sense of altruism, inequality aversion, value

[49]: Falk and Kosfeld (2006), 'The Hidden Costs of Control'

State- (or situation-)dependent preferences

If a person's valuation of states (outcomes) depends on the state or situation which the person is currently experiencing, we say that their preferences are state-dependent (or situation-dependent; this latter expression is closer to the way psychologists use the term).

During the COVID 19 pandemic of 2020-2023, surveys in Germany found that people had a more favorable attitude towards vaccinations and other public health policies if they were voluntary than if they were legally required ("mandated"), an example of control aversion. Katrin Schmelz, a pscyhologist and economist, found that older people, those who had grown up in Communist-ruled East Germany and had experienced extensive controls over their lives, including many mandatory vaccinations, were less control averse than other German people [87].

[87]: Schmelz (2021), 'Enforcement May Crowd Out Voluntary Support for COVID-19 Policies'

of self-image or other reasons for positively valuing providing effort is captured by α.

1. Write down an expression giving the agent's level of effort conditional on whether control is imposed or not.

2. Assuming that the control was not binding (the agent chose to provide more effort than the lower bound when control was imposed), what restrictions on the values of β and α are consistent with observed behavior in the experiment?

3. If the agent provided effort at the level of the lower bound when control was imposed, can you say anything about the parameters of the agent's utility function?

Answers.

1. The first order condition of the level of effort e maximizing the agent's utility is

$$u_e = 0 \Rightarrow e = \alpha + \lambda\beta$$

Therefore, depending on whether control is imposed or not, the agent would wish to contribute the amounts:

$$e = \begin{cases} e^A = \alpha + \lambda & \text{control is not imposed} \\ e^C = \alpha - \lambda & \text{control is imposed} \end{cases}$$

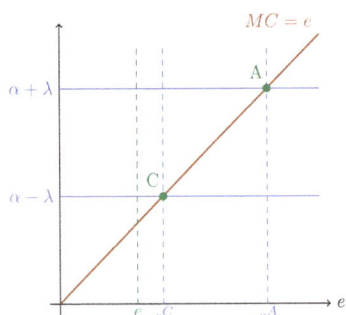

Figure 3.8: When the minimum level of effort $\underline{e}$ is not binding, we can measure the degree of control aversion by taking the difference in the levels of effort chosen by the agent in the two scenarios

$$e^A - e^C = 2\lambda$$

2. Suppose the principal sets the minimum level of effort to be $\underline{e}$. If the control is not binding (i.e., $e^C > \underline{e}$), then we can measure the degree of control aversion by taking the difference in the levels of effort chosen by the agent in the two scenarios $e^A - e^C = 2\lambda$, as shown in Figure 3.8. In other words, the effect of control on preferences can be inferred from the effect of control on experimental behavior. Notice that the degree of control aversion is the product of two terms: the degree of reciprocity of the agent (λ) and the effect of the imposition of control on the agent's evaluation of the type of the principal (the difference in the value of β if the principal imposes control or does not impose control, namely $1 - (-1) = 2$).

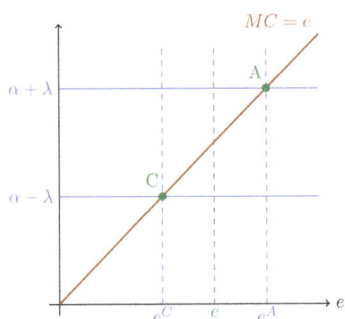

Figure 3.9: When the minimum level of effort $\underline{e}$ is binding, we do not observe what the agent would choose had they been given the choice with the belief that control will be imposed. We could only say that the effect of control on preferences is no less than

$$e^A - \underline{e} = \alpha + \lambda - \underline{e}$$

3. If $e^C < \underline{e} < e^A$, then when control is imposed, we observe only the mandated minimum level of effort $\underline{e}$ that the principal sets. We do not observe the level of effort the agent would prefer to contribute under these conditions. As Figure 3.9 demonstrates, we could only say that the effect of control on preferences is no less than $e^A - \underline{e}$. If $e^C < e^A < \underline{e}$, then experimental behavior provides no information at all about the effect of control on preferences, because in this case neither e^A nor e^C are observable.

Public Goods, Mechanism Design, and the Social Multiplier 4

Homo sapiens is an exceptionally social species. In the previous chapter we illustrated one aspect of our social nature: the fact that we care about each other (including sometimes, negatively). Here we take up a second and less obvious aspect of our sociality: only a relatively small part of our interactions with each other are governed by complete contracts. Our actions, as a result, confer uncompensated external benefits or costs on others.

Public goods and common property resources illustrate these external effects, and they present a challenge: how do you design policies that will overcome the coordination failures (or market failures) that result when, in choosing an action, people do not take account of their external effects (positive or negative) on others? In this chapter we focus for the most part on public goods, treating common property resources in the next two chapters (in this chapter, Section 4.6 is also about a common property resource problem, team production).

To explore policies to address the coordination failures arising from these uncompensated external effects we take up the tools of mechanism design. In most economic problems we have some initial conditions — resources owned by players, technologies, preferences — and then, given some rules of the game, we determine one or more likely outcomes (typically by identifying the Nash equilibria of the game).

The field of mechanism design inverts this process. It starts with some desired outcome or a set of desiderata for a good outcome such as Pareto efficiency and fairness and then reverse-engineers the rules of the game that will support this outcome as a Nash equilibrium. Mechanism design is a modern variant of the approach taken by classical economists — David Hume, Adam Smith, Jeremy Bentham, and others — who sought to design institutions that would result in socially desirable or at least acceptable outcomes, taking account of what people are like (their preferences and beliefs) and the fact that people are free to make their own choices given the resources and technologies available to them.

We also introduce power, here represented by the advantages of being the first mover in a game about the division of labor within the home (specifically, how much each will contribute to producing the public good of cleaning and other housework).

Some background for the problems in this chapter is found in Chapter 4 of Bowles [14] and Chapter 16 of Bowles and Halliday [29].

We begin with the problem facing a social planner who recognizes the social nature of consumption — that is, that our preferences depend on what others are consuming. Section 5.3 is another problem dealing with consumption as a social rather than merely individual activity.

Figure 4.1: Kenneth Arrow (1921–2017) was an American economist who by the age of 30 had proved three theorems that were to shape the development of economics and the other social sciences ever since: the two Fundamental Welfare ("invisible hand") Theorems and his Impossibility Theorem. The latter theorem showed that, if citizens' preferences are ordinal (they rank outcomes rather than assigning cardinal numbers to them) and are not comparable across individuals, then it is impossible to design a system of voting that can meet a set of criteria broadly capturing our idea of how a democracy should work. He also made major contributions to understanding the economic importance of learning-by-doing. Wikimedia Commons, CC BY 3.0, https://commons.wikimedia.org/wiki/File:Kenneth_Arrow,_Stanford_University.jpg

[14]: Bowles (2004), *Microeconomics*

[29]: Bowles and Halliday (2022), *Microeconomics*

4.1 The social multiplier of a tax on cigarettes

Suppose we want to determine the effect of a cigarette tax on the amount of smoking that people do. We know that the amount that an individual will smoke varies inversely with the price of cigarettes and positively with the amount that others smoke (because smoking is a social activity — it is more enjoyable when done with others).

Social multiplier

The social multiplier measures the indirect effects of some exogenous change, in which an individual's action ($a_i(s)$) is affected not only by the exogenous variations in some parameter (s) but also by the actions taken by others ($a_{-i}(s)$) in response to variations in s.

Then, the direct effect on an individual's smoking of a price increase experienced (hypothetically) only by that single individual will be less than the total effect (that is, the effect on the Nash equilibrium) on that same individual's smoking of a tax-induced general price increase. The reason is that in addition to the direct effect on the individual — making smoking more costly — a tax will also have an indirect effect, making smoking less enjoyable via the reduction of others' smoking. The social multiplier measures the difference between these direct and total effects (we will see presently that the multiplier may enlarge the direct effect, as in this case, or reduce it).

Econometric estimates suggest that the social multiplier may be substantial in magnitude. A study of "heavy drinking" by Russian men, for example, estimated that the effect of a 50 percent permanent increase in the price of vodka would reduce heavy drinking by about 30 percent, and that the social multiplier — that is the indirect effect of reduced peers' drinking on one's own alcohol consumption — accounts for one third of this effect [111].

The social multiplier measures the indirect effects of some exogenous change, in which an individual's action ($a_i(s)$) is affected not only by the exogenous variations in some parameter (s) but also by the actions taken by others ($a_{-i}(s)$) in response to variations in s. When this is the case, the effect on the Nash equilibrium actions may differ from the effect on a single individual considered in isolation (e.g. were we to hypothetically assume no change in others' actions in response to either the individual's own actions or the change in the exogenous parameter). Thus individual i's best response function $a_i(\cdot)$ is $a_i = a_i(s, a_{-i})$ and the Nash equilibrium action of all individuals, indicated by the N superscript, is given by $a^N = a_i^N(s, a_{-i}^N)$.

[111]: Yakovlev (2018), 'Demand for Alcohol Consumption in Russia and Its Implication for Mortality'

The action of each citizen, a_i, is the amount of smoking (number of cigarettes smoked per week). Denoting the citizen's income as y, the pre-tax price of a cigarette as p, and the effect of the tax on the price (expressed as a fraction of the pre-tax price of cigarettes) as τ, each (identical) citizen's utility is

$$u_i = \ln(y_i - p(1 + \tau)a_i) + a_i(\alpha + \beta a_{-i}) \tag{4.1}$$

where α and β are positive constants.

Other studies of the social multiplier concern the effect of schooling on wages, the effect of friendship networks on scholastic achievement, and tax evasion [52, 55, 75]. An application of the social multiplier idea to the problem of optimal subsidies for the provision of a public good is in Bowles and Hwang [30].

1. Give the first order condition for the citizen's utility maximization problem and explain its economic meaning, including how the amount of smoking by others affects the individual's choice.

[52]: Galbiati and Zanella (2012), 'The Tax Evasion Social Multiplier'
[55]: Glaeser, Sacerdote, and Scheinkman (2003), 'The Social Multiplier'
[75]: Melo (2014), *Peer Effects Identified Through Social Networks: Evidence from Uruguayan Schools*

2. Use this expression to derive a closed-form best response function showing

[30]: Bowles and Hwang (2008), 'Social Preferences and Public Economics'

   a) how the individual's choice depends on the choices of others, that is $\partial a_i / \partial a_{-i}$; and

   b) the effect of the tax on the choice of the individual (holding constant the level of smoking of the others), that is $\partial a_i / \partial \tau$.

3. Find the effect of the tax on a^N, that is $da^N/d\tau$, and explain why it differs from the partial effect of the tax on citizen i's smoking (holding the smoking level of others constant).

4. Suppose that the Nash equilibrium is stable. Show that the social multiplier is positive, i.e.,

$$m = \frac{da^N/d\tau - \partial a_i/\partial \tau}{\partial a_i/\partial \tau} > 0$$

Answers.

1. The first order condition is

$$\alpha + \beta a_{-i} = \frac{p(1 + \tau)}{y_i - p(1 + \tau)a_i}$$

The left-hand side is the marginal benefit of smoking. Since $\beta > 0$, the amount of smoking by others would increase the marginal benefit of smoking. The right-hand side is the marginal cost of smoking.

2. From the first order condition above, we have

$$a_i = \frac{y_i}{p(1 + \tau)} - \frac{1}{\alpha + \beta a_{-i}}$$

a) The individual's choice depends positively on the choices of others since

$$\frac{\partial a_i}{\partial a_{-i}} = \frac{\beta}{(\alpha + \beta a_{-i})^2} > 0 \qquad (4.2)$$

b) The effect of the tax on the choice of the individual (holding constant the level of smoking of the others) is

$$\frac{\partial a_i}{\partial \tau} = -\frac{y}{p(1 + \tau)^2} < 0$$

3. Let $a_{-i} = a_i = a^N$, we have

$$a^N = \frac{y}{p(1 + \tau)} - \frac{1}{\alpha + \beta a^N}$$

then

$$\frac{da^N}{d\tau} = \frac{\partial a_i}{\partial \tau} + \frac{\partial a_i}{\partial a_{-i}} \frac{da^N}{d\tau}$$

which is different from the partial effect of the tax on citizen i's smoking holding the smoking level of others constant. This is because each individual's smoking will also be influenced by the change of smoking of others induced by the tax.

4. It is laborious to calculate the value of the Nash equilibrium of this problem; but we can calculate the multiplier directly. Since

$$\frac{da^N}{d\tau} = \frac{\partial a_i}{\partial \tau} + \frac{\partial a_i}{\partial a_{-i}} \frac{da^N}{d\tau} = \left(1 - \frac{\partial a_i}{\partial a_{-i}}\right)^{-1} \frac{\partial a_i}{\partial \tau}$$

Then,

$$m = \frac{da^N/d\tau}{\partial a_i/\partial \tau} - 1 = \left(1 - \frac{\partial a_i}{\partial a_{-i}}\right)^{-1} - 1$$

is the social multiplier.

In order for the Nash equilibrium to be stable, the smoking of any i cannot be too responsive to the smoking of the others, i.e., the absolute value of $\partial a_i/\partial a_{-i}$ at the Nash equilibrium should be less than 1. When this is the case we say that the dynamic process is characterized by negative feedback: if for some reason one person smokes more, others will also smoke more but not by as much more as the initial person's additional smoking.

The stability of the Nash equilibrium implies that the slope of the best response function is "not too steep." See Section 5.3 for details.

Together with (4.2) using the above expression for m, we have

$$0 < \frac{\partial a_i}{\partial a_{-i}} < 1 \Rightarrow \left(1 - \frac{\partial a_i}{\partial a_{-i}}\right)^{-1} > 1$$

and therefore, $m > 0$.

Coordination failure

A coordination failure occurs when the non-cooperative interaction of two or more people results in an outcome that is worse for at least one of those involved and not better for any.

Rival

A good is rival if one person's use of the good reduces the availability of the good to others.

Excludable

A good is excludable if a would-be user may be denied access to the good at a low or zero cost.

Common property resource

A common property resource is rival and non-excludable.

Public good

A public good generates benefits that are non-rival and non-excludable.

4.2 Public goods and common property resources

To better understand the kinds of coordination problems that we face and how we might design effective remedies, we classify goods along two dimensions: rivalness and excludability. If a good is rival, one person's use of the good reduces the availability of the good to others. If a good is excludable, a would-be user may (at low or zero cost) be denied access to the good (excluded from its use).

These two distinctions give us the 2×2 taxonomy shown in Table 4.1. The four categories shown there are "pure cases" introduced to clarify distinctions. In reality many goods or resources have some aspects of a public good (they may be a little bit rival and a little bit excludable). The same is true of the other three categories.

Consider the following case. A group with n members has a common project to which each member may contribute effort and from which they all may benefit. The utility function of member j (identical for all members) is

$$u_j = z_j - \delta(e_j)$$

Table 4.1: Public, private, common property, and club goods. In parentheses are examples of the kinds of goods

	Excludable	Non Excludable
Rival	Private good (clothing, food)	Common property (pool) resource (fishing stocks, potential buyers)
Non Rival	Club good (streaming music, online movies)	Public good (global climate, rules of calculus)

where $e_j \geq 0$ is the effort devoted to the project by the jth member, where $\delta(e_j)$ is increasing and convex in its argument and

$$z_j = be_j + c\gamma$$

The total supply of the public good, γ, is a function of the total effort provided by the members:

$$\gamma = \gamma \left(\sum_{k=1}^{n} e_k \right)$$

γ is increasing in the sum of contributions of the members, so $\gamma' > 0$.

1. Give the values of the parameters of the individuals' utility functions such that the good in question is a (pure) public good or a (pure) private good.

2. How would you define the term "public bad"? Illustrate your definition by choosing values for one or more of the parameters of the utility function such that we have a public bad that would be (over-)provided by people.

3. The location in Table 4.1 of any particular good or service depends on legal practices as well as the nature of the good itself. So the same or very similar goods may be located in any of the four cells of the Table. Locate the following types of information in that 2×2 taxonomy:

   a) A piece of information that guarantees winning a contest.

   b) Signaling high income by "conspicuous consumption" so as to improve one's social status.

   c) General knowledge under patent or copyright.

   d) General knowledge not covered by patent of copyright.

Answers.

1. Pure public good: $b = 0, c > 0$; Pure private good $b > 0, c = 0$.

2. A "public bad" mirrors the idea of a public good: it generates costs ("bads") that are non-rival and non-excludable, so for the case of a "pure public bad" we have $c < 0$. Public bads might be produced if there was some private benefit to doing so (that is $b > 0$). Section 5.3 is about a public bad that the American economist and sociologist Thorsten Veblen called "conspicuous consumption," for example, luxury clothing or housing that conveys the superiority of the buyer over others.

3. The four types of information are presented in Table 4.2.

Table 4.2: Information can be a private, public or club good or a common property resource.

	Excludable	Non Excludable
Rival	A piece of information that guarantees winning a contest (private good).	Signaling high income by "conspicuous consumption" so as to improve one's social status (common property resource).
Not Rival	General knowledge under patent or copyright (club good).	General knowledge not covered by patent of copyright (public good).

4.3 Private under-provision of a public good

This section illustrates why self-regarding individuals will jointly provide a lower level of a public good than is Pareto-efficient.

Suppose that each of n identical citizens may contribute to a public good. Their identical utility functions are

Sections 4.3 and 4.4 address the same problem — private under-provision of a public good — with differing functions translating the citizens' contributions into the supply of the public good.

$$u_i = f\left(\sum_{k=1}^{n} a_k\right) + sa_i - \frac{1}{2}a_i^2 \qquad (4.3)$$

where a_i, for $i = 1, \ldots, n$, is the citizen's non-negative contribution to the public good, the first term on the right-hand side of the equation is the total benefit of the public good to each citizen (with $f' > 0$ and $f'' < 0$), the cost of contributing is $a_i^2/2$, and individual i may receive a subsidy introduced by a social planner that amounts to sa_i.

1. Give the first order condition indicating citizen i's utility maximizing contribution.

2. Are the citizens' contributions to the public good strategic complements or substitutes?

3. If $s = 0$, is mutual non-contribution ($a_i = 0$ for $i = 1, \ldots, n$) a Nash equilibrium? Explain why or why not.

4. What is the symmetric Nash equilibrium level of contributions, namely $a_i^N = a^N$ for all i?

5. Using the first order conditions that define the Nash equilibrium, show that it is not Pareto-efficient.

Now let's give the benefit function for the public good a specific form where $f(\cdot)$ in the above utility function is simply a positive constant f. Suppose that a social planner wishes to maximize the total benefits from the project net of the costs of contributing, denominated as ω (the subsidy is just a transfer and so is neither a benefit nor a cost in the planner's evaluation of the optimal subsidy).

6. Give:

   a) the first order conditions for the contribution levels of each citizen that the social planner would like to implement;

b) the value of s (call it s^*) that implements this result; and

c) explain in words the economic (not mathematical) reason why this subsidy maximizes the benefits of the project.

Answers.

1. For the citizen i, the problem is

$$\max_{a_i} \quad u_i = f\left(\sum_{k=1}^{n} a_k\right) + sa_i - \frac{1}{2}a_i^2$$

The first order condition for the choice of a_i is

$$f'\left(\sum_{k=1}^{n} a_k\right) + s - a_i = 0 \Rightarrow f'\left(\sum_{k=1}^{n} a_k\right) + s = a_i \qquad (4.4)$$

That is, the marginal individual benefit of contributing $f' + s$ equals the marginal individual cost a_i.

2. The citizen's contributions are strategic substitutes since

$$\frac{\partial^2 u_i}{\partial a_i \partial a_j} = f'' < 0$$

Or, by total differentiation of (4.4), we have

$$f''\left(\sum_{k=1}^{n} a_k\right)\left(\sum_{k=1}^{n} da_k\right) = da_i \Rightarrow \frac{da_i}{da_j} = \frac{f''}{1 - f''} < 0$$

for $j \neq i$, since $f'' < 0$ and $1 - f'' > 0$ by the second order condition.

> Note that the second order condition is
> $$\frac{\partial^2 u}{\partial a_i^2} = f'' - 1 < 0$$
> which implies $1 - f'' > 0$.

3. If $s = 0$, mutual non-contribution ($a_i = 0$ for $i = 1, \ldots, n$) is not a Nash equilibrium. In this situation, for citizen i, the marginal individual benefit of contribution is $f'(0) > 0$, while the marginal individual cost is 0. Therefore, they have the incentive to increase a_i.

Alternatively, we could prove that it is not a Nash equilibrium by contradiction. Suppose, on the contrary, that it is a Nash equilibrium. Then equation (4.4) holds for $s = 0$ and $a_i = 0$, $\forall i$. That is, $f'(0) = 0$, which is contradicted with $f' > 0$. Therefore, it is not a Nash equilibrium.

4. The condition for the Nash equilibrium is

$$f'\left(\sum_{k=1}^{n} a_k^N\right) + s = a_i^N$$

By symmetry, $a_i^N = a_k^N = a^N$, so we have

$$f'\left(na^N\right) + s = a^N$$

5. At the Nash equilibrium, we have

$$\frac{\partial u_i}{\partial a_i} = 0, \quad i = 1, \ldots n$$

However,

$$\frac{\partial u_i}{\partial a_j} = f'\left(\sum_{k=1}^{n} a_k\right) > 0, \quad \forall j \neq i, i = 1, \ldots n$$

Therefore, a mutual marginal increase in contributions $da_i > 0, i = 1, \ldots n$ would be a Pareto-improvement, as

$$du_i = \frac{\partial u_i}{\partial a_i} da_i + \sum_{j \neq i} \frac{\partial u_i}{\partial a_j} da_j = \sum_{j \neq i} \frac{\partial u_i}{\partial a_j} da_j > 0, \quad i = 1, \ldots n.$$

Thus, the Nash equilibrium is not Pareto-efficient.

6. The social planner's objective function is

$$\omega = \sum_{i=1}^{n}\left(f\sum_{k=1}^{n} a_k - \frac{1}{2}a_i^2\right) = n\left[fna - \frac{1}{2}a^2\right]$$

The first order condition for the contribution levels of each citizen that the social planner would like to implement is

$$\frac{\partial \omega}{\partial a} = n(nf - a) = 0 \Rightarrow a^* = nf = f + (n-1)f$$

which implies that private marginal costs (a^*) equal total marginal benefits (that is, private marginal benefits, f, plus the marginal benefits conferred on the $n-1$ others, $(n-1)f$). Note that the first order condition for the individual's choice of a level of contribution (4.4) is now just

$$a_i = f + s$$

To implement $a_i = a^*, i = 1, \ldots, n$, the social planner chooses s^* so that

$$f + s^* = a^* = nf \Rightarrow s^* = (n-1)f$$

This subsidy maximizes the benefits of the project because it internalizes the external benefits of each member's public goods contribution.

4.4 An optimal subsidy for public goods provision

This section illustrates how a mechanism designer could identify a subsidy that would motivate self-regarding individuals acting independently to provide a Pareto-efficient level of public goods.

Each of n identical citizens may contribute to a public good. Their identical utility functions are

$$u_i = f \ln \left(\sum_{k=1}^{n} a_k \right) + sa_i - ga_i \qquad (4.5)$$

where $f > 0$ and $g > 0$ are constants.

1. Give the first order condition indicating citizen i's utility-maximizing contribution.

2. What is the symmetric Nash equilibrium level of contributions, namely $a_i^N = a^N$ for all i?

3. Effect of variations in s:

   a) What is the partial effect of variations in s on a citizen's level of contribution ("partial" here means holding constant the other citizens' contributions)?

   b) What is the effect of variations in s on the symmetric Nash equilibrium level of contributions (a_i^N)?

   c) Why is the effect of the subsidy on the Nash equilibrium different from the partial effect?

4. Strategic substitutes and the social multiplier.

   a) Are contribution to the public good complements or substitutes?

   b) Write down an expression for m, the social multiplier, compute its value and explain its sign.

5. Suppose you are the social planner and you wish to select a level of subsidy to maximize the sum of the citizen's benefits from the public good net of the costs of their contributions. (Note that the planner's objective function ignores the contribution of the subsidy to the citizens' utility functions, sa_i, as this is simply a transfer. We also assume that there is no cost to administering the subsidy.) Give the first order conditions for the contribution levels of each citizen that you would like to implement and the value of s (call it s^*) that implements this result.

6. As before, you are the social planner, but while you can observe the total benefit of the public project for each citizen, that is, the first term on the right-hand side of the utility function at the outset, you cannot observe individual contributions. As a result, you cannot implement a subsidy based on the individual's contribution. Is there some other subsidy mechanism by which you could implement the socially optimal level of contributions (assuming no change in the citizens' utility functions and other aspects of the setup of the problem above)? If so, explain what it is. If not, say why it is impossible.

Answers.

1. For citizen i, the problem is

$$\max_{a_i} \quad u_i = f \ln \left(\sum_{k=1}^{n} a_k \right) + s a_i - g a_i$$

The first order condition for the choice of a_i is

$$\frac{f}{\sum_{k=1}^{n} a_k} + s = g \Rightarrow \sum_{k=1}^{n} a_k = \frac{f}{g - s} \qquad (4.6)$$

Or

$$a_i = \frac{f}{g - s} - \sum_{j \neq i} a_j \qquad (4.7)$$

2. The condition for the Nash equilibrium is

$$\sum_{k=1}^{n} a_k^N = \frac{f}{g - s}$$

By symmetry $a_k^N = a^N$, we have

$$n a^N = \frac{f}{g - s} \Rightarrow a^N = \frac{f}{n(g - s)} \qquad (4.8)$$

3. a) The partial effect of variation in s on citizen i's contribution is

$$\frac{\partial a_i}{\partial s} = \frac{f}{(g - s)^2}$$

from the best response function (4.7).

   b) The effect of variations in s on the symmetric Nash equilibrium level of contributions (a^N) is

$$\frac{\partial a^N}{\partial s} = \frac{f}{n(g - s)^2}$$

from (4.8).

   c) The effect of the subsidy on the Nash equilibrium includes the effect of the change in one's contributions on the others, which is excluded in the partial effect by holding constant other citizens' contributions.

4. a) From (4.7), we have

$$\frac{\partial a_i}{\partial a_j} = -1 < 0$$

Contributions to the public good are thus substitutes. This is the case due to the diminishing marginal benefit of contributions to the public good (the level of the public good is concave in the total contributions by the citizens.)

b) The social multiplier m is given by

$$\frac{da_i^N}{ds} = (1+m)\frac{\partial a_i}{\partial s} \qquad (4.9)$$

That is,

$$\frac{f}{n(g-s)^2} = (1+m)\frac{f}{(g-s)^2}$$

Then

$$m = \frac{1}{n} - 1$$

which is negative for $n \geq 2$.

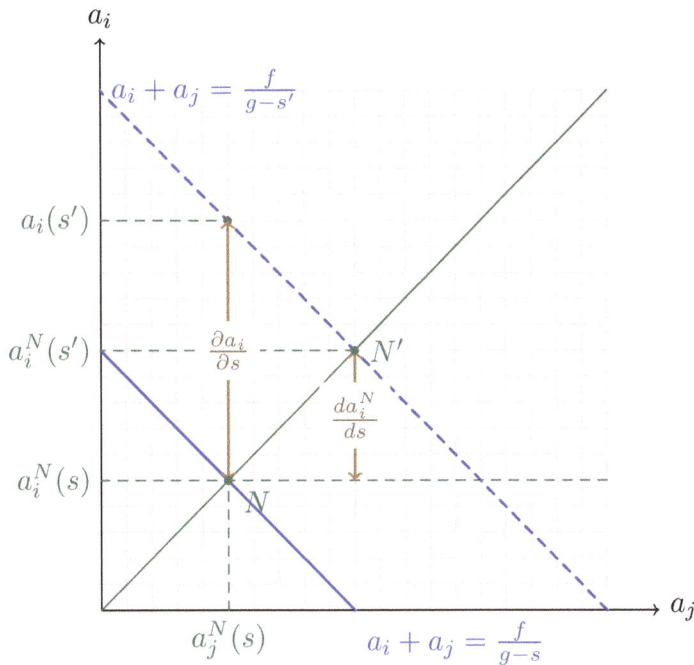

Figure 4.2: The social multiplier in the public goods game. The curve

$$a_i + a_j = \frac{f}{g-s}$$

is the best response function and N the symmetric Nash equilibrium. Suppose the social planner increases the subsidy to s'. Then the best response function shifts upward to

$$a_i + a_j = \frac{f}{g-s'}$$

and the symmetric Nash equilibrium becomes N'. It can be seen that

$$a_i(s') - a_i^N(s) = \frac{\partial a_i}{\partial s}$$

is greater than

$$a_i^N(s') - a_i^N(s) = \frac{da_i^N}{ds}$$

With $f = 1$, $g = 3$, $s = 1$ and $s' = 2$, we have

$$a_i^N(s) = a_j^N(s) = \frac{1}{4}$$

and

$$a_i^N(s') = a_j^N(s') = \frac{1}{2}$$

If contributions to the public good are strategic substitutes, i.e., $\partial a_i/\partial a_j < 0$, then we have

$$\frac{da_i^N}{ds} = \frac{\partial a_i}{\partial s} + \sum_{j \neq i}\frac{\partial a_i}{\partial a_j}\frac{da_j^N}{ds} < \frac{\partial a_i}{\partial s} \qquad (4.10)$$

which implies a negative social multiplier. Intuitively, an increase in subsidy would also induce the other citizen j to contribute more, which discourages citizen i's contribution as they are strategic substitutes, as shown in Figure 4.2.

From (4.10) and the symmetry of Nash equilibrium, we have

$$\frac{da_i^N}{ds} = \frac{1}{1 - \sum_{j \neq i}\partial a_i/\partial a_j}\frac{\partial a_i}{\partial s}$$

Given the definition of social multiplier (4.9),

$$m = \frac{1}{1 - \sum_{j \neq i}\partial a_i/\partial a_j} - 1$$

$$= \frac{\sum_{j \neq i}\partial a_i/\partial a_j}{1 - \sum_{j \neq i}\partial a_i/\partial a_j}$$

which is negative if $\partial a_i/\partial a_j < 0$.

5. The social planner's objective function is

$$\omega = \sum_{i=1}^{n}\left[f\ln\left(\sum_k a_k\right) - ga_i\right] = n[f\ln(na) - ga]$$

The first order condition for the contribution levels of each citizen that they would like to implement is

$$\omega_a = n\left(\frac{f}{a} - g\right) = 0 \Rightarrow a^* = \frac{f}{g}$$

Implementing $a_i = a^*$, $i = 1, \ldots, n$ in the first order condition (4.6), we have

$$\frac{f}{g - s^*} = na^* = \frac{nf}{g} \Rightarrow s^* = g\left(1 - \frac{1}{n}\right)$$

6. Observing the total benefit $B = f\ln(\sum_{k=1}^{n} a_k)$, the social planner can provide a subsidy $S = (n-1)B$ to each citizen to implement the socially optimal level of contribution a^*. The problem of the citizen becomes

$$\max_{a_i} \quad u_i = f\ln\left(\sum_{k=1}^{n} a_k\right) - ga_i + S = nf\ln\left(\sum_{k=1}^{n} a_k\right) - ga_i$$

The first order condition is

$$\frac{nf}{\sum_{k=1}^{n} a_k} - g = 0 \Rightarrow \sum_{k}^{n} a_k = \frac{nf}{g}$$

Then, considering the symmetric Nash equilibrium $a_i = a^S$, we have

$$na^S = \frac{nf}{g} \Rightarrow a^S = \frac{f}{g} = a^*$$

which is the socially optimal level of contribution. The optimal subsidy compensates the citizen for the external benefits of their contribution to the public good conferred on the $(n-1)$ other citizens. In Section 4.6 you will find a question about an optimal contract that is based on the same logic.

An alternative solution. The social planner could set

$$S = w\sum_{k=1}^{n} a_k$$

where w is a constant to be determined. Then the problem of the citizen becomes

$$\max_{a_i} \quad u_i = f\ln\left(\sum_{k=1}^{n} a_k\right) - ga_i + S = f\ln\left(\sum_{k=1}^{n} a_k\right) - ga_i + w\sum_{k=1}^{n} a_k$$

The first order condition is

$$\frac{f}{\sum_{k=1}^{n} a_k} - g + w = 0 \Rightarrow \sum_{k}^{n} a_k = \frac{f}{g - w}$$

Then, considering the symmetric Nash equilibrium $a_i = a^S$, we have

$$na^S = \frac{f}{g - w} \Rightarrow a^S = \frac{f}{n(g - w)}$$

To implement the socially optimal contribution, $a^* = f/g$, the social planner finds the value of w such that

$$a^S = a^* \Rightarrow \frac{f}{n(g-w)} = \frac{f}{g} \Rightarrow w = \left(1 - \frac{1}{n}\right)g$$

Therefore, the social planner could set

$$S = \left(1 - \frac{1}{n}\right)g \sum_{k=1}^{n} a_k$$

to implement the socially optimal level of contribution a^*.

How does it work? The previous optimal subsidy and this alternative subsidy both address the problem of uncompensated external effects, but in different ways. The previous subsidy compensates the citizen for the benefits that their contribution to the public good conferred on the $n-1$ other members of the population, while the alternative subsidy instead compensates the citizen for the cost they have borne in contributing to the public good. Under the alternative subsidy, instead of bearing the full cost ga_i of their contribution, the citizen bears just $1/n$ of the cost, that is, the same fraction of the cost that the citizen is as a member of the population of n.

4.5 Conflict over who will produce a household public good

Two people — i and j — share a home and may engage in housework in amounts a_i, a_j. The housework produces a public good (e.g. a clean house, a beautiful garden) that is valuable to each, but producing it incurs a disutility g, as is represented by the following utility function:

$$u_k(a_i, a_j) = f \ln(a_i + a_j) - ga_k, \quad k \in \{i, j\} \qquad (4.11)$$

where $a_k \geq 0$ and f and g are positive constants.

1. Give the first order condition for the choice of a_i and i's best response function.

2. Are the housework levels of the two substitutes or complements? Explain your answer.

3. Suppose the two people i and j play non-cooperatively as a simultaneous-moves game. Identify all the Nash equilibria.

4. Suppose i is the first mover and j, as the second mover, has no reservation option (they must participate in the game). What would be the resulting housework level of the first mover, a_i^F?

5. Tired of fighting about housework, they consult a marriage counselor. Give the first order condition for the housework levels that the counselor (acting as a social planner) would suggest to maximize the sum of their utilities.

6. Having followed the counselor's advice, the two people eventually come to love each other, valuing the utility of the other as much as their own. What would be the housework levels at equilibrium?

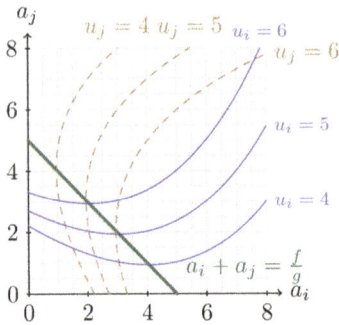

Figure 4.3: The best response in the Household Public Goods Game. The indifference curves

$$u_i(a_i, a_j) = f \ln(a_i + a_j) - g a_i = \bar{u}$$

and

$$u_j(a_i, a_j) = f \ln(a_i + a_j) - g a_j = \bar{u}$$

and the best response functions

$$a_i + a_j = \frac{f}{g}$$

with $f = 5$, $g = 1$ and $\bar{u} = 4, 5, 6$. The two best response functions are the same segment, so that any point in the segment is a Nash equilibrium.

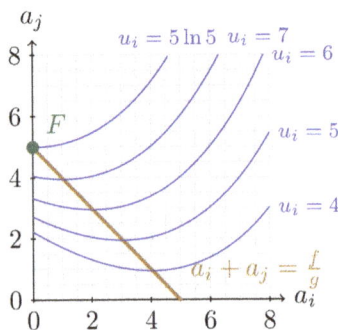

Figure 4.4: The first mover's choice in the Household Public Goods Game. The first mover i's indifference curves

$$u_i(a_i, a_j) = f \ln(a_i + a_j) - g a_i = \bar{u}$$

and the second mover j's best response functions

$$a_i + a_j = \frac{f}{g}$$

with $f = 5$ and $g = 1$. Facing j's best response function, the first mover would choose F to maximize their utility, where $a_i^F = 0$.

Answers.

1. The first order condition the choice of a_i is

$$\frac{\partial u_i}{\partial a_i} = \frac{f}{a_i + a_j} - g = 0$$

Therefore, we have the best response function

$$a_i = \frac{f}{g} - a_j$$

2. Because $da_i/da_j = -1$, it is clear that the housework levels of the two are perfect substitutes: the more work j does the less i does.

3. Played non-cooperatively as a simultaneous-moves game, there are infinitely many Nash equilibria. The two best response functions do not intersect. They are the same segment as shown in Figure 4.3.

4. As first mover, i will choose the housework level to maximize their utility subject to j's best response function. That is

$$\max_{a_i} \quad u_i(a_i, a_j) = f \ln(a_i + a_j) - g a_i$$

$$\text{s.t.} \quad a_j = \frac{f}{g} - a_i$$

Substituting in the constraint, we have

$$\max_{a_i \geq 0} \quad u_i = f \ln\left(\frac{f}{g}\right) - g a_i$$

Therefore, $a_i^F = 0$, as shown in Figure 4.4.

5. The program of the counselor is

$$\max_{a_i, a_j \geq 0} \quad u_i + u_j = 2f \ln(a_i + a_j) - g(a_i + a_j)$$

The first order condition is

$$\frac{2f}{a_i + a_j} - g = 0 \Rightarrow a_i + a_j = \frac{2f}{g}$$

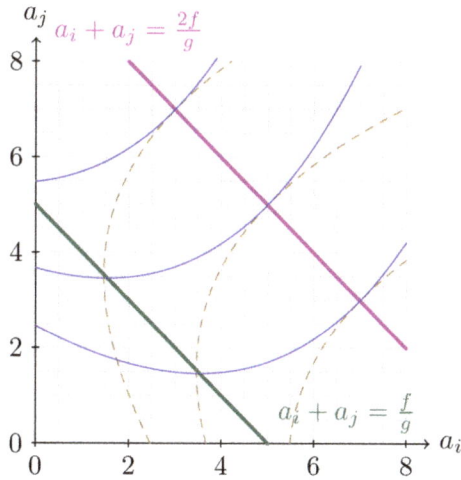

Figure 4.5: The socially optimal allocation in the Household Public Goods Game. The indifference curves

$$u_i(a_i, a_j) = \bar{u}$$

and

$$u_j(a_i, a_j) = \bar{u}$$

with $f = 5$ and $g = 1$. The segment

$$\{(a_i, a_j) \mid a_i + a_j = \frac{f}{g}, a_i, a_j \geq 0\}$$

is the set of Nash equilibria for the selfish couple, while the segment

$$\{(a_i, a_j) \mid a_i + a_j = \frac{2f}{g}, a_i, a_j \geq 0\}$$

is the set of Nash equilibria for the couple who values each other's utility as much as their own, which is also the set of socially optimal allocations.

6. For i, the problem becomes

$$\max_{a_i} \quad u_i + u_j = 2f \ln(a_i + a_j) - g(a_i + a_j)$$

The first order condition for the choice of a_i is now

$$\frac{2f}{a_i + a_j} - g = 0 \Rightarrow a_i + a_j = \frac{2f}{g}$$

which is same as the socially optimal allocation suggested by the counselor, as shown in Figure 4.5.

4.6 Teamwork and optimal contracts

Lower and Upper work together, devoting effort e and E respectively to their work tasks (you may consider e and E to be fractions of a day). Because the two work independently and do not observe each other's activities, the effort levels of the two cannot be made subject to an enforceable contract. Their levels of consumption, c and C, are simply an equal share of the joint output (Q) of their work (that is, $c = C = Q/2$). Output varies positively with the sum of their work, and the marginal productivity of the effort of Lower varies positively with the amount of effort that Upper has supplied (and vice versa). Thus

$$Q = \alpha(e + E) + \beta eE \tag{4.12}$$

where $\alpha > 0, \beta > 0$ and $e, E \in [0, 1]$. The only cost to the workers is the disutility of their own effort, which is just the square of the amount of effort they have provided. The utility of each is increasing in the amount they consume, each unit of the product consumed contributing $\mu > 0$ to their utility. The utility of Lower is given by

$$u = \mu c - e^2 = \frac{1}{2}\mu[\alpha(e + E) + \beta eE] - e^2 \tag{4.13}$$

1. Is the team production problem a public goods problem, a common property problem, or something else?

2. If the two interact non-cooperatively, maximizing u and U, respectively, what is the first order condition for Lower? Explain its economic meaning.

3. Give the best response function of Lower (that is, $e^* = e^*(E; \alpha, \beta, \mu)$). Are the actions of the two substitutes or complements? Why?

4. Using what you know about the first order conditions defining the two best response functions, show that the Nash equilibrium is not Pareto-efficient.

5. Suppose as before their effort levels cannot be subjected to a contract and that rather than their current rule for sharing output, the two adopt the following contract: The income of each is the entire output of the team, minus a constant R sufficient to ensure that the output of the team is not less than the total incomes paid out. Show that this contract is optimal.

Optimal contract

A contract is said to be optimal if the one or more Nash equilibria of a game played non-cooperatively under this contract are Pareto-efficient.

Answers.

1. It is a common property resource problem because the output of the team is rival, and team members cannot be excluded from claiming a share of the output (even if they do not contribute work).

2. The first order condition for Lower is

$$\frac{\partial u}{\partial e} = \frac{1}{2}\mu(\alpha + \beta E) - 2e = 0 \qquad (4.14)$$

That is, marginal benefit equals marginal cost:

$$\frac{1}{2}\mu(\alpha + \beta E) = 2e$$

3. From (4.14), we have the best response function

$$e^* = \frac{1}{4}\mu(\alpha + \beta E)$$

The actions of the two are complements since

$$\frac{de^*}{dE} = \frac{1}{4}\mu\beta > 0.$$

as shown in Figure 4.6.

4. At the Nash equilibrium, we have $\partial u/\partial e = 0$ and $\partial U/\partial E = 0$. By

$$\frac{\partial u}{\partial E} = \frac{1}{2}\mu(\alpha + \beta e^*) > 0$$
$$\frac{\partial U}{\partial e} = \frac{1}{2}\mu(\alpha + \beta E^*) > 0$$

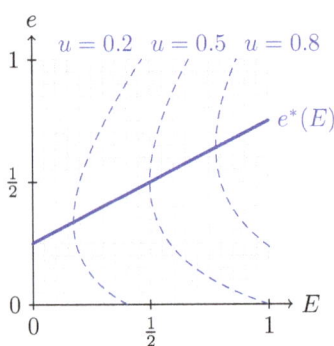

Figure 4.6: The best response functions in the teamwork game. The indifference curves of Lower

$$u(e, E) = \bar{u}$$

and the best response function

$$e^*(E) = \frac{1}{4}\mu(\alpha + \beta E)$$

with $\mu = \alpha = 1$, $\beta = 1$, and $\bar{u} = 0.2$, 0.5, 0.8. The actions of the two e and E are complements since the best response function slopes upwards.

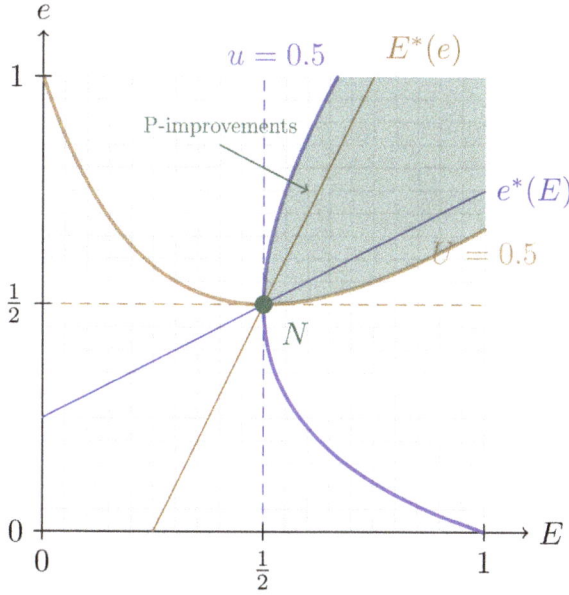

Figure 4.7: The Nash equilibrium in the teamwork game. The intersection of the best response functions

$$e^*(E) = \frac{1}{4}\mu(\alpha + \beta E)$$

and

$$E^*(e) = \frac{1}{4}\mu(\alpha + \beta e)$$

is the Nash equilibrium N, with $\mu = \alpha = 1$, $\beta = 1$. The curves $u = 0.5$ and $U = 0.5$ are indifference curves through N, which is not Pareto-efficient since any point in the shaded region is a Pareto-improvement.

we have

$$du = \frac{\partial u}{\partial e} de + \frac{\partial u}{\partial E} dE = \frac{\partial u}{\partial E} dE > 0$$

$$dU = \frac{\partial U}{\partial e} de + \frac{\partial U}{\partial E} dE = \frac{\partial U}{\partial e} de > 0$$

for marginal increases in effort $de, dE > 0$. That is, it would make both better off to mutually increase the level of effort. Therefore, the Nash equilibrium is not Pareto-efficient, as shown in Figure 4.7.

5. With the new contract, Lower's problem is

$$\max_e \quad u = \mu[\alpha(e + E) + \beta eE - R] - e^2 \qquad (4.15)$$

and the first order condition is

$$\mu(\alpha + \beta E) = 2e \qquad (4.16)$$

If we can show that this condition is identical to the one that maximizes social welfare, then the outcome of the new contract is the same as the socially optimal outcome and thus Pareto-efficient.

Let ω be the total social welfare that the social planner would maximize by selecting appropriate levels of e and E:

$$\omega = u + U = \mu c - e^2 + \mu C - E^2 = \mu Q - (e^2 + E^2)$$

the first order condition of effort level of both Lower and Upper are

$$\frac{\partial \omega}{\partial e} = \mu(\alpha + \beta E) - 2e = 0$$

$$\frac{\partial \omega}{\partial E} = \mu(\alpha + \beta e) - 2E = 0 \qquad (4.17)$$

which is the same as (4.16). Therefore, the new contract would induce Lower and Upper to provide the socially optimal levels of

Pareto-improving lens

The set of allocations that are (at least weakly) Pareto-superior to the fallback options of the players is the Pareto-improving lens.

effort $(\tilde{e}, \tilde{E})$, which is Pareto-efficient.

How does it work? Paying each team member the entire output (minus a constant) internalizes all of the external effects: each team member will receive the total marginal benefit of their effort and so they will implement the social optimum. A similar problem with an optimal contract based on the same logic is in Section 4.4.

Coordination Failures: A Taxonomy | 5

Going beyond the problem of public goods in the previous chapter, we illustrate in this chapter the general problem of uncompensated external effects and the resulting coordination failures, beginning with the case of over–exploitation of an environmental resource, namely over-harvesting a stock of fish. We then move on to coordination problems arising from tax competition among nation states, luxurious lifestyles that Thorsten Veblen called "conspicuous consumption" as a "public bad" (another example of the social nature of consumption, like cigarette smoking in the previous chapter), and finally the residential segregation already studied in Section 5.4 using a different model (also inspired by the work of Thomas Schelling).

These problems illustrate a taxonomy of coordination problems based on the nature of the effects of one's actions on others. We distinguish between positive and negative uncompensated external effects, on the one hand, and strategies that are either complements or substitutes on the other. The taxonomy provides a clarification of both the common mathematical structure underlying seemingly quite different coordination problems and their distinctive character. In Chapter 6 we provide a taxonomy of policies to address one of these coordination problems, the Tragedy of the Fishers.

These problems also allow us to study the exercise of bargaining power as first movers with the (to some) surprising result that a second mover may be better off following a first mover than in a game with simultaneous moves. This illustrates that unequal power is not only a source of inequality and sometimes injustice; it is also a resource for solving coordination problems.

Some background for the problems in this chapter is found in Chapter 5 in Bowles and Halliday [29] and Chapter 4 in Bowles [14].

Figure 5.1: **Thomas Schelling** (1921–2016) was an American economist who won the Nobel Prize in Economics in 2005 for his contributions to our understanding of conflict and cooperation in what are now called "non-market social interactions" that go beyond simple exchanges of the type typically taught in economics courses. He sought to establish "an inter-disciplinary [...] theory of bargaining [...] that could be useful to people concerned with practical problems."[86] Wikimedia Commons, CC BY-SA 4.0, https://commons.wikimedia.org/wiki/File:Thomas_Schelling_.png

[86]: Schelling (1980), *The Strategy of Conflict*

[29]: Bowles and Halliday (2022), *Microeconomics*

[14]: Bowles (2004), *Microeconomics*

5.1 The tragedy of fishers: A common property resource coordination failure

Fish markets were once a favorite textbook example of perfect competition with complete contracts. But without switching species we can focus on a quite different aspect of economics.

Suppose the fishing technology and abundance of fish is such that, letting H_A and H_B be the number of hours worked by Alfredo and Bob respectively, the number of kilos of fish caught by each is

$$F_n = 100 \frac{\sqrt{H_n}}{\sqrt{H_A + H_B}}, \quad n = A, B$$

Let the disutility of working H_n hours be δH_n^2, $n = A, B$.

©2025 Samuel Bowles and Weikai Chen, CC BY-NC 4.0

https://doi.org/10.11647/OBP.0466.05

Taking into account both the value they place on the fish that they catch and the fact that the time and effort they spend fishing is onerous, we can write the utility of the two as the number of fish caught minus the subjective cost of effort. That is

$$U_n = 100\frac{\sqrt{H_n}}{\sqrt{H_A + H_B}} - \delta H_n^2, \quad n = A, B \tag{5.1}$$

"Right now, my only incentive is to go out and kill as many fish as I can [...] any fish I leave is just going to be picked by the next guy." — John Sorlien, Rhode Island lobsterman [102]

[102]: Tierney (2000), 'A Tale of Two Fisheries'

Suppose $\delta = 0.1$ and there are only two choices Alfredo and Bob can make: fish 4 hours or fish 9 hours. (We relax this assumption in Chapter 6, allowing the fishers to vary their fishing hours over the entire length of the day.)

1. Give the payoff matrix for the two and

   a) Confirm that both fishing 9 hours is the strictly dominant strategy, and that both fishing 4 hours is a Pareto-improvement over the dominant strategy.

   b) Identify the Pareto-efficient outcomes in this game.

Tragedy of the commons

The tragedy of the commons is a term used to describe a coordination problem in which self-interested individuals acting non-cooperatively and adopting their dominant strategies deplete a common property resource, lowering the payoffs of all.

Fallback position

A player's fallback position (or reservation option) is the payoff they receive in their next best alternative.

2. Now suppose the World Cup is on, so the subjective cost of the time they spend fishing increases to $\delta = 0.3$. They would rather be watching the giant screen in the town square than peering at the radar screens on their boats, looking for fish. The opportunity cost of their time fishing is no longer sitting in the square just having a coffee; it is missing the World Cup! Is their interaction still a Prisoners' Dilemma (PD) Game? Explain why or why not.

3. Find a restriction on the values of δ such that the game is a Prisoners' Dilemma.

4. Suppose that Bob is first mover and can commit to fishing 9 hours some fraction p of the time and 4 hours the rest of the time (the World Cup is no longer on, so once again: $\delta = 0.1$). Find the fraction p^* he will choose.

5. If Bob has take-it-or-leave-it (TIOLI) power, he can set not only the fraction of time that he will fish 9 hours but also the fraction of time that Alfredo will fish 9 hours. Alfredo can either accept Bob's proposal, or reject, in which case Alfredo will fish 9 hours with certainty, the dominant strategy if the game is played non-cooperatively. What proposal will Bob make to Alfredo?

Take-it-or-leave-it power

A player with take-it-or-leave-it (TIOLI) power in a two-person bargaining game can specify the entire terms of the exchange — for example, both the quantity to be exchanged and the price — in an offer, to which the other player responds by choosing to accept ("take it") or reject ("leave it" and as a result receive their fallback option).

6. Now suppose that as before Bob has TIOLI power but in addition to dictating the fraction of the time, he can demand a payment (in kilos of fish) from Alfredo.

   a) Rewrite their utility functions to reflect this fact.

   b) What offer will he make (hours of each, and any possible payment)?

7. If the resulting two allocations differ (the case where payments are possible and where they are impossible), explain why. If they do not, explain why not.

Answers.

1. Given the utility function and $\delta = 0.1$, we have the payoff matrix as Table 5.1.

   a) It is a symmetric game, so we only need to confirm that fishing 9 hours is a dominant strategy for Alfredo. As we can see in the payoff matrix, $75.1 > 69.1$ and $62.6 > 53.9$. That is, for Alfredo, the payoff to fishing 9 hours is higher than that to fishing 4 hours, no matter what Bob plays. Therefore, fishing 9 hours is the dominant strategy. However, the payoff to both fishing 4 hours (69.1) is greater than the dominant strategy (both fishing 9 hours, 62.6). Therefore, fishing 4 hours is a Pareto-improvement over the dominant strategy.

   b) There are three Pareto-efficient outcomes in this game. They are (Fish 4 Hours, Fish 4 Hours), (Fish 4 Hours, Fish 9 Hours), (Fish 9 Hours, Fish 4 Hours), as shown in Figure 5.2.

2. Table 5.2. The game is no longer a Prisoners' Dilemma Game since the dominant strategy equilibrium (Fish 4 Hours, Fish 4 Hours) is now Pareto-efficient.

3. For the game to remain a Prisoners' Dilemma, by the material introduced in Section 2.1, we should have

$$U_n(4,9) < U_n(9,9) < U_n(4,4) < U_n(9,4)$$
$$U_n(4,9) + U_n(9,4) < 2U_n(4,4)$$

for $n = A, B$. Given the utility function (5.1), we can solve that $0 < \delta < 0.192$ gives the values of δ such that the interaction is a Prisoners' Dilemma.

4. Independently of the value of p that Bob chooses, Alfredo's best response is to fish 9 hours all the time since Fish 9 Hours is the dominant strategy as shown in Table 5.1. Then the payoff to Bob by choosing p is

$$\pi_B(p) = 53.9(1 - p) + 62.6p = 8.7p + 53.9$$

Therefore, Bob will choose to fish 9 hours, that is $p^* = 1$.

5. Suppose that Bob can offer (p, q) where p is the fraction of time that he will spend fishing 9 hours himself and q is the corresponding fraction for Alfredo. Then given the payoff matrix in Table 5.1, the payoff to them is

$$\pi_A(p, q) = 69.1(1 - p)(1 - q) + 53.9p(1 - q) + 75.1(1 - p)q + 62.6pq$$
$$= 2.7pq - 15.2p + 6q + 69.1$$
$$\pi_B(p, q) = 2.7pq + 6p - 15.2q + 69.1$$

Table 5.1: The Game of Tragedy of the Fishers, with $\delta = 0.1$. The numbers in bold indicate the best response

	Bob	
Alfredo	4 Hours	9 Hours
4 Hours	69.1, 69.1	53.9, **75.1**
9 Hours	**75.1**, 53.9	**62.6, 62.6**

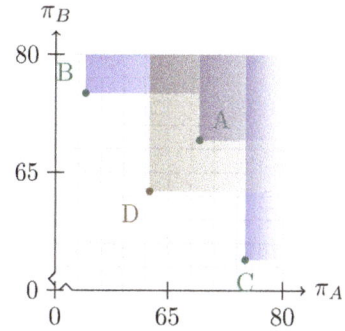

Figure 5.2: Pareto-efficient outcomes in the Tragedy of the Fishers. Denote the four ordered pairs of payoffs in the payoff matrix by A, B, C, and D. D is Pareto dominated by A, since A locates in the upper-right corner of D. All the outcomes are Pareto-efficient except D.

Table 5.2: The Game of Tragedy of the Fishers, with $\delta = 0.3$. The numbers in bold indicate the best response.

	Bob	
Alfredo	4 Hours	9 Hours
4 Hours	**65.9, 65.9**	50.7, **58.9**
9 Hours	58.9, **50.7**	46.4, 46.4

Dominant strategy equilibrium

A dominant strategy equilibrium is a strategy profile in which all players play a dominant strategy.

Since Bob has TIOLI power and Alfredo's fallback position (should he reject Bob's proposal) will be the dominant strategy equilibrium (Fish 9 Hours, Fish 9 Hours), Bob's optimization problem is

$$\max_{0 \leq p, q \leq 1} \quad \pi_B = 2.7pq + 6p - 15.2q + 69.1$$

$$\text{s.t.} \quad \pi_A = 2.7pq - 15.2p + 6q + 69.1 \geq 62.6$$

Next, we solve Bob's problem using the Lagrangian. Let

$$\mathcal{L} = \pi_B + \lambda(\pi_A - 62.6) + \mu(1 - p) + \gamma(1 - q)$$

The Kuhn-Tucker conditions are

$$\mathcal{L}_p = 2.7q + 6 + \lambda(2.7q - 15.2) - \mu \leq 0 \tag{5.2}$$

$$\mathcal{L}_q = 2.7p - 15.2 + \lambda(2.7p + 6) - \gamma \leq 0 \tag{5.3}$$

$$p\mathcal{L}_p = q\mathcal{L}_q = \lambda(\pi_A - 62.6) = \mu(1 - p) = \gamma(1 - q) = 0 \tag{5.4}$$

$$p, q, \lambda, \mu, \gamma \geq 0, \quad \pi_A \geq 62.6 \tag{5.5}$$

Note that the shadow prices on the constraints that q and p not exceed 1 are γ and μ respectively, while the shadow price on Alfredo's participation constraint is λ. As a first step towards determining Bob's proposal we will show that $0 < p < 1$ and $q = 0$ using a proof by contradiction.

▶ Suppose $p = 1$. Then by

$$\pi_A(1, q) = 53.9(1 - q) + 62.6q \geq 62.6$$

we have $q = 1$. Then (5.2) and (5.3) become

$$8.7 - 12.5\lambda - \mu = 0 \Rightarrow \lambda = \frac{8.7 - \mu}{12.5} \leq \frac{8.7}{12.5}$$

$$-12.5 + 8.7\lambda - \gamma = 0 \Rightarrow \lambda = \frac{12.5 + \gamma}{12.5} \geq \frac{12.5}{8.7}$$

which is a contradiction. Therefore, $p < 1$, meaning that the constraint on p not exceeding 1 is not binding. The shadow price on that constraint is therefore $\mu = 0$.

▶ Suppose $p = 0$. Then

$$\pi_A(0, q) = 69.1(1 - q) + 75.1q > 62.6$$

so by (5.4) we have $\lambda = 0$. Then (5.2) becomes $2.7q + 6 \leq 0$, which cannot be true — contradiction. Therefore, we have $0 < p < 1$, $\mathcal{L}_p = 0$, and $\lambda > 0$ (otherwise $\mathcal{L}_p = 2.7q + 6 > 0$ is contradicted).

▶ Suppose $q = 1$. Then by $p < 1$ we have

$$\pi_A(p, 1) = 75.1(1 - p) + 62.6p > 62.6$$

implying $\lambda = 0$ by (5.4). This contradicts $\lambda > 0$, so we have $q < 1$ and $\gamma = 0$.

▶ Finally, suppose $0 < q < 1$. Then $\gamma = 0$ and $\mathcal{L}_q = 0$ by (5.4), which is inconsistent with $\mathcal{L}_p = 0$. Therefore, $q = 0$.

Note that

$$\mathcal{L}_p = 0 \Rightarrow \lambda = \frac{2.7q + 6}{15.2 - 2.7q} < \frac{8.7}{12.5}$$

is contradicted with

$$\mathcal{L}_q = 0 \Rightarrow \lambda = \frac{15.2 - 2.7p}{2.7p + 6} > \frac{12.5}{8.7}$$

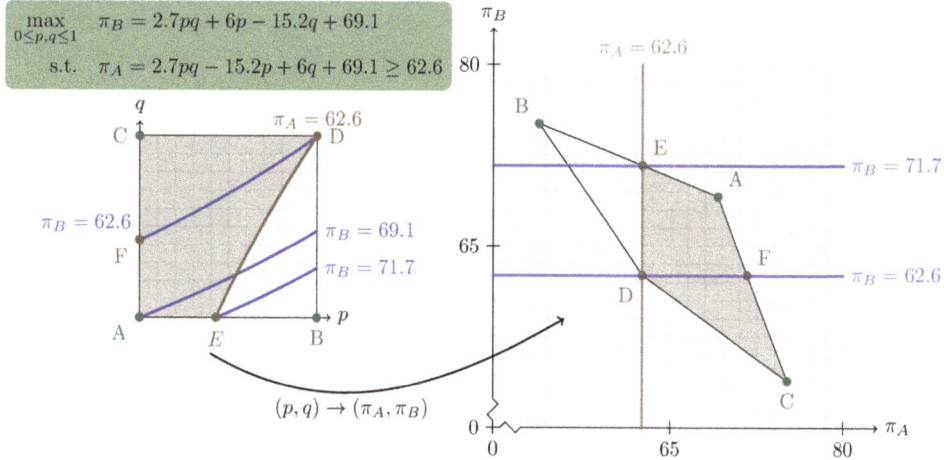

Figure 5.3: Tragedy of the Fishers with TIOLI power. Bob's optimizing problem when he has TIOLI power. Left panel: Fraction of time fishing 9 hours for Bob (p) and Alfredo (q) and Bob's iso-profit loci (blue). Right panel: Payoffs. In both panels the feasible set is shaded. Denote the four ordered pairs of payoffs in the payoff matrix by A, B, C, and D. Bob has the TIOLI power and offers (p, q). The expected payoff function $(p, q) \rightarrow (\pi_A, \pi_B)$ maps any point in left panel to the point in the right. $\pi_A = c$ and $\pi_B = c$ are indifference curves, and the shaded region $\{(p, q) \mid \pi_A(p, q) \geq 62.6\}$ is the feasible set. Point E maximizes π_B, representing the offer he will make $(p^*, q^*) = (0.43, 0)$.

Then by $\pi_A(p, 0) = 62.6$, we have

$$p = \frac{69.1 - 62.6}{15.2} \approx 0.43$$

Thus, Bob will offer $(p^*, q^*) = (0.43, 0)$ if he has TIOLI power. As a result, $\pi_A = 62.6$ and $\pi_B = 71.7$, as shown in the left panel of Figure 5.3.

The right panel of Figure 5.3 illustrates the solution using the feasible set defined by Alfredo's participation constraint (fallback option) and Bob's iso-payoff loci. The participation constraint is shown by the vertical line DE, and the highest up it can be is in the boundary of the feasible set given by the line segment BA. The payoff to Alfredo is the weighted average of that at point A (62.6) and that at point B (69.1). Given that at point E the payoff to Alfredo is 62.6, we have

$$69.1(1 - p) + 53.9p = 62.6 \Rightarrow p \approx 0.43$$

6. Denote Bob's offer by (p, q, y) where p and q are the fractions of time to fish 9 hours for Bob and Alfredo as defined above, and y is the payment from Alfredo to Bob.

   a) The utility functions for Alfredo and Bob are

   $$\pi_A(p, q, y) = 2.7pq - 15.2p + 6q + 69.1 - y$$
   $$\pi_B(p, q, y) = 2.7pq + 6p - 15.2q + 69.1 + y$$

   b) Bob's problem is

   $$\max_{0 \leq p, q \leq 1, y} \quad \pi_B = 2.7pq + 6p - 15.2q + 69.1 + y$$
   $$\text{s.t.} \quad \pi_A = 2.7pq - 15.2p + 6q + 69.1 - y \geq 62.6$$

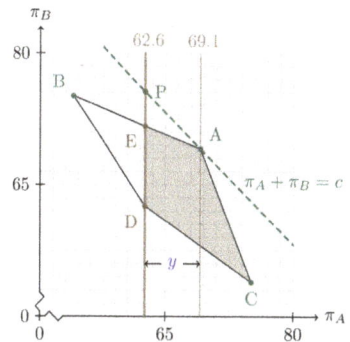

Figure 5.4: Allocation and distribution in the Tragedy of the Fishers. Bob's optimizing problem when he has TIOLI power and payments are possible. This is an extension of the right panel of the previous figure. Denote the four ordered pairs of payoffs in the payoff matrix by A, B, C, and D.

$$\pi_A + \pi_B = c$$

is the level curve of the objective function, which obtains its maximum at point A, i.e., $p = q = 0$, the allocation in which neither Bob nor Alfredo fish 9 hours. We then use the participation constraint $\pi_A = 62.6$ to determine the payment $y = 6.5$ and the final distribution P. Recall that E is the outcome when payments are impossible, which is different from both A and P.

The constraint must be binding, otherwise a slightly higher y with the same p and q would give Bob higher utility and would still satisfy the constraint. Therefore,

$$y = 2.7pq - 15.2p + 6q + 6.5$$

The problem becomes

$$\max_{0 \le p,q \le 1} \quad \pi_B = 5.4pq - 9.2p - 9.2q + 75.6$$

Since $\partial \pi_B / \partial p = 5.4q - 9.2 < 0$ and $\partial \pi_B / \partial q = 5.4p - 9.2 < 0$, the solution is $(p^*, q^*) = (0, 0)$, and $y^* = 6.5$. Therefore, Bob will make the offer $(0, 0, 6.5)$, i.e., both fish 4 hours, and Alfredo pays Bob 6.5 kilos of fish. As a result, $\pi_A = 62.6$ and $\pi_B = 75.6$.

7. The two allocations differ as shown in Figure 5.4. When payments are impossible, allocation and distribution are inseparable: Bob can alter the distribution of income in his favor only by fishing more than Alfredo. When payments are possible, allocation and distribution can be separated. In this case, the player with TIOLI power (Bob) has the incentive to implement the socially optimal allocation of fishing times since his TIOLI bargaining power allows him to capture the total benefit subject only to the participation constraint of Alfredo.

5.2 Footloose jobs and fiscal competition

The day after a cut in the U.S. corporate tax rate from 35 percent to 21 percent was signed into law, the *New York Times* reported:

> To President Trump [...] the overhaul of the tax code that became law on Friday will make the U.S. a better place to do business. To the rest of the world, it has the potential to challenge the global economic order [...] setting off a race among countries to cut corporate taxes.
>
> "It's a huge incentive to governments around the world who want to see more investment to be part of that," said Andrew Mackenzie, the chief executive of the mining giant BHP, which has its headquarters in Australia and major operations in North and South America. "They will have to follow suit." (*New York Times*, Dec 22, 2017. [97])

[97]: Stevenson and Ewing (2017), 'U.S. Tax Bill May Inspire Cuts Globally, While Fueling Trade Tensions'

Consider two nations, Here and There, whose governments each select a rate of taxation to finance an unconditional income grant to all members of their respective populations. The grant is very popular in both countries, so to increase their chances of being reelected the governments select the level of the tax which maximizes the grant. Population size is fixed. The problem facing each government is that investment is mobile between countries and the level of employment depends on the size of the capital stock, which, due to capital mobility, varies inversely with the tax rate.

We call this the Fiscal Competition Game. (Lower-case letters refer to Here, while upper-case letters refer to There.)

A general model, including fiscal competition, is Sinn [94].

[94]: Sinn (1997), 'The Selection Principle and Market Failure in Systems Competition'

The tax rates in each country, t and T, are levied as a fraction of income produced in each country and vary between 0 and 1. The income produced in each country (y and Y) is the product of the exogenously given level of productivity (q and Q) and the number of people employed (n and N), that is,

$$Y = QN \text{ and } y = qn$$

so the total payments for the grant in each country are

$$g = tqn \text{ and } G = TQN$$

The dependence of the level of employment on the tax rates of the two countries for Here (lower-case letters) is expressed by

$$n = \underline{n}(1 + m(T - t) - rt)$$

where $\underline{n}$, r, and m are positive constants, the last reflecting the degree of openness of the economy, and the consequent loss of producers associated with tax rates higher than the other country. (A closed economy is one for which $m = 0$ and a completely open economy is one for which $m = +\infty$.) The employment equation for There is analogous, with identical parameters m and r.

1. Assuming that the two countries interact non-cooperatively and that neither country is either completely closed or open ($0 < m < +\infty$), derive the two countries' best response functions and graph them. Give an explicit expression for the effect on t^* (the tax rate selected by Here) of variations in T, sign this term (if possible), and explain what it means.

2. Do you have enough information to determine if an increase in the openness of one economy will increase, leave unchanged, or decrease the responsiveness of its own selected tax rate to variations in the tax rate of the other country? If you have enough information, derive the appropriate expression and explain what it means. If not, explain why not.

3. What is the symmetric Nash equilibrium?

4. Using the first order conditions defining the two best response functions, show why it must be that at the Nash equilibrium there is some increase in both tax rates that is Pareto-improving.

5. What would be the selected tax rate if the two nations instead played cooperatively and agreed to adopt a common tax rate? Compare your answer to the selected tax rate for a closed economy and explain why they are similar or different.

6. First mover advantage. Now consider an asymmetry of power between the two countries such that Here can commit to its tax rate in advance of There selecting its tax rate (Here is first mover). What tax rate will Here select? What tax rate will There select in response?

Compare them with the tax rates in Nash equilibrium. Here clearly benefits from its first mover advantage, but is it at There's expense? Is There better off or worse off following Here as first mover, in comparison to the Nash equilibrium of the simultaneous moves games with no power asymmetries? Explain your response.

7. An "imperial" solution. Imagine that Here (a powerful country) dictates tax policy to There, and that There complies because There believes Here's threat that it will adopt the Nash equilibrium tax rate if There does not comply. (So Here has TIOLI power.) What constrained choice problem would Here solve to determine the tax rate to impose on There and to adopt for itself? Are the two tax rates imposed by Here (i.e., the solution to the above constrained choice problem) Pareto-efficient? Explain why, why not, or why you cannot say.

TIOLI: Take-it-or-leave-it

8. Evaluation. Using whatever graphs or other reasoning you have presented above, rank the outcomes resulting from the four solution concepts (Nash, cooperative with identical tax rates, first mover, and "imperial") for each country. (For Here indicate which solution gives the highest level of total tax revenues, the next highest, and so on, and then do the same for There.) Where possible, Pareto-rank the outcomes.

Answers.

1. For Here, taking T as exogenous, to maximize

$$g = tq\underline{n}[1 + m(T - t) - rt]$$

the first order condition is

$$g_t = q\underline{n}(1 + mT - 2mt - 2rt) = 0 \Rightarrow t^* = \frac{1 + mT}{2(m + r)}$$

which is the best response function. Similarly, There's best response function is

$$T^* = \frac{1 + mt}{2(m + r)}$$

as shown in Figure 5.5. The effect on t^* of variations in T is

$$\frac{dt^*}{dT} = \frac{m}{2(m + r)} > 0$$

which means that the tax rates of the two counties are strategic complements. An increase in the rate of tax in There will lead Here to increase its tax rate.

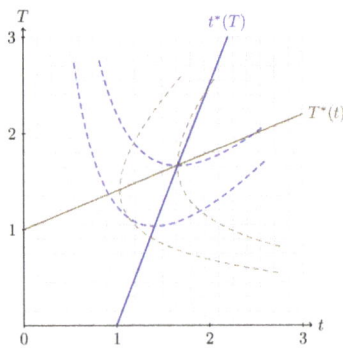

Figure 5.5: The best response functions in the Fiscal Competition Game. The figure shows the indifference curves (iso-total-tax loci) of Here (blue) and There (brown) with parameters $m = 0.4$, $r = 0.1$, $q = \underline{n} = 1$. The best response functions are

$$t^*(T) = \frac{1 + mT}{2(m + r)}$$

and

$$T^*(t) = \frac{1 + mt}{2(m + r)}$$

Notice that the indifference curves are respectively flat and vertical where they intersect the best response functions of Here and There.

2. The responsiveness of one country's own selected tax rate to variations in the tax rate of the other country expressed as an elasticity is

$$\varepsilon = \frac{dt^*}{dT} \frac{T}{t^*} = \frac{m}{2(m + r)} \frac{T}{\frac{1 + mT}{2(m+r)}} = 1 - \frac{1}{1 + mT}$$

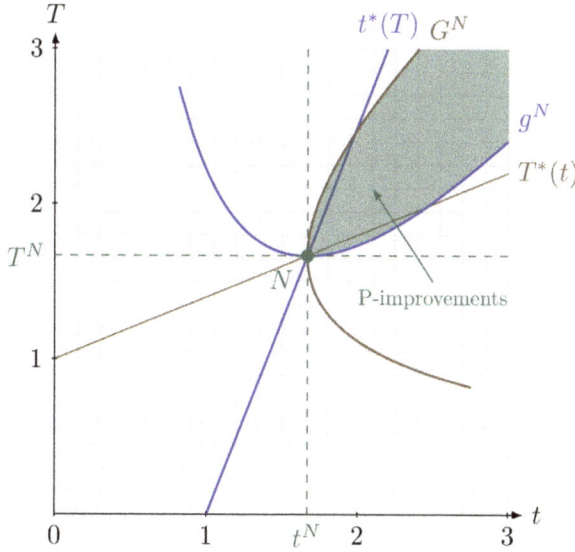

Figure 5.6: The Nash equilibrium in the Fiscal Competition Game. The Nash equilibrium is the intersection of the best responses,

$$t^N = \frac{1}{m + 2r} = T^N$$

which is not Pareto-efficient since any point in the shaded region is a Pareto-improvement. The shaded region — termed the Pareto-improving lens — must exist because at the Nash equilibrium the indifference curve of Here is horizontal and of There is vertical (because the Nash equilibrium must be on the best response function of each).

Then we have

$$\frac{d\varepsilon}{dm} = \frac{T}{(1 + mT)^2} > 0,$$

so an increase in the openness of one country will increase the responsiveness of its own selected tax rate to variations in the tax rate of the other country.

3. Let the symmetric Nash equilibrium be $t^N = T^N = x$. Then by the best response function we have

$$x = \frac{1 + mx}{2(m + r)} \Rightarrow x = \frac{1}{m + 2r}$$

Therefore, the Nash equilibrium for both countries is

$$(t^N, T^N) = \left(\frac{1}{m + 2r}, \frac{1}{m + 2r} \right)$$

as shown in Figure 5.6.

4. The Nash equilibrium is a point common to both best response functions, and we know that along each of these (from the first order condition defining the best response functions) we must have

$$g_t = G_T = 0$$

It is also the case that

$$g_T = t^N q \underline{n} m > 0 \quad \text{and} \quad G_t = T^N Q \underline{N} m > 0$$

Therefore, for some small increase $dt > 0$ and $dT > 0$ in each tax rate, we have

$$dg = g_t dt + g_T dT = g_T dT > 0$$
$$dG = G_t dt + G_T dT = G_t dt > 0$$

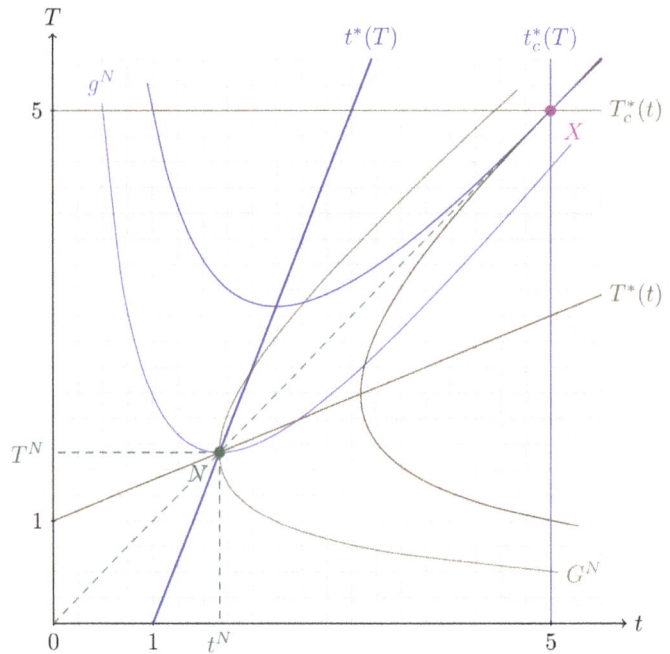

Figure 5.7: The common tax rate in the Fiscal Competition Game. The common tax rates

$$(x, x) = (\frac{1}{2r}, \frac{1}{2r})$$

are the same as the Nash equilibrium tax rates in close economy, which is the intersection of the best response functions

$$t_c^* = \frac{1}{2r}$$

and

$$T_c^* = \frac{1}{2r}$$

It follows that at the Nash equilibrium there is some increase in both tax rates that is Pareto-improving, as shown in Figure 5.6.

5. Let $t = T = x$. Then $g = xq\underline{n}(1 - rx)$ and $G = xQ\underline{N}(1 - rx)$. From $g_x = G_x = 0$, we have

$$x = \frac{1}{2r}$$

so both countries will adopt a common tax rate $x = 1/2r$. In a closed economy, $m = 0$, from the best response functions, we have

$$t_c^* = T_c^* = \frac{1}{2r}$$

Therefore, the result of a common tax rate is the same as that in the closed economy case, as shown in Figure 5.7. This is because the adoption of a common tax rate eliminates the possible incentives for investment to move. When the Fiscal Competition Game is played non-cooperatively, an increase in one country's tax rate confers an uncompensated external effect (a benefit) on the other country. The failure of each government to take account of this effect (to internalize it) is the source of the coordination failure arising in fiscal competition.

Uncompensated external effects

Uncompensated external effects (also called externalities, external economies and dis-economies, or simply external effects) are benefit or costs experienced by others as the result of an action taken by some individual.

6. As first mover, Here solves this constrained choice problem, maximizing tax revenues subject to the best response function of There.

$$\max_t \quad g = tq\underline{n}[1 + m(T - t) - rt]$$

$$\text{s.t.} \quad T = \frac{1 + mt}{2(m + r)}$$

That is to maximize

$$g = tq\underline{n}\left[1 + m\left(\frac{1 + mt}{2(m + r)} - t\right) - rt\right]$$

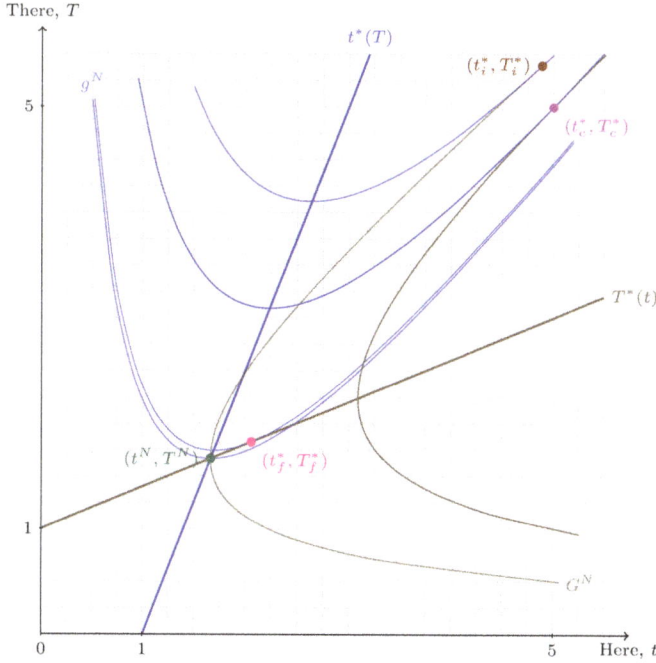

Figure 5.8: The four allocations in the Fiscal Competition Game. The four allocations are:

(i) the Nash equilibrium (t^N, T^N);

(ii) the common tax rates (t_c^*, T_c^*);

(iii) the first mover solution (t_f^*, T_f^*);

(iv) the imperial solution (t_i^*, T_i^*).

The first order condition is

$$g_t = q\underline{n}[1 + m(T - t) - rt] + tq\underline{n}[m(T' - 1) - r] = 0$$

Note that

$$T = \frac{1 + mt}{2(m + r)} \text{ and } T' = \frac{m}{2(m + r)}$$

It can be solved using $g_t = 0$ that

$$t_f^* = \frac{3m + 2r}{2(m^2 + 4mr + 2r^2)} > t^N = \frac{1}{m + 2r}$$

Thus Here sets a higher tax rate than in the Nash equilibrium. Then There responds by setting

$$T_f^* = T^*(t_f^*)$$

Since the best response function $T^*(t)$ is increasing and $t_F^* > t^N$, we have

$$T_f^* = T^*(t_f^*) > T^*(t^N) = T^N$$

Therefore, when Here is the first mover, both set a higher tax rate than that at the Nash equilibrium. As shown in Figure 5.8, following Here as first mover (who increases the tax rate and is as a result better off), There would also increase the tax rate since the tax rates of the two countries are strategic complements. Therefore, There is also better off compared to the Nash equilibrium as the first mover (Here).

Notice that

$$\frac{t_f^*}{t^N} = \frac{(3m + 2r)(m + 2r)}{2(m^2 + 4mr + 2r^2)}$$

$$= \frac{3m^2 + 8mr + 4r^2}{2m^2 + 8mr + 4r^2}$$

Since the numerator is larger than the denominator when $m > 0$, we have

$$\frac{t_f^*}{t^N} > 1 \Rightarrow t_f^* > t^N$$

7. Here's constrained choice problem is

$$\max_{t,T} \quad g = tq\underline{n}(1 - rt)$$

$$\text{s.t.} \quad G = TQ\underline{N}(1 - rT) \geq G^N$$

where G^N is the size of the grant at the Nash equilibrium. Since Here maximizes its payoff subject to There's reservation indifference curve, the two indifference curves are tangent at the solution (t_i^*, T_i^*), implying that (t_i^*, T_i^*) is Pareto-efficient.

8. As shown in Figure 5.8, for Here,

$$g(t^N, T^N) < g(t_f^*, T_f^*) < g(t_c^*, T_c^*) < g(t_i^*, T_i^*)$$

and for There,

$$G(t^N, T^N) = G(t_i^*, T_i^*) < G(t_f^*, T_f^*) < G(t_c^*, T_c^*)$$

Allocations (t_c^*, T_c^*), (t_f^*, T_f^*) and (t_i^*, T_i^*) are Pareto-superior to (t^N, T^N), (t_i^*, T_i^*) is Pareto-superior to (t_f^*, T_f^*), and we cannot Pareto-rank (t_c^*, T_c^*) and (t_i^*, T_i^*).

Figure 5.9: Thorstein Veblen (1857–1929) was an American economist and sociologist who coined the term "conspicuous consumption." Veblen's seminal work, *The Theory of the Leisure Class*, published in 1899, examined the influence of social norms on individual behavior, i.e., the social and economic implications of extravagant spending as a display of status and power. In addition to his work on consumption, Veblen explored the impact of institutions on economic coordination. Wikimedia Commons, public domain https://commons.wikimedia.org/wiki/File:Veblen3a.jpg

The Conspicuous Consumption Game is based on the model in Oh, Park, and Bowles [79], and was inspired by Veblen's theory of what he termed "conspicuous consumption," a precursor to the contemporary models of costly signalling of otherwise unobservable qualities initiated in economics by Spence [96] and in biology by Zahavi [115]. (See also Bowles and Park [32].)

[79]: Oh, Park, and Bowles (2012), 'Veblen Effects, Political Representation, and the Reduction in Working Time over the 20th Century'

[96]: Spence (1973), 'Job Market Signaling'

[115]: Zahavi (1975), 'Mate Selection—A Selection for a Handicap'

[32]: Bowles and Park (2005), 'Emulation, Inequality, and Work Hours'

5.3 Conspicuous consumption as a "public bad"

In 1992, almost a century after Thorsten Veblen's *The Theory of the Leisure Class*, Juliet Schor published *The Overworked American*. Both works view consumption as a social activity aimed at least in part at establishing and maintaining one's social standing relative to others. Here is a problem in the Veblen-Schor tradition, based on what we call the Conspicuous Consumption Game. The problem about the effect of a tax on the extent of cigarette smoking in Section 4.1 is another example of consumption as a social activity.

Suppose individuals differ in some trait that influences hourly wages and that they choose their time at work (h) to maximize a utility function, the arguments of which are leisure (which we normalize as $1 - h$) and what we term effective consumption, c^*, defined as their own consumption level (c) minus the product of a constant $v > 0$ (for Veblen) times the consumption level of some higher-income reference group ($\bar{c}$).

The individual's reference group might be the very rich or it might be an intermediate group. The reference group's rank in the income distribution is taken as exogenous, as is the Veblen constant v. It may be convenient to think of each individual as belonging to a homogeneous income class, each member of which takes the next highest income class as its reference group (the richest class have no reference group). Together, the reference group and v measure the nature and intensity of the relevant social comparisons. Individuals do not save, so $c = wh$, where w is the wage rate (the earnings of a person who took no leisure).

Thus for some individual not in the richest group we have

$$u = u(c^*, h) = u((wh - v\bar{c}), h) \tag{5.6}$$

where $u_c^* > 0$, $u_{c^*c^*} < 0$, $u_h < 0$, and $u_{hh} < 0$. Leisure and consumption are complements so $u_{c^*h} < 0$.

1. Show that the uncompensated external effect from the reference group's consumption is negative, and the effect of the reference group's consumption is to increase the hours of work of less well-off groups.

Now consider the specific utility function for a game with just two players denoted by subscripts j and k whose valuation of leisure (average and marginal) is equal to λ. Thus the utility of each is

$$
\begin{aligned}
u_j &= \ln(wh_j - vwh_k) + (1 - h_j)\lambda \\
u_k &= \ln(wh_k - vwh_j) + (1 - h_k)\lambda
\end{aligned}
\tag{5.7}
$$

Suppose they are able to choose their own work hours and (until indicated otherwise below) they do so independently and simultaneously.

2. Write down the first order conditions for j's choice of work hours and, using this and the analogous first order condition for k, derive the two best response functions: $h_j(h_k)$ and $h_k(h_j)$.

3. What is the effect on j's hours of work of variations in k's hours of work, i.e., dh_j/dh_k? Explain whether work hours are complements or substitutes.

4. Give the hours worked by each in the Nash equilibrium, h_k^N and h_j^N. Does this expression for the Nash hours of work place any restriction on the size of the "Veblen coefficient" v? Recall that time of work (called "hours") is restricted to the unit interval.

5. Given the restriction you impose on v above, is the resulting Nash equilibrium stable? Explain your answer.

6. Using the results you have already derived, show that the Nash equilibrium outcome is not Pareto-efficient.

7. The Leisure is Lovely Party surprisingly wins office and it invests in public parks, music festivals and other things that enhance the marginal and average utility of leisure. (The public finance of the policy has no effects on the workers' choice of hours.)

   a) Give the partial effect of the policy on j's working time (conditional on a given working time by k), and that on the Nash equilibrium level of j's work hours. Explain why they are different.

   b) Define the social multiplier in this case and give its value, m. Explain why it is positive or negative (whichever it is), and why it depends on v the way it does.

   The social multiplier is explained in Section 4.1 and Section 4.4.

8. Suppose that one of the workers, j, is the first mover. What optimization problem will they solve and what would be the resulting hours of work: h_j^F and $h_k(h_j^F)$? Explain the effect of j's first mover advantage on k's utility.

9. The workers form a political party (Workers of the World Unite, You have Nothing to Lose but Your Overwork!). They defeat the incumbent LLP party and implement an alternative policy to limit working hours: each may not work more than $\underline{h}$ hours, having chosen $\underline{h}$ so as to maximize their utilities. Solve the optimizing problem of the workers. Why does solution $\underline{h}^*$ not depend on v? Show that $\underline{h}^* < h_j^F < h_j^N$ and explain both inequalities.

Answers.

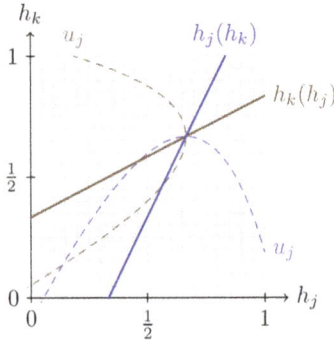

Figure 5.10: best response functions in the conspicuous consumption. Shown in the figure are the indifference loci of the two and their best response functions

$$h_j(h_k) = v h_k + \frac{1}{\lambda}$$

and

$$h_k(h_j) = v h_j + \frac{1}{\lambda}$$

for the case where $v = 0.5, \lambda = 3$ and $w = 1$. The same parameter values are used in the other figures for the Conspicuous Consumption Game.

Note that from $c^* = wh - v\bar{c}$, we have

$$\frac{dc^*}{d\bar{c}} = w\frac{dh}{d\bar{c}} - v$$

Since

$$u_{c^*c^*} < 0, u_{hh} < 0, u_{c^*h} < 0$$

both the numerator and denominator of $dh/d\bar{c}$ are negative.

1. Given the utility function (5.6), we have

$$\frac{\partial u}{\partial \bar{c}} = -v u_{c^*} < 0$$

Therefore, the externality from the reference group consumption is negative. The first order condition for the choice of h is

$$u_{c^*} w + u_h = 0 \tag{5.8}$$

which defines an implicit function $h = h(\bar{c})$.

Then, to find the effect of variations in $\bar{c}$ (the consumption level of the reference group) on work hours we totally differentiate the equilibrium condition (5.8) with respect to $\bar{c}$ and set the result equal to zero. Then we have

$$0 = w\left(u_{c^*c^*}\frac{dc^*}{d\bar{c}} + u_{c^*h}\frac{dh}{d\bar{c}}\right) + \left(u_{hc^*}\frac{dc^*}{d\bar{c}} + u_{hh}\frac{dh}{d\bar{c}}\right)$$
$$= (w u_{c^*c^*} + u_{hc^*})\frac{dc^*}{d\bar{c}} + (w u_{c^*h} + u_{hh})\frac{dh}{d\bar{c}}$$
$$= (w u_{c^*c^*} + u_{hc^*})(w\frac{dh}{d\bar{c}} - v) + (w u_{c^*h} + u_{hh})\frac{dh}{d\bar{c}}$$

Thus,

$$\frac{dh}{d\bar{c}} = \frac{(w u_{c^*c^*} + u_{c^*h})v}{w^2 u_{c^*c^*} + 2w u_{c^*h} + u_{hh}} > 0.$$

Therefore, the effect of the reference group's consumption is to increase the hours of work of less well-off groups.

2. To maximize $u_j = \ln(wh_j - vwh_k) + (1 - h_j)\lambda$, the first order condition is

$$\frac{\partial u_j}{\partial h_j} = \frac{w}{w(h_j - vh_k)} - \lambda = 0 \Rightarrow \frac{1}{h_j - vh_k} = \lambda \tag{5.9}$$

which means that on the best response function the marginal utility of working hours equals the marginal utility of leisure time.

From equation (5.9), we have the following best response functions

$$h_j(h_k) = v h_k + \frac{1}{\lambda}$$

and similarly

$$h_k(h_j) = v h_j + \frac{1}{\lambda}$$

as shown in Figure 5.10.

3. The effect on j's hours of work of variations in k's hours of work

$$\frac{dh_j}{dh_k} = v > 0$$

Therefore, work hours are strategic complements. Indeed, by definition strategic complement means

$$\frac{\partial^2 u_j}{\partial h_j \partial h_k} > 0$$

which is equivalent to

$$\frac{dh_j}{dh_k} = v > 0$$

assuming the second order condition holds.

4. Given the best response function, we have

$$h_j^N = v\left(vh_j^N + \frac{1}{\lambda}\right) + \frac{1}{\lambda} = \frac{1}{\lambda(1-v)} = h_k^N$$

By $0 < h_j \leq 1$ we have

$$\lambda(1-v) \geq 1 \Rightarrow v \leq 1 - \frac{1}{\lambda}$$

5. From

$$0 < \frac{dh_j}{dh_k} = v \leq 1 - \frac{1}{\lambda} < 1$$

we know that the Nash equilibrium is stable, since no one will "overreact" to a small deviation of the other as shown in Figure 5.11. Mathematically, consider the following dynamic system,

$$h_j^{t+1} = h_j(h_k^t)$$
$$h_k^{t+1} = h_k(h_j^t)$$

then the Nash equilibrium (h_j^N, h_k^N) is the steady state. It is stable if and only if the eigenvalue of the derivative matrix

$$\begin{bmatrix} v & 0 \\ 0 & v \end{bmatrix}$$

is less than one in absolute value, i.e., if $|v| < 1$, which we know to be the case.

6. At the Nash equilibrium, from the first order conditions defining the two best response functions, we have

$$\frac{\partial u_j}{\partial h_j} = \frac{\partial u_k}{\partial h_k} = 0$$

Total differentiating the first order condition (5.9) gives

$$\frac{\partial^2 u_j}{\partial h_j^2} dh_j + \frac{\partial^2 u_j}{\partial h_j \partial h_k} dh_k = 0$$

and so

$$\frac{dh_j}{dh_k} = -\frac{\frac{\partial^2 u_j}{\partial h_j \partial h_k}}{\frac{\partial^2 u_j}{\partial h_j^2}} > 0$$

since the numerator is positive by the definition of strategic complement and the denominator is negative by the second order condition

$$\frac{\partial^2 u_j}{\partial h_j^2} < 0$$

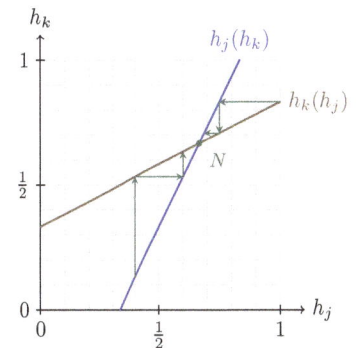

Figure 5.11: The stability of the Nash equilibrium in the conspicuous consumption. The slope of the best response function is less than one, as

$$\frac{dh_j(h_k)}{dh_k} = v < 1$$

and

$$\frac{dh_k(h_j)}{dh_j} = v < 1$$

which means that no one will overreact to a small deviation of the other. Thus, the Nash equilibrium N is asymptotically stable.

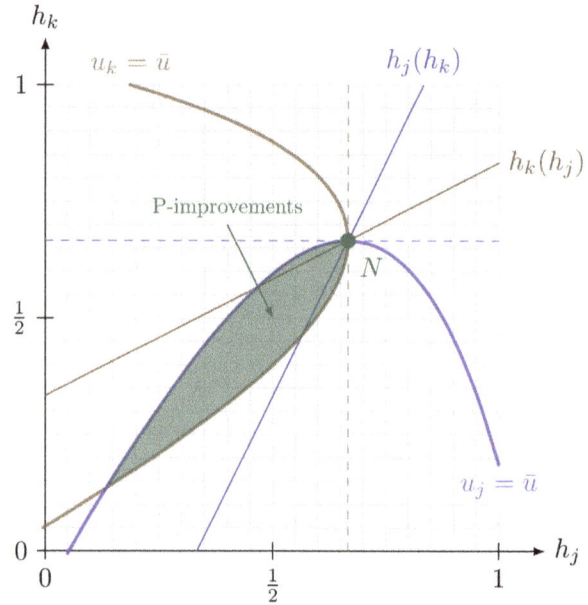

Figure 5.12: The inefficiency of the Nash equilibrium in the conspicuous consumption. At the Nash equilibrium N, the tangent line of the indifference curve $u_k = \bar{u}$ is horizontal and that of $u_j = \bar{u}$ is vertical, since by the first order conditions defining the two best response functions

$$\frac{du_k}{dh_k} = 0, \quad \frac{du_j}{dh_j} = 0$$

Then the two indifference curves can not be tangent with each other, therefore, N is not Pareto-efficient and any point in the shaded region is a Pareto-improvement.

while

$$\frac{\partial u_j}{\partial h_k} = -\frac{v}{h_j - vh_k} < 0 \quad \text{and} \quad \frac{\partial u_k}{\partial h_j} = -\frac{v}{h_k - vh_j} < 0$$

Thus,

$$du_j = \frac{\partial u_j}{\partial h_j}dh_j + \frac{\partial u_j}{\partial h_k}dh_k = \frac{\partial u_j}{\partial h_k}dh_k > 0$$

$$du_k = \frac{\partial u_k}{\partial h_j}dh_j + \frac{\partial u_k}{\partial h_k}dh_k = \frac{\partial u_j}{\partial h_k}dh_j > 0$$

for $dh_k, dh_j < 0$. That is, by reducing the working hours together, both j and k will be better off than in the Nash equilibrium. Thus, the Nash equilibrium is not Pareto-efficient, as shown in Figure 5.12.

7. a) Since $h_j = vh_k + 1/\lambda$, the partial effect of the policy on j's working time is

$$\frac{\partial h_j}{\partial \lambda} = -\frac{1}{\lambda^2}$$

While the effect of the policy on the Nash equilibrium level of j's work hours is

$$\frac{\partial h_j^N}{\partial \lambda} = -\frac{1}{\lambda^2(1-v)}$$

The two effects are different as shown in Figure 5.13 because

$$\frac{\partial h_j^N}{\partial \lambda} = \frac{\partial h_j}{\partial \lambda} + \frac{\partial h_j}{\partial h_k}\frac{\partial h_k^N}{\partial \lambda} \tag{5.10}$$

That is, the effect of the policy on the Nash equilibrium level of j's work hours includes the direct effect (conditional on a given working time by k) and their reaction to k's response.

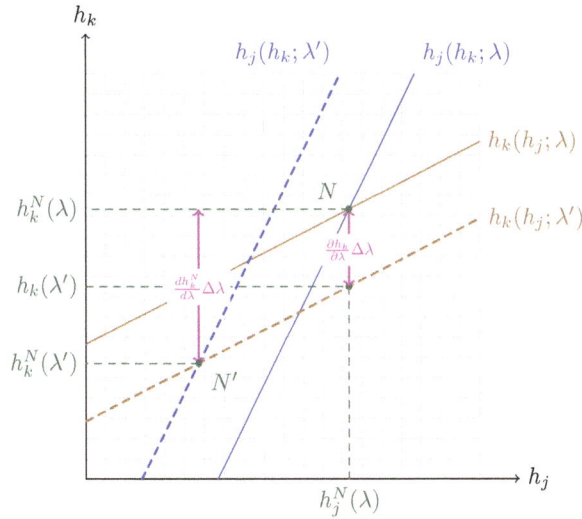

Figure 5.13: The social multiplier in conspicuous consumption. The Nash equilibrium N is the intersection of the two best response functions

$$h_j(h_k;\lambda) = vh_k + \frac{1}{\lambda}$$

and

$$h_k(h_j;\lambda) = vh_j + \frac{1}{\lambda}$$

Suppose the public policy increases the marginal and average utility of leisure from λ to λ'. The best response functions shift and the symmetric Nash equilibrium becomes E', with $v = 0.5$, $\lambda = 3$, and $\lambda' = 7$. It can be seen that

$$h_k(\lambda') - h_k^N(\lambda) = \frac{\partial h_k}{\partial \lambda}\Delta\lambda$$

is different from

$$h_k^N(\lambda') - h_k^N(\lambda) = \frac{dh_k^N}{d\lambda}\Delta\lambda$$

b) The social multiplier m is defined by

$$(1+m)\frac{\partial h_j}{\partial \lambda} = \frac{\partial h_j^N}{\partial \lambda}$$

Therefore, we have

$$m = \frac{\partial h_j^N/\partial \lambda}{\partial h_j/\partial \lambda} - 1 = \frac{v}{1-v} > 0$$

Alternatively, by the symmetry of the Nash equilibrium, the decomposition (5.10) becomes

$$\frac{\partial h_j^N}{\partial \lambda} = \frac{\partial h_j}{\partial \lambda} + \frac{\partial h_j}{\partial h_k}\frac{\partial h_k^N}{\partial \lambda}$$

and then, dividing both sides by $\partial h_j/\partial \lambda$ gives

$$(1+m) = 1 + v(1+m)$$

and therefore

$$m = \frac{v}{1-v}$$

The multiplier is positive since working hours are strategic complements. The change in the work time of j will induce a change in that of k in the same direction, which will reinforce the change in that of j, and so on. Thus, the effect of the policy on the Nash equilibrium level is greater than the direct effect conditional on a given working time by the other.

The multiplier is increasing in v. A larger v means a larger effect of one's work time on the other's, and then a larger indirect effect and thus a greater multiplier.

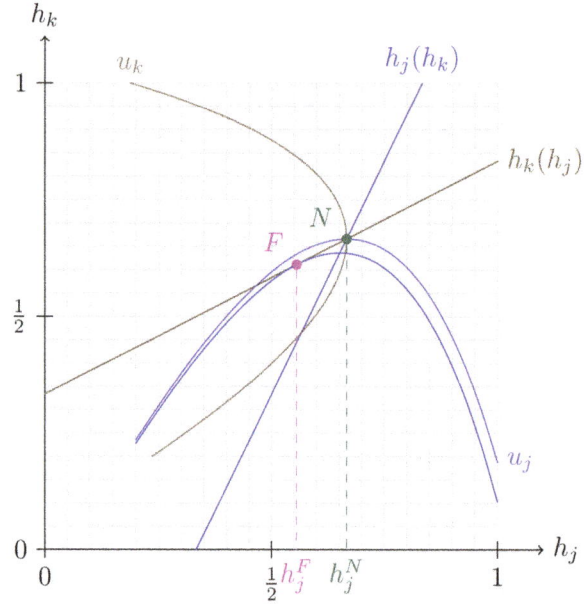

Figure 5.14: The first-mover's constrained choice problem and its solution. The first-mover's problem is to maximize their utility

$$u_j = \ln(wh_j - vwh_k) + (1 - h_j)\lambda$$

subject to the other's best response

$$h_k(h_j) = vh_j + \frac{1}{\lambda}$$

The solution

$$h_j^F = \frac{1 - v^2 + v}{\lambda(1 - v^2)}$$

is given by point F where the indifference curve and the best response are tangent with each other.

8. The constrained choice problem for the first mover j is

$$\max_{h_j} \quad u_j = \ln(wh_j - vwh_k) + (1 - h_j)\lambda$$

$$\text{s.t.} \quad h_k = vh_j + \frac{1}{\lambda}$$

That is

$$\max_{h_j} \quad u_j = \ln\left[wh_j - vw\left(vh_j + \frac{1}{\lambda}\right)\right] + (1 - h_j)\lambda$$

The first order condition is

$$\frac{w(1 - v^2)}{w[h_j^F - v(vh_j^F + \frac{1}{\lambda})]} - \lambda = \frac{1 - v^2}{(1 - v^2)h_j^F - \frac{v}{\lambda}} - \lambda = 0$$

Therefore,

$$h_j^F = \frac{1 - v^2 + v}{\lambda(1 - v^2)}$$

as shown in Figure 5.14. When j is the first mover, they would be better off by reducing their hours of work, which would lead k to also lower their hours of work due to the strategic complementary of work hours in this game. Therefore, k would be better off as well.

9. The new constrained choice problem for the two acting cooperatively (the game is symmetrical so maximizing the utility of either one is sufficient) is

$$\max_{\underline{h}} \quad \ln(w\underline{h} - vw\underline{h}) + (1 - \underline{h})\lambda = \ln[(1 - v)w\underline{h}] + (1 - \underline{h})\lambda$$

The first order condition is

$$\frac{1}{\underline{h}} - \lambda = 0 \Rightarrow \underline{h}^* = \frac{1}{\lambda}$$

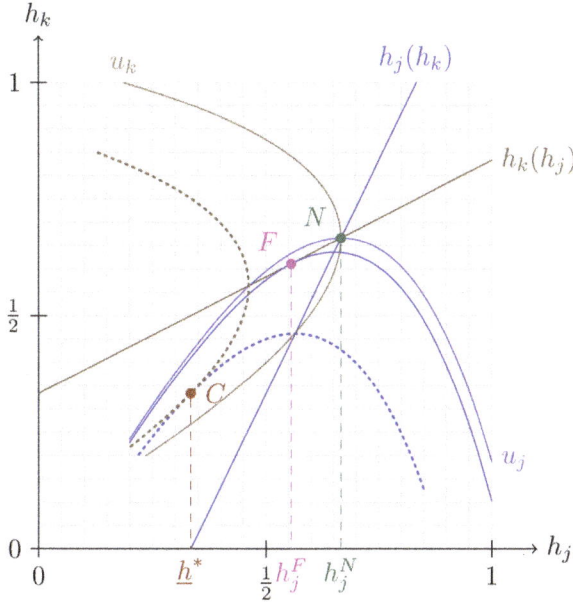

Figure 5.15: The three allocations in the conspicuous consumption. The three allocations with $v = 0.5$, $\lambda = 3$ and $w = 1$ are: (i) the Nash equilibrium N where

$$h_j^N = \frac{1}{\lambda(1 - v)} = h_k^N$$

(ii) the solution when k is the first-mover F where

$$h_j^F = \frac{1 - v^2 + v}{\lambda(1 - v^2)}$$

and (iii) the solution of the worker union, C where

$$\underline{h}^* = \frac{1}{\lambda}$$

It can be seen that

$$\underline{h}^* < h_j^F < h_j^N$$

which is identical to the first order condition for the individual choice in the absence of the Veblen effect, that is when $v = 0$ in equation (5.9).

Comparing the hours of work in the three cases, since

$$h_j^F = \frac{1 - v^2 + v}{\lambda(1 - v^2)} = \frac{1 + v}{\lambda(1 - v^2)} - \frac{v^2}{\lambda(1 - v^2)} = h_j^N - \frac{v^2}{\lambda(1 - v^2)}$$

and

$$h_j^F = \frac{1 - v^2 + v}{\lambda(1 - v^2)} = \frac{1}{\lambda} + \frac{v}{\lambda(1 - v^2)} = \underline{h}^* + \frac{v}{\lambda(1 - v^2)}$$

we have

$$\underline{h}^* < h_j^F < h_j^N$$

as shown in Figure 5.15.

> Note that
> $$\frac{1 + v}{\lambda(1 - v^2)} = \frac{1 + v}{\lambda(1 - v)(1 + v)} = h_j^N$$

5.4 Residential segregation as a coordination failure

Consider a single neighborhood (one of many) in which all housing units are equally desirable to all members of the population. Individuals' preferences for living in this neighborhood depend solely on the composition of the neighborhood. In this neighborhood and in the surrounding population, "Greens" prefer to live in a mixed neighborhood in which there are slightly more "Greens" than "Blues", and "Blues" correspondingly do not prefer segregation but would rather not be a minority of the neighborhood.

A related model of segregation (like this one, inspired by the work of Thomas Schelling) is in Section 2.5.

Some background for this question is in Section 7.16 of [29] and Chapter 2 of [14].

[29]: Bowles and Halliday (2022), *Microeconomics*

[14]: Bowles (2004), *Microeconomics*

These preferences are expressed by the price, p_g and p_b, that Greens and Blues, respectively, would be willing to pay for a house in the neighborhood, each depending on the fraction of homes in the neighborhood occupied by Greens, $f \in [0, 1]$.

$$p_b = \frac{1}{2}(f + \delta) - \frac{1}{2}(f + \delta)^2 + p$$
$$p_g = \frac{1}{2}(f - \delta) - \frac{1}{2}(f - \delta)^2 + p \tag{5.11}$$

with $\delta \in (0, 1/2)$ where p is a positive constant reflecting the intrinsic value of the identical homes. Examples of two equations are shown in Figure 5.16.

Suppose that during each time period some fraction α of both the Greens and the Blues in this neighborhood consider selling their house to a member of the surrounding population. Prospective buyers from outside the neighborhood visit the neighborhood in proportion to the current composition of the neighborhood. The fraction of prospective buyers who are Green, like the fraction of prospective sellers, is thus f.

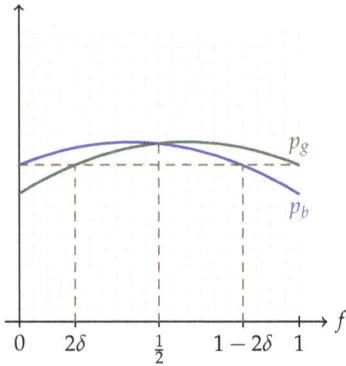

Figure 5.16: The prices of the house as functions of the fraction of homes in the neighborhood occupied by Greens. For the Blues,

$$p_b = \frac{1}{2}(f + \delta) - \frac{1}{2}(f + \delta)^2 + p$$

and the Greens,

$$p_g = \frac{1}{2}(f - \delta) - \frac{1}{2}(f - \delta)^2 + p$$

Note that $p_b(0) = p_b(1 - 2\delta)$, $p_g(2\delta) = p_g(1)$ and

$$p_b(\tfrac{1}{2}) = p_g(\tfrac{1}{2})$$

In this figure, we assume $p = 0.5$ and $\delta = 0.1$.

Prospective buyers and sellers are randomly matched; imagine that the house-hunting visitors just knock on the door of a randomly selected house. Thus, the expected number of Greens seeking to sell their house who are contacted by a house-hunting Blue in any period is $\alpha f(1 - f)$. Each prospective seller meets just one buyer per period, either making a sale or not; the probability of making the sale depends on the difference between the buyer's valuation of the home and the seller's valuation, assuming the former exceeds the latter. Thus, if a Blue considering selling meets a Green and if f is such that $p_g > p_b$ then the probability that a sale will take place is $\beta(p_g - p_b)$ where β is a positive constant relating the price difference to the probability of sales.

The process of change in f is described by the following replicator equation:

$$\Delta f = f' - f = \alpha f(1 - f)\beta(p_g - p_b) \tag{5.12}$$

If the Blue's price exceeds the Green's price, αf is the number of Greens seeking to sell, of these $(1 - f)$ will be matched with a Blue, and the sale will take place with probability $\beta(p_g - p_b)$. Analogously, if the Green's price exceeds the Blue's price, $\alpha(1 - f)$ is the number of Blues seeking to sell, of these f will be matched with a Green, and the sale will take place with probability $\beta(p_g - p_b)$.

If you are curious about replicator equations (and replicator dynamics in general) have a look at Sandholm [85].

[85]: Sandholm (2010), *Population Games and Evolutionary Dynamics*

1. Find all the equilibria of the house market and indicate which (if any) of the equilibria are stable in the replicator dynamic given by the equation above.

2. For $\delta < 1/4$, show that there exists a value of $\epsilon > 0$ such that a law permitting house sales only if $f \in [1/2 - \epsilon, 1/2 + \epsilon]$ would implement an outcome that is Pareto-superior to the stable equilibria.

3. What accounts for the market failure in this situation?

4. Suppose that the Greens have the same preferences as in equation (5.11), with $\delta = 0.1$ and $p = 1$, but the Blues have all converted to the Love Everybody Equally religion and as a consequence are

indifferent to the types of their neighbors and simply value all homes at $p_b = 1.12$. Indicate all the equilibria of the resulting housing market and indicate which are stable in the replicator dynamic (i.e., determine the sign of $d\Delta f/df$ for each stationary value of f).

Answers.

1. By (5.11), we have $p_g - p_b = \delta(2f - 1)$, then

$$\Delta f = \alpha\beta\delta f(1 - f)(2f - 1)$$

Let $\Delta f = 0$ we have $f = 0$, $f = 0.5$, or $f = 1$. As shown in Figure 5.17, both $f = 0$ and $f = 1$ are stable (in the neighborhood of $f = 0$ f is decreasing, while in the neighborhood of $f = 1$ f is increasing).

2. From the price equations (5.11) it can be seen that

$$p_b(1) < p_b(0) = p_b(1 - 2\delta)$$

and

$$p_g(0) < p_g(1) = p_g(2\delta)$$

as shown in Figure 5.18. Thus, for any f between 2δ and $1 - 2\delta$, we have

$$p_b(1) < p_b(0) = p_b(1 - 2\delta) < p_b(f)$$

and

$$p_g(0) < p_g(1) = p_g(2\delta) < p_g(f)$$

Then for any ϵ such that

$$\begin{cases} \frac{1}{2} - \epsilon > 2\delta \\ \frac{1}{2} + \epsilon < 1 - 2\delta \end{cases} \Leftrightarrow \epsilon < \frac{1}{2} - 2\delta$$

at any possible outcome $f \in [1/2 - \epsilon, 1/2 + \epsilon] \subset (2\delta, 1 - 2\delta)$, both prices are greater than the prices at either $f = 0$ or $f = 1$, i.e., any possible outcome is Pareto-superior to the stable equilibria.

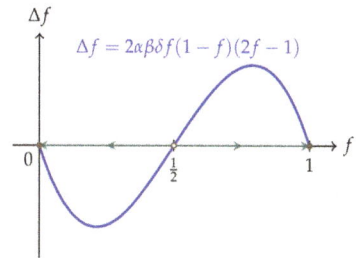

Figure 5.17: The stable equilibria in the dynamics of residential segregation. The replicator dynamics

$$\Delta f = \alpha\beta\delta f(1 - f)(2f - 1)$$

has 3 equilibria, i.e.,

$$f = 0, f = 0.5 \text{ and } f = 1$$

Both $f = 0$ and $f = 1$ are stable, while $f = 0.5$ is unstable. In this figure, we assume $\delta = 0.1$.

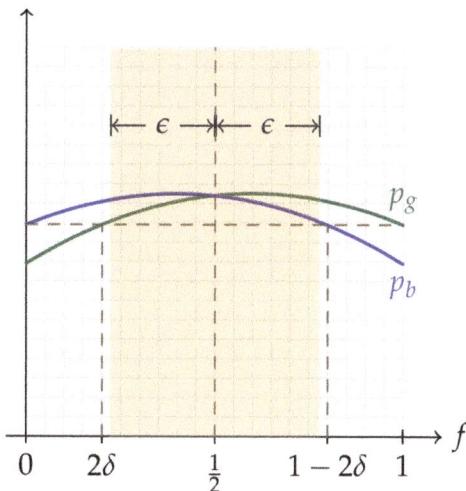

Figure 5.18: The value of housing as function of racial composition of the neighborhood. For the Blues,

$$p_b(f) > p_b(0)$$

for all $0 < f < 1 - 2\delta$, and the Greens,

$$p_g(f) > p_g(1)$$

for all $1 > f > 2\delta$. Thus, if

$$\epsilon < \frac{1}{2} - 2\delta$$

then for any outcome $f \in [1/2 - \epsilon, 1/2 + \epsilon]$, both prices would be greater than the prices at the stable equilibria. In this figure, we assume $\delta = 0.1$.

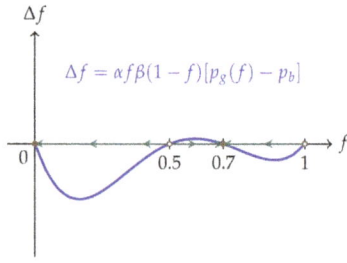

$$\Delta f = \alpha f \beta (1-f)[p_g(f) - p_b]$$

Figure 5.19: The stable equilibria in the dynamics of residential segregation with the Love Everybody Equally religion. The replicator dynamics

$$\Delta f = \alpha f \beta (1-f)[p_g(f) - p_b]$$

has 4 equilibria, i.e.,

$$f = 0, f = 0.5, f = 0.7 \text{ and } f = 1$$

Both $f = 0$ and $f = 0.7$ are stable, while $f = 0.5$ and $f = 1$ are unstable. In this figure, we assume $\delta = 0.1$.

3. Uncompensated external effects. When one person purchases or sells a house, it will also affect others as it changes the composition of the neighborhood.

4. By $\Delta f = 0$ we have $f = 0$, $f = 1$ or $p_g = p_b$. Given that $\delta = 0.1$, $p = 1$ and $p_b = 1.12$, we have

$$p_g = p_b \Rightarrow (f - 0.1) - (f - 0.1)^2 = 0.24 \Rightarrow f = 0.5 \text{ or } f = 0.7$$

Therefore, there are four equilibria, and as shown in Figure 5.19, $f = 0$ and $f = 0.7$ are stable.

5.5 Interdependence and coordination: A taxonomy

Four of the games we have presented in this and the previous chapter — The Tragedy of the Fishers, Fiscal Competition, Conspicuous Consumption, and Household Public Goods — differ along two dimensions: the nature of the uncompensated external effect between the actors (positive or negative) and the way in which the choices of one actor affect the best responses of the other (whether their actions are complements or substitutes). This problem explores the resulting 2×2 taxonomy of coordination problems.

Consider two individuals — lower and Upper — who each take an action — a and A in $[0, \infty)$ — which is costly to them to do, while also yielding a benefit to the actor as well as affecting the utility of the other (positively or negatively). Thus let

$$\begin{aligned} u &= u(A, a) \\ U &= U(a, A) \end{aligned} \tag{5.13}$$

Suppose the above utility functions take this form

$$\begin{aligned} u &= \alpha + \beta a + \gamma A + \delta aA - \lambda a^2 \\ U &= \alpha + \beta A + \gamma a + \delta aA - \lambda A^2 \end{aligned} \tag{5.14}$$

1. Give the equation defining lower's best response function $a(A)$.

2. Find the Nash equilibrium (i.e., a^N and A^N).

3. Give (sufficient) conditions on the parameters of the utility functions above under which (a) the external effect u_A and U_a is positive or negative and (b) the two strategies a and A are substitutes or complements.

Notation:

$$u_A = \frac{\partial u}{\partial A}, \quad u_a = \frac{\partial u}{\partial A}$$

$$u_{aA} = \frac{\partial^2 u}{\partial a \partial A}, \quad U_{aA} = \frac{\partial^2 U}{\partial a \partial A}$$

4. The fact that external effects u_A and U_a can be of either sign and the actions taken by the two may be either substitutes or complements given by the sign of u_{aA} and U_{Aa} means that there are four possible types of interaction. Locate the games in this and the previous chapter — Tragedy of the Fishers, Fiscal Competition, Conspicuous

Consumption, and Household Public Goods — in the associated 2×2 taxonomy as shown in Table 5.3

Strategies	External effects	
	Positive: $u_A > 0$	Negative: $u_A < 0$
Complements: $u_{aA} > 0$ Substitutes: $u_{aA} < 0$		

Table 5.3: A taxonomy of coordination problem

5. What is the first order condition for a symmetric Pareto-efficient allocation? (This is the hypothetical rule governing the actors' choice of an action that would result in their implementing a Pareto-efficient allocation were they to play non cooperatively.)

   a) How does this hypothetical first order condition differ from the first order condition that you derived above (from the actors' utility function)? Show that the additional term(s) represent the uncompensated external effects of the actor's choices on the other's utility.

   b) Use this first order condition and your expression for the Nash equilibrium above to show that a^* and A^* exceed the Pareto-efficient levels if and only if the external effect is negative. Explain why this is so.

6. Assuming that the Nash equilibrium is in pure strategies, show that there will always be a first mover advantage, and that the second mover will do worse (than in the Nash equilibrium of the simultaneous moves game) if strategies are substitutes and better if strategies are complements. Explain why this is so.

7. In the games shown here could it ever be advantageous to be second mover rather than first mover? If yes, provide an example, and explain why going second would be an advantage.

Answers.

1. The first order condition to maximize u is

$$u_a = \beta + \delta A - 2\lambda a = 0 \Rightarrow a = \frac{\beta + \delta A}{2\lambda}$$

2. Similarly, we have

$$A = \frac{\beta + \delta a}{2\lambda}$$

Then, using the fact that the game is symmetrical, the Nash equilibrium is

$$a^N = A^N = \frac{\beta}{2\lambda - \delta}$$

Similarly, we have

$$U_a = \gamma + \delta A$$

Figure 5.20: A taxonomy of coordination problem. The indifference curves and best response function with

$$u = \alpha + \beta a + \gamma A + \delta aA - \lambda a^2$$

The utility of the upper is symmetric:

$$U = \alpha + \beta A + \gamma a + \delta Aa - \lambda A^2$$

Figure (a) and (b) show strategic complements with

$$u_{aA} = \delta > 0$$

while (c) and (d) show strategic substitutes with

$$u_{aA} = \delta < 0$$

In (a) and (c) we have positive external effect by

$$u_A > 0$$

while in (b) and (d) we have negative external effect by

$$u_A < 0$$

By symmetry, we have the best response function of the Upper $A^*(a)$. In all the cases, the intersection of $A^*(a)$ and $a^*(A)$ is the Nash equilibrium N,

$$a^* = A^* = \frac{\beta}{2\lambda - \delta}$$

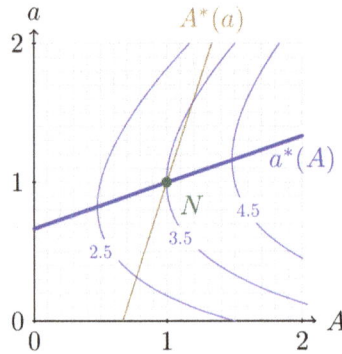

(a) Positive external effect and strategic complements with $u = 1 + 2a + A + aA - 1.5a^2$.

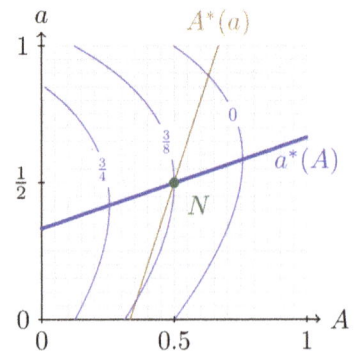

(b) Negative external effect and strategic complements with $u = 1 + a - 2A + aA - 1.5a^2$.

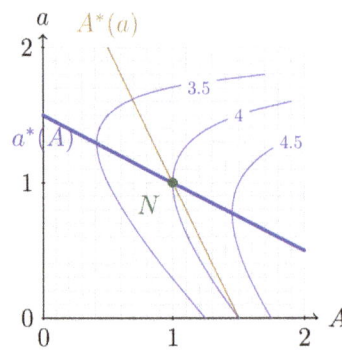

(c) Positive external effect and strategic substitutes with $u = 1 + 3a + 2A - aA - a^2$.

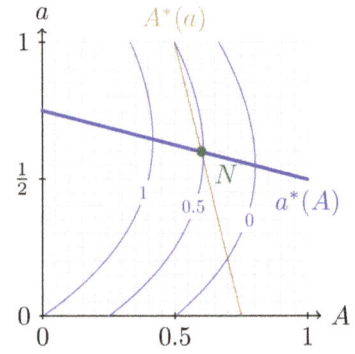

(d) Negative external effect and strategic substitutes with $u = 1 + 3a - 2A - aA - 2a^2$.

3. The external effect is

$$u_A = \gamma + \delta a$$

Since $a \in [0, \infty)$, if $\gamma, \delta > 0$, then $\gamma + \delta a > 0$ and the external effect is always positive; if $\gamma, \delta < 0$, then $\gamma + \delta a < 0$ and the external effect is always negative. From

$$u_{Aa} = U_{aA} = \delta$$

we have a and A are strategic complements if $\delta > 0$, and strategic substitutes if $\delta < 0$, as shown in Figure 5.20.

Table 5.4: A taxonomy of coordination games

	External effects	
Strategies	Positive: $u_A > 0$	Negative: $u_A < 0$
Complements: $u_{aA} > 0$	Fiscal Competition	Conspicuous Consumption
Substitutes: $u_{aA} < 0$	Household Public Goods	Tragedy of the Fishers

Note that

$$\omega = u(x, x) = U(x, x)$$

Suppose that ω does not achieve its maximum at (x, x). Then there exists (x', x') such that

$$u(x', x') > u(x, x)$$

and

$$U(x', x') > U(x, x)$$

Then (x', x') is Pareto-superior to (x, x).

4. The 2×2 taxonomy is given in Table 5.4.

5. If $(a^*, A^*) = (x^*, x^*)$ is a symmetric allocation that is Pareto-efficient, then it maximizes $\omega(x) = u(x, x) = U(x, x)$:

$$x^* = \arg\max_x \quad \omega(x) = \alpha + (\beta + \gamma)x + (\delta - \lambda)x^2$$

The first order condition is

$$\omega_x(x^*) = \beta + \gamma + 2(\delta - \lambda)x^* = 0 \Rightarrow x^* = \frac{\beta + \gamma}{2(\lambda - \delta)} \qquad (5.15)$$

a) The first order condition (5.15) can be rewritten as

$$2\lambda x^* = (\beta + \delta x^*) + (\gamma + \delta x^*)$$

where the first part in the right-hand side corresponds to the private marginal benefit $u_a = \beta + \delta A^* = \beta + \delta x^*$, while the second terms represents the uncompensated external effects $u_A = \gamma + \delta a^* = \gamma + \delta x^*$ at (x^*, x^*).

b) If the external effect is negative, then at the Nash equilibrium there exists a common decrease in the action that will benefit both players, as shown in Figure 5.21. That is, at the Nash equilibrium, for $da < 0, dA < 0$, we have

$$du = u_a da + u_A dA = u_A dA > 0,$$

and

$$dU = U_A dA + U_a da = U_a da > 0$$

since u_a and U_A equal 0 at the Nash equilibrium, and $U_a < 0$ and $u_A < 0$ because the external effect is negative.

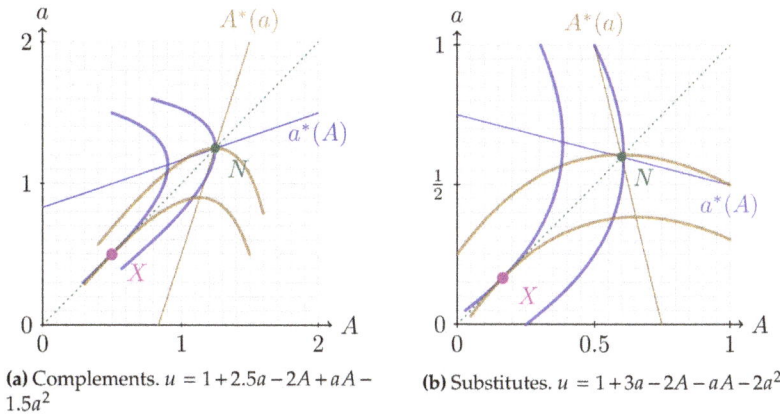

(a) Complements. $u = 1 + 2.5a - 2A + aA - 1.5a^2$

(b) Substitutes. $u = 1 + 3a - 2A - aA - 2a^2$

Figure 5.21: The symmetric efficient outcome. The Nash equilibrium levels

$$a^* = A^* = \frac{\beta}{2\lambda - \delta}$$

exceed the symmetric Pareto-efficient action levels

$$x^* = \frac{\beta + \gamma}{2(\lambda - \delta)}$$

if and only if the external effect is negative, regardless of (a) whether strategies are complements (left panel) or (b) substitutes (right panel). The utility functions under the two panels give examples of lower's utility function (Upper's is analogous) illustrating the case.

6. Suppose lower is the first mover. Denote the solution to the constrained choice problem

$$\begin{aligned} \max_a \quad & u(a, A) \\ \text{s.t.} \quad & A = A(a) \equiv \arg\max_A U(A, a) \end{aligned} \qquad (5.16)$$

by a^F and $A^F = A(a^F)$. We first show that there will always be a first mover advantage, i.e.,

$$u(a^F, A^F) > u(a^N, A^N)$$

where (a^N, A^N) is the Nash equilibrium. At the Nash equilibrium (a^N, A^N), we have $u_a = 0$. Therefore, there exists a Δa such that

$$\Delta u = u_A \frac{dA}{da} \Delta a > 0 \qquad (5.17)$$

Since (a^N, A^N) satisfies the constraint, i.e., $A^N = A(a^N)$, it is easy to see that

$$u(a^F, A^F) \geq u(a^N, A^N)$$

otherwise, lower would just choose the Nash equilibrium.

It can be seen that $\Delta a > 0$ if and only if

$$u_A \frac{dA}{da} > 0$$

That is the external effect is positive and the two strategies are complements, or the external effect is negative and the two strategies are substitutes.

by $u_A \frac{dA}{da} \neq 0$. We know this expression cannot be zero because we are looking at cases where external effects (of either sign) exist — so u_A cannot be zero — and where the action taken by each depends on the action taken by the other — so dA/da cannot be zero.

Then, from (5.17), there exists $a' = a^* + \Delta a$ such that $u(a', A(a')) > u(a^*, A^*)$. Thus,

$$u(a^F, A^F) \geq u(a', A(a')) > u(a^*, A^*).$$

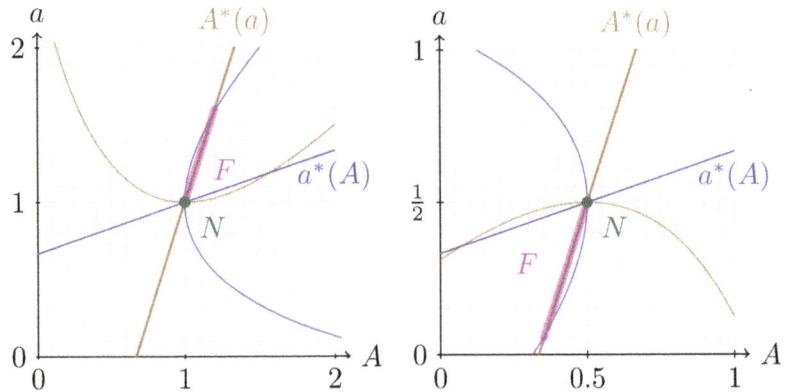

(a) Positive external effect and strategic complements with $u = 1 + 2a + A + aA - 1.5a^2$

(b) Negative external effect and strategic complements with
$u = 1 + a - 2A + aA - 1.5a^2$

(c) Positive external effect and strategic substitutes with $u = 1 + 3a + 2A - aA - a^2$

(d) Negative external effect and strategic substitutes with $u = 1 + 3a - 2A - aA - 2a^2$

Figure 5.22: The programming problem of the first mover in four cases. The programming problem of the lower as the first mover is to maximize

$$u = \alpha + \beta a + \gamma A + \delta aA - \lambda a^2$$

subject to the Upper's best response $A^*(a)$. To satisfy Upper's participation constraint, the solution must be located in the purple segment on the best response function intersected by the indifference curve through the Nash equilibrium N,

$$F = \{(A^*(a), a) \mid u(A, a) > u(N)\}$$

In all the four cases, there is always a first mover advantage. In figure (a) and (c) with strategic complements the second mover will do better, while in figure (b) and (d) with strategic substitutes the second mover will do worse.

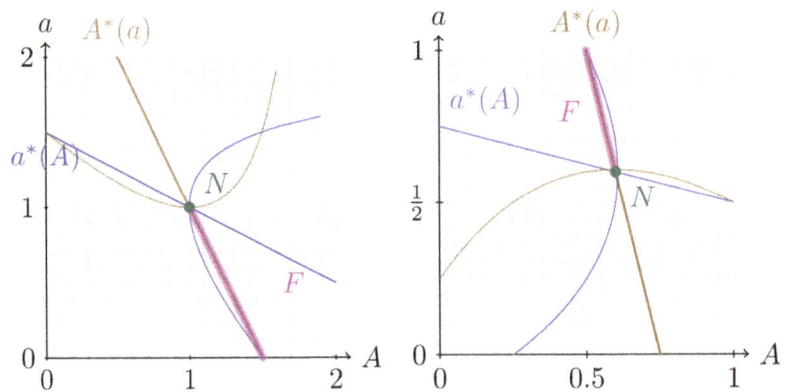

Now consider the second mover. On the graph of the best response function $(a, A(a))$, we have

$$U_A = 0$$

then

$$\frac{dU(A(a), a)}{da} = U_A \frac{dA}{da} + U_a da = U_a da$$

Thus by the Newton-Leibniz formula

Suppose $F'(x) = f(x)$. Then we have

$$F(b) - F(a) = \int_a^b f(x)dx$$

$$U(A^F, a^F) - U(A^*, a^*) = \int_{a^*}^{a^F} \frac{dU(A(a), a)}{da} da = \int_{a^*}^{a^F} U_a da$$

From (5.17) we know that

$$a^F > a^* \Leftrightarrow u_A \frac{dA}{da} > 0$$

Therefore, if strategies are substitutes (i.e., if $dA/da < 0$), then

$$a^F > a^* \Leftrightarrow u_A < 0 \Leftrightarrow U_a < 0$$

Thus

$$U(A^F, a^F) - U(A^*, a^*) = \int_{a^*}^{a^F} U_a da < 0$$

and so the second mover will do worse than in the Nash equilibrium.

While if strategies are complements (i.e., if $dA/da > 0$), then

$$a^F > a^* \Leftrightarrow u_A > 0 \Leftrightarrow U_a > 0$$

Thus

$$U(A^F, a^F) - U(A^*, a^*) = \int_{a^*}^{a^F} U_a da > 0$$

that is, the second mover will do better than in the Nash equilibrium, as shown in Figure 5.22.

Intuitively, there will always be a first mover advantage because the first mover could at least choose the Nash equilibrium which is not Pareto-efficient, and so must be able to do better by choosing some other action. Therefore, the first mover will always change their action in the direction that makes them better off. If strategies are substitutes, then the second mover will change their action in the opposite direction and do worse than in the Nash equilibrium. If strategies are complements, then the second mover will change their action in the same direction and do better than in the Nash equilibrium.

7. Yes, considering the case in which we regard the two utility functions as cardinal and interpersonally comparable, it is possible that the second mover gains more than the first mover. Consider the example shown in Figure 5.23 where (a) strategies are complements, (b) the external effect is positive, and (c) the best response function is pretty "flat" i.e., the first mover has to change a lot to affect the second mover's action. Then the second mover could gain more than the first mover compared with the Nash equilibrium.

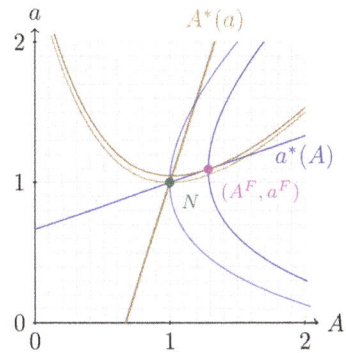

Figure 5.23: The example of interaction in which the second mover gains more than the first mover. The programming problem of Upper as the first mover is to maximize

$$U = 1 + 2A + a + aA - 1.5A^2$$

subject to lower's best response function

$$a^*(A) = \frac{2}{3} + \frac{1}{3}A$$

The solution in this case is

$$(A^F, a^F) = (1.285, 1.095)$$

and their utilities are

$$U^F = 3.595, u^F = 4.085$$

Both are higher than the utility level at Nash equilibrium

$$U^N = u^N = 3.5$$

but lower gains as the second mover.

Environmental Coordination Failures and Institutional Responses 6

Returning to the theme of mechanism design introduced in Chapter 4, we illustrate the adoption of policies to address the Pareto inefficient outcomes that arise in the presence of uncompensated external effects.

Discussions of alternative policies to address coordination failures often center on the appropriate balance of solutions implemented by markets — such as changes in property rights — and governmental interventions, such as taxes, transfers, or prohibitions. In Figure 6.2 we expand the space of policies and institutions to address coordination failures by adding to the poles — government and market — a third dimension that we term civil society. We call the figure the governance simplex: the vertices are differing types of rules of the game that jointly govern our social interactions.

The set of social interactions making up civil society — relationships taking place in families, firms, neighborhoods, identity groups, and other face-to-face settings — are strikingly dissimilar. But they have in common that they are personal and enduring (even involuntary) and that other-regarding preferences (for better or worse) are important motives for behavior.

While these characteristics of civil society are not absent in the social interactions governed by markets and states, they play a lesser role, and in most economic models are entirely absent. In this respect, civil society as a conceptual construct differs from markets and states whose proper functioning is consistent with ephemeral and impersonal interactions motivated entirely by self-interest.

Figure 6.1: Elinor Ostrom (1933–2012), a political scientist, won the Nobel Prize in economics for her work demonstrating the importance of the social norms and institutions of civil society in addressing local environmental problems. Holger Motzkau 2010, Wikimedia Commons, CC BY-SA 3.0, https://commons.wikimedia.org/wiki/File:Nobel_Prize_2009-Press_Conference_KVA-30.jpg

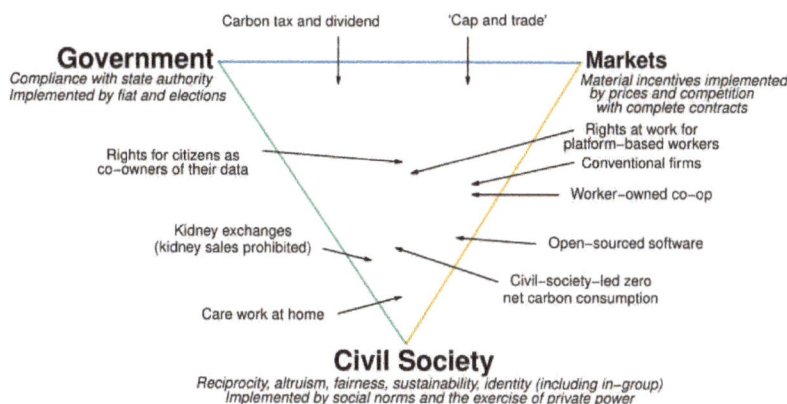

Figure 6.2: The governance triangle: Government, market, and civil society. An expanded space for policies and institutions. At each vertex are shown the kinds of motivations and mechanisms implementing outcomes that are characteristic of the vertex. The coordinates of any point in the triangle sum to one and so can be considered to be weights indicating the relative importance of each of the sets of institutions on the vertices. A point closer to a vertex represents a policy or institution for which the vertex in question is more important. You can read more about this approach in [17].

[17]: Bowles and Carlin (2020), 'Shrinking Capitalism'

Here we illustrate three approaches to environmental coordination failures based respectively on markets, on governmental policies, and on both other-regarding preferences and repeated interactions in civil society. We also provide a model of the adoption of electric vehicles and policies

©2025 Samuel Bowles and Weikai Chen, CC BY-NC 4.0

https://doi.org/10.11647/OBP.0466.06

In mathematical terminology, we are converting a one-dimensional simplex, the Government Market line, to the two-dimensional simplex, the triangle shown in the figure.

[14]: Bowles (2004), *Microeconomics*

[29]: Bowles and Halliday (2022), *Microeconomics*

[15]: Bowles (2016), *The Moral Economy*

To find out how fish markets really work, have a look at Gallegati, Giulioni, et al. [53] and Graddy [56].

[53]: Gallegati, Giulioni, et al. (2011), 'What's That Got to Do with the Price of Fish?'

[56]: Graddy (2006), 'Markets'

This problem is similar to the Tragedy of the Fishers in Section 5.1 except that we now allow the fishers to vary their fishing time continuously rather than being restricted to just two discrete hours of fishing.

to disrupt a coordination failure constituted by carbon trap in which all or most vehicles are based on internal combustion engines.

Some background for the problems in this chapter is found in Chapter 4 in Bowles [14], Chapters 5 and 16 in Bowles and Halliday [29], and Bowles [15].

6.1 The Tragedy of the Fishers revisited

This preliminary section sets up the model that will be used in the remaining sections of this chapter, and gives you the opportunity to exercise the modeling skills you developed in the previous chapter, or if you have not worked those problems, to familiarize you with some modeling methods that will help in what follows.

We return to the Tragedy of the Fishers example with two fishers, now called Upper and Lower for ease of notation, who fish in the same lake, using their labor and their nets. They consume their catch and do not engage in any kind of exchange, nor do they make any agreements about how to pursue their economic activities. Yet the activities of each affect the well-being of the other: the more Upper fishes, the harder it is for Lower to catch fish, and conversely. To be specific (using lower-case letters for Lower, upper-case for Upper):

$$y = [\alpha - \beta(e + E)]e$$
$$Y = [\alpha - \beta(e + E)]E \quad (6.1)$$

where y and Y are the amount of fish caught by Lower and Upper respectively over some given period; α and β are positive constants; and e and E are the amount of time (fraction of a twenty-four-hour day) that Lower and Upper each spend fishing. Each derives well-being from eating fish and experiences a loss of well-being from additional effort, according to the utility functions:

$$u = y - \frac{1}{2}e^2$$
$$U = Y - \frac{1}{2}E^2 \quad (6.2)$$

1. Show Lower's best response function $e(E)$.

2. Find the symmetric Nash equilibrium (e^N, E^N).

3. Find the allocation $(e^\sim, E^\sim)$ that maximizes the joint surplus $\omega = u + U$.

4. Consider the allocations (i) at the Nash equilibrium, (ii) at the social welfare optimum (your answer to the previous question), (iii) when Lower is first mover committing to some given effort level, and (iv) when Lower makes a take-it-or-leave-it offer specifying their own effort level as well as Upper's. Which allocations can you Pareto rank?

5. Can you think of a modification of the fishing technology such that the allocation where Lower has first mover advantage would be a Pareto-improvement over the Nash equilibrium?

   a) Provide an alternative to equations (6.1) — a change in the parameters α and or β — such that the interaction would have this property.

   b) In the hypothetical case you have invented (given the new fishing technology) would the Nash equilibrium of the simultaneous moves game be Pareto-efficient?

   c) The change in technology that you have introduced shifts the nature of the coordination problem in the typology presented in Figure 5.22 and Tables 5.3 and 5.4. Describe the shift (for example, from which cell to which cell in the tables?).

Answers.

1. To maximize $u = y - e^2 = [\alpha - \beta(e + E)]e - e^2/2$, we have

$$u_e = (\alpha - \beta E) - 2\beta e - e = 0$$

which says that effort should be set so as to equate the marginal cost of effort (which is e itself) with the marginal benefit of effort (the remaining terms) taking account of the negative effect on one's own productivity imposed by the level of fishing done by the other. Rearranging gives a closed form expression for the best response function:

$$u_e = (\alpha - \beta E) - (1 + 2\beta)e = 0 \Rightarrow e = \frac{\alpha - \beta E}{1 + 2\beta}$$

Similarly, we have

$$U_E = 0 \Rightarrow E = \frac{\alpha - \beta e}{1 + 2\beta}$$

2. For symmetric Nash Equilibrium $e^N = E^N$ we have

$$\alpha - \beta e^N - (1 + 2\beta)e^N = 0 \Rightarrow e^N = \frac{\alpha}{1 + 3\beta} = E^N$$

3. To maximize the joint surplus

$$\omega = u + U = [\alpha - \beta(e + E)]e - \frac{1}{2}e^2 + [\alpha - \beta(e + E)]E - \frac{1}{2}E^2$$

we have

$$\omega_e = (\alpha - \beta E) - (1 + 2\beta)e - \beta E = 0$$
$$\omega_E = (\alpha - \beta e) - (1 + 2\beta)E - \beta e = 0$$

Then

$$e^{\sim} = \frac{\alpha}{1 + 4\beta} = E^{\sim}$$

at which the utilities are denoted by $u^{\sim} = U^{\sim}$, as shown in Figure 6.3.

Figure 6.3: The four allocations in the Tragedy of the Fishers. Assuming $\alpha = 1$, $\beta = 0.5$, the four allocations are

(i) the Nash equilibrium

$$e^N = E^N = \frac{\alpha}{1+3\beta} = \frac{2}{5}$$

(ii) the social optimum

$$e^{\sim} = E^{\sim} = \frac{\alpha}{1+4\beta} = \frac{1}{3}$$

(iii) the first-mover allocation
(iv) the take-it-or-leave-it allocation

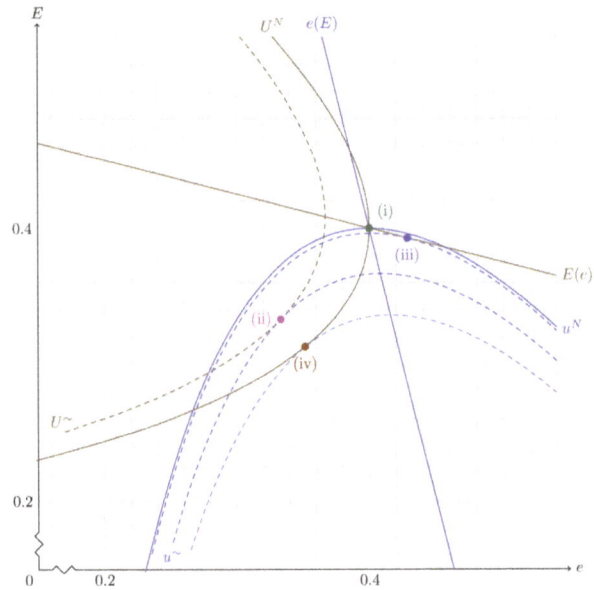

4. As shown is Figure 6.3, we have

$$(ii) > (i); (iv) > (i); (ii) > (iii); (iv) > (iii);$$

where $>$ means "is Pareto-superior to" using the preferences (6.2). We can not rank (iv) with (ii), nor the pair of (i) and (iii).

5. a) The second mover benefits from the other player's status as first mover (compared to the simultaneous move game) if the fishing efforts of each are strategic complements, in which case the game is a Stag Hunt (fishing is a group activity and one's catch and hence one's marginal utility of effort varies positively with the effort level of the other). That is

$$u_{eE} = U_{eE} = -\beta > 0 \Rightarrow \beta < 0$$

   b) No. The Nash equilibrium of the simultaneous moves game is not Pareto-efficient as the external effect is positive, i.e.,

$$u_E = -\beta e > 0, \quad U_e = -\beta E > 0$$

and thus the increases in the amounts of fishing time would make both better off.

   c) With the original technology we have negative external effect and strategic substitutes. With the new technology, the external effect is positive and both actions are strategic complements. Therefore, it shifts from the Tragedy of Fishers to Fiscal Competition in Table 5.4, or from panel (d) to panel (a) in Figure 5.22.

6.2 Averting the tragedy: Privatization

Using the same set up as in Section 6.1, suppose one of the fishers (Lower, say) owned the lake and as owner could exclude Upper, or could regulate the amount that Upper fished. In this case, Lower will maximize their utility by varying both e and E. Assume that Upper's options are such that their utility is zero in the next-best alternative.

An obvious constraint on Lower's constrained choice problem is the requirement that if Upper is to do any fishing at all, Upper must receive at least as much as their next best alternative. This restriction is Upper's *participation constraint*. We assume that Upper's next best alternative is to do no fishing and to acquire no fish.

Two types of interaction among the fishers might take place under privatization. Lower might issue a *permit* allowing Upper to continue to fish independently but to catch not more than a given amount of fish, requiring Upper to pay for the permit a sum sufficient to not violate the participation constraint. Alternately, Lower might offer Upper an *employment contract* under which Upper would fish under Lower's direction, and the fish caught by Upper would be Lower's property, Upper's compensation being a wage (paid in the fish caught by the two of them) sufficient to offset the disutility of Upper's labor and thus to satisfy the participation constraint.

> **Participation constraint**
>
> A participation constraint is an expression giving the minimal conditions under which an actor will voluntarily participate in an exchange or other economic interaction.

> Here and throughout, for simplicity, we assume that if a participation constraint is satisfied, but only weakly (that is, as an equality), the actor participates.

1. For the permit case, give

    a) the maximization problem that Lower will solve and the first order conditions for Lower's choices, and

    b) the fee that Lower will collect from Upper as a condition for Upper's fishing in the lake.

2. For the employment case, give

    a) the maximization problem that Lower will solve,

    b) the first order conditions for Lower's choices, and

    c) the total wages that Lower will pay Upper.

3. In both cases explain why Lower did not simply exclude Upper from fishing on the lake.

4. Explain why in both cases the owner selects the allocation that maximizes the total utility of the two fishers.

Answers.

1. a) In the permit case, Lower determines both levels of fishing effort ($e^\sim$ and $E^\sim$) and then issues Upper a permit to fish at level $E^\sim$ in return for Upper paying a permit price of F. To take account of the participation constraint, we express Lower's offer to Upper as the solution of a standard constrained maximization problem, namely, to vary e and E to maximize Lower's utility subject to the Upper's participation constraint. That is

$$\max_{e,E,F} \quad \omega = [\alpha - \beta(e + E)]e - \frac{1}{2}e^2 + F$$
$$\text{s.t.} \quad [\alpha - \beta(e + E)]E - \frac{1}{2}E^2 - F \geq 0 \tag{6.3}$$

b) We know that satisfying Upper's participation constraint will be costly to Lower (the two are not satiated, nor do they love work so much that providing for the other is costless), so the constraint will be satisfied as an equality.

$$F = [\alpha - \beta(e + E)]E - \frac{1}{2}E^2$$

Thus, using this expression to substitute out F in the maximization problem (6.3) becomes

$$\max_{e,E} \quad \omega(e, E) = [\alpha - \beta(e + E)]e - \frac{1}{2}e^2 + [\alpha - \beta(e + E)]E - \frac{1}{2}E^2 \tag{6.4}$$

The first order conditions are

$$\omega_e = (\alpha - \beta E) - (1 + 2\beta)e - \beta E = 0$$
$$\omega_E = (\alpha - \beta e) - (1 + 2\beta)E - \beta e = 0$$

Thus,

$$e^\sim = \frac{\alpha}{1 + 4\beta} = E^\sim$$

Therefore, the solution to problem (6.3) is $e = e^\sim$, $E = E^\sim$ and $F = [\alpha - \beta(e^\sim + E^\sim)]E^\sim - (E^\sim)^2/2$.

2. For the employment case, suppose the wage is W. Then Upper's utility is

$$U = W - \frac{1}{2}E^2$$

and Lower's problem is

$$\max_{e,E,W} \quad \omega = [\alpha - \beta(e + E)]e - \frac{1}{2}e^2 + [\alpha - \beta(e + E)]E - W$$
$$\text{s.t.} \quad W - \frac{1}{2}E^2 \geq 0$$

Knowing that the participation constraint is satisfied as an equality allows us to use the fact that the wage paid must just offset Upper's disutility of effort or $W = E^2/2$. Then the problem becomes identical to the permit case, i.e., (6.4), and thus

$$e^{\sim} = \frac{\alpha}{1 + 4\beta} = E^{\sim}$$

and $W = (E^{\sim})^2/2$.

3. The reason (in both cases) is that the marginal cost of compensating Upper's fishing effort goes to zero as E goes to zero (remember, the marginal disutility of Upper's fishing effort is E itself), so setting some positive level of E will be advantageous to Lower. Informally: exploiting Upper is better (for Lower) than excluding Upper.

4. Privatization supports Pareto-efficient outcomes because the decision maker maximizes their own payoff subject to the other's binding participation constraint. The reason why the decision maker (Lower in this case) chooses an allocation that maximizes total utility (a different question) is that the utility gained by the other is just their next best alternative, so the question of distribution between the two is settled in advance. As a result, the owner — as residual claimant on the total surplus — maximizes their utility by choosing an allocation which maximizes the total utility of the two. The key here is that the owner is powerful enough to determine the distribution of gains independently of the allocation of fishing times and so has no incentive to adopt any but the most efficient allocation.

Remember, in a two-person interaction an allocation that maximizes the utility of the actor subject to a binding constraint on the utility of the other is by definition Pareto-efficient.

The take home message here is that if one party has sufficient power to claim the entire surplus then what we call "the larger piece of a smaller pie" syndrome does not occur. But in the next and latter chapters we provide examples where conflicts over distribution result in inefficient outcomes. The reason is that the parties to the conflict can alter the distribution in their favor by implementing an inefficient outcome.

6.3 Averting the tragedy: Optimal taxes and government regulation

It is typically impossible for a single actor to own an entire common property resource (imagine establishing property rights in fish in the open ocean). Moreover, even were private ownership possible, the Pareto efficiency properties of the private ownership-based allocation would have to be weighed against the highly unequal distributional consequences (the owner captures all of the surplus and others receive only their fallback option). In this case a government or some other third party may be able to improve on the Nash equilibrium of the non-cooperative private ownership game described above. As with privatization, two alternatives suggest themselves.

Direct regulation. The planner (the government), knowing all the relevant information, could select e and E to maximize the total surplus. The planner might then implement this outcome by *direct regulation*, simply issuing a fishing permit allowing each fisher to catch a given amount of fish.

1. Using the same set up as in Section 6.1 here and in the subsequent questions, give the first order conditions for the planner's choice of $e^{\sim}$ and $E^{\sim}$ and explain how they are different from the first order

conditions for the two fishers acting independently (explain what the additional term or terms in the first order conditions represent).

Optimal taxes. Rather than implementing the optimal allocational plan by fiat, however, the planner might let the fishers each decide how much to fish, but alter the incentives facing them in such a way that the Nash equilibrium of the modified game is socially optimal (the above allocation that maximizes the sum of utilities).

So, the planner proposes a tax on fishing designed to eliminate the discrepancy between the social and private marginal costs and benefits of fishing. Assume that the proceeds will be given back to the fishers as a lump sum, and that they ignore this lump sum in their calculations (as they would were there two thousand rather than just two fishers, as in a more realistic case). The problem is thus for the planner to select a tax that will maximize the sum of the fishers' utilities when the fishers independently choose how much to fish, given the tax.

This is a standard mechanism design problem: define some desired outcome and then devise a mechanism (rules of the game) such that the desired outcome is a unique Nash equilibrium of the game when played non-cooperatively.

2. What is the optimal tax? (Hint: you'll have to "reverse engineer" this by asking what the first order conditions for the individuals would have to look like in order that the actors maximizing their individual utility would implement the social optimum.)

Answers.

1. Direct regulation. For the social planner, the problem is again (6.4), and the first order condition for the choice of effort levels as shown above are

$$\omega_e = (\alpha - \beta E) - (1 + 2\beta)e - \beta E = 0$$
$$\omega_E = (\alpha - \beta e) - (1 + 2\beta)E - \beta e = 0$$

They are different from that for the two fishers acting independently, i.e.

$$u_e = (\alpha - \beta E) - (2\beta + 1)e = 0$$
$$U_E = (\alpha - \beta e) - (2\beta + 1)E = 0$$

The additional terms $-\beta E$ and $-\beta e$ are the external effects of each fisher's action on the other's utility that constitute the basis for the coordination failure.

2. Optimal taxes. Given the tax τ, the utility (for Lower) becomes

$$u^\tau = [\alpha - \beta(e + E)]e - \frac{1}{2}e^2 - \tau e$$

Then the first order condition is

$$u_e^\tau = (\alpha - \beta E) - (1 + 2\beta)e - \tau = 0$$

To mimic that implied by joint surplus maximization, namely

$$\omega_e = (\alpha - \beta E) - (1 + 2\beta)e - \beta E = 0$$

the optimal tax must be $\tau = \beta E$.

6.4 Averting the tragedy: Civil society

Addressing a common property resource coordination failure by means of privatization may be impossible (or lead to unacceptable differences in power and wealth). Moreover, even if governments place a high priority on environmental sustainability (and mitigating other coordination failures) they may lack the information necessary to define and implement either direct regulation or the optimal taxes. The enduring personal interactions that make up civil society provide a third set of options: other-regarding preferences and repeated interactions.

Other-regarding preferences. To see how a concern for the states experienced by others might help mitigate the underlying coordination problem imagine that the utility function of each fisher was as defined above in equation (6.2), plus some weight $a \in [0, 1]$ placed on the utility of the other, so that Lower's utility would now be

$$v = u + aU = [\alpha - \beta(e + E)]e - \frac{1}{2}e^2 + aU \qquad (6.5)$$

and analogously for Upper.

1. Given these utility functions, what are the best response functions of the two? What is the symmetric Nash equilibrium?

2. Is there some degree of altruism, a, such that the fishers (playing cooperatively) would implement the social optimum without either privatization and/or government intervention?

3. Suppose that, although both fishers are altruistic, a is less than 1. Can you think of a way they could address the over-fishing coordination failure?

Repeated interactions. Even in the absence of other-regarding preferences or converting the interaction to a cooperative game, there is another way the coordination failure might be addressed by a community of people who interact frequently and over a long period. If they play the Tragedy of the Fishers game repeatedly, day after day, year after year, then even if mutual over-fishing is a Nash equilibrium in the one-shot game, it may not be in the repeated game.

To see this, suppose that Table 6.1 represents the stage game (played in a single period) that will be repeated with probability P. The payoffs of the stage game are such that mutual fishing for 12 hours a day (over-fishing) is the dominant strategy equilibrium. The stage game is a prisoners' dilemma.

But the repeated game may be an assurance game with limited fishing (10 hours a day) being a Nash equilibrium that would be sustainable in the absence of government regulation or privatization. Suppose that the strategies available in the repeated game are unconditional Defect (overfish) and Grim Trigger (cooperate by limiting fishing on the first

Elinor Ostrom documented many examples of communities that, when faced with an environmental coordination failure, found ways to change the rules of the game to address the problem [81].

[81]: Ostrom (1990), *Governing the Commons*

Table 6.1: Payoffs for one-shot Prisoners' Dilemma Game. Row player's payoff in the symmetric game, with $b > a > c > d$

	10 hours	12 hours
10 hours	a	d
12 hours	b	c

round and continue as long as the other does not defect, in which case defect for all future rounds of the game).

4. At the beginning of any period, what is the expected duration of the game (in periods)?

5. Write down the payoff matrix for the repeated game with strategies Defect and Grim Trigger (assuming that the players do not discount the future, but they do take account of the likelihood that the repeated game will end).

6. What condition on the entries in the payoff matrix of the repeated game is necessary and sufficient for the repeated game to be an Assurance Game? If the payoffs are $b = 5, a = 2, c = 1, d = 0$, what is the least value of P such that the interaction is an Assurance Game?

7. If the payoffs are $b = 5, a = 2, c = 1, d = 0$, what is the least value of P such that for both fishing 10 hours is the risk-dominant equilibrium?

Answers.

1. To maximize the utilities in (6.5), we have

$$(\alpha - \beta E) - (1 + 2\beta)e - a\beta E = 0$$
$$(\alpha - \beta e) - (1 + 2\beta)E - a\beta e = 0$$

Then best response functions of the two are

$$e = \frac{\alpha - (1 + a)\beta E}{1 + 2\beta}$$

$$E = \frac{\alpha - (1 + a)\beta e}{1 + 2\beta}$$

and the Nash equilibrium in this case is

$$e^a = \frac{\alpha}{1 + (3 + a)\beta} = E^a$$

2. Note that (e^a, E^a) is equal to (e^N, E^N) when $a = 0$, and the socially optimal $(e^\sim, E^\sim)$ when $a = 1$, as shown in Figure 6.4.

3. If we take the model literally, then seeing that they are fishing in the same lake and have altruistic feelings toward each other, they might decide not to play non-cooperatively and instead to just agree on the social optimum level of fishing. But remember, we do not intend to take the model literally: we use a 2-person game to represent interactions among a large number of people among whom such an agreement would probably not be possible given the incentives for free riding (fishing 12 hours in violation of the agreement to limit fishing to 10 hours).

Let X be the number of periods as a random variable, then

$$X \sim G(1 - P)$$

the geometric distribution with probability $1 - P$. Therefore,

$$E[X] = \frac{1}{1 - P}$$

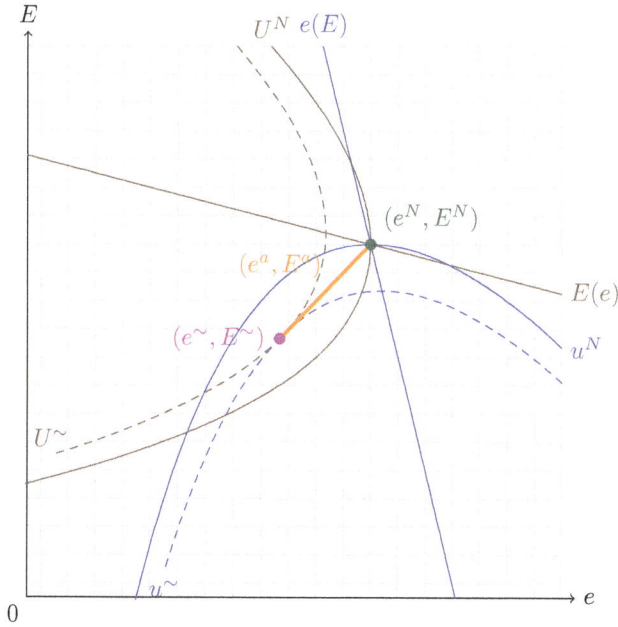

Figure 6.4: The solution in averting fisher's tragedy with altruism. The solutions with altruism $a \in [0, 1]$ is

$$e^a = \frac{\alpha}{1 + (3 + a)\beta} = E^a$$

the segment between the Nash equilibrium

$$e^N = \frac{\alpha}{1 + 3\beta} = E^N$$

and the socially optimal allocation

$$e^{\sim} = \frac{\alpha}{1 + 4\beta} = E^{\sim}$$

4. Since the game will be repeated with probability P, the expected duration of the game is $1/(1 - P)$.

5. The payoff matrix for the repeated game is given in Table 6.2, which is derived as follows.

	Grim Trigger	Defect
Grim Trigger	$a/(1 - P)$	$d + cP(1 - P)$
Defect	$b + cP/(1 - P)$	$c/(1 - P)$

Table 6.2: Payoffs for the repeated Prisoners' Dilemma Game. The game will be repeated with probability P. Row player's payoff in the symmetric game, with $b > a > c > d$.

▶ The expected payoff to playing Defect against Defect is $c/(1 - P)$, the stage game payoff times the expected duration.
▶ The expected payoff to playing Grim Trigger against Grim Trigger is $a/(1 - P)$, the stage game payoff times the expected duration.
▶ The expected payoff to playing Grim Trigger against Defect is $d + cP/(1 - P)$ i.e., the payoff of the first period d plus the payoff (c) times the expected duration $1/(1 - P) - 1$.
▶ The expected payoff to playing Defect against Grim Trigger is $b + cP/(1 - P)$, i.e., the payoff of the first period b plus the payoff (c) times the expected duration.

6. To make the repeated game an Assurance Game, the payoff to playing Defect against Grim Trigger should be less than the payoff to playing Grim Trigger against itself. That is,

$$b + c\left(\frac{P}{1 - P}\right) < \frac{a}{1 - P} \Rightarrow P > \frac{b - a}{b - c} \qquad (6.6)$$

Given that $b = 5$, $a = 2$, $c = 1$, and $d = 0$, we have

$$P > \frac{5 - 2}{5 - 1} = \frac{3}{4}$$

7. To make both playing Grim Trigger (both would fish 10 hours) the risk-dominant equilibrium, the expected payoff to playing Grim Trigger against the other playing Grim Trigger and Defect with equal probability

$$\frac{1}{2}\left(\frac{a}{1-P}\right) + \frac{1}{2}\left(d + \frac{cP}{1-P}\right) = \frac{1}{2}\left(d + \frac{a+cP}{1-P}\right)$$

must be greater than that to Defect

$$\frac{1}{2}\left(b + \frac{cP}{1-P}\right) + \frac{1}{2}\left(\frac{c}{1-P}\right) = \frac{1}{2}\left(b + c\frac{1+P}{1-P}\right)$$

That is,

$$d + \frac{a+cP}{1-P} > b + c\frac{1+P}{1-P} \Rightarrow P > 1 - \frac{a-c}{b-d}$$

Given that $b = 5$, $a = 2$, $c = 1$, $d = 0$, we have

$$P > 1 - \frac{2-1}{5-0} = \frac{4}{5}$$

which is greater than $3/4$, the least value of P such that the interaction is an Assurance Game.

This question is based on one of the models environmental problems with multiple equilibria and tipping points in Unit 8 of *The Economy 2.0 Macroeconomics* by the CORE Project available at www.core-econ.org.

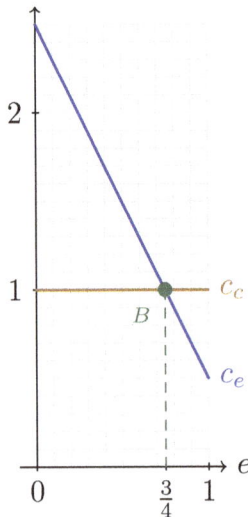

Figure 6.5: The cost functions of the two types of vehicles and the break-even point. The blue line represents the cost of owning and using an e-vehicle

$$c_e(e) = 2.5 - 2e$$

The orange line represents the costs of owning and operating a conventional vehicle $c_c = 1$. And point B is the break-even point at which

$$c_e(e) = c_c$$

6.5 Disrupting a carbon trap to promote electronic vehicle adoption

Shifting away from carbon-based internal combustion engines for our vehicles would significantly help in curbing global warming. However, achieving this shift faces a significant challenge: without public policies to disrupt it, our carbon-dependent transportation system remains in a stable equilibrium, at least in the short term. Efforts to break free from this system will be hindered by various negative feedback mechanisms that reinforce the existing carbon-based equilibrium. In this section, we set up a model and provide questions for you to explore the carbon trap and examine strategies for shifting away from it.

Here are the assumptions in the model. There are two types of vehicles: those powered by conventional carbon-based internal combustion engines (c-vehicles) and those powered by electric batteries (e-vehicles). The cost of owning and using an e-vehicle (per kilometer traveled), denoted by c_e, decreases as the number of other e-vehicle users increases. In other words, $c_e(e)$ is a decreasing function of e, where $e \in [0, 1]$ represents the fraction of households using electric vehicles. This phenomenon occurs for two main reasons:

▶ **Infrastructure development**: When there are few e-vehicle users, it is not profitable to build many charging stations. Consequently, these stations will be sparse, increasing the time required to travel to a charging station and possibly wait for an available charger. This scarcity also complicates trip planning, potentially necessitating the use of alternative transportation for longer journeys.

▶ **Economies of scale and learning by doing**: As the number of e-vehicles on the road increases, economies of scale and learning by doing in production reduce the cost of manufacturing e-vehicles. This results in lower sale prices, making e-vehicles more affordable and further encouraging their adoption.

In contrast, the costs of owning and operating a conventional vehicle, denoted by c_c, do not depend on the mix of internal combustion and e-vehicles on the road.

Let the period be sufficiently long so that we can assume households purchase a new car every period to replace the old one. Their decision to choose between an electric or conventional vehicle is influenced not only by the costs $c_e(e)$ and c_c but also by their value for reducing their carbon footprint, denoted as g, which varies among individuals. They will choose an e-vehicle when the green value is greater than or equal to the cost disadvantage of the e-vehicle, represented by the condition

$$g \geq c_e(e) - c_c \tag{6.7}$$

and a c-vehicle otherwise.

Given the fraction of household using e-vehicles e_t at period t, the fraction at the next period $t + 1$ is

$$e_{t+1} = Pr\{g \geq c_e(e_t) - c_c\} \tag{6.8}$$

That is, all the households with green values no less than the cost disadvantage in this period will adopt e-vehicles at next period.

For simplification, assume further that $c_e(e) = 2.5 - 2e$, $c_c = 1$ and g is uniformly distributed between 0 and 1, i.e., $g \sim U(0, 1)$.

1. Derive the cumulative distribution function (cdf) of g and use it to find the *adoption dynamics function* $e_{t+1} = A(e_t)$.

2. Find all the equilibrium values of e satisfying $e = A(e)$, and say whether each is stable or not.

3. Show that the e-based equilibrium $e = 1$ is Pareto-superior to the carbon-trap equilibrium $e = 0$.

4. Suppose that 10% of households are staunch conventional vehicle users who will never buy an e-vehicle regardless of costs, and another 10% are EV enthusiasts who will always choose e-vehicles even if they cost a lot more. Find the equilibria in this case. Is the e-based equilibrium still Pareto-superior to the carbon-trap equilibrium? Why or why not?

Breaking a society out of the carbon trap could be accomplished by the three approaches introduced in Figure 6.2.

The structure of interaction here is similar to the game of Planting in Palanpur in Section 2.4; the carbon trap for transportation is similar to the stable equilibrium in which all of the farmers plant late when they would all be better off if all planted late.

The government of the city of Beijing has implemented a license plate lottery policy to control the number of vehicle purchase permits issued each year. To encourage the adoption of electric vehicles, the policy allocates separate purchase permits for conventional vehicles and electric vehicles, with a preference for electric vehicles over conventional vehicles. This means that while conventional vehicles purchasers must compete for a limited number of permits, electric vehicles purchasers have dedicated permits, thereby promoting a higher fraction of electronic vehicles usage in the population. [116]

[116]: Zhuge, Wei, et al. (2020), 'The Role of the License Plate Lottery Policy in the Adoption of Electric Vehicles'

5. The government can simply require the switch to electric vehicles by for example restricting the sale of conventional vehicles so that a large enough fraction of the population use e-vehicles rather than conventional ones at period t. What is the smallest quota (in percentage) for e-vehicles of the total new cars that can disrupt the carbon trap?

6. Suppose that the government reduces the cost disadvantage of the e-vehicles by subsidies for their purchase, or for research and development of better vehicles (and batteries) and the production of the vehicles, or for expanding the network of charging stations, so that the cost disadvantage becomes $0.5 - 2e$. Find the equilibrium value and characterize its stability.

7. Suppose that the government invests in an environment awareness campaign and shift the distribution of green values to be $g \sim U(1, 2)$. Find the equilibrium value and characterize its stability.

Answers.

1. By $g \sim U(0, 1)$, the cumulative distribution function is

$$G(x) = Pr\{g < x\} = \begin{cases} 0 & x \leq 0 \\ x & 0 < x < 1 \\ 1 & x \geq 1 \end{cases}$$

Then

$$e_{t+1} = Pr\{g \geq 1.5 - 2e\} = 1 - Pr\{g < 1.5 - 2e\} = 1 - G(1.5 - 2e)$$

Therefore, the adoption dynamic function is

$$A(e) = 1 - G(1.5 - 2e) = \begin{cases} 0 & 0 \leq e \leq 0.25 \\ 2e - 0.5 & 0.25 < e < 0.75 \\ 1 & 0.75 \leq e \leq 1 \end{cases} \quad (6.9)$$

as shown in Figure 6.6.

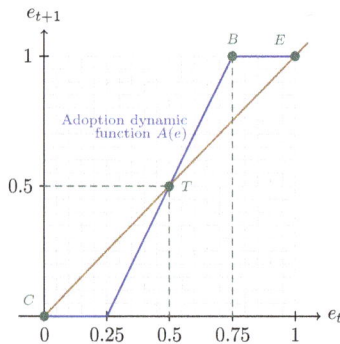

Figure 6.6: The adoption dynamics curve with the three equilibria. The blue curve represents the adoption dynamic function

$$A(e) = \begin{cases} 0 & 0 \leq e \leq 0.25 \\ 2e - 0.5 & 0.25 < e < 0.75 \\ 1 & 0.75 \leq e \leq 1 \end{cases}$$

The orange line is the 45-degree line from the origin, where $e_{t+1} = e_t$. This represents the stationarity condition, according to which the fraction of the population that owns e-vehicles remains unchanged from period to period. The three intersections of the blue curve and the orange line give the three equilibria, that is, stationary values of e: (i) the carbon-based equilibrium C; (ii) the tipping point T; and (iii) the e-vehicle equilibrium E. The cost break even point B, defined by $c_e(e_t) = c_c$, is at the right of the tipping point because people's green values lead them to switch to electric even if e-vehicles are somewhat more expensive.

2. Let $e = A(e)$ we have three equilibria: (i) the carbon trap equilibrium (C) $e^* = 0$; (ii) the tipping point (T) where

$$e^* = 2e^* - 0.5 \Rightarrow e^* = 0.5$$

and (iii) the e-vehicle equilibrium (E) $e^* = 1$. Both (B) are (E) stable, while (T) is unstable since at $e^* = 0.5$

$$\frac{dA}{de} = 2 > 1$$

3. Since the cost at the e-based equilibrium, $c_e(1) = 0.5$ is less than that at the carbon-based equilibrium $c_c = 1$, all would be better-off at the e-based equilibrium.

4. The range of e becomes $[0.1, 0.9]$ and the new adoption dynamics in this case is

$$e_{t+1} = 0.1 + 0.8[1 - G(1.5 - 2e)] = \begin{cases} 0.1 & 0.1 \leq e \leq 0.25 \\ 1.6e - 0.3 & 0.25 < e < 0.75 \\ 0.9 & 0.75 \leq e \leq 0.9 \end{cases}$$

and the three stationary values are: (i) the carbon trap $e^* = 0.1$, (ii) the tipping point $e^* = 0.5$ and (iii) the e-vehicle equilibrium $e^* = 0.9$ as shown in Figure 6.7. The e-based equilibrium $e^* = 0.9$ is Pareto-superior to the carbon trap equilibrium $e^* = 0.1$ because:

▶ Staunch conventional vehicle users are not worse off in the e-based equilibrium compared to the carbon trap equilibrium since they can still purchase c-vehicles at the same cost; and

▶ The remaining households benefit as the cost of e-vehicles is reduced.

5. The unstable equilibrium $e^* = 0.5$ is the tipping point, so the quota for e-vehicles should be no less than 50% in order to promote the shift to the e-based equilibrium.

6. With new cost disadvantage $0.5 - 2e$, the adoption dynamics function becomes

$$e_{t+1} = Pr\{g \geq 0.5 - 2e\} = \begin{cases} 2e + 0.5 & 0 \leq e \leq 0.25 \\ 1 & 0.25 < e \leq 1 \end{cases} \quad (6.10)$$

Then $e^* = 1$ is the unique equilibrium, which is stable as shown in Figure 6.8.

7. With the new distribution of green values $g \sim U(1, 2)$, the cumulative distribution function is

$$G_1(x) = Pr\{g < x\} = \begin{cases} 0 & x \leq 1 \\ x & 1 < x < 2 \\ 1 & x \geq 2 \end{cases}$$

and then the adoption dynamics function becomes

$$e_{t+1} = 1 - G_1(1.5 - 2e) = \begin{cases} 2e + 0.5 & 0 \leq e \leq 0.25 \\ 1 & 0.25 < e \leq 1 \end{cases}$$

which is the same adoption dynamics function as the one induced by the shift in the cost function, (6.10), though the shift in this case is induced by a change in values, not costs. Therefore, we have the same unique and stable equilibrium $e^* = 1$.

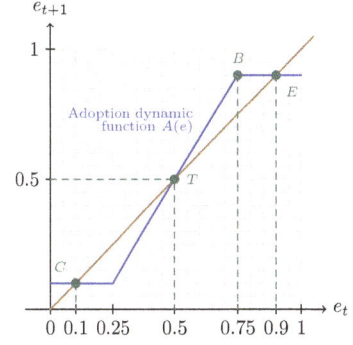

Figure 6.7: The adoption dynamics curve with staunch users. The blue curve represents the adoption dynamic function

$$A(e) = \begin{cases} 0.1 & 0.1 \leq e \leq 0.25 \\ 1.6e - 0.3 & 0.25 < e < 0.75 \\ 0.9 & 0.75 \leq e \leq 0.9 \end{cases}$$

The three intersections of the blue curve and the orange line give the three equilibria: (i) the carbon-based equilibrium C; (ii) the tipping point T; and (iii) the e-vehicle equilibrium E. The cost break even point B, defined by $c_e(e_t) = c_c$, is at the right of the tipping point because people's green values lead them to switch to electric even if e-vehicles are somewhat more expensive.

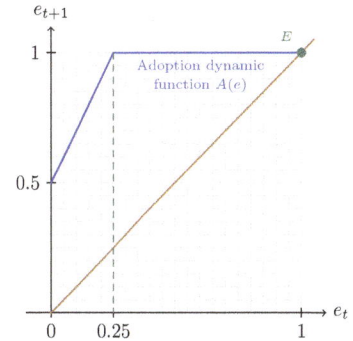

Figure 6.8: The new adoption dynamics curve with the unique equilibrium (E). The blue curve represents the new adoption dynamic function

$$A(e) = \begin{cases} 2e + 0.5 & 0 \leq e \leq 0.25 \\ 1 & 0.25 < e \leq 1 \end{cases}$$

The orange line is the 45 degree line from the origin with $e_{t+1} = e_t$.

Bargaining: Mutual Gains and conflicts over their Distribution

7

If two people voluntarily engage in some exchange or other economic interaction, then it must be the case that each of them expects to benefit from undertaking the transaction compared to the payoffs associated with their next best alternative (not engaging in the exchange). Here we consider bargaining as a way of determining how the mutual gains from the exchange will be distributed. We show how the outcome of the bargain will depend on the rules of the game — for example, that one of the actors may be first mover — and the initial rights held by the players.

Rights in this case may consist of the ownership of property, but it may also refer to the set of actions that a person may legitimately take, as illustrated by the curfew in Section 7.1 below. In that set of problems we see that a combination of governmental intervention (by the "social planner") followed by private bargaining may support better outcomes than could be achieved by either private or public action alone.

Bargaining is a way of re-allocating rights in ways that can be Pareto-improving, as was pointed out by Ronald Coase (from which this process gets the name, Coasean bargaining). Bargaining is an example of a social interaction in civil society (introduced in the previous chapter): it occurs among private parties, but unlike markets is dyadic (involving just 2 parties, e.g. members of a couple, employer and trade union) and is not directly impacted by market-like competition.

In these problems, you will see that the outcome of bargaining depends on the fallback position of each player. As a result, players have an incentive to divert some of the resources at their disposal away from production toward improving their next best alternative (their fallback option) or diminishing the fallback position of the party they are bargaining with.

Conflict over the distribution of mutual gains may thus result in a reduced amount of goods to distribute, an outcome that we termed the "larger piece of a smaller pie" syndrome in the previous chapter. This is exactly the point of the statements by Pareto in the margin notes here and by Hirschleifer in Section 7.4.

An example is the war of attrition game (also in Section 7.4), in which (under plausible assumptions) the amount invested by players to enhance their bargaining power exactly equals the value of the "prize" over which they are contesting, so the value of the prize is entirely dissipated by the bargaining process. The larger piece of a smaller pie syndrome is also illustrated in Sections 7.2 and 7.3.

Some background for the problems in this chapter is found in Chapter 5 in Bowles [14] and Chapter 14 in Bowles and Halliday [29].

"[T]he efforts of men are utilized in two different ways: they are directed to the production or transformation of economic goods, or else to the appropriation of goods produced by others." — Vilfredo Pareto, *Manual of Political Economy* (1905)

Figure 7.1: Vilfredo Pareto (1848–1923), an Italian economist and sociologist, earned a degree in engineering for his research on the concept of equilibrium in physics. He is mostly remembered for his criterion for ranking allocations and the related concept of Pareto efficiency. He wanted economics and sociology to be fact-based sciences, similar to the physical sciences he had studied when he was young. His empirical investigations led him to another important contribution, on allocations of wealth. The distribution of wealth did not seem to resemble the familiar bell curve, with a few rich, a few poor, and a large middle-income class. Instead, he proposed what came to be called Pareto's law, according to which there would be very few rich people and a lot of poor people. Wikimedia Commons, CC BY-SA 3.0, https://commons.wikimedia.org/wiki/File:Vilfredo_Pareto_1870s2.jpg

[14]: Bowles (2004), *Microeconomics*

[29]: Bowles and Halliday (2022), *Microeconomics*

©2025 Samuel Bowles and Weikai Chen, CC BY-NC 4.0

https://doi.org/10.11647/OBP.0466.07

7.1 Deadheads vs. nerds: Coasean bargaining and state intervention as complements

Bargaining among private agents is sometimes seen as an alternative to government intervention. It can also be a complement: the superior information of private parties and the superior enforcement capacities of the state, combined, can support a better outcome then either policy pursued separately. This is an example of complementarity between two of the vertices — State and Civil Society — in the governance simplex (the triangle in the introduction to Chapter 6).

Consider two neighbors, A and B, with conflicting late-night habits attempting to agree on a curfew (a time at night later than which loud music will not be played). We also introduce a social planner who represents an impartial body (perhaps the mayor of the town that they live in) who might also introduce a curfew. The two neighbors have the following utility functions (A's first and B's second):

$$u(x, y) = y - \alpha(a - x)^2$$
$$v(x, y) = -y - \beta(b - x)^2 \tag{7.1}$$

This problem is inspired by Farrell [50] whose own inspiration, it seems, comes from first-hand experience. Farrell writes: "I once tried to bribe some noisy neighbors to be quiet, and the response was a puzzled and angry rebuff."

[50]: Farrell (1987), 'Information and the Coase Theorem'

where x is the time of the curfew and y is an amount of money that B may transfer to A (if y is negative, then it represents a transfer from A to B). Normalize the time over which the curfew may be set so that $x \in [0, 1]$ (think of 0 as a 6 p.m. curfew, and 1 as a 6 a.m. curfew), and let $a = 1/4$ and $b = 3/4$, i.e., 9 p.m. and 3 a.m., respectively. Assume they both care equally about the time of the curfew, so set both $\alpha = \beta = 1$.

1. Show that the social planner maximizing the sum of the utilities of the two individuals will set $x^* = 1/2$, namely, midnight.

Suppose, instead, the curfew had been set at 3 a.m. (to the Deadhead's delight) and B can make a take-it-or-leave-it (TIOLI) offer to A promising (we'll assume credibly) to voluntarily submit to an earlier curfew in return for a side payment from A (equal to $-y$).

We call B a "Deadhead" — an American expression for a follower of the (very loud) band The Grateful Dead — because B would like to play loud music until 3 a.m. We can call A a "nerd" — another American expression, in this case for someone who wants to study all the time — because A's studying is disrupted by the music that B plays late at night.

2. If B designs an offer that will maximize their utility, what offer will B make? Explain why the curfew that B proposes is identical to that implemented by the social planner.

3. Explain why, had the initial curfew been set at 1/4 (the nerd's revenge), the selection of x as a result of Coasean bargaining (as above with B as first mover with TIOLI power) would have been the same as that resulting from the imposed curfew being the Deadhead's delight or the social planner's optimum. This is what Coase [41] meant when he wrote that

[41]: Coase (1960), 'The Problem of Social Cost'

> "all that matters (questions of equity aside) is that the rights of the various parties should be well defined and the results of legal actions easy to forecast."[41, p. 19]

Assume that A has limited resources and cannot make a payment to B in excess of $\bar{y}$. (The official curfew is still 3 a.m.)

4. What is the smallest value of $\bar{y}$ that will induce B to implement the socially optimal outcome (assuming, as above that he can make a take-it-or-leave-it offer to A)?

5. Now assume that A rather than B is in a position to make the take-it-or-leave-it offer. What is the smallest value of $\bar{y}$ that will induce A to implement the social optimum? Why are your answers to this and the previous question different?

In Chapter 11 we explore the ways that limited wealth may limit the opportunities for mutually beneficial exchanges, and how an egalitarian redistribution of wealth might address the resulting Pareto inefficiencies.

Suppose that the amount A has available to make a side payment to B is positive, but it is too small to support a bargain between the two resulting in the social optimum curfew when the curfew is set at 3 a.m. and B can make a take-it-or-leave-it offer to A. Recognizing that the limited wealth of A makes it impossible to achieving the social optimum by Coasean bargaining, the social planner considers imposing a somewhat earlier curfew that in combination with bargaining might implement the social optimum.

6. Show that there exists some official curfew (earlier than 3 a.m. but later than the social optimum) that, if imposed by the social planner, would allow the social optimum bargained curfew to be implemented under one of the bargaining rules above.

7. Why can a redistribution of initial rights by the social planner (declaring a somewhat earlier curfew) plus Coasean bargaining together accomplish what Coasean bargaining alone could not accomplish in this case?

8. Consider four possible cases: either A or B has TIOLI power and the curfew is set at either 9 p.m. or 3 a.m. Can you order the outcomes of these four cases (from worst to best) for the two?

Answers.

1. For the social planner, the problem is

$$\max_{x} \quad \omega = u + v = -\alpha(a - x)^2 - \beta(b - x)^2$$

The first order condition is

$$2[\alpha(a - x) + \beta(b - x)] = 0 \Rightarrow x^* = \frac{\alpha a + \beta b}{\alpha + \beta}$$

With $a = 1/4, b = 3/4$ and $\alpha = \beta = 1$, we have $x^* = 1/2$.

2. When B has the TIOLI power, the problem becomes

$$\max_{x,y} \quad v = -y - \beta(b - x)^2$$

$$\text{s.t.} \quad y - \alpha(a - x)^2 \geq u\left(\frac{3}{4}, 0\right)$$

Using the fact that the PC (participation constraint) must be binding, we have

$$y = \alpha(a - x)^2 + u\left(\frac{3}{4}, 0\right)$$

Then the problem becomes

$$\max_{x,y} \quad -u\left(\frac{3}{4}, 0\right) - \alpha(a - x)^2 - \beta(b - x)^2$$

The first order condition is

$$2[\alpha(a - x) + \beta(b - x)] = 0 \Rightarrow x^* = \frac{\alpha a + \beta b}{\alpha + \beta}$$

With $a = 1/4$, $b = 3/4$ and $\alpha = \beta = 1$, we have $x^* = 1/2$, which is identical to the social optimum, as shown in Figure 7.2. This is because the utility function is assumed to be quasi-linear, so that the marginal rate of substitution remains the same at $x = x^*$ regardless of the change in y. By substituting x^* into the participation constraint, we have the value of y^*

$$y^* = \left(\frac{1}{4} - x^*\right)^2 + u\left(\frac{3}{4}, 0\right) = -\frac{3}{16}$$

that is, A would transfer 3/16 to B.

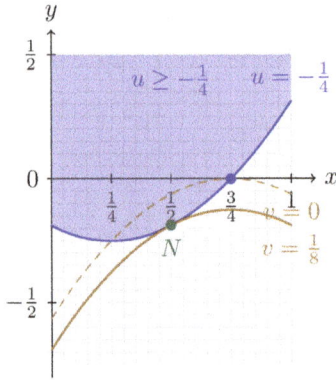

Figure 7.2: The allocation with TIOLI power in curfew conflict, case I. When the curfew is set at 3/4 (3 a.m.), A's fallback option (their utility if no change in the curfew is agreed upon) is

$$u(x, y) = u\left(\frac{3}{4}, 0\right) = -\frac{1}{4}$$

and the shaded region is the feasible set. B, having TIOLI power, maximizes their utility subject to the participation constraint. The solution is N where

$$x^* = \frac{1}{2}, \quad y^* = -\frac{3}{16}$$

3. When the curfew is set at 1/4, B's problem becomes

$$\max_{x,y} \quad v = -y - \beta(b - x)^2$$

$$\text{s.t.} \quad u = y - \alpha(a - x)^2 \geq u\left(\frac{1}{4}, 0\right)$$

Similarly, we have the solution $x^* = 1/2$, as shown in Figure 7.3. Again, by substituting x^* into the participation constraint, we have the value of y,

$$y^* = \alpha(a - x^*)^2 + u\left(\frac{3}{4}, 0\right) = \frac{1}{16}$$

that is, B would transfer 1/16 to A. Therefore, the difference in property rights (the curfew) alters the distribution of benefits from the interaction.

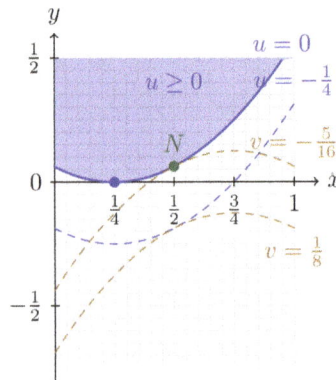

Figure 7.3: The allocation with TIOLI power in curfew conflict, case II. When the official curfew is set at 1/4 (9 p.m.), A's fallback position is

$$u(x, y) = u(1/4, 0) = 0$$

and the shaded region is the feasible set. B, having TIOLI power, maximizes their utility subject to the participation constraint. The solution is N where

$$x^* = \frac{1}{2}, \quad y^* = \frac{1}{16}$$

4. As shown in part 2, we know that in order to induce B to implement the socially optimal outcome $x^* = 1/2$, A should transfer 3/16 to B. Suppose that $\bar{y} < 3/16$ as shown in Figure 7.4. Then the outcome x^* at the corner solution is greater than the socially optimal outcome 1/2. Therefore, the smallest value of A's resource sufficient to implement the socially optimal outcome is

$$\bar{y}_1 = \frac{3}{16}$$

5. Note that when the curfew is set at 3/4 or 3 a.m., the fallback position of B is $v(3/4, 0) = 0$. When A has the TIOLI power, the problem becomes:

$$\max_{x,y} \quad u = y - \left(\frac{1}{4} - x\right)^2$$

$$\text{s.t.} \quad -y - \left(\frac{3}{4} - x\right)^2 \geq 0$$

The solution is $x^* = 1/2$ and $y^* = -1/16$. That is, A should transfer $1/16$ to induce B to implement the socially optimal outcome $x^* = 1/2$. Therefore, the smallest value of A's resource is

$$\bar{y}_2 = \frac{1}{16}$$

which is different from $\bar{y}_1$. This is because in this setting, A with TIOLI power will get joint surplus after compensating B to their fallback position, but in the case where B has TIOLI power, A must have enough wealth to ensure the joint surplus can be transferred to B.

6. Suppose the official curfew is $x_0 \in (1/2, 3/4)$ and B has TIOLI power. To reach the social optimum $x^* = 1/2$, A would pay $y(x_0)$ such that

$$u\left(\frac{1}{2}, -y(x_0)\right) = u(x_0, 0)$$

Therefore, we have

$$y(x_0) = -\frac{1}{16} + \left(\frac{1}{4} - x_0\right)^2$$

Given any $\bar{y} \in (0, 3/16)$, we would like to show that there exists an $x_0^* \in (1/2, 3/4)$ such that

$$y(x_0^*) = \bar{y}$$

which holds by the intermediate value theorem. Therefore, when A has limited resource that is not sufficient to induce B to implement the socially optimal outcome, i.e.,

$$\bar{y} < \bar{y}_1 = \frac{3}{16}$$

the social planner could impose the new official curfew x_0^* earlier than 3 a.m. but later than the social optimum, i.e.,

$$\frac{1}{2} < x_0^* < \frac{3}{4}$$

that allows the social optimum to be implemented.

7. In this case the social planner can "reallocate" the wealth by changing the official curfew, therefore — together with Coasean bargaining — overcoming the wealth constraint and accomplishing what Coasean bargaining alone could not. This combination of a state intervention (the change in the curfew) plus private bargaining

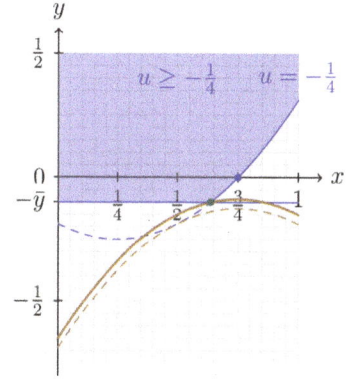

Figure 7.4: The allocation with TIOLI power and limited resources in the curfew conflict. When the official curfew is set at 3/4 (3 a.m.), A's fallback position is

$$u(x, y) = u\left(\frac{1}{4}, 0\right) = 0$$

and the shaded region is the feasible set

$$\{(x, y) \mid u(x, y) \geq 0 \ \& \ -y \leq \bar{y}\}$$

In this case, A's resources $\bar{y}$ are not sufficient to support the socially optimal outcome.

Note that $y(x_0)$ is increasing in x_0 in the interval $(1/2, 3/4)$ and range is given by

$$y\left(\frac{1}{2}\right) = 0, \quad y\left(\frac{3}{4}\right) = \frac{3}{16}$$

The intermediate value theorem guarantees that any value in the range could be achieved by some x_0^*.

might be an effective strategy if the social planner did not have enough information to implement the social optimum directly but did know that the A's lack of wealth was limiting the capacity of A and B to come to a private agreement implementing the social optimum. (The planner could have accomplished the same result if instead of changing the curfew they had transferred some of B's wealth to A.)

8. The four cases are presented in Table 7.1 and Figure 7.5, from which it can be seen that the for A, the nerd, $a > b > c > d$. For B, the deadhead, the opposite ordering holds.

Table 7.1: The four cases of the interaction between the deadhead and the nerd

	TIOLI power	
Curfew	A	B
9 p.m.	a	b
3 a.m.	c	d

Figure 7.5: The allocations with TIOLI power in curfew conflict. The blue curves are A's indifference curves, and the orange curves represent B's indifference curves. The thick curves are the participation constraint in the following four cases with the tangent points from a to d:

(a) The curfew is set at 1/4 (9 p.m.), and A has TIOLI power.

(b) The curfew is set at 1/4 (9 p.m.), and B has TIOLI power.

(c) The curfew is set at 3/4 (3 a.m.), and A has TIOLI power.

(d) The curfew is set at 3/4 (3 a.m.), and B has TIOLI power.

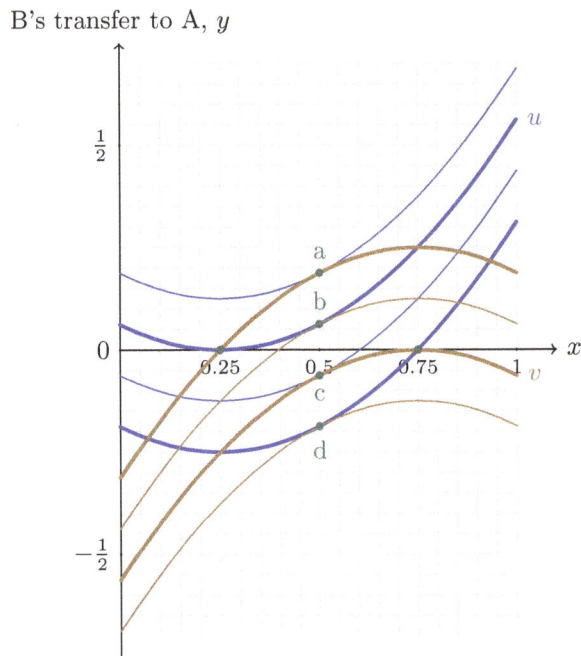

7.2 Bargaining power in the Nash solution

Considering the case of the fishers in Chapter 5 where e and E are the fishing effort of Lower and Upper, $v(e, E)$ and $V(e, E)$ are their respective utilities, and z and Z are their respective fallback positions, the Nash solution to the bargaining problem is defined as the allocation (e^*, E^*) which maximizes the "Nash product" ω where

$$\omega = [v(e^*, E^*) - z]^\alpha [V(e^*, E^*) - Z]^{1-\alpha} \tag{7.2}$$

subject to the constraint represented by the feasible set of outcomes, the boundary of which is sometimes called the *Pareto frontier* (or the bargaining frontier). This subset of outcomes is summarized by the differentiable function Γ as follows:

$$\Gamma(v, V) = 0$$

The two terms in square brackets in equation 7.2 are the rents (utilities above their fallback options) of the two bargainers. The exponent $\alpha \in [0, 1]$ (which is 1/2 in the conventional Nash bargain, that is, in the case of symmetry) is sometimes termed the bargaining power of Lower.

1. Show that the allocation which maximizes equation (7.2) above (for $\alpha \in (0, 1)$) is that which distributes utilities to Lower and Upper as follows:

$$\frac{\alpha}{1 - \alpha} = \frac{(v - z)\Gamma_v}{(V - Z)\Gamma_V}$$

A simplification will make this result a bit more transparent. Assume the Pareto frontier can be expressed by $\Gamma(v, V) = v + V - 1 = 0$ (the bargainers are dividing a dollar, say). Thus the joint surplus is $1 - (z + Z)$ and $\Gamma_v = 1 = \Gamma_V$.

2. Maximizing the Nash product above, derive an expression for Lower's utility resulting from Nash bargaining. (Denote this v^n, with the lower-case n superscript indicating the Nash bargaining solution.)

Endogenous bargaining power. Suppose two individuals engage in a joint production process, both supplying one unit of an input and producing an output (net of costs). They have agreed on a Nash bargain solution as the division of the resulting joint surplus. The two (Upper and Lower) have fallback positions of Z and z, respectively, and the bargaining power of Lower is given by α. The supply of the input is not verifiable and Lower (but not Upper) discovers that, by spending some fraction μ of their input to enhance bargaining power (employing lawyers, game theorists, etc.) rather than in production, α may be raised. As a result, $\alpha = \alpha(\mu)$ with $\alpha' > 0$ and $\alpha'' < 0$. Of course, diverting resources to a nonproductive use will lower the joint surplus, which we assume is just the sum of the inputs devoted to production or $2 - \mu$. Then the Pareto frontier is assumed to be

$$\Gamma(v, V) = v + V - (2 - \mu) = 0$$

3. Give the first order condition for Lower's choice of μ and explain what it means.

4. Suppose that $z = Z = 0$, $\mu \in [0, 1)$, and

$$\alpha(\mu) = \frac{1}{2}(1 + \sqrt{\mu})$$

so that $\alpha \in [1/2, 1)$. Give Lower's choice of μ, the level of the joint surplus, and the division of the joint surplus between the two.

Answers.

1. The problem is

$$\max_{v,V} \quad \omega = (v - z)^\alpha (V - Z)^{1-\alpha}$$

$$\text{s.t.} \quad \Gamma(v, V) = 0$$

Bargaining power

In the Nash bargaining model the share of the total rents gained by one of the two bargainers is termed their *bargaining power*. The term is something of a misnomer as it appears to refer to an explanation of the share of the surplus that a bargainer gets, but is really just a description of the outcome of the bargain.

Let the Lagrangian function be

$$\mathscr{L} = \omega + \lambda\Gamma$$

then the first order conditions for the Nash solution (e^*, E^*) are

$$\mathscr{L}_v = \omega_v + \lambda\Gamma_v = 0$$
$$\mathscr{L}_V = \omega_V + \lambda\Gamma_V = 0$$
$$\mathscr{L}_\lambda = \Gamma(v, V) = 0$$

Therefore, we have the marginal rate of substitution equal to the marginal rate of transformation

$$-\frac{w_v}{w_V} = -\frac{\Gamma_v}{\Gamma_V}$$

as shown in Figure 7.6. That is

$$\frac{\alpha(v - z)^{\alpha-1}(V - Z)^{1-\alpha}}{(1 - \alpha)(v - z)^\alpha(V - Z)^{-\alpha}} = \frac{\Gamma_v}{\Gamma_V}$$

which implies

$$\frac{\alpha}{1 - \alpha} = \frac{(v - z)\Gamma_v}{(V - Z)\Gamma_V}$$

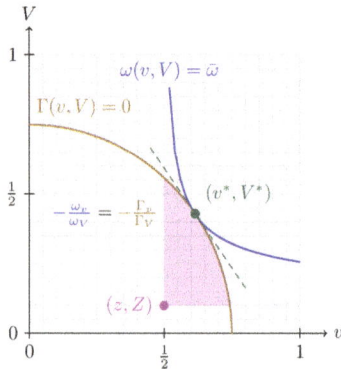

Figure 7.6: The Nash bargaining solution. The figure illustrates the case where $z = 0.5$, $Z = 0.1$, $\alpha = 1/3$. The shaded region represents the bargaining set. The orange curve is the Pareto frontier given by

$$\Gamma(v, V) = v^2 + V^2 - \frac{9}{16} = 0$$

and the blue curve is one of the family of iso-ω loci. To maximize the Nash product

$$\omega(v, V) = (v - z)^\alpha(V - Z)^{1-\alpha}$$

subject to the Pareto frontier, the solution is the point of tangency (v^n, V^n) in which MRS = MRT,

$$-\frac{\omega_v}{\omega_V} = \frac{\Gamma_v}{\Gamma_V}$$

2. With $\Gamma(v, V) = v + V - 1 = 0$, we have

$$\frac{\alpha}{1 - \alpha} = \frac{v - z}{V - Z} \Rightarrow V - Z = \frac{1 - \alpha}{\alpha}(v - z)$$

Then the joint surplus is

$$1 - (z + Z) = (v - z) + (V - Z) = \left(1 + \frac{1 - \alpha}{\alpha}\right)(v - z) = \frac{1}{\alpha}(v - z)$$

Therefore,

$$v^n = z + \alpha[1 - (z + Z)] \tag{7.3}$$

The expression (7.3) means that the Lower's utility is their fallback utility z plus a share of the joint surplus $[1 - (z + Z)]$. The share is exactly α, which is why it is termed the bargaining power of the Lower.

3. In this case, the total surplus is $2 - \mu - (z + Z)$. Then, by (7.3), we have

$$v = z + \alpha(\mu)[2 - \mu - (z + Z)]$$

The first order condition for Lower's choice of μ is

$$v_\mu = \alpha'(\mu)[2 - \mu - (z + Z)] - \alpha(\mu) = 0 \tag{7.4}$$

The first term in the middle expression is the marginal change in the share (α') associated with a change in μ, times the joint surplus, i.e., the marginal benefit, while the second is the marginal change in the joint surplus, which is -1, times the share (α), i.e., the marginal cost.

4. Given $z = Z = 0$ and $\alpha = (1 + \sqrt{\mu})/2$ for $\mu < 1$, the first order condition (7.4) becomes

$$\frac{1}{4\sqrt{\mu}}(2 - \mu) = \frac{1}{2}(1 + \sqrt{\mu})$$

That is

$$2 - \mu = 2\sqrt{\mu} + 2\mu \Rightarrow 3\mu + 2\sqrt{\mu} - 2 = 0$$

Then we have

$$\sqrt{\mu} = \frac{\sqrt{7} - 1}{3} \Rightarrow \mu = \frac{8 - 2\sqrt{7}}{9} \approx 0.3$$

7.3 Investing in bargaining power with transaction-specific assets

Here is another example of the "larger piece of a smaller pie" syndrome.

Consider a production process that requires two inputs, labor and a machine. The productivity of each input depends on the extent to which it has been designed or trained specifically for this particular production process (the *transaction specificity* of each). Revenue is defined by

$$Y(a, b) = \mu(Aa^\alpha + Bb^\beta) \tag{7.5}$$

where A and B are the number of units of labor and machines, respectively, and a and b are the degrees of transaction specificity, the values of both restricted to the unit interval $[0, 1]$.

> **Transaction specificity**
>
> An asset is *transaction-specific* to the extent that its value in its current use exceeds the value in its next best alternative.

The alternative use of the inputs yields revenue of $1 - a$ and $1 - b$ respectively for each unit of the input, that is, e.g. 1 if they are entirely unspecific ($a = 0 = b$) and 0 if they are entirely specific to this particular purpose. Notice that this means that a maximally specific input is worthless in its next-best alternative use, while an input with zero specificity is worthless in the production process under consideration.

Making each input more specific is resource-using for the input's owner, with costs rising linearly from 0 to c as a or b vary from 0 to 1 (training for the worker whose specificity is b costs bc, and correspondingly for the degree of specificity of the machine).

The Robinson Crusoe case. Suppose a single owner of one unit of both inputs is considering how best (through engineering their machine and training their labor) to design the inputs for the production process. Should production be economically viable, they will vary a and b to maximize revenues minus costs or $Y(a, b) - c(a + b)$.

1. Give the first order conditions for this constrained maximization problem, and indicate the profit-maximizing levels of specificity if $\alpha = \beta = 1/2$, $c = 1$, and $\mu = 2$.

A Nash bargaining solution. Now assume that the supplier of labor and the supplier of the capital goods are two different people who will make their design decisions (a and b) independently, then jointly produce, and then bargain over the resulting output. Suppose they have agreed on a symmetrical Nash bargaining outcome, that is, the division of the surplus which maximizes the Nash product. Their fallback position is the value of the input in its next best use.

2. If each owner varies the degree of asset specificity to maximize their income, give the relevant first order conditions, and, using the numerical values given above, indicate the levels of specificity selected by the two.

3. Compare the first order conditions of the bargaining and Robinson Crusoe case and explain why they differ.

4. What is the source of the coordination failure faced by the two owners in the bargaining?

Answers.

1. The constrained maximization problem of the single owner of both inputs (Robinson Crusoe) is

$$\max_{a,b} \quad Y(a,b) - c(a+b) = \mu(a^\alpha + b^\beta) - c(a+b)$$

The first order condition for the above is

$$Y_a = c = Y_b \implies \mu\alpha a^{\alpha-1} = c = \mu\beta b^{\beta-1} \tag{7.6}$$

Given $\alpha = \beta = 1/2$, $c = 1$ and $\mu = 2$, we have

$$a^{-1/2} = 1 = b^{-1/2} \implies a = b = 1$$

2. With specificity a and b, their fallback values are $z = 1 - a$ and $Z = 1 - b$ respectively. Assuming symmetrical Nash bargaining (equal "bargaining power"), each will get their fallback value plus half of the surplus $Y(a,b) - (z+Z)$. Then the income of the supplier of labor is

$$u = z + \frac{1}{2}[Y(a,b) - (z + Z)] - ca$$

The first order condition for the choice of a is

$$z_a + \frac{1}{2}(Y_a - z_a) - c = 0 \implies \frac{1}{2}(Y_a + z_a) = c \tag{7.7}$$

We have $Y_a = \mu\alpha a^{\alpha-1}$ by (7.5), and $z_a = -1$ since $z = 1 - a$. Then the first order condition (7.7) becomes

$$\frac{1}{2}(\mu\alpha a^{\alpha-1} - 1) = c$$

Given the numerical values, we have

$$\frac{1}{2}(a^{-1/2} - 1) = 1 \implies a = \frac{1}{9}$$

Symmetrically, the income of the supplier of capital is

$$U = Z + \frac{1}{2}[Y(a, b) - (z + Z)] - cb$$

and the first order condition for the choice of b is

$$\frac{1}{2}(Y_b + Z_b) = c \Rightarrow \frac{1}{2}(\mu\beta b^{\beta-1} - 1) = 1 \Rightarrow b = \frac{1}{9}$$

we have $b = 1/9$.

3. Take the choice of a, for example. The first order conditions (7.7) and (7.6), i.e.,

$$Y_a = c$$

$$\frac{1}{2}(Y_a + z_a) = c$$

differ in two ways. First, in the Robinson Crusoe case, the marginal benefit of greater specialization is Y_a, while in the case of bargaining, the actor who makes their own input more specific gains only half of the benefit due to the greater productivity of more specific inputs: $Y_a/2$. Secondly, the marginal cost of making the input more specific is just c in the single owner case, while in the bargaining case making the input more specific incurs an additional cost because it also reduces the fallback value of their input: $z_a < 0$. The reduced fallback value lowers the income directly since the fallback value is part of the income. This effect is only partially offset by the increase in the total surplus made possible by the greater specificity, so the net marginal cost of greater specificity is $c + z_a/2$.

4. The suppliers of labor and of machines face a coordination problem: making their own input more transaction-specific increases the output of the team, benefiting the other player, but it reduces the fallback value of their input, and their income after the Nash bargain is their fallback plus their share of the total surplus. So the actor who makes their own input more specific shares half of the benefit (with the other actor) but bears all of the cost (the reduced fallback option). This uncompensated external benefit that specializing their own input transfers to the other actor is the source of the coordination failure, resulting in too little specialization.

7.4 The war of attrition: How bargaining may exhaust the potential gains to cooperation

These games were first modeled by John Maynard Smith [95] and other evolutionary biologists.

[95]: Smith (1974), 'The Theory of Games and the Evolution of Animal Conflicts'

The war of attrition game is a distant cousin of the Hawk Dove game introduced in Chapter 15. It can be applied to a broad class of competitive rent-seeking behaviors leading to an escalation of unproductive expenditures. Examples include influencing governmental decisions or allocations within firms, firm strategies when competing for market shares, cramming for examinations on which only the relative grade

"... The balance between these modes of economic activity — the one leading to greater aggregate wealth and the other to conflict over who gets the wealth — provides the main story line of human history[...] Karl Marx, though a flop as an economist, did appreciate the importance of the dark side, the conflict option." — Jack Hirshleifer, (1994) Presidential Address, Western Economic Association [61]

[61]: Hirshleifer (1994), 'The Dark Side of the Force'

A variant of this model shows that depending on the relationship between the individual investment and the probability of winning the prize, total costs expended may exceed, equal or fall short of the prize.

For a detailed explanation of this property, refer to Section 2.3.

counts, and acquiring redundant educational credentials. The underlying structure is that individuals undertake an unproductive investment attempting to get a prize in a tournament-like setting.

Consider a case where one of two employees will be given a promotion worth v. Both understand that the employer will choose between the two based on their estimate of the employee's diligence and dedication to the firm, indicated by the number of hours worked during the period prior to the promotion. Let c be the cost to each employee of working an additional hour. At the beginning of the period each begins work and continues working until one of them stops and the other is promoted.

1. Show that there is no symmetric pure strategy equilibrium in this game. (Hint: during the U.S. steelworkers long strike at Ravenswood, Illinois, they adopted the slogan: "How long will we fight? One day longer than the company!")

2. Show that a symmetric Nash equilibrium can be based on a mixed strategy — at the end of each period, stop working with probability p, otherwise continue working. What is the equilibrium quitting probability, p^*?

3. If both players adopt the mixed-strategy Nash equilibrium, what is t^*, the expected duration of the game? (You may simplify by defining a period as short enough to be able to ignore the likelihood that the two quit simultaneously.)

4. Show that the expected total costs invested by the two players — $2t^*c$ — will exactly equal the magnitude of the prize.

Answers.

1. There is no symmetric pure strategy Nash equilibrium, as the best response to the other working t hours is to work either $t + 1$ (and win) or 0 (and avoid any costs).

2. For a mixed strategy to be a Nash equilibrium, it must be that all of the pure strategies in its support (making it up) have the same expected payoff. Were this not the case, the pure strategy with the highest expected payoff would be the best response, rather than the mixed strategy itself. Therefore, against the p-player the payoff to staying in must be the same as that to dropping out. That is,

$$p(v - c) - (1 - p)c = 0 \Rightarrow p^* = \frac{c}{v}$$

3. If each player quits with probability p^*, the probability that the game ends after each round, recalling that periods are sufficiently brief that we can ignore the probability that both quit in the same period (p^2) is

$$P = 1 - (1 - p^*)^2 = 2p^* - p^{*2} \approx 2p^*$$

and the expected duration of the game, t^*, is just the inverse of this probability, i.e.,

$$t^* = \frac{1}{P} \approx \frac{1}{2p^*} = \frac{v}{2c}$$

4. Since $t^* \approx v/2c$, the expected total costs invested by the two players is $2t^*c = 2 \times v/2c \times c = v$.

Principals and Agents: Contracts, Norms, and Power | 8

Working the problems in this chapter will familiarize you with the common properties of principal agent models and the many seemingly unrelated economic interactions to which they apply — a buyer purchasing a good of variable quality from a sub-contractor, a landlord renting an apartment to a tenant, or the rental of a truck to move your belongings. Similar models will later be applied to employers and workers and to lenders and borrowers, providing essential tools for the analysis of labor and credit markets.

There are two broad classes of principal–agent models. Hidden action (or moral hazard) models concern something the agent may *do* (or fail to do)—such as exerting effort or delivering high-quality goods—that is not subject to contract. Hidden attributes (or adverse selection) models concern characteristics of what the agent *is*—such as having a pre-existing health condition—that are not known to the principal or are otherwise not contractible. The problems below concern hidden action models.

You will discover that, in contrast to the conventional Walrasian model, a single difference in the institutional set up — the lack of a complete contract guaranteeing the enforcement of all the terms of an exchange of interest to either party — introduces fundamental changes in how markets work, even in a perfectly competitive equilibrium. Included are the following:

- ▶ the market does not clear in equilibrium, even though there are no impediments to entry by competitors and no "price rigidities" or other "frictions;"
- ▶ agents who succeed in making transactions receive rents — payments or other benefits in excess of their next best alternative — that are not competed away by the less fortunate agents who do not find a transaction;
- ▶ principals exercise power over agents even though the agents are free to walk away from the transaction;
- ▶ the preferences of agents (their intrinsic motivation to provide high quality goods for example) will affect the payoff of principals, who therefore have an interest in altering agents' preferences; and
- ▶ the resulting allocation is neither technically nor Pareto-efficient despite there being no impediments to competition and none of the usual externalities (such as environmental spillovers).

Some background for the problems in this chapter is found in Chapters 7 in Bowles [14] and 10 in Bowles and Halliday [29].

Figure 8.1: Herbert Simon (1916–2001) was a Nobel Laureate in economics though his undergraduate and PhD degrees were in political science. He was a pioneer in fields as diverse as artificial intelligence and organizational theory and is best known for stressing people's limited cognitive capacities and incomplete information when making decisions, what he termed "bounded rationality." He was the author in 1951 of one of the first principal agent models — about the conflict of interest between an employer and an employee [91]. He favored replacing taxes on wages and salaries with a tax on the value of land. Photo from News and Events, published by the Rochester Institute of Technology (RIT). Wikimedia Commons, public domain, https://commons.wikimedia.org/wiki/File:Herbert_Simon,_RIT_NandE_Vol13Num11_1981_Mar19_Complete.jpg

[91]: Simon (1951), 'A Formal Theory of the Employment Relationship'

[14]: Bowles (2004), *Microeconomics*

[29]: Bowles and Halliday (2022), *Microeconomics*

8.1 An incomplete contract: Difficult-to-measure quality

A supplier of some good or service may offer either low or high quality, costing the supplier $\underline{c}$ and $\bar{c}$ respectively. The quality will be tested by

©2025 Samuel Bowles and Weikai Chen, CC BY-NC 4.0

https://doi.org/10.11647/OBP.0466.08

the buyer and, if the quality supplied is low, this will be detected with a probability τ. In this case, the buyer will refuse the goods and the supplier will have to search for another buyer which will result in an expected payoff of $z - \underline{c}$. We assume that the cost of the quality test is sufficiently small to be ignored so that if $\tau = 1$ we say the contract is complete. The structure of this interaction is given in the game tree shown in Figure 8.2.

In answering the questions below you may assume that both principal and agent are entirely self-regarding, and that each anticipates just a single transaction with the other (it is a one-shot interaction).

1. Write down the *incentive compatibility constraint* for the provision of high quality, that is, the condition on the price offered such that the supplier will provide high quality.

2. Show that, if this is the price offered and $\tau < 1$, the supplier will receive a rent, that is, a payment superior to their fallback position.

3. Assume that the test determining whether low quality is detected is perfect so that $\tau = 1$. What is the least price consistent with the supplier providing high quality?

4. If the principal could devote some resources to reducing the fallback position of the supplier by one dollar, what is the maximum amount they would pay to do this?

5. Now suppose that the test for quality makes both Type I and Type II errors: not only does it sometimes fail to detect low quality, but with the same probability it mistakenly identifies high quality as low. Re-draw the above game tree and indicate what the new price that the buyer will offer is under these conditions, assuming $\tau > 0.5$.

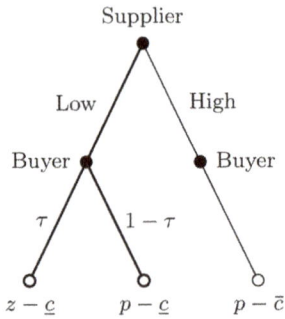

Figure 8.2: The quality game, with the agent's payoffs. The game tree gives the order of play (from the top down), the actions taken at each node (branching point) in the tree, and the agent's payoffs that will result from each path through the tree.

A variant of this model will be used in later chapters to model the labor market and the credit market.

Incentive compatibility constraint

The incentive compatibility constraint, ICC, describes the limits on the outcomes that a first mover may implement, showing how a second mover will respond to each of the actions (or strategies) that the first mover might take (including incentives designed to alter the second mover's behavior), also known as the second mover's best response function.

Enforcement rent

In a principal–agent relationship, an enforcement rent is the excess of the value of the transaction to the agent over the agent's fallback option. The prospect of losing the enforcement rent if the principal terminates the transaction induces the agent to act in the principal's interest.

Answers.

1. The incentive compatibility constraint for the provision of high quality requires that the payoff to providing high quality not be less than the expected payoff to providing low quality. Because this constraint will always be binding, we express it as an equality:

$$p - \bar{c} = \tau(z - \underline{c}) + (1 - \tau)(p - \underline{c}) \Rightarrow p = z + \frac{\bar{c} - \underline{c}}{\tau} \quad (8.1)$$

2. From (8.1), for $\tau < 1$ we have

$$p = z + \frac{\bar{c} - \underline{c}}{\tau} > z + \bar{c} - \underline{c} \Rightarrow p - \bar{c} > z - \underline{c}$$

so the agent receives more than their fallback position. This difference is termed an *enforcement rent*.

3. When $\tau = 1$, we have $p = z + \bar{c} - \underline{c}$ according to (8.1). In this case (a complete contract) the principal offers a price such that the agent's payoff when providing high quality is identical to their fallback option: $p - \bar{c} = z - \underline{c}$.

4. From (8.1), we have

$$\frac{dp}{dz} = 1$$

therefore, the principal would at most pay one dollar to reduce the fallback position of the supplier by one dollar.

5. The new game tree is shown in Figure 8.3. The supplier's expected payoff to provide high quality becomes

$$(1 - \tau)(z - \bar{c}) + \tau(p - \bar{c}) = (1 - \tau)z + \tau p - \bar{c}$$

and that to low quality is

$$(1 - \tau)(p - \underline{c}) + \tau(z - \underline{c}) = (1 - \tau)p + \tau z - \underline{c}$$

Therefore, the incentive compatibility constraint for the provision of high quality is

$$(1 - \tau)z + \tau p - \bar{c} = (1 - \tau)p + \tau z - \underline{c} \Rightarrow p = z + \frac{\bar{c} - \underline{c}}{2\tau - 1}$$

The new price is higher than the one in (8.1),

$$z + \frac{\bar{c} - \underline{c}}{2\tau - 1} \geq z + \frac{\bar{c} - \underline{c}}{\tau}$$

since $2\tau - 1 \leq \tau$. The equality holds when $\tau = 1$, in which case we have $p = z + \bar{c} - \underline{c}$.

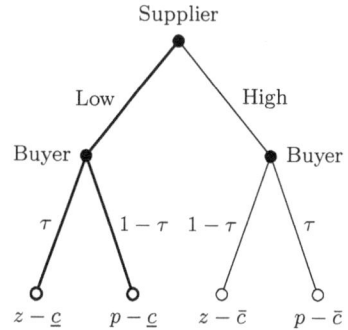

Figure 8.3: The quality game, with both types of errors. Even with high quality, the buyer could refuse the goods when the test mistakenly identifies high quality as low.

8.2 Renter as agent, landlord as principal

Abby is spending the summer vacation working at a job in her home town and would like to rent an apartment for two months. She finds a place that is available and she would be willing to pay at most v dollars per month if no other place were available. She also has the option of living with her parents which she values per month at $z < v$.

She approaches the landlord, Bob, who offers the apartment at a rent of r_1 per month and r_2 for the two months (no other contract, for example, including a security deposit, is possible). But he is concerned about the upkeep of the apartment and so adds that there will be an unannounced inspection sometime during the first month, the result of which will determine if Abby gets to rent the place for the second month. If she is evicted, she will spend the second month with her parents. (She could also stay there the first month, but would prefer to avoid staying there altogether). The subjective cost to Abby of devoting effort (e) to maintaining the apartment is

$$\delta(e) = \frac{1}{2}\underline{\delta}e^2, \quad e \in [0, 1]$$

Bob would like to maximize the total rent he receives minus the cost $c(e)$ of the necessary repairs or cleaning resulting from Abby's not taking proper care of the apartment, which is decreasing and convex in its argument. He tells Abby that he will terminate her lease after the first month with probability $t(e) = 1 - e$ (Bob cannot observe e so his termination schedule is based on the condition of the apartment when he monitors it which will be better the more effort that Abby has devoted). If Bob terminates her lease, the apartment will remain unrented for the second month. Both Abby and Bob are entirely self-regarding; the passage of time is so limited (just two months) that neither of them time-discount the costs and benefits associated with their transaction.

1. How much effort will Abby devote to maintaining the apartment in the second month?

2. Write down the first order condition of Abby's maximization problem and the resulting best response function.

3. What is Bob's maximization problem? What constraint(s) must he satisfy? (Show both the participation constraint (PC) and incentive compatibility constraint (ICC).)

4. Suppose that

$$c(e) = \frac{1}{2}(e - 1)^2$$

and that $z = \underline{\delta} = 1$ and $v = 2$. What rents will Bob charge?

5. Why does Bob charge a lower rent for the second month?

Answers.

1. Given (r_1, r_2), Abby's utility function is

$$u = v - r_1 - \delta(e_1) + [1 - t(e_1)][v - r_2 - \delta(e_2)] + t(e_1)z$$

Since
$$\frac{\partial u}{\partial e_2} = -[1 - t(e_1)]\delta'(e_2) = -\underline{\delta}e_1e_2 \le 0$$

Abby will set $e_2 = 0$. Or, more simply: taking proper care of the apartment in the second month is costly to Abby and yields no benefit (she will leave anyway at the end of the month), so she will devote no effort to this.

2. Given $e_2 = 0$, Abby's maximization problem is

$$\max_{e_1} \quad u = v - r_1 - \frac{1}{2}\underline{\delta}e_1^2 + e_1(v - r_2) + (1 - e_1)z$$

The first order condition is

$$\frac{\partial u}{\partial e_1} = -\underline{\delta} e_1 + (v - r_2 - z) = 0$$

Therefore (rearranging the first order conditions), the best response function is

$$e_1 = \frac{v - r_2 - z}{\underline{\delta}}$$

3. Bob's maximizing problem is

$$\max_{r_1, r_2} \quad \pi = r_1 - c(e_1) + e_1[r_2 - c(0)]$$

$$\text{s.t.} \quad u = v - r_1 - \delta(e_1) + e_1(v - r_2) + (1 - e_1)z \geq 2z \quad \text{(PC)}$$

$$e_1 = \frac{v - r_2 - z}{\underline{\delta}} \quad \text{(ICC)}$$

4. It is clear that the PC must be binding, otherwise Bob can always raise the rent in the first month r_1. Therefore, we have

$$r_1 = v - \frac{1}{2}\underline{\delta} e_1^2 + e_1(v - r_2 - z) - z$$

By the ICC, we have $de_1/dr_2 = -1/\underline{\delta}$. Then

$$\frac{dr_1}{dr_2} = -\underline{\delta} e_1 \frac{de_1}{dr_2} - e_1 + \frac{de_1}{dr_2}(v - r_2 - z) = -\frac{v - r_2 - z}{\underline{\delta}} = -e_1$$

and therefore the first order condition is

$$\frac{d\pi}{dr_2} = \frac{dr_1}{dr_2} - c'(e_1)\frac{de_1}{dr_2} + \frac{de_1}{dr_2}[r_2 - c(0)] + e_1$$

$$= -e_1 + \frac{c'(e_1)}{\underline{\delta}} - \frac{r_2 - c(0)}{\underline{\delta}} + e_1$$

$$= \frac{1}{\underline{\delta}}[c'(e_1) - r_2 + c(0)] = 0$$

Since

$$c(e) = \frac{1}{2}(e - 1)^2$$

we have $c'(e) = e - 1$ and so

$$\frac{v - r_2 - z}{\underline{\delta}} - 1 = r_2 - c(0) \Rightarrow r_2^* = \frac{v - z - \underline{\delta}[1 - c(0)]}{1 + \underline{\delta}}$$

With $z = \underline{\delta} = 1$ and $v = 2$, we have $r_2 = 1/4$, so $e_1 = 3/4$ and $r_1 = 41/32$.

5. The lower rent in the second month motivates Abby to devote effort to maintaining the apartment in the first month so as to avoid Bob terminating the contract at the end of the first month.

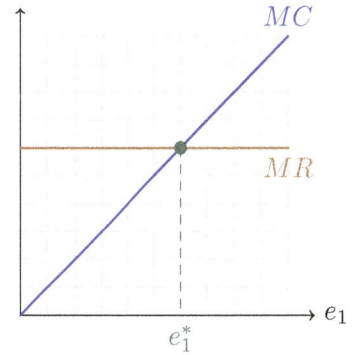

Figure 8.4: Abby's choice in the Rental Housing Market: she would choose an effort level e_1^* to equate marginal cost and marginal benefit, where

$$MC = \delta'(e_1) = \underline{\delta} e_1$$

and

$$MB = t'(e_1)(v - r_2 - z)$$

8.3 Quality control: The Benetton model

The Benetton family — three brothers and a sister born during the Great Depression and the Second World War — founded a small company selling sweaters to shops near the town of Treviso in northern Italy. Benetton grew to become one of the world's largest designers, producers, and sellers of casual wear and other garments. A key to its early success was a highly decentralized system of production: the labor-intensive aspects of production — primarily sewing — were carried out by hundreds of small subcontractors, working to designs and schedules and with materials supplied by Benetton.

A few processes were done by Benetton itself — notably dyeing, performed at the last minute so as to keep the product in tune with fashion trends. In 2020, Benetton's subcontractors outnumbered their employees by a factor of 17 to 1. Importantly, *quality control* and marketing were centralized, performed by Benetton's own staff. Sub-contractors who reliably produced goods of the specified quality benefited from permanent orders, quick payment by Benetton, and other benefits of their long-standing relationship with the company.

Consider the supplier of a good of variable quality, like one of Benetton's subcontractors, selling to the demander, Benetton. The supplier's per period utility depends solely on the price paid by the demander of the good (only one of which, at most, will be supplied), and the quality of the good supplied ($q \in [0, 1]$). Thus we can express the supplier's utility as $u = u(p, q)$. Providing quality requires effort and hence is onerous, so u is increasing and concave in its first argument and decreasing and convex in its second. In particular, assume that

$$u(p, q) = p - \frac{\delta}{1 - q} \tag{8.2}$$

where $\delta > 0$ is a constant.

The demander of the good buys such goods from n identical suppliers, transforms them somehow (perhaps by putting labels on them), and then sells them to consumers. The quality of the good is not subject to a costlessly enforceable contract.

Faced with contractual incompleteness, the buyer offers the supplier a contingent renewal contract as follows: the buyer announces a price p with a promise to continue the transaction in subsequent periods unless the buyer finds the quality of the goods provided to be inadequate, in which case the transaction will be terminated, the latter occurring with probability $t(q) = 1 - q$.

Denote the value of the supplier's next best alternative (the fallback position) by z, and the supplier's rate of time preference by i.

1. Explain the economic meaning of the parameter δ.

2. Give the value of the transaction to the supplier, v. You will find it simpler if you assume that the price is paid and the disutility of providing quality is experienced at the end of each period.

3. Using this expression, derive the first order condition for the supplier's choice of a level of quality and the resulting best response to the buyer's price offer. Explain the meaning of the first order condition on which the best response function is based. To simplify you may assume that $z = i = 0$.

4. Give the buyer's first order condition if they seek to set p to minimize p/q, knowing the supplier's best response function. What is the equilibrium price, p^N, and the resulting equilibrium level of quality supplied, q^N?

5. At this equilibrium, give the per period level of utility of the supplier, the expected duration of the transaction (in periods), and the value of the transaction.

6. Using the first order conditions you have derived, show that the Nash equilibrium in Figure 8.6 is not Pareto-efficient.

7. Suppose δ is endogenous, so the subjective cost of supplying quality (some combination of the disutility of effort, pride in the quality of one's work, and related motivations) can be altered by actions taken by the buyer. If the buyer could reduce δ for a single period, at a cost, what would be the largest cost the buyer would be willing to pay? (Hint: Use the equilibrium price of quality to answer this.)

Answers.

1. The parameter δ is the disutility for the supplier to provide a good of zero quality $q = 0$.

2. The value of the transaction to the supplier (simplified by assuming that $z = i = 0$) is

$$v = \frac{u + (1 - t)v + tz}{1 + i} = u + (1 - t)v = \frac{u}{t} \qquad (8.3)$$

3. The first order condition is

$$v_q = \frac{u_q t - u t'}{t^2} = 0 \Rightarrow u_q = t'\frac{u}{t} = t'v$$

That is, the supplier selects q to equate the marginal disutility of supplying quality (u_q) to the marginal effect of higher quality on the probability of retaining the transaction (t') times the enforcement rent (v). See Figure 8.5. Given the utility function (8.2) and $t = 1 - q$, we have

$$-\frac{\delta}{(1 - q)^2} = -1\frac{(p - \frac{\delta}{1-q})}{(1 - q)} \Rightarrow \delta = p(1 - q) - \delta \Rightarrow q = 1 - \frac{2\delta}{p}$$

Therefore, the supplier's best response to the buyer's price offer is

$$q(p) = 1 - \frac{2\delta}{p}.$$

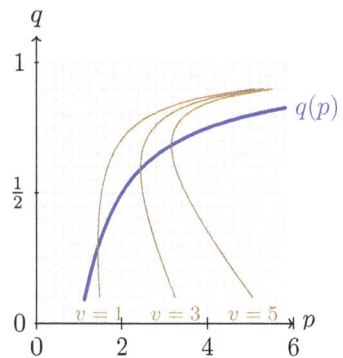

Figure 8.5: The supplier's indifference curves and best response function. The supplier's indifference curves are

$$v(p, q) = \frac{u(p, q)}{t(q)} = \bar{v}$$

and the best response function with $\delta = 0.5$ is

$$q(p) = 1 - \frac{2\delta}{p}$$

Figure 8.6: Maximizing p/q subject to the supplier's best response function. The curve labeled $v = 2$ is one of the supplier's indifference curved and $q(p)$ is their best response function. The green ray from the origin shows combinations of q and p that result in the same unit cost of quality: it is an "iso-cost-of-quality" locus with slope being q/p. The buyer would like an allocation on the steepest possible ray, but only points on or below the seller's best response function $q(p)$ are feasible. The first order condition to $\min_p p/q$, or $\max_p q/p$, is

$$q'(p) = \frac{q(p)}{p}$$

the green ray is tangent with the best response function. The price and level of quality supplied at equilibrium is

$$(p^N, q^N) = \left(4\delta, \frac{1}{2}\right)$$

with $\delta = 0.5$. It is not Pareto-efficient and any point in the shaded region is a Pareto-improvement.

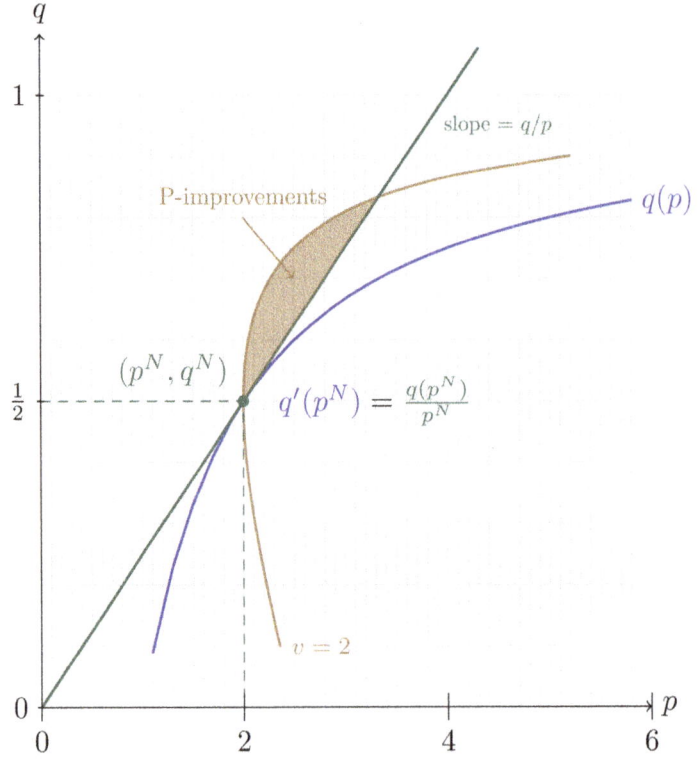

4. To $\min_p p/q(p)$, the first order condition is

$$\frac{q(p) - pq'(p)}{[q(p)]^2} = 0 \Rightarrow q'(p) = \frac{q(p)}{p}$$

Therefore

$$\frac{2\delta}{p^2} = \frac{1}{p} - \frac{2\delta}{p^2} \Rightarrow p^N = 4\delta$$

$$\Rightarrow q^N = 1 - \frac{2\delta}{4\delta} = \frac{1}{2}.$$

Let X be the number of periods as a random variable, then

$$X \sim G(t(q^N))$$

the geometric distribution with probability $t(q^N)$. Therefore,

$$E[X] = \frac{1}{t(q^N)}$$

5. Since $p^N = 4\delta$ and $q^N = 1/2$, we have

$$u = p^N - \frac{\delta}{1 - q^N} = 2\delta$$

and the expected duration of the transaction is

$$\frac{1}{t(q^N)} = \frac{1}{1 - q^N} = 2$$

Therefore, from (8.3), the value of the transaction is

$$v = \frac{u}{t} = \frac{2\delta}{1/2} = 4\delta.$$

6. To show that the Nash equilibrium is not Pareto-efficient, consider

a new outcome $(p^N + dp, q^N + dq)$ such that $dq > 0$ and

$$\frac{p^N}{q^N} \cdot dq \geq dp > 0 \qquad (8.4)$$

Then we have

$$dv = v_p dp + v_q dq = v_p dp > 0$$

since $v_q = 0$ at the Nash equilibrium and $v_p = u_q/t = 1/t > 0$, and

$$\frac{p^N + dp}{q^N + dq} \leq \frac{p^N}{q^N}$$

by (8.4). Therefore, $(p^N + dp, q^N + dq)$ is Pareto-superior to the Nash equilibrium (p^N, q^N) and thus the latter is not Pareto-efficient as shown in Figure 8.6.

> Note that from (8.4) we have
>
> $$q^N dp \leq p^N dq$$
>
> and then
>
> $$p^N q^N + q^N dp \leq p^N q^N + p^N dq$$
>
> which is
>
> $$q^N(p^N + dp) \leq p^N(q^N + dq)$$
>
> Therefore,
>
> $$\frac{p^N + dp}{q^N + dq} \leq \frac{p^N}{q^N}$$

7. We know that the level of quality at Nash equilibrium is $q^N = 1/2$ for any $\delta > 0$. Therefore, the change in δ affects the buyer's payoff only through the price. Since the equilibrium price is $p^N = 4\delta$, the benefit from reducing δ is

$$\Delta p^N = 4\Delta\delta$$

Therefore, the largest cost (per unit of δ) the buyer would be willing to pay to reduce δ for a single period is 4.

> This illustrates a common case in which a principal has the incentive to deliberately alter the preferences of the agent. Incomplete contracts and the principal agent relationships based on them are another reason for economists to study endogenous preferences.

8.4 Rental of capital goods as a principal agent problem

Where the care of a capital good is not verifiable, conventional rental contracts are often unattractive to the owner. This is a reason (as one of us found, while visiting New Zealand) why instead of renting bicycles, some companies sell the bikes to the user and then buy them back at the end of the contracted period, with the price depending on the condition of the bike.

Here is another vehicular example: a wealthy principal, P, owns a truck worth $1 which is to be used by the agent A; it may be run at speed f, resulting in a probability

$$\psi(f) = \frac{1}{2}f^2 \text{ for } f \in [0, 1]$$

that the truck will be wrecked (in which case its scrap value is zero). If the truck is not wrecked, its value at the end of the period is undiminished and still worth $1. The benefits to the agent are βD, where D is the distance traveled in the period (which, normalizing the hours of work of the agent to 1, is just f). The agent experiences a cost (of effort or anxiety) of cf. The fallback option of the agent is to receive z at the end of the period (i.e., if they were not transacting with the principal, they would get z). The above information is common knowledge, but it is impossible to write contracts in f. Both P and A are *risk neutral* and self-regarding.

Risk neutrality

A risk neutral person is indifferent between receiving x dollars with certainty and playing an uncertain lottery with the same expected value. A risk neutral person is not risk averse.

P offers the following contract (r, s) to A: at the beginning of the period, A pays r to P for the use of the truck, and at the end of the period the truck (if it survives) will be sold and A will be given a share, $s > 0$, of the proceeds.

The opportunity cost to the agent of paying r to the principal is $r(1 + \rho')$ and the value to the principal of the payment (evaluated at the end of the first period) to the principal is $r(1 + \rho)$. Assume that because the wealth levels of the two are different (rich principal, poor agent), the subjective cost of capital or the rate of time preference of the less wealthy person is higher, so $\rho' > \rho$.

The principal varies (r, s) to maximize expected income while the agent either rejects the contract offered by the principal or, given the terms of the contract, varies f to maximize expected utility.

1. What is the participation constraint (PC) for A's participation in the exchange?

2. What is the incentive compatibility constraint (ICC), that is the first order condition governing A's choice of f? Compare this with the f which would be chosen if A owned the truck outright, and show that if $s = 1$ the chosen speed would be the same in the two cases.

3. Write down the principal's optimization problem. Give the first order conditions. Letting s^N be the agent's share of the value of the truck in the Nash equilibrium, show that if $\rho' = \rho$ then s^N is 1 and if $\rho' > \rho$, $s^N < 1$.

4. If $\rho' = \rho$ and therefore $s^N = 1$, the agent is the residual claimant on the entire effect of his choice of f on the value of the truck, so there is no uncompensated external effect of their choice of f. If $\rho' > \rho$ (so $s^N < 1$), is the Nash equilibrium of this interaction Pareto-efficient? Explain why or why not.

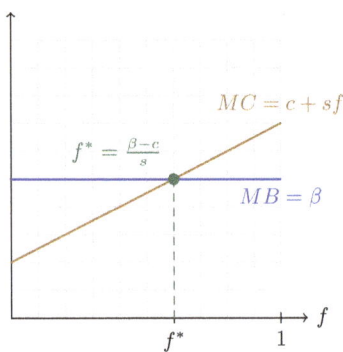

Figure 8.7: The first order condition of the agent's choice of speed. The marginal benefit from the additional distance traveled in the period is

$$MB = \beta$$

while the marginal cost consists of the marginal cost of effort or anxiety, c, and the cost arising from the reduced probability that the agent will make a sale of the truck at the end of the period, sf. That is,

$$MC = c + sf$$

Answers.

1. The participation constraint for A is

$$u = \beta f - c f + \left(1 - \frac{1}{2}f^2\right)s - r(1 + \rho') \geq z$$

2. For A, the problem is to

$$\max_f \quad u = \beta f - c f + (1 - \frac{1}{2}f^2)s - r(1 + \rho')$$

The first order condition is

$$\beta - c - s f = 0 \Rightarrow f = \frac{\beta - c}{s}$$

which is A's incentive compatibility constraint, as shown in Figure 8.7.

If A owned the truck, the problem becomes

$$\max_{f} \quad u = \beta f - c f + \left(1 - \frac{1}{2}f^2\right)$$

The first order condition is

$$\beta - c - f = 0 \Rightarrow f = \beta - c$$

which is the same as the one derived above with $s = 1$. Therefore, if $s = 1$, the chosen speed would be the same in the two cases. In this case, the agent has effectively purchased the truck, and the problem is no longer a principal agent relationship.

3. For P, the problem is to vary r and s to maximize v subject to both the participation and incentive compatibility constraints of the agent:

$$\max_{r,s\le 1} \quad v = r(1+\rho) + (1-s)\left(1 - \frac{1}{2}f^2\right)$$

$$\text{s.t.} \quad u = (\beta - c)f + s\left(1 - \frac{1}{2}f^2\right) - r(1+\rho') \ge z$$

$$f = \frac{\beta - c}{s}$$

First, substitute the ICC into u to get

$$u = s + \frac{(\beta - c)^2}{2s} - r(1+\rho')$$

Secondly, the participation constraint must be binding; otherwise, P can set a higher rent without A rejecting the contract. Suppose instead that the participation constraint is not binding. Then, by continuity, there exists some $r' > r$ that still satisfies the participation constraint for the same value of s. Since the incentive compatibility constraint is independent of r, and the principal's objective function is increasing in r, the contract (r', s) would be feasible and would yield higher expected income for the principal. Therefore, the participation constraint must bind (i.e., $u = z$), which implies

$$r = \frac{1}{1+\rho'}\left[s + \frac{(\beta - c)^2}{2s} - z\right]$$

Then substitute r and $f = (\beta - c)/s$ into P's objective function v to get

$$v(s) = \frac{1+\rho}{1+\rho'}\left[s + \frac{(\beta - c)^2}{2s} - z\right] + (1-s)\left[1 - \frac{(\beta - c)^2}{2s^2}\right]$$

Let s^N be the agent's share of the value of the truck that maximizes $v(s)$, where the superscript indicates a Nash equilibrium value. Then the first order condition is

$$v'(s^N) = 0 \quad \text{if } s^N \in (0,1)$$

$$v'(s^N) \ge 0 \quad \text{if } s^N = 1$$

Substitute $f = (\beta - c)/s$ into u to get

$$u = \frac{(\beta - c)^2}{s} + s\left[1 - \frac{1}{2}\frac{(\beta - c)^2}{s^2}\right]$$

$$- r(1+\rho')$$

$$= s + \frac{(\beta - c)^2}{2s} - r(1+\rho')$$

where

$$v'(s) = \frac{1+\rho}{1+\rho'}\left[1 - \frac{(\beta-c)^2}{2s^2}\right] - \left[1 - \frac{(\beta-c)^2}{2s^2}\right]$$

$$+ (1-s)\frac{(\beta-c)^2}{s^3}$$

$$= \frac{\rho-\rho'}{1+\rho'}\left[1 - \frac{(\beta-c)^2}{2s^2}\right] + \frac{(1-s)(\beta-c)^2}{s^3}$$

$$= \frac{\rho-\rho'}{1+\rho'}(1-\phi) + \frac{(1-s)(\beta-c)^2}{s^3}$$

and

$$\phi = \frac{(\beta-c)^2}{2s^2}$$

▶ If $\rho' = \rho$, we have

$$v'(s) = \frac{(1-s)(\beta-c)^2}{s^3} > 0 \quad \forall s \in (0,1)$$

and $v'(1) = 0$, so $s^N = 1$.

▶ If $\rho' > \rho$, we have

$$v'(1) = \frac{\rho-\rho'}{1+\rho}(1-\phi) < 0$$

so $v'(s^N) = 0$ for some $s^N < 1$.

4. If $\rho' > \rho$, then $s^N < 1$. In this case, the Nash equilibrium of this interaction is not Pareto-efficient, since both would be better off with a small decrease in f and a small increase in s, as shown in Figure 8.8. Consider $s' = s^N + ds$ and $f' = f^N + df$ with $df < 0$ and

$$0 < ds < -\frac{f^N(1-s^N)}{1 - \frac{1}{2}(f^N)^2}df \tag{8.5}$$

then we have

$$du = u_f df + u_s ds = \left[1 - \frac{1}{2}(f^N)^2\right]ds > 0$$

and

$$dv = v_f df + v_s ds = -(1-s^N)f^N df - \left[1 - \frac{1}{2}(f^N)^2\right]ds > 0$$

by (8.5). Therefore, (r', s') together with f' is an allocation Pareto-superior to the Nash equilibrium.

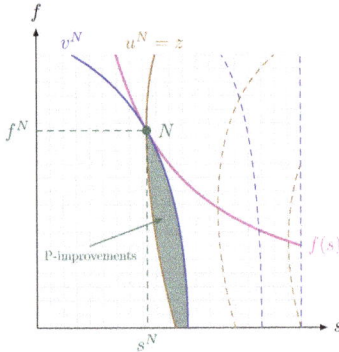

Figure 8.8: The Nash equilibrium of interaction between the wealthy truck owner and the agent. The orange curves are the indifference curves of the agent

$$(\beta-c)f + s(1 - \frac{1}{2}f^2) - r(1+\rho') = \bar{u}$$

the blue curves are the indifference curves of the principal

$$r(1+\rho) + (1-s)(1 - \frac{1}{2}f^2) = \bar{v}$$

and

$$f(s) = \frac{\beta-c}{s}$$

is the agent's best response function. The tangency of the principal's indifference curve and the agent's best response function (s^N, f^N) is the Nash equilibrium when $\rho' > \rho$ so $s^N < 1$. At the Nash equilibrium, the principal would choose the rent r^N such that the participation constraint is binding,

$$u^N = z$$

The Nash equilibrium is not Pareto-efficient as any point in the green shaded area (allocations with a lower f and higher s) is Pareto-superior to it.

Economic Classes and Incomplete Contracts | 9

Institutions are often described as integrated and organic wholes, more or less like a member of a species. Everyone can tell an elephant from a dog, and similarly, capitalism, feudalism, and socialism are not likely to be mixed up, at least when speaking abstractly. But when one studies institutions empirically, one encounters a vast diversity of often highly local arrangements. Individual farmers often work under as many as three distinct contracts, for example, working one's own land, hiring out as wage labor, and farming on land rented from another owner (possibly under a fixed rent, a crop share, or other distinct contract). In this chapter we use principal agent models to study how differences in institutions — the incomplete nature of contracts, or the exercise of coercion by some actors — result in differing levels of economic inequality.

Like all principal-agent relationships, these are structurally asymmetric in the game-theoretic sense: the principals and agents have distinct strategy sets. In the Benetton model of Section 8.3, for example, the principal sets the price and the agent sets the quality. Here we turn to principal agent relationships between members of different economic classes that are asymmetric in another sense: the principal is typically wealthy and the agent not, for example, owners of substantial tracts of farmland as principals and the farmers they engage as employees or sharecroppers as agents. In Chapter 10 we introduce principal agent relationships between owners of firms and their employees and in Chapter 11 between owners of banks and borrowers. The problems in Chapter 11 will allow you to explore why principals — whether landlords, employers, or owners of banks — are often the wealthy.

While social scientists and historians regularly use the term "class" to refer to landlords, employees, or owners of firms, economists typically eschew such categorical representations. Discrete groupings often convey less information than continuously measured variables such as income and wealth, an example being the use of the term "middle class" to mean nothing more than middle income. It is partly for this reason that the classical economists' concept of class — which was a staple not only of Marxian economics but of the economics of Ricardo and Smith as well — fell into disuse among economists during the last century.

The contemporary theory of incomplete contracts provides a reason to revive the classical economists' categories. It provides a theory of economic classes in which discrete class categories convey information not captured by wealth or other continuous measures. Members of a class have more in common than their wealth (which need not even be similar). This is because their relationship to other classes is the same: an economic class is a set of people who engage in similar contracts with members of other classes.

Thus all employees — whether highly paid or minimum wage — have in common that they interact on an ongoing basis with an employer who directs their work activities; they receive income in the form of a wage or salary, they do not own the goods they produce, and their employment can

Figure 9.1: Joan Robinson (1903–1983) taught economics at the University of Cambridge and developed one of the first models of what she called "imperfect competition." The term "monopsony" is also due to her, as were many colorful turns of phrase. Concerning debates between critics and defenders of capitalism she wrote: "No one is conscious of his own ideology anymore than he can tell the smell of his own breath." And "the misery of being exploited by capitalists is nothing compared to not being exploited at all" (that is, being without a job). Her heated "capital controversy" with American economists Paul Samuelson, Robert Solow, and others raised doubts about the general equilibrium model of perfect competition. A letter to a female student in 1970 from Paul Samuelson, perhaps the most influential economist of the 20th century, concluded: "P.S. Do study economics. Perhaps the best economist in the world happens also to be a woman (Joan Robinson)." Photo Courtesy of Nancy Folbre

Economic class

An economic class is a set of people who engage in similar contracts with members of other classes.

©2025 Samuel Bowles and Weikai Chen, CC BY-NC 4.0   https://doi.org/10.11647/OBP.0466.09

be terminated by their employer. Another class, independent producers who neither hire others nor are hired by others, may not differ from employees in wealth or income. They differ because they engage with other economic actors primarily in the buying of inputs and selling of outputs, and their income takes the form of revenues derived from selling the goods or services they produce.

Some background for the problems in this chapter is found in Chapter 10 in Bowles [14], Wright [110], and Naidu [78].

[14]: Bowles (2004), *Microeconomics*

[110]: Wright (2000), *Class Counts*

[78]: Naidu (2026), *Terms of Service*

9.1 Sharecropping and incomplete labor contracts

A farmer produces goods with the production function $Q = f(L)$, with f increasing and concave in its argument L, the amount of time the farmer works. The farmer values goods and finds spending time at work onerous according to $u = y - v(L)$, where y is the farmer's income (in units of output) and both v' and v'' are positive.

1. If the farmer is the residual claimant on the crop, how much time will they spend working? Give the first order condition of their choice of L^*.

2. If the farmer is a wage worker whose reservation utility is z and L is contractible, show that the farmer's income-maximizing employer-landowner will offer a contract implementing the same level of labor time as that given in your answer above, i.e., $L_w^N = L^*$. Explain why the Nash equilibrium of this interaction (W^N, L_w^N) is or is not Pareto-efficient.

Suppose that contracts in L cannot be written and that the landowner offers the farmer a share contract, according to which the farmer's income is $y = sQ$ and the owner receives the remainder of the crop or $(1 - s)Q$.

3. How much time will the farmer now spend working? Use the first order condition for their maximization problem to write down the farmer's best response to the owner's choice of s.

In some of the problems below in this chapter and in Chapter 10 we introduce the distinction between hours of working time L and the amount of work (meaning effort devoted to production) actually done. In this question L is just the time spent working.

4. To maximize their income (assuming the landlord bears no other costs), give the first order condition for the landlord's choice of s.

5. Explain why the equilibrium (s^N, L_s^N) is or is not Pareto-efficient.

6. Will the Nash equilibrium amount of labor L_s^N done by the farmer be greater or less than the equilibrium amounts L_w^N when labor is contractible?

7. Is there a Pareto-efficient contract the landlord could offer in this case (assuming as before that no contracts can be written in L)? Say what it is and why it works.

Imagine that the landlord can rent a device that makes information concerning the farmer's working hours (L) verifiable.

Verifiable information

Information that can be used in legal proceedings to enforce a contract or other agreement is termed verifiable information.

8. How much is the most they would be willing to pay to rent this device for a single period if the alternative was (i) sharecropping (that is assigning a share s to the farmer) or (ii) the efficient contracting you devised in the last part of your previous answer?

Answers.

1. Since the farmer is the residual claimant on their crop, we have $y = Q = f(L)$. Then the problem is to

$$\max_{L} \quad u = y - v(L) = f(L) - v(L)$$

The first order condition is

$$u_L = f' - v' = 0 \Rightarrow f'(L^*) = v'(L^*) \tag{9.1}$$

that is, the marginal benefit equals the marginal cost, as shown in Figure 9.2. This is another Robinson Crusoe case (the decision maker is RC = residual claimant) that we introduce here as a useful benchmark allowing us to see what is distinctive about the principal-agent cases that follow.

2. Suppose that the contract is (W, L), where W is the total wage (not the hourly wage) and L is the hours of labor hired. The problem for the employer-landowner is to

$$\max_{W,L} \quad \pi = f(L) - W \tag{9.2}$$
$$\text{s.t.} \quad W - v(L) \geq z$$

Note that for any solution to this maximization problem, the constraint must be binding; otherwise there would be different contract with slightly lower W and the same L that the worker would accept and would yield higher profit. Therefore, we have $W = v(L) + z$. Then, using the participation constraint (expressed as an equality), the problem becomes

$$\max_{L} \quad \pi = f(L) - v(L) - z$$

The first order condition is

$$f'(L) - v'(L) = 0 \tag{9.3}$$

which is identical to equation (9.1). Therefore, the farmer's profit-maximizing employer-landowner will offer a contract implementing the same level of labor as that when the farmer is the residual claimant. Note that the Nash equilibrium (W^N, L_w^N) maximizes the sum of both utilities,

$$\pi + [W - v(L)] = f(L) - W + [W - v(L)] = f(L) - v(L)$$

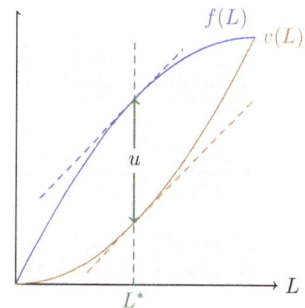

Figure 9.2: The first order condition of farmer's choice of labor as the residual claimant. Assume that

$$v(L) = L^2$$

and

$$f(L) = 2L - L^2$$

Then, at $L^* = 0.5$, we have the marginal benefit equal to the marginal cost

$$f'(L^*) = v'(L^*)$$

which maximizes the utility

$$u = f(L) - v(L)$$

by the first condition (9.3). Therefore, it is Pareto-efficient. Otherwise, if there existed an allocation (W', L') that is Pareto-superior to the Nash equilibrium, then the sum of utilities would be greater than that at the Nash. But because (W^N, L_w^N) satisfies (9.3), no such allocation can exist. Graphically, as shown in Figure 9.3, the Nash equilibrium (W^N, L_w^N) is at the tangency of the indifference curves of the two actors, so it must be Pareto-efficient.

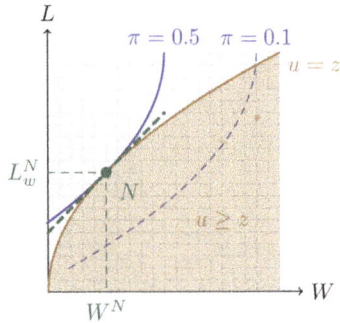

Figure 9.3: The equilibrium when labor is contractible. The shaded region

$$\{(L, W) \mid u(L, W) = W - v(L) \geq z\}$$

is the feasible set, and

$$\pi(L, W) = f(L) - W = \bar{\pi}$$

are the iso-profit curves. Then the tangency (L_w^N, W^N) is the solution with

$$MRT = f'(L_w^N) = v'(L_w^N) = MRS$$

The figure has been constructed with

$$v(L) = L^2, \quad f(L) = 2L - L^2$$

and $z = 0$.

Differentiating both sides of

$$sf' - v' = 0$$

with respect to s, we have

$$f' + sf''\frac{dL}{ds} - v''(L)\frac{dL}{ds} = 0$$

which implies that

$$\frac{dL}{ds} = \frac{f'}{v'' - sf''} > 0$$

since $f' > 0$, $v'' > 0$ and $f'' < 0$.

---

3. Given $y = sQ = sf(L)$, the farmer's problem is

$$\max_L \quad u = sf(L) - v(L)$$

The first order condition (again, expressing the requirement that the marginal benefit of working more hours be equal to the marginal disutility of working additional hours) is

$$u_L = sf' - v' = 0 \Rightarrow sf'(L) = v'(L) \tag{9.4}$$

which defines an implicit function $L = L(s)$ for $s > 0$. When $s = 0$, we have $L = 0$ as the farmer's best response, as shown in Figure 9.4. From the first order condition, we can see that

$$f' + (sf'' - v'')\frac{dL}{ds} = 0 \Rightarrow \frac{dL}{ds} = \frac{f'}{v'' - sf''} > 0 \tag{9.5}$$

so as expected the larger the share of the crop the farmer keeps, the more hours they will work.

4. The landlord's problem is to select s to maximize profits subject to the farmers best response function, or

$$\max_{s \in [0,1]} \quad \pi = (1 - s)f(L)$$
$$\text{s.t.} \quad sf'(L) - v'(L) = 0 \tag{9.6}$$

which, using the implicit function $L(s)$, becomes

$$\max_{s \in [0,1]} \quad \pi = (1 - s)f(L(s))$$

and the first order condition of the interior solution $s \in (0, 1)$ is

$$\pi_s = (1 - s)f'\frac{dL}{ds} - f = 0 \tag{9.7}$$

By rearranging (9.7) we have

$$MRT = \frac{dL}{ds} = \frac{f}{(1 - s)f'(L)} = MRS$$

which means that the profit-maximizing landlord will set s such that the marginal rate of transformation of the farmer's share into the farmer's hours of work equals the marginal rate of substitution between s and L in the landlord's iso-profit locus based on their profit function, as shown by the tangency at (s^N, L_s^N) in the figure 9.4. Substituting (9.5) into (9.7), we get the first order condition

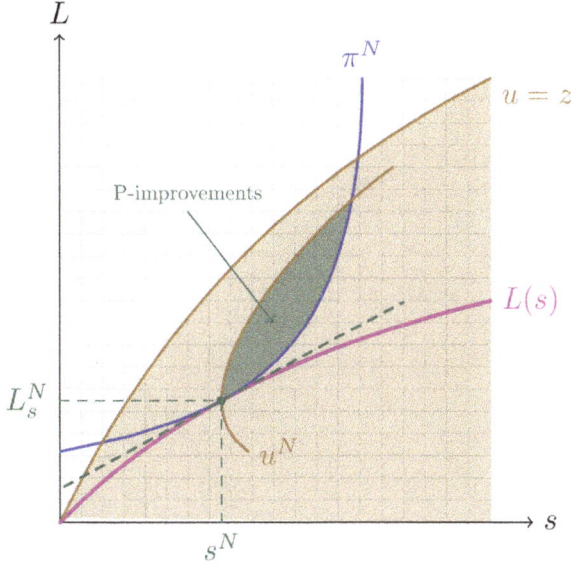

Figure 9.4: The equilibrium sharing contract when labor is not contractible. The shaded region

$$\{(s, L) \mid u(s, L) \geq z\}$$

is the feasible set determined by the participation constraint, which contains the best response function $L(s)$ defined by

$$s f'(L) = v'(L)$$

and

$$\pi(s, L) = (1 - s)f(L) = \bar{\pi}$$

is one of the landlord's iso-profit curves. Then the tangency (s^N, L_s^N) is the solution to the landlord's problem (maximize profit subject to the best response function), and therefore is the Nash equilibrium of this problem, at which

$$MRT = \frac{dL}{ds} = \frac{f}{(1 - s)f'} = MRS$$

The solution here is not Pareto-efficient: any point in the green shaded region is a Pareto-improvement over the Nash equilibrium. As before, we have used

$$v(L) = L^2, \quad f(L) = 2L - L^2$$

and $z = 0$.

for the landlord's choice of s:

$$\frac{(1 - s)(f')^2}{v'' - s f''} = f$$

5. The Nash equilibrium (s^N, L_s^N) is not Pareto-efficient. Consider the allocation (s', L') such that

$$s' = s^N + ds, \quad L' = L_s^N + dL$$

with $dL > 0$ and

$$0 < ds < \frac{(1 - s^N)f'(L_s^N)}{f'(L_s^N)} \tag{9.8}$$

Then we have

$$du = u_L dL + u_s ds = f(L_s^N)ds > 0$$

and

$$d\pi = \pi_L dL + \pi_s ds$$
$$= (1 - s^N)f'(L_s^N)dL - f(L_s^N)ds > 0$$

> Note that at Nash equilibrium,
>
> $$\frac{\partial u}{\partial L}(L_s^N) = 0$$
>
> therefore
>
> $$du = u_s ds = f(L_s^N)ds$$

by (9.8). Thus, (L', s') is Pareto-superior to the Nash equilibrium as shown in Figure 9.4. This means that there exists some increase in both the farmer's working time and the share of the crop they retain that would make both parties better off (the Pareto-improving lens is to the "north east" of the Nash equilibrium in this case).

6. The first order condition determining the labor time chosen by

the farmer when labor time is contractible (9.3) is identical to the analogous first order condition for non-contractible labor time when the share kept by the farmer is $s = 1$. We also know that $dL/ds > 0$ from (9.5) and that the landlord will set a value of $s < 1$. So the amount of time worked by the farmer under the share cropping arrangement with labor time not contractible is less than the time the farmer would work with contractible labor time (or, equivalently, if the farmer owned the entire crop that they produce).

We can show this letting L_w^N be the equilibrium amount when labor is contractible, and L_s^N be that when it is not. Then, from (9.3) and (9.4), we have

$$f'(L_w^N) - v'(L_w^N) = 0 = s^N f'(L_s^N) - v'(L_s^N)$$

As $s^N < 1$,

$$f'(L_s^N) - v'(L_s^N) > s^N f'(L_s^N) - v'(L_s^N)$$
$$= f'(L_w^N) - v'(L_w^N)$$

and thus $L_w^N > L_s^N$ by $f'' - v'' < 0$. That is, the farmer will do more labor in the Nash equilibrium than when labor is contractible, as shown in Figure 9.5.

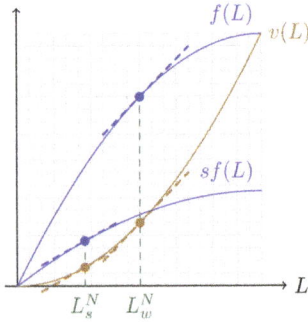

Figure 9.5: The farmer will do more when labor is contractible in the share-cropping game. When labor is contractible, the labor in equilibrium is L_w^N such that

$$f'(L_w^N) = v'(L_w^N)$$

while when labor is not contractible, the equilibrium labor becomes L_s^N such that

$$sf'(L_s^N) = v'(L_s^N)$$

Then we have $L_s^N < L_w^N$. The figure shows the case that $v(L) = L^2$ and $f(L) = 2L - L^2$.

7. There is a Pareto-efficient contract such that the farmer is the residual claimant on the entire crop and pays the landlord a fixed rent r. Then, to maximize the utility $u = f(L) - v(L) - r$, the farmer would choose $L = L^*$ (satisfying $f' = v'$) when $u \geq z$ is satisfied.

The landlord would choose a maximum rent subject to the participation constraint, that is

$$\begin{aligned} \max_r \quad & r \\ \text{s.t.} \quad & f'(L) - v'(L) = 0 \\ & f(L) - v(L) - r \geq z \end{aligned} \quad (9.9)$$

Then $r^* = f(L^*) - v(L^*) - z$. This result is Pareto-efficient, because r^* maximizes the landlord's profits subject to the farmer's binding participation constraint, as shown in Figure 9.6.

8. With the device to monitor, the landlord can offer a complete contract, so the problem is the same as (9.2) whose value is

$$\pi^w = f(L_w^N) - v(L_w^N) - z$$

a) With the sharecropping contract, the value of the problem (9.6) is

$$\pi^s = (1 - s^N)f(L_s^N)$$

Then the most they would be willing to pay to rent this device is

$$p^{max} = \pi^w - \pi^s$$

Since $u = s^N f(L_s^N) - v(L_s^N) \geq z$, we have

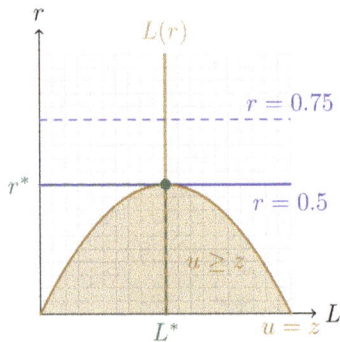

Figure 9.6: The equilibrium rent in the sharecropping game. The shaded region

$$\{(L, r) \mid u(L, r) = f(L) - v(L) - r \geq z\}$$

is the feasible set, $r = \bar{r}$ is an iso-rent curve, and the line $L(r)$ determined by

$$f'(L) = v'(L)$$

is the best response. Then (L^*, r^*) is the solution assuming $v(L) = L^2, f(L) = 2L - L^2$, and $z = 0$.

$$p^{max} \geq [f(L_w^N) - v(L_w^N)] - [f(L_s^N) - v(L_s^N)] > 0$$

where the first bracket represents the surplus when labor is contractible, and the second bracket the surplus in the share-cropping equilibrium. Therefore, the maximum willingness to pay for the device is greater than the difference in surplus between the scenarios where labor is contractible and where it is subject to sharecropping.

b) With the fixed rent contract, the value of the problem (9.9) is

$$r^* = f(L^*) - v(L^*) - z$$

where, as before, $L^* = L_w^N$ is the quantity of labor satisfying $f' = v'$. Therefore, the most they would be willing to pay to rent this device is $p^{max} = \pi^w - r^* = 0$.

By $u \geq z$ we have

$$s^N f(L_s^N) \geq v(L_s^N) + z$$

and therefore

$$\pi^s = f(L_s^N) - s f(L_s^N)$$
$$\leq f(L_s^N) - [v(L_s^N) + z]$$

Then

$$\pi^w - \pi^s \geq \pi^w - [f(L_s^N) - v(L_s^N) - z]$$
$$= [f(L_w^N) - v(L_w^N)] - [f(L_s^N)$$
$$- v(L_s^N)]$$

which is positive since $f - v$ achieves its maximum at L_w^N.

9.2 Class conflict and the choice of contracts

This question concerns the mix of contracts that may exist in equilibrium. Table 9.1 gives the distribution of contracts engaged in by households of differing wealth levels in Palanpur, the Indian village you will have encountered if you studied Section 2.4. (Notice how little wealth the villagers have: those with more than half an acre are considered wealthy.) You can see that three-quarters of those owning no land mostly take jobs working for others ("hires out"), but occasionally they are employers, too ("hires in"). Working for others is uncommon among the wealthiest group (less than 1 in 5).

Land owned (acres)	Hires in	Hires in and hires out	Hires out only
None	0.25	0.21	0.54
≤ 0.47	0.30	0.37	0.33
> 0.47	0.81	0.15	0.04

Table 9.1: Land ownership and wage labor in Palanpur. The entries are the fraction of the wealth class hiring labor, hiring themselves out, and both hiring in and hiring out. Source: Bowles [14, p. 351]

[14]: Bowles (2004), *Microeconomics*

Consider a landowner with ten units of land that they do not farm. The owner can offer access to their land to farmers who do not own land under two types of contracts, sharecropping and wage labor. The utility of prospective farmers and the landlord alike is simply $y - e^2$, where y is income (in units of agricultural output) and e is effort over a given period. Each farmer, when working full-time, farms one hectare of land. (The farmers can split their time between wage work and sharecropping.) Output is proportional to the level of effort of the farmer, so the production function on each hectare of the land is simply $q = e$, where q is the level of output.

If wage labor is used, the monitoring is done by the landlord, who experiences a disutility occasioned by the associated level of effort. Sufficient monitoring is done so that $e = 1/2$ for each worker hired for wages, and the amount of the landlord's effort needed to perform the monitoring to enforce this level of worker effort is $e = 1/8$ per worker. (Wages are not used to induce higher levels of effort, so the wage is simply the minimum necessary to secure the supply of labor time, namely, the wage that gives the worker the utility attainable in the neighboring sharecropping contracts.)

There are neighboring landlords identical to this one offering sharecropping contracts, but because these are absentee owners they cannot oversee wage work (monitoring the effort levels) and hence do not offer wage contracts. They all engage farmers under sharecropping contracts.

The landlord is trying to decide how much land to rent to sharecroppers, how much to farm using wage labor, and what contracts to offer each. Local traditions preclude very complex contracts, so the landlord simply has to determine what the sharecropper's share, s, should be in the sharecropping contracts, what the wage w should be in the wage labor contracts, and how many hectares of land should be devoted to cultivation by wage labor, n. (An amount of land, in hectares, equal to $10 - n$ will be cultivated by sharecroppers.) The landlord first must determine how the tenants' effort levels will be affected by s, the share that the farmer retains of the crop they produce.

1. What is the sharecropper's best response function: $e^* = e^*(s)$? What share will the landlord offer (setting $s = s^*$ to maximize their utility)?

2. Turning now to the possibility of hiring wage labor, and assuming that all landlords in the area are offering sharecropping contracts with sharecropper's share s^*, indicate the wage the landlord will offer, w^*.

3. Given s^*, $e^*(s^*)$, and w^*, determine the landlord's utility-maximizing number of hectares that they will select to be farmed by wage labor, n. Call this n^*. At the equilibrium (e^*, s^*, w^*, n^*), what are the utility levels of the three types of agents: landlord, worker, and sharecropper?

4. Is the result given by (e^*, s^*, w^*, n^*) Pareto-efficient?

5. **A Coasean bargain.** Explain an offer that one or more of the (non-colluding) agents might make to the landlord that would result in a Pareto-improvement and explain why this Pareto-improvement is possible. (Hint: Begin by indicating how much one of the farmers would be willing to pay the landlord per period to rent a unit of land and become the residual claimant on what they produce. What is the least amount the landlord would be willing to receive to give up one hectare? Then indicate any Pareto-improving offers.)

Imagine now that the ten cultivators (sharecroppers and wage workers alike) and their comrades from surrounding farms are angry at what they consider to be their exploitation. They meet to plan a collective strategy. Before long they have succeeded in securing a binding agreement of all cultivators in the area to refuse any contract with $s < 0.6$.

6. **Collective action.** If all sharecropping contracts in the area were revised so that $s = 0.6$ (and other parameters were to remain unchanged), indicate the resulting new equilibrium values: e', w', and n'. (The value of n' need not be an integer.) Why does the change in s alter the wage rate? Compare the levels of utility now obtained by the three types of agents (the landlord, the sharecroppers and the wage workers) in the new equilibrium with their utility levels before the collective action.

A Pareto-improving revolution. As an alternative to the strategy of increasing the sharecropper's share, one of the ten cultivators suggests that they simply occupy the landlord's land forcibly and farm it themselves as owners of individual plots and residual claimants on the crops they produce. The revolutionary cultivator claims that they could pay the (possibly soon to be ex) landlord an amount sufficient so that the landlord's utility would be no less after the revolution than in the initial situation (prior to the increment in the sharecropper's share), thereby securing the landlord's support or at least attenuating their opposition.

7. If no compensation were paid to the landlord, what would be the effort levels and resulting utility levels of the farmers?

8. If they agreed that each of the farmers would pay an equal lump sum (per period) to provide the minimal compensation to the landlord necessary to allow them to attain a level of utility not less than in the previous equilibrium, how much would each pay?

9. If transfer of assets with compensation is Pareto-improving, why is a revolution necessary to implement it? Why are (Pareto-inefficient) sharecropping contracts so common (instead of rental contracts)? Why do the farmers not simply purchase the land? Is there something missing from the model?

Answers.

1. For the sharecropper, $u^s = sq - e^2 = se - e^2$, so the problem is

$$\max_e \quad u^s = se - e^2$$

The first order condition is

$$u_e^s = s - 2e = 0$$

which gives the sharecropper's best response function

$$e^*(s) = \frac{1}{2}s \qquad (9.10)$$

For the landlord, considering just their utility based on the work of a single sharecropper, the problem is to maximize the utility from dealing with a *single* sharecropper $v^s = (1 - s)e$ subject to the sharecropper's best response function. That is

$$\max_s \quad v^s = (1 - s)e^*(s) = \frac{1}{2}(1 - s)s$$

Notations. We denote the landlord's utility from dealing with a *single* agent by the lower-case v, and that from dealing with n agents by upper-case $V(n)$. The superscript s or w indicates that the agents are sharecroppers or workers.

The first order condition is

$$v_s^s = \frac{1}{2}(1 - 2s) = 0$$

and therefore $s^* = 1/2$. Then $e^* = 1/4$, $u^{s^*} = 1/16$, $v^{s^*} = 1/8$, and the utilities from dealing with n sharecropper at equilibrium is

$$V^{s^*}(n) = nv^{s^*} = \frac{1}{8}n \tag{9.11}$$

2. Receiving a wage w while exerting effort $1/2$, the workers' utility function is

$$u^w = w - \left(\frac{1}{2}\right)^2 = w - \frac{1}{4}$$

The workers' fallback position is the utility of the sharecroppers in the surrounding area $u^{s^*} = 1/16$. For the landlord to hire workers, they need to perform the monitoring requiring the landlord to exert effort $e = 1/8$ to get $e = 1/2$ from each worker hired for wages, then the landlord's utility of hiring n workers is

$$V^w(n) = \left(\frac{1}{2} - w\right)n - \left(\frac{1}{8}n\right)^2$$

To maximize $V^w(n)$ subject to the worker's participation constraint

$$u^w \geq u^{s^*} \Rightarrow w - \frac{1}{4} \geq \frac{1}{16}$$

which will be satisfied as an equality, the worker's utility is

$$u^{w^*} = u^{s^*} = 1/16 \tag{9.12}$$

and as a result the landlord will offer

$$w^* = \frac{1}{16} + \frac{1}{4} = \frac{5}{16}$$

Thus,

$$V^{w^*}(n) = \left(\frac{1}{2} - w^*\right)n - \left(\frac{1}{8}n\right)^2 = \frac{3n}{16} - \frac{n^2}{64} \tag{9.13}$$

3. The landlord now decides on n, the number of hectares of land that will be cultivated by wage laborers (the remaining $10 - n$ hectares will be cultivated by sharecroppers). The landlord's utility (now summing over all ten of the farmers, whether wage workers or sharecroppers), is

$$V(n) = V^{w^*}(n) + V^{s^*}(10 - n) = \frac{1}{64}[84 - (n - 2)^2]$$

which reaches its maximum at $n^* = 2$. Thus at the equilibrium (e^*, s^*, w^*, n^*), the utility of the landlord is

$$V^* = \frac{21}{16} = 1.3125$$

and that of the workers and sharecroppers is $u^{w^*} = u^{s^*} = 1/16$

From (9.11) and (9.13),

$$V(n) = V^{w^*}(n) + V^{s^*}(10 - n)$$

$$= \frac{3n}{16} - \frac{n^2}{64} + \frac{10 - n}{8}$$

$$= \frac{1}{64}(80 + 4n - n^2)$$

$$= \frac{1}{64}[84 - (n - 2)^2]$$

from (9.12).

4. The result is not Pareto-efficient (as you probably anticipated if you had studied Figure 9.4 in one of the earlier questions in this chapter). Consider a small increase in both s and e in the interaction between the landowner and the sharecroppers. At the new allocation (e', s', w^*, n^*) with $s' = s^* + ds$, $e' = e^* + de$, $ds > 0$, and $de > 0$, we have

$$du^s = \frac{\partial u^s}{\partial s}ds + \frac{\partial u^s}{\partial e}de = \frac{\partial u^s}{\partial s}ds > 0$$

and

$$dv^s = \frac{\partial v^s}{\partial s}ds + \frac{\partial v^s}{\partial e}de = \frac{\partial v^s}{\partial e}de > 0$$

Therefore, $u^{s'} > u^{s^*}$, $v^{s'} > v^{s^*}$, and thus $V' > V^*$. That is, the landowner and the sharecroppers are all better off. Note that the utility of the workers remains the same (receiving the same wage w^*). Then the new allocation (e', s', w^*, n^*) is Pareto-superior to the equilibrium (e^*, s^*, w^*, n^*). Therefore, the result given by (e^*, s^*, w^*, n^*) is not Pareto-efficient.

Note that at e^*,

$$\frac{\partial u^s}{\partial e} = 0, \frac{\partial u^s}{\partial s} = e^* > 0$$

and similarly, at s^*,

$$\frac{\partial v^s}{\partial s} = 0, \frac{\partial v^s}{\partial e} = 1 - s^* > 0$$

Note that from $v^{s'} > v^{s^*}$, we have

$$V^{s'}(n) = nv^{s'} > nv^{s^*} = V^{s^*}(n), \forall n$$

and therefore,

$$V' = V^{w^*}(n^*) + V^{s'}(10 - n^*)$$
$$> V^{w^*}(n^*) + V^{s^*}(10 - n^*) = V^*$$

5. Consider the contract such that the farmer pays a price p per period to acquire the ownership of a hectare of land (this could be a purchase or a rental contract; what is important is that the farmer becomes the residual claimant on the crop they produce). By buying the land, the farmer's utility as a function of effort becomes $u^p = e - e^2$. To maximize utility, they will choose $e = 1/2$ and get $u^{p*} = 1/4$. Therefore, the maximum price the farmers would like to offer to get the ownership of a unit of land in one period is

$$p^* = u^{p*} - u^{s^*} = \frac{1}{4} - \frac{1}{16} = \frac{3}{16}$$

That is, the transaction at price lower than p^* would make the farmer better off.

For the landlord, after selling one unit of land, they would choose n to maximize the utility from the remaining 9 units of land

$$V^{w^*}(n) + V^{s^*}(9 - n) = \frac{1}{64}(72 + 4n - n^2)$$

which again achieves its maximum 19/16 at $n^* = 2$. Therefore, the least amount the landlord would be willing to receive per period to give up a hectare is

$$p^l = V^* - \frac{19}{16} = \frac{1}{8}$$

That is, the transaction at a price higher than p^l would make the landlord better off. Therefore, a transfer of residual claimancy rights to the sharecropper at the price $p \in [p^l, p^*] = [1/8, 3/16]$ would be a Pareto-improving reallocation.

6. Given $s = 0.6$, from the best response function (9.10), we have

$$e' = \frac{1}{2} \cdot 0.6 = 0.3$$

Then the fallback position of the workers becomes

$$u^{w'} = se' - e'^2 = 0.09$$

and the (per worker) utility of the landlord gained by sharecropping is

$$v^{s'} = (1 - s)e' = 0.12$$

For the landlord, they will offer the new wage to the worker

$$w' = \frac{1}{4} + u^{w'} = 0.34$$

due to the change in the worker's fallback position.

To maximize

$$V(n) = \left(\frac{1}{2} - w'\right)n - \frac{n^2}{64} + (10 - n)V^{s'}$$
$$= 1.2 + 0.04n - \frac{1}{64}n^2$$

the landlord will choose $n' = 1.28$, and they will get $V' = 766/625 = 1.2256$ units of utility. The levels of utility gained by the three types of agents in the new equilibrium compared with their utility levels before the collective action are summarized in Table 9.2.

7. If no compensation were paid, the farmers would choose e to maximize $u = e - e^2$. Then $e^{f*} = 1/2$ and $u^{f*} = 1/4$ as a result.

8. Note that, after the revolution, the landlord exerts no effort and thus their utility equals the total compensation they receive, which must be no less than their utility in the previous equilibrium ($V^* = 21/16$). Therefore, each farmer would pay an equal lump sum

$$c = \frac{V*}{10} = \frac{21}{160} = 0.13125$$

Therefore, the utility of the farmer becomes

$$u^c = u^{f*} - c = 0.11875$$

The level of utilities and the change after revolution are presented in Table 9.2.

9. The Pareto-improving transfer of residual claimancy from the landlord to the farmers (either through outright purchase of the land or by a rental contract) is unlikely to occur for two reasons.

   ▸ The farmers are unlikely to have the wealth to purchase the land, and without wealth would be unable to borrow the necessary amounts, for reasons that you will explore in Chapter 11.

Table 9.2: Levels of utility gained by the three types of agents before and after the collective action, and after the farmers become owners. Note that the total in the last column shows the sum of utilities of the landlord and the 10 agents.

	Landlord	Worker	Sharecropper	Total
Before	1.3125	0.0625	0.0625	1.9375
Collective Action				
After	1.2256	0.09	0.09	2.1256
Gains	-0.0869	0.0275	0.0275	0.1881
Revolution				
After	1.3125	0.11875	0.11875	2.5
Gains	0	0.05625	0.05625	0.5625

> ► The rental contract circumvents this problem, but residual claimancy on the full value of the crop produced, while providing effort incentives for the farmer, also exposes them to greater risk, which would deter risk-averse farmers from accepting the rental contract. You will learn more about the relationship between wealth and risk aversion in Chapter 12.

So yes, there are several somethings missing from the model: first is the fact that limited wealth restricts the ability of less well-off people to borrow on favorable terms; and second is risk aversion, which is associated with having limited wealth, and may make ownership unattractive to less well-off people.

This is another case in which measures to reduce inequality (here a redistribution of wealth to the less well-off) could facilitate Coasean bargaining that would result in assets being owned by those who would use them in the most productive ways.

See the last part of Section 13.2 for a similar example where the efficiency-equality trade-off does not hold.

9.3 Constrained choice under contrasting contracts

This problem is both a survey of seven distinct contracts and a chance to exercise and test your understanding about how they work. In this problem there are two types of actors, agents and owners. The term "agent" here means a person who is not an owner, not necessarily an agent in a principal-agent problem.

Each agent has an identical utility function $u(y, e)$, where y is hourly income measured in units of goods (all payments are made in units of goods), e is work effort per hour, and the function is increasing and concave in the first and decreasing and concave in the second argument. Goods (Q) may be produced on an hourly basis according to the production function $Q(E)$, where E is the sum of effort devoted to the production of goods (either by a single worker or by the combined members of a team) and the function is increasing and concave in its argument.

The level of effort is not verifiable. Property rights consist of permission to use the production function (there are no inputs other than effort, but use of the production function requires permission from the "owner"). Where property rights are held by someone other than the agent (say an owner), you may assume that the property owner maximizes profits. Suppose that, for each agent, the alternative to working under the contract in question is to receive zero utility. Consider the following situations:

a. The agent owns the right to use the production function and owns the output resulting from their work.

b. The agent works under a contract, receiving a fraction s of the output while the rest is claimed by the owner who also determines s.

c. The agent pays a fixed sum k per period to the owner for permission to use the production function above, and owns the residual income. The owner determines k.

To answer this question about contingent renewal contracts (and the one below), you may want to first answer the questions in Section 10.2.

d. The owner offers the agent (who is a member of a team of n identical agents) a contingent renewal contract, with wage w.

e. The agent is one of a team of n identical agents who share equally the product resulting from their efforts.

f. The owner employs a team of workers, offering to pay each worker $Q - x$ per period, where x is some positive constant.

g. The owner offers the agent (one of a team of identical workers) a contingent renewal contract, charging the agent a one-time fee equal to B for permission to begin work.

1. For the above 7 types of contract:
   ▶ Describe how the level of effort of each agent will be determined under the above situations. Give the relevant maximization problem or problems and derive the associated first order conditions, adding whatever additional information you need to do this.
   ▶ Describe how the values of $w, s, k, x,$ and B will be determined in the above situations.
   ▶ In each of the above situations, determine if the agent's level of effort and income determined by the relevant first order conditions is or is not Pareto-efficient. Explain why the results differ.

2. Consider a population in which there are no economies of scale and every member is very rich, so rich that each is risk neutral and can finance any investment at a subjective cost equal to the economy-wide risk-free interest rate (the rate of return on a riskless asset). To keep things simple, assume that, though very rich, each member nonetheless places an undiminished value on gaining additional income. In this population, which of the above contracts, if any, would you expect to observe in a competitive equilibrium? Explain your answer.

Answers.

1. Below we use the convention that e_i is the level of effort in contract $i \in \{a, b, c, d, e, f, g\}$.

   a. The problem is to

   $$\max_{e} \quad u(y, e) = u(Q(e), e)$$

   The first order condition for this maximization problem is

   $$u_y(e)Q'(e) + u_e(e) = 0 \qquad (9.14)$$

   and the value of e satisfying this equation is $e^* = e_a$, the level of effort in contract a. The term Pareto efficiency does not apply here as there is just a single actor.

   b. The worker's problem is to

   $$\max_{e} \quad u(sQ(e), e)$$

   The first order condition of the choice of e_b is

   $$su_yQ' + u_e = 0 \Rightarrow e^* = e_b(s) \qquad (9.15)$$

   The owner's problem is

   $$\max_{s} \quad (1 - s)Q(e^*)$$

   $$\text{s.t.} \quad e^* = e_b(s)$$

   Substituting $e_b(s)$ into the objective function, the first order condition is

   $$-Q + (1 - s)Q'e_b' = 0 \Rightarrow s = s^*$$

   The result $(s^*, e_b(s^*))$ is not Pareto-efficient, as shown in Figure 9.7.

   c. The agent's problem is

   $$\max_{e} \quad u(Q(e), e) - k$$

   and the first order condition is

   $$u_yQ' + u_e = 0 \Rightarrow e^* = e_c \qquad (9.16)$$

   which is the same as (9.14) under contract a and thus $e_c = e_a$. The owner's problem is to maximize k subject to the agent's participation constrain, i.e.

   $$u(y, e) - k \geq 0 \Rightarrow k^* = u(Q(e_c), e_c)$$

   The result (e_c, k^*) is Pareto-efficient.

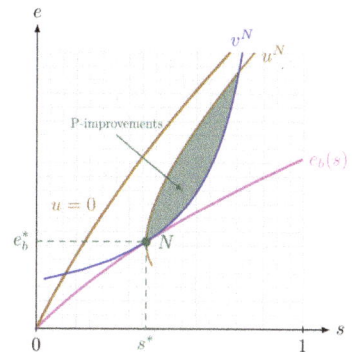

Figure 9.7: The solutions under contract b. The orange curves are the indifference curves of the agent

$$u(sQ(e), e) = \bar{u}$$

the blue curves are the indifference curves of the owner

$$(1 - s)Q(e) = \bar{v}$$

and $e_b(s)$ is agent's best response function. The tangency of the owner's indifference curve and the agent's best response function (s^*, e_b^*) is the solution, which is not Pareto-efficient as any point in the green shaded area is Pareto-superior to it. This figure is constructed using $u = y - e^2/2$ and $Q = \ln(1 + e)$.

d. Suppose that the owner will terminate the contract with probability $t(e) = 1 - e$, and that the discount factor is zero. Then the worker's problem is

$$\max_{e} \quad v = u(w,e) + [1-t(e)]v = \frac{u(w,e)}{t(e)}$$

and the first order condition is

$$v_e = \frac{u_e t - u t_e}{t^2} = 0 \Rightarrow u_e = \frac{u t_e}{t} \Rightarrow e^* = e_d(w) \qquad (9.17)$$

The owner's problem is

$$\max_{w} \quad Q(n e_d(w)) - nw$$

and the first order condition is

$$nQ'e_d' - n = 0 \Rightarrow Q'e_d' = 1 \Rightarrow w^* = w_d$$

The result is not Pareto-efficient as shown in Section 10.2.

e. Agent j's problem is

$$\max_{e_j} \quad u\left(\frac{1}{n}Q\left(\sum_i e_i\right), e_j\right)$$

The first order condition is

$$\frac{1}{n}u_y Q' + u_e = 0 \Rightarrow e^* = e_e \qquad (9.18)$$

The result is not Pareto-efficient since, for $de_k > 0$,

$$du_j = \sum_{k \neq j} \frac{\partial u_j}{\partial e_k} de_k > 0$$

by

$$\frac{\partial u_j}{\partial e_j} = 0 \quad \text{and} \quad \frac{\partial u_j}{\partial e_k} = \frac{1}{n}u_y Q' > 0, \forall k \neq j$$

That is, all agents would be better off if they mutually increase their effort.

f. Agent j's problem is

$$\max_{e_j} \quad u\left(Q\left(\sum_i e_i\right) - x, e_j\right)$$

The first order condition is

$$u_y Q' + u_e = 0 \Rightarrow e^* = e_f \qquad (9.19)$$

The owner's problem is to maximize x subject to the agent's participation constrain, i.e.,

$$u(Q(n e_f) - x, e_f) \geq 0$$

Therefore, the owner would choose x^* such that

$$u(Q(ne_f) - x^*, e_f) = 0$$

The result is Pareto-efficient since it maximizes the joint utility of the worker and the owner.

g. Suppose that the owner will terminate the contract with probability $t(e) = 1 - e$, and that the discount factor is zero. Then the worker's problem is

$$\max_e \quad v = \frac{u(w, e)}{t(e)} - B$$

and the first order condition is

$$\frac{u_e t - u t'}{t^2} = 0 \Rightarrow e^* = e_g(w)$$

which is the same as the condition (9.17) under contract d. The owner's problem is

$$\max_{w, B} \quad Q(ne_g(w)) - nw + nB$$

$$\text{s.t.} \quad u(w, e_g(w)) - B \geq 0$$

The participation constraint in the problem above must be binding at the optimum, since otherwise the owner could increase B and obtain a higher level of utility at no cost. Thus, substituting the constraint into the owner's problem:

$$\max_w \quad Q(ne_g(w)) - nw + nu(w, e_g(w))$$

The first order condition defining the wage w^* that will be chosen by the owner is

$$nQ'e'_g - n + n(u_w + u_e e'_g) = 0 \Rightarrow w^* = w_g \qquad (9.20)$$

The fee that will be chosen by the owner is, in turn

$$B^* = u(w_g, e_g(w_g))$$

The resulting allocation (e_g, w_g, B^*) is Pareto-efficient because, by satisfying equation (9.20), it maximizes the owner's utility subject to the worker's participation constraint, which is binding.

2. Only contract a would be observed in a competitive equilibrium in such a rich population. First, since every member is so rich that each can finance any investment, no one would produce as a worker with contract b or c, under which they give up a portion of the surplus for permission to use the production technology Q. Second, since $Q(ne) < nQ(e)$ (because $Q'' < 0$), no one would produce in a team if they could produce alone; this rules out contracts $d, e, f,$ and g.

Work and Wages | 10

By an ironic twist in the history of economics, the modern theory of the firm and labor markets based on principal-agent models finds its origins in the works of two writers at the opposite end of the political spectrum. The first is Ronald Coase, whom *Forbes Magazine* termed "the greatest of the many great University of Chicago economists." (*Forbes* calls itself "the capitalist tool.") The other is Karl Marx, the 19th-century author of the *Communist Manifesto*.

Marx introduced the idea that the labor market was unlike the market for bread, shirts, and other commodities. The reason is that the contract governing employment is incomplete: it specifies the hours and wages of the worker, but not how hard the worker works. "Only by misuse," Marx [73, p. 275] wrote, could the work performed for the employer "have been called any kind of exchange at all."

Coase, too, stressed the difference between markets and firms: the organization of the firm — a hierarchical system of command — represented the employer's response to the incomplete nature of the contract:

> If a workman moves from department Y to department X, he does not go because of a change in prices but because he is ordered to do so. [...] the distinguishing mark of the firm is the suppression of the price mechanism. [40, pp. 387, 389]

Working through the problems in this chapter will introduce you to the principal-agent relationship between worker and employer that replaces what used to be a "black box" theory of production in which, as Walras put it, we "consider the productive services as being, in a certain sense, exchanged directly for one another." [106, p. 225] To provide a contrast with the models to follow, Section 10.1 illustrates what such a Walrasian model would look like.

In its place, we have an explicit model of conflicts over the gains from cooperation arising from employment in which the following results hold (in contrast to the Walrasian model where the quality and quantity of a worker's effort is subject to contract). In a perfectly competitive Nash equilibrium of the labor discipline model,

- ▶ the labor market does not clear (Section 10.2);
- ▶ the wage rate, the level of effort provided by workers, work hours, and working conditions provided by the employer are both technically inefficient and Pareto-inefficient (Section 10.2);
- ▶ the employer exercises power (in a well defined sense) over the worker (Section 10.2);
- ▶ social norms — including reciprocity and inequality aversion or other fairness concerns — affect wage setting and worker effort (Section 10.4); and
- ▶ the choice of technology by a profit-maximizing employer will be both technically inefficient and Pareto-inefficient (Sections 10.5 and 10.7).

[73]: Marx (1973), *Grundrisse*

[40]: Coase (1937), 'The Nature of the Firm'

[106]: Walras (1954), *Elements of Pure Economics*

Figure 10.1: Ronald Coase (1910–2013). In accepting the Nobel Prize in 1992, he reminisced that as a young man he had wondered: "How did one reconcile the views expressed by economists on the role of the pricing system and the impossibility of successful central economic planning with the existence [...] of these apparently planned societies, firms, operating within our own society." Both legal practice and economic theory have been shaped by his model of the firm as a mini-planned economy and his theory of bargaining. Photo taken at and by University of Chicago Law School (2003). Wikimedia Commons, https://commons.wikimedia.org/wiki/File:Coase_profile_2003_(cropped).jpg

©2025 Samuel Bowles and Weikai Chen, CC BY-NC 4.0

https://doi.org/10.11647/OBP.0466.10

These models — and especially the "no-shirking condition" (Section 10.7) — provide an analytical link between the behavior of individual employers and workers and macroeconomic outcomes such as the presence of involuntary unemployment in the equilibrium of a competitive aggregate labor market. Other applications include policy issues such as the employment effects of monopsony and the minimum wage (Section 13.6).

[40]: Coase (1937), 'The Nature of the Firm'

[14]: Bowles (2004), *Microeconomics*

[29]: Bowles and Halliday (2022), *Microeconomics*

Some background for the problems in this chapter is found in Coase [40], Chapter 9 Bowles [14] and Chapter 12 in Bowles and Halliday [29].

10.1 A Walrasian labor market equilibrium

To understand the importance of incomplete contracts, let's begin with the Walrasian model of complete contracts and (as he put it, above) "consider the productive services as being, in a certain sense, exchanged directly for one another."

Assume that enforceable contracts can be written concerning worker effort and that an employer and employee engage in a one-shot (non-repeated) interaction. There are many other identical workers whom the employer may also hire. Let $e \in [0, 1]$ be effort per hour of work (it could be simply the fraction of the hour in which the worker is "working" as opposed to "not working"). The worker varies e to maximize utility. The employer varies the hourly wage, w, and the hours of workers' time hired, h, to maximize accounting profit

$$\pi = y(he) - wh$$

that is, revenues (y) minus costs, the former of which is increasing and concave in the total amount of effort the workers provide he. (We simplify by assuming labor effort is the only input, and that the employer will hire workers for just one hour, so h is the number of workers.)

1. What kind of contract would the employer offer?

2. Assume the workers' utility function is $u(w, e) = w - e^2$, Suppose the worker's next-best alternative is to be unemployed, that the unemployment benefit is equal to 1/4, and that, if unemployed, $e = 0$ (so that, if unemployed, the worker's utility is 1/4). What is the relevant constraint on the employer's profit maximization problem? What wage would the profit-maximizing employer offer?

3. Show that the resulting wage and effort level is Pareto-efficient and the labor market clears in equilibrium.

Answers.

1. The employer will offer the contract (w, e) which specifies both the wage rate and the effort level.

2. The participation constraint limiting the employer's profit maximization is

$$u(w, e) = w - e^2 \geq \frac{1}{4}$$

The employer will offer the contract (w, e) and decide the employment level h to maximize expected profit subject to the participation constraint. That is

$$\max_{w,e,h} \quad \pi = y(he) - wh$$

$$\text{s.t.} \quad u(w, e) = w - e^2 \geq \frac{1}{4}$$

Note that the participation constraint will be satisfied as an equality, i.e., $w = 1/4 + e^2$. Any allocation for which this were not true could not be the solution to the employer's maximization problem above because the employer could then decrease w for a given e to obtain a higher profit. Then, substituting the participation constraint into the profit function, the problem becomes

$$\max_{e,h} \quad \pi = y(he) - \left(\frac{1}{4} + e^2\right)h$$

The first order conditions are

$$\pi_e = y'h - 2eh = 0$$

$$\pi_h = y'e - \left(\frac{1}{4} + e^2\right) = 0$$

From these equations we have $y' = 2e$ and then

$$2e^2 = \frac{1}{4} + e^2 \Rightarrow e^* = \frac{1}{2}$$

Then $w^* = 1/4 + e^2 = 1/2$. Therefore, the contract that the profit-maximizing employer would offer is $(w^*, e^*) = (0.5, 0.5)$, as shown in Figure 10.2.

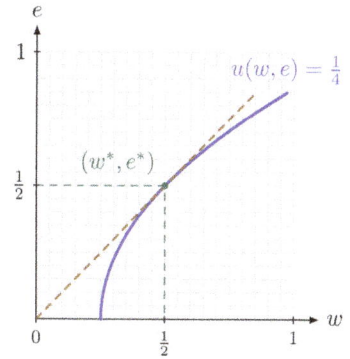

Figure 10.2: The Walrasian labor market equilibrium. The blue curve is the worker's indifference curve when the participation constraint is binding, i.e.

$$u(w, e) = w - e^2 = \frac{1}{4}$$

The orange ray from the origin represents the iso-cost curve whose slope is the inverse of the average cost w/e. The tangent point between the orange ray from the origin and the participation constraint (w^*, e^*), minimizing the average cost, is the Walrasian labor market equilibrium.

3. The employer's utility is maximized subject to a binding participation constraint for the worker. The allocation resulting from this maximum problem must be Pareto-efficient, by definition. We can also prove this statement by contradiction. Suppose that the solution is not Pareto-efficient and is dominated by (w', e'), i.e.,

$$u(w', e') \geq u(w^*, e^*) = \frac{1}{4}$$

and

$$\pi(w', e') \geq \pi(w^*, e^*)$$

and at least one of the inequalities holds strictly. Then (w', e') satisfies the participation constraint, and thus $\pi(w', e') \leq \pi(w^*, e^*)$ as (w^*, e^*) is the solution to the maximization problem. Therefore, we have

$$u(w', e') > u(w^*, e^*) = \frac{1}{4}$$

and

$$\pi(w', e') = \pi(w^*, e^*)$$

Since both u and π are continuous in w and $u_w > 0$, $\pi_w < 0$, there exists a new wage w'' slightly less than w' such that

$$u(w', e') > u(w'', e') > u(w^*, e^*) = 1$$

and

$$\pi(w'', e') > \pi(w^*, e^*)$$

That is, the new outcome (w'', e') satisfies the participation constraint and yields higher profit, which is contradicted with the assumption that (w^*, e^*) is the solution to the employer's profit maximum problem.

Given the wage rate $w^* = 0.5$ and $e^* = 0.5$, there is no involuntary unemployment because, the participation constraint being satisfied as an equality, the worker is indifferent to whether they have the job or not. This means that the labor market clears in equilibrium.

10.2 Employment and labor discipline

The model of employment and the labor market to follow is a variant of what may be termed the *effort regulation* or *labor discipline model* based on *contingent renewal* [11, 14, 90].

[11]: Bowles (1985), 'The Production Process in a Competitive Economy: Walrasian, Neo-Hobbesian, and Marxian Models'
[14]: Bowles (2004), *Microeconomics*
[90]: Shapiro and Stiglitz (1984), 'Equilibrium Unemployment as a Worker Discipline Device'

Work effort (not hours of work) is an argument in the production function of the employer. But unlike hours of work, effort cannot be contracted for because information concerning an employee's effort is known to the employer at best very imperfectly and is not verifiable (not admissible in court). So the employer has to devise a method to secure effort from the worker.

The problem would not arise in the case of independent production (self-employment) because then the worker is the residual claimant on the results of their own efforts, but fixed costs or economies of scale generally make team production a necessity. (To capture these economies of scale, assume that engaging in production at any level requires one unit of capital, perhaps the cost of owning a patent necessary to use a particular production process, and that this requirement makes individual production unprofitable.)

Let $e \in [0, 1]$ be effort per hour of work. Per period output is

$$y = y(he) \quad \text{with } y' > 0 \text{ and } y'' < 0 \tag{10.1}$$

where h is the number of worker "hours" hired (assumed to be a single "hour" per worker, so that h is also the number of identical workers hired). Output is contractible, but the input levels of particular workers cannot be inferred from the output levels because of the team nature of production.

The employer engages the employee in a contingent renewal interaction, in which employment may continue for many periods conditional on the worker's performance. From past experience or experimentation, the principal (the employer) knows the agent's (worker's) best-effort response, $e(w, m; z)$, given each wage rate w and level of monitoring m, with an exogenously determined worker's fallback position z. At the beginning of a period, the employer selects (so as to maximize profits) and announces: a termination probability $t(e, m) \in [0, 1]$ with $t_e < 0$ and $t_m > 0$ over the economically relevant ranges; a wage rate w; and a level of monitoring per hour of labor hired m. Both the wage and the monitoring inputs are measured in the same units as per period output.

Notation alert: Arguments of a function to the right of the semicolon are exogenous.

The worker, following the employer's announcement of their labor discipline strategy, and hence knowing the above, selects e so as to maximize the present value of their lifetime utility. At the end of the period, the worker is paid and experiences the utility incurred as a result of their effort and pay, and their employment is renewed or terminated, the latter occurring with probability $t(e, m)$. If the worker's job is terminated, they obtain a present value of lifetime utility of z and the worker is replaced by an identical worker from the unemployment pool. If the worker retains the job, the interaction is repeated the next period (with the same strategies implemented by the two parties); thus, the interaction is stationary (or time-invariant).

The model as set up described here is used in the other questions in the chapter except for Section 10.7.

The worker's per period utility function is

$$u = u(w, e) \tag{10.2}$$

with $u_w \geq 0$ and $u_e \leq 0$ over the economically relevant ranges. The worker varies e to maximize the present value of expected utility over an infinite horizon, given a rate of time preference i:

$$v = \frac{u(w, e) + [1 - t(e, m)]v + t(e, m)z}{1 + i}$$
$$= \frac{u(w, e) - iz}{i + t(e, m)} + z \tag{10.3}$$

Solving v from equation

$$v = \frac{u + (1 - t)v + tz}{1 + i}$$

gives

$$v = \frac{u + tz}{i + t} = \frac{u - iz}{i + t} + z$$

1. In equation (10.3), identify the employment rent and explain why it is called a rent.

2. Give the first order condition determining the level of effort chosen by the worker, e^*, and explain its economic meaning.

3. Taking z as exogenous, present and explain the economic meaning of the first order conditions that (for a profit-maximizing employer) determine the level of monitoring m^*, the wage rate w^*, and the level of hiring h^*. You may assume the market price of the output produced is 1.

Technical efficiency

An allocation is technically efficient if there is no alternative allocation in which the same output is produced with less of one input and not more of any.

4. Show that the resulting wage (w^*) and effort level (e^*) are not Pareto-efficient.

5. Show that the allocation (e^*, w^*) is not *technically efficient*.

Power

Agent B has power over A if, by imposing or threatening to impose sanctions on A, B is capable of affecting A's actions in ways that advance B's interests, while A lacks this capacity with respect to B.

6. Show that in the Nash equilibrium of this model the labor market does not clear.

7. Using the definition of *power* in the margin note, show that in the equilibrium of this labor discipline model the employer exercises power over the worker.

Answers.

1. The rent is the first term on the right-hand side of the equation and it is the excess of the worker's present value of lifetime utility if employed over their next best alternative, consistent with the conventional definition of a rent.

2. The worker varies e to maximize (10.3), so differentiating that equation with respect to e and setting the result equal to zero we have:

$$u_e = t_e(v - z) \Rightarrow e^* = e(w, m; z) \qquad (10.4)$$

This is the best response function of the worker expressed as an implicit function (all of the terms in the equation are functions of e except z), rather than the closed form expressions that you have seen in the best response functions in previous chapters. That is, the worker will choose the level of effort that equates the marginal cost of effort to the marginal benefit of effort represented by the effect of working harder on not getting fired, times the value of the job (the employment rent).

From $v = [u+(1-t)v+tz]/(1+i)$, the first order condition $v_e = 0$ implies

$$0 = \frac{u_e + (1 - t)v_e - t_e v + t_e z}{1 + i}$$

$$= \frac{u_e - t_e v + t_e z}{1 + i}$$

so

$$u_e - t_e(v - z) = 0$$

3. The employer, who faces a competitive market for the output in which the given price is 1, varies m, w, and h to maximize economic profit:

$$\pi = y(he(w, m; z)) - (w + m)h - \rho \qquad (10.5)$$

where ρ is the exogenously given per period cost of the fixed input including the opportunity cost of capital. The first order conditions for a maximum are,

$$\pi_h = y'e^* - (w^* + m^*) = 0$$
$$\pi_w = y'h^*e_w - h^* = 0$$
$$\pi_m = y'h^*e_m - h^* = 0$$

from which we can see that a profit maximum requires that,

$$e_w = \frac{e^*}{w^* + m^*} = e_m \qquad (10.6)$$

$$y' = \frac{w^* + m^*}{e^*} \qquad (10.7)$$

The former (called the Solow condition) requires that the average level of effort per dollar of expenditure on labor be equal to the marginal impact of variations in both wages and monitoring expenditures, as shown in Figure 10.3.

The other first order condition is analogous to the familiar condition for a profit maximum that the firm hires more labor as long as the marginal revenue product of (an hour of) labor exceeds the (market determined) wage. With effort endogenous, this condition requires that firm hires more labor as long as the marginal revenue

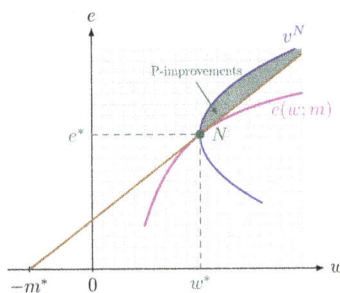

Figure 10.3: The Solow condition in the labor discipline model. The green shaded area is the Pareto-improving lens showing all the pairs of wages (w) and effort (e) that are preferred by both employer and worker over the Nash rquilibrium (w^*, e^*).

product of effort exceeds the cost of a unit of effort (including the cost of monitoring) determined by the Solow condition (not by the market).

4. At (e^*, w^*), by the first order conditions we have

$$v_e = 0, \quad \pi_w = 0$$

but

$$\pi_e = y'h^* = \frac{(w^* + m^*)h^*}{e^*} > 0$$
$$v_w = \frac{u_w}{i + t(e, m)} > 0$$

Thus for $dw, de > 0$,

$$dv = v_w dw > 0$$
$$d\pi = \pi_e de > 0$$

There exists a small increase in effort accompanied by a small increase in the wage that would be Pareto-improving.

5. The Nash equilibrium allocation is *technically efficient* if there is no alternative allocation in which the same output is produced with less of one input and not more of any.

Suppose that the employer who has implemented the Nash equilibrium labor discipline strategy were hypothetically required to raise the wage by Δw and then to lower the level of monitoring by an amount Δm just sufficient to restore effort to the equilibrium level, such that

$$e(w^*, m^*; z) = e(w^* + \Delta w, m^* - \Delta m; z)$$

At the hours of employment as before, output will be unchanged. But one of the inputs, monitoring, has been reduced: the resources represented by Δm are now freed up for productive use. So the competitive equilibrium (e^*, w^*, m^*, h^*) is technically inefficient.

A similar demonstration of the technical inefficiency of the Nash equilibrium allocation appears in Section 10.5.

The key here is that the use of society's resources (supervisory labor, surveillance equipment) to monitor the workers' effort levels is a social cost (these resources could be productive in some other use) while the payment of the wage to the worker is a private cost to the employer but not a social cost: it is a transfer.

6. For the employer to employ the worker, the worker must be expected to provide some effort, and we know from equation (10.4) that in order for the worker to provide effort it must be the case that $v - z > 0$, meaning that the employed worker receives a rent. This could not be the case if the market cleared, meaning that a worker terminated from the current job could (without a spell of unemployment) find an equivalent job (remember, workers are identical).

7. There are three parts of the definition. The employer

In Section 1.4 we observed that post-Walrasian economics necessarily draws on insights from other disciplines. Here is an example: if the exercise of power is an essential aspect of wage determination (even in a perfectly competitive model) then economists will have a lot to learn from sociology and political science.

(1) imposes (or threatens) sanctions on the worker for insufficient effort

(2) that cause the worker to act in a way benefiting the employer, and

(3) the worker is not capable of affecting the employer's actions in an analogous way.

From equation (10.4) we see two things. First, to induce the worker to work the employer pays a rent $v - z$ to the worker, the withdrawal of which by the employer is a credible threat, satisfying point (1) in the definition. Second, in the absence of this threat ($v - z = 0$ or $t_e = 0$) the worker would provide no effort (in equation (10.4) the worker would set $u_e = 0$), so the threat and the worker's best response to it advance the interests of the employer, satisfying part (2) of the definition. Third, in the equilibrium of the model there are identical workers ready to work under the same terms as an incumbent worker (we know this from $v - z > 0$), so in contrast to the credible threat wielded by the employer, termination of the relationship by the worker imposes no costs on the employer, satisfying part (3) of the definition.

10.3 Employment and labor discipline: Applications

Use the same setup as in Section 10.2 when answering the questions below.

A Walrasian equilibrium of the labor discipline model. The Walrasian equilibrium is a special case of the competitive equilibrium in the contingent renewal model. You may wish to consider the case in which there is some level of effort $\underline{e}$ that the worker will provide in the absence of a threat of termination, and if, working at this level of effort, the worker is paid $\underline{w}$, they will work at effort level $\underline{e}(\underline{w})$ and be indifferent between having the job and their fallback option.

1. Exactly what is a Walrasian equilibrium in this model? Under what conditions will the Walrasian equilibrium be a Nash equilibrium of this model (that is, still assuming that e is not verifiable)?

The determination of aggregate employment. For simplicity, we now assume that there is no monitoring expenditure, i.e., $m = 0$ so that a signal of the workers effort is costless to the employer. Suppose that aggregate employment is given by

Notation alert. Be careful here: h is the employment level of a particular firm, and because firms are identical, we use the same notation for the employment level of all firms. But when a single firm selects its employment level, it does not determine the employment levels of all of the firms; each firm regards the other firms' employment levels as exogenous. This is why, in the firm's profit equation (10.5) in Section 10.2 used to model the employer's profit maximization problem, z is represented as exogenous.

$$H = nh$$

where n is the number of identical firms. (You may think of H as the number of workers hired, each one for a single hour, or instead let h represent the firm's level of employment in worker days rather than worker hours, so that H is the number of workers hired on a day if that simplifies your thinking about the problem.) Because aggregate employment is determined by firms' hiring decisions (h), it follows that z is endogenously determined by

$$z = z(H,b) \quad z_H > 0; z_b > 0 \tag{10.8}$$

where b represents the level of unemployment benefits. The signs of the two derivatives shown follow because, respectively, an increase in total employment increases the probability that a worker who is currently unemployed will find a job and the workers' level of utility while unemployed is increasing in the level of the unemployment benefit.

Suppose the relevant markets are perfectly competitive in the sense that there are no barriers to entry or exit. Firms enter if economic profits are positive, while negative profits induce firms to exit. Therefore, the firm's zero economic profit condition is

$$\pi = y(he(w,z)) - wh - \rho = 0 \tag{10.9}$$

where ρ, as above, is the given per period cost of the fixed input including the opportunity cost of capital.

2. Explain the determination of the competitive equilibrium aggregate employment level, H^*.

3. Use your answers to the previous question to explain the effect on the equilibrium level of aggregate employment of

   a) An increase in the unemployment benefit b.

   b) A reduction in the workers' marginal disutility of effort.

   c) Mortality among workers (due to some illness unrelated to their wages, effort, or other aspects of their work) so that the probability of death at the end of each period is δ.

Monitoring technology to the rescue! Assume that the employer discovers a monitoring technology which allows them to costlessly monitor the workers (the information acquired is verifiable).

4. What optimization problem will the employer solve (to maximize profits)?

5. Give the relevant first order conditions.

6. If the monitoring device is owned by others, how much would the employer pay to rent it for one period?

7. Suppose all firms permanently adopt this costless monitoring technology.

   a) Will there be involuntary employment in equilibrium?

   b) Will employers still exercise power over their employees?

   Explain your answers to both questions.

Answers.

1. A Walrasian equilibrium would be characterized by the absence of an employment rent (meaning that the labor market clears), so both the Solow condition (equation (10.6)) and the equality $v = z$ would have to obtain. How could this occur? If we rewrite the Solow condition as an inequality stating that $e_w \leq e/(w + m)$, then if we had

$$e_w \leq \frac{\underline{e}}{\underline{w} + m^*}$$

this would mean that, when paid the wage $\underline{w}$, the worker would work at effort level $\underline{e}$ and gain a present value of $v = z$. The Solow condition expressed as a strong inequality ($<$ above) means that raising the wage above $\underline{w}$ would raise the cost of a unit of effort to the employer (it would lower $e/(w + m)$).

There are two conditions under which this Walrasian equilibrium could occur:

a) *The Stakhanovite condition* (see the margin picture): the level of effort provided by the worker in the absence of the threat of losing the employment rent ($\underline{e}$) is sufficiently large as shown in Figure 10.5; and

b) *The counter-cultural condition*: the worker provides some level of effort even in the absence of the threat of termination, and because the worker's marginal utility of consuming material goods is virtually zero (the worker is a counter-cultural hippie), the effect of wage increases on the effort provided (e_w) is sufficiently limited (the best response function is sufficiently "flat") as shown in Figure 10.6.

So the labor discipline model would return a Walrasian equilibrium if employees love to work, and/or were sufficiently counter-cultural (or wealthy) that they did not care about increasing their incomes.

2. The aggregate level of employment is determined by the zero-profit condition and the fact that the rate of profit is a monotonically decreasing function of the employment rate. Here is the process. With n firms producing, each employ h units of labor as defined by the first order conditions (10.7) (i.e., $y'(he^*) = w^*/e^*$). The aggregate employment level is $H = nh$. Now suppose that the number of firms is such that $\pi > 0$, inducing the entry of additional firms. The resulting additional employment raises H, which raises z, which in turn raises the unit cost of effort and decreases the rate of profit. Firm entry continues until the zero profit condition (10.9) is satisfied, thus determining the equilibrium aggregate employment level H.

3. a) An increase in the unemployment benefit b raises the fallback position as $z_b > 0$, which in turn decreases the effort $e(w, z)$ for any w. Therefore, the unit cost of effort rises and the profit rate falls for a given level of employment, which would induce firms to exit and reduce the aggregate level of employment.

Figure 10.4: Aleksey Stakhanov (1906–1977) was a coal miner in the Soviet Union who was legendary for taking pleasure in the enormous amount of coal he could mine in a single shift. The term Stakhanovite now refers to an exceptionally hardworking person. Photo by Eleazar Langman (unknown date). Wikimedia Commons, public domain, https://commons.wikimedia.org/wiki/File:Stakhanov.JPG

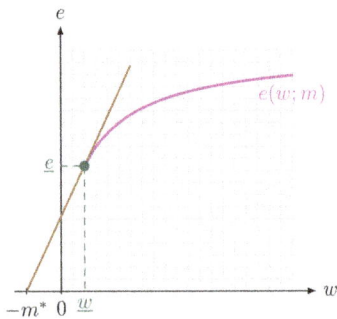

Figure 10.5: The Stakhanovite condition. The level of effort provided by the worker in the absence of the threat of losing the employment rent ($\underline{e}$) is sufficiently large, so at the solution (w^*, e^*) the Solow condition is satisfied as an inequality

$$e_w < \frac{e}{m + w}$$

b) A reduction in the worker's marginal disutility of effort would raise the effort $e(w, z)$ for any given pair (w, z). Therefore, the unit cost of effort decreases and the profit rate rises for a given level of employment, which would induce firms to enter and raise the aggregate level of employment.

c) With the probability of death at the end of each period $\delta > 0$, the worker's expected utility becomes

$$v = \frac{u + (1 - \delta)[(1 - t)v + tz]}{1 + i}$$
$$= \frac{u - (i + \delta)z}{i + \delta + (1 - \delta)t} + z$$

and then the first order condition becomes

$$u_e = (1 - \delta)t_e(v - z) \Rightarrow e^{\delta}(w, z)$$

Therefore, for any given pair (w, z) the effort level $e^{\delta}(w, z) < e(w, z)$. Then the unit cost of effort rises and profit rate falls for a given level of employment, which would induce firms to exit and reduce the aggregate level of employment.

4. With the monitoring technology, the employer's optimization problem becomes

$$\max_{h, e, w} \quad \pi = y(he) - wh \tag{10.10}$$
$$\text{s.t.} \quad u(w, e) = z$$

5. Let the Lagrangian function be:

$$\mathcal{L} = y(he) - wh + \lambda[u(w, e) - z]$$

The first order conditions are

$$\mathcal{L}_h = y'e - w = 0 \tag{10.11}$$
$$\mathcal{L}_e = y'h + \lambda u_e = 0 \tag{10.12}$$
$$\mathcal{L}_w = -h + \lambda u_w = 0 \tag{10.13}$$
$$\mathcal{L}_\lambda = u - z = 0 \tag{10.14}$$

which implies that $u(w, e) = z$ and

$$\frac{e}{w} = -\frac{u_w}{u_e}$$

6. The most that the employer would pay to rent the monitoring device is the extra profit they would gain by employing the worker with a complete contract compared to an incomplete one, that is, the difference between the profit from maximizing (10.5) in Section 10.2 and the maximum profit from the problem (10.10).

7. If all firms use this costless monitoring technology, the situation is the same as Walrasian model of complete contracts in Section 10.1.

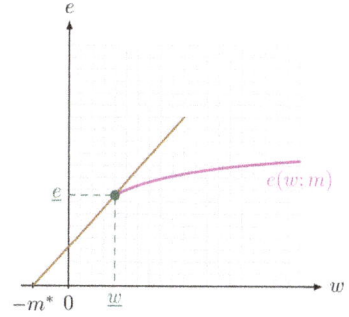

Figure 10.6: The counter-cultural (or hippie) condition The worker provides some level of effort even in the absence of the threat of termination, and because the worker's marginal utility of consuming material goods is virtually zero, the effect of wage increases on the effort provided (e_w) is sufficiently limited (the best response function is sufficiently "flat"). Therefore, at the solution (w^*, e^*) the Solow condition satisfies as an inequality

$$e_w < \frac{e}{m + w}$$

Equation (10.13) implies that $h = \lambda u_w$. Substituting it into (10.12), we have

$$y'\lambda u_w + \lambda u_e = 0 \Rightarrow \frac{1}{y'} = -\frac{u_w}{u_e}$$

From equation (10.11) we have $1/y' = e/w$. Therefore,

$$\frac{e}{w} = -\frac{u_w}{u_e}$$

a) There is no involuntary unemployment because, the participation constraint being satisfied as an equality, the worker is indifferent to whether they have the job or not. This means that the labor market clears in equilibrium.

b) As the worker is indifferent to whether they have the job or not, the employer cannot impose or threaten sanctions on workers. Therefore, the employers will not exercise power over their employees.

10.4 Fair wages: Inequality-averse norms and best responses

George Akerlof and Janet Yellen pioneered the literature on social preferences — reciprocity and fairness norms — and wage setting [2, 3].

[2]: Akerlof (1982), 'Labor Contracts as Partial Gift Exchange'
[3]: Akerlof and Yellen (1990), 'The Fair Wage-Effort Hypothesis and Unemployment'

Another example of the point made in Section 1.4 about interdisciplinary pluralism: Social norms such as a commitment to reciprocity or fairness have been studied by sociologists, anthropologists, and others; economists' models of wage determination can incorporate insights from these fields. Examples are found in Bowles, Gintis, and Osborne [28].

[28]: Bowles, Gintis, and Osborne (2001), 'The Determinants of Earnings'

Consider an individual for whom their wage level is a "good" and work is a "bad" whose disutility depends not only on the level of effort but also (inversely) on how fairly it is rewarded. Suppose the employee's utility function is

$$u = w - \frac{w^f}{w} \frac{a}{1-e} \tag{10.15}$$

where a is a positive constant and w^f is an exogenous wage norm called the "fair wage". The disutility of effort represented by the second term is rising in effort (at an increasing rate). Note that it is also declining in the wage relative to the fair wage, indicating that hard work that is fairly rewarded may be less onerous than less effort at a wage considered to be unfair. The underlying motivation may reflect a variant of the reciprocal preference function introduced in Chapter 3: the employee may take the wage offer as an indication of the employer's type and experience less disutility of effort in working hard for a generous or fair boss.

Suppose the information available to the employer about the worker's level of effort is not verifiable so as before e is non contractible, monitoring is absent and the termination function is simply $t = 1 - e$. The above utility function means that, for any finite wage, the disutility of effort becomes infinite as e approaches 1. Therefore, the employee will not choose $e = 1$, and as a result we know that $t > 0$. Assume that the employee's fallback position is normalized to zero and the rate of time preference is also zero (this simplification gives a closed-form expression for the best response function but is obviously unrealistic).

1. If the employee maximizes the above utility function, what is their best response function?

2. What is the Solow condition (the first order condition for the employer's choice of the wage)?

3. If $a = 1$ and $w^f = 24$, what wage will the employer offer (relative to the fair wage)?

4. If $a = 1$, is there a value of the fair wage such that the profit-maximizing wage will be the fair wage?

5. Under what conditions will the employer offer a wage higher than the fair wage?

Answers.

1. Given the worker's per period utility function (10.15), $t = 1 - e$, and $i = z = 0$ we have

$$v = \frac{u(w,e) - iz}{i + t(e,m)} + z = \frac{u(w,e)}{t(e)} = \frac{w}{1-e} - \frac{w^f}{w} \frac{a}{(1-e)^2}$$

and the first order condition (10.4) $u_e = t_e v$ becomes

$$-\frac{w^f}{w} \frac{a}{(1-e)^2} = -\left[\frac{w}{1-e} - \frac{w^f}{w} \frac{a}{(1-e)^2}\right]$$

and thus

$$e = 1 - \frac{2aw^f}{w^2} \tag{10.16}$$

which is the worker's best response function.

2. Given $m = 0$, the Solow condition $e_w = e/w$ becomes

$$\frac{e}{w} = \frac{1}{w}\left(1 - \frac{2aw^f}{w^2}\right) = \frac{4aw^f}{w^3} = e_w$$

which implies that $w^* = \sqrt{6aw^f}$.

3. If $a = 1$ and $w^f = 24$, then

$$w^* = \sqrt{6 \cdot 24} = \sqrt{144} = 12$$

which is half the fair wage w^f.

4. If $a = 1$ and $w^f = w^*$, we must have

$$w^f = \sqrt{6w^f} \Rightarrow w^f = 6$$

Therefore, when the fair wage is $w^f = 6$, it will be equal to the profit-maximizing wage.

5. From $w^* > w^f$ we have

$$\sqrt{6aw^f} > w^f \Rightarrow 6aw^f > (w^f)^2 \Rightarrow w^f < 6a$$

Therefore, if the fair wage is less than $6a$, it is profitable for the employer to exceed the fair wage norm.

10.5 Endogenous technology and workplace amenities with incomplete contracts

The two parts of this question use the same model as in Section 10.2.

Endogenous technology. Now consider a more general production function with a non-labor input, $y(k, E)$ where k is the per period input of the non-labor input, $E = he$ is the total input of effort, and as before the function is increasing and concave in its arguments. Suppose that variations in k are associated with differing spatial or other arrangements of the production process affecting the ease of monitoring the work process. For example, highly capital-intensive processes such as the assembly lines that Henry Ford pioneered may be "machine-paced," greatly simplifying the identification of low-effort workers. (This is what Charlie Chaplin made clear in his 1936 film, *Modern Times*.)

To reflect this fact, the termination function is now $t = t(e, m, k)$. An example of which might be $t = \eta(m, k)(1 - e)$ where $\eta(m, k)$ is the probability that a non-working employee will be detected. As before, the probability of low effort being detected $\eta(\cdot)$ is increasing in m. If η is increasing in k (as the assembly line example suggests) then $t_{ek} < 0$; because the more k-intensive technology facilitates the monitoring process it augments the (negative) effect of effort on the probability of termination.

In this case we might say that the k-intensive production process is more "transparent" from the standpoint of the monitor and that a less k-intensive process is more "opaque". Opposite cases also exist; the important point is not the sign of t_{ek} but the fact that the choice of technology will generally affect the ease of monitoring one way or the other, namely $t_{ek} \neq 0$. (A related problem, on how conflicts over the distribution of the gains from cooperation may result in the inefficient choice of technology, is in Section 10.7.)

In the California food processing industry of the late 19th century, the highly skilled tinsmiths called "cappers" who put the caps on the tins of fruit or vegetables had extraordinary bargaining power because they were difficult to replace, and by striking just after harvest they could inflict substantial costs on their employers. The canning company owners invested in a new mechanical device — called Cox's capper, after its inventor — designed to replace the human cappers. Writing a quarter of a century after its invention, Cox explained why the cannery owners avidly took up the device even though it did not really work. "It was this helplessness of the [owner] that made him a willing advocate of every mechanical means and made possible the working out, through frequent failures and heavy losses the perfected means now in use." The owners did not even use the machines initially, they kept them on hand to limit the human cappers' bargaining power. [12, 36]

[12]: Bowles (1988), *Capitalist Technology*
[36]: Brown and Philips (1986), 'The Historical Origin of Job Ladders in the US Canning Industry and Their Effects on the Gender Division of Labour'

1. Write down the new best-response function of the employee.

2. Letting ρ be the per period rental price of a unit of k, what is the employer's first order condition for the selection of k?

3. Show that e_k takes the sign of $-t_{ek}$. (Hint: try using the second order condition for the employee's utility maximization problem.)

4. Show that the employer will select a more k-intensive technology if increasing k makes the production process more "transparent" (increases the effectiveness of monitoring).

5. Show that, unless $t_k = 0$, the employer's profit-maximizing choice, k^*, is both Pareto-inefficient and technically inefficient.

Under-provision of workplace amenities. The analysis of endogenous selection of a technology by the employer is a template for other, seemingly unrelated questions. Consider, for example, the question of workplace amenities, such as a respectful and safe work environment. The employer will of course take into account the employee's preferences about workplace amenities; if there is an inexpensive way to make the job more valuable to the worker, this will allow a reduction in wages without reducing the incentive to provide effort.

To study this case, suppose the employee's utility function is expanded to include α, a measure of work amenities provided (per hour of work),

$$u = u(w, \alpha, e)$$

with $u_\alpha > 0$ over the relevant range, and that amenities cost $p\alpha$ for the employer to provide.

6. Write down the new best response function of the employee.

7. What is the first order condition for the employer's choice of profit-maximizing levels of workplace amenities, α^*?

8. Show that the level of amenities provided is Pareto-inefficient, namely, that there exists an improvement in workplace amenities coupled with an increase in worker effort that would benefit both parties to the interaction.

Answers.

1. The best response function of the employee, expressed as an implicit function, is still $u_e = t_e(v - z)$, but since t_e is a function of k, the best response function of the employee now depends on k.

2. The employer's economic profit function is $\pi = y(E, k) - wh - mh - \rho k$. Hence, the employer's first order condition for the selection of k is

$$\pi_k = y_k + y_E h e_k - \rho = 0$$

The employer will choose the level of the k-input such as to equate the rental price of k to the marginal productivity of k, plus the marginal effect of k on the worker's level of effort, times the marginal productivity of effort.

3. Using the new termination function and differentiating the employee's best response function $u_e = t_e(v - z)$ totally with respect to k and e, we have

$$e_k = \frac{(v - z)t_{ek}}{u_{ee} - (v - z)t_{ee}}$$

Using the second order condition for the employee's maximization problem

$$u_{ee} - (v - z)t_{ee} < 0$$

we see that e_k takes the sign of $-t_{ek}$.

From $v = [u+(1-t)v+tz]/(1+i)$ and $v_e = 0$, the second order condition $v_{ee} < 0$ implies

$$0 > \frac{u_{ee} - t_{ee}v - t_e v_e + t_{ee}z}{1 + i}$$

$$= \frac{u_{ee} - (v - z)t_{ee}}{1 + i}$$

so

$$u_{ee} - (v - z)t_{ee} < 0$$

4. If increasing k makes the production process more transparent, then $t_{ek} < 0$, which implies, by the previous part, $e_k > 0$. Hence, by the employer's first order condition, the employer would select a more k-intensive technology.

5. At equilibrium, by the first order conditions, we have

$$v_e = 0, \pi_k = 0$$

but

$$\pi_e = y'h > 0$$

From $v = [u + (1 - t)v + tz]/(1 + i)$, we have

$$v_k = \frac{-t_k v + (1 - t)v_k + t_k z}{1 + i}$$

That is

$$(1 + i)v_k = (1 - t)v_k - (v - z)t_k$$

so

$$v_k = -\frac{(v - z)t_k}{i + t}$$

and

$$v_k = -\frac{(v - z)t_k}{i + t} \neq 0$$

unless $t_k = 0$. Then there exist small changes de and dk that would be Pareto-improving. Therefore, the profit-maximizing level of k is Pareto-inefficient.

It is technically inefficient if there is an alternative allocation in which the same output is produced with less of one input and not more of any. At the same hours h^* of employment as before, output is unchanged when k is reduced and wage w is increased just sufficiently to restore effort to the equilibrium level.

$$e(w^*, m^*, k^*; z) = e(w^* + \Delta w, m^*, k^* - \Delta k; z)$$

In this new situation, the same effort is being provided (and so output is unchanged) with less of one input (k) and not more of any, demonstrating that the profit-maximizing choice of the level of k is technically inefficient.

A similar demonstration of the technical inefficiency of the Nash equilibrium allocation appears in Section 10.2

6. The employee's best response function is $e(w, m, \alpha, z)$, expressed by the implicit function

$$u_e(w, \alpha, e) = t_e(v - z)$$

7. Abstracting from inputs other than labor effort, the employer's profit function is

$$\pi = y(he) - p\alpha h - wh - mh$$

Thus, the first order condition for the employer's choice of a^* is

$$\pi_\alpha = y'he_\alpha - hp = 0$$

8. Workplace amenities are valued by the worker and costly for the employer to provide. The same reasoning of why profit-maximizing employer's wage offer is Pareto-inefficient (demonstrated in Section 10.2) applies here as well, because from the first order conditions of the employer and the worker at the Nash equilibrium (e^*, w^*, a^*, m^*), we have

$$\pi_\alpha = 0 \text{ and } v_\alpha > 0$$
$$v_e = 0 \text{ and } \pi_e > 0$$

Hence, a small improvement in workplace amenities along with a small increase in effort would be Pareto-improving.

10.6 Buy this job: Can rent-seeking employers clear the labor market?

The labor discipline principal-agent model based on the incomplete employment contract appears to show that involuntary unemployment must exist in the equilibrium of a competitive labor market with profit-maximizing employers and flexible wages and prices. Many have interpreted the model as having provided a piece of analysis missing from the original Keynesian theory of employment.

But Lorne Carmichael pointed out that the model excludes the possibility that the employer might require a non-refundable payment, a job fee, as a condition of employment. (This is sometimes called a bond, but the term is misleading as bonds are often refundable upon the performance of a contract.) If firms could sell jobs, Carmichael pointed out, the profit-maximizing price they would set would be such that an unemployed worker would be indifferent between taking the job and remaining unemployed, meaning that any unemployment would be voluntary [39].

[39]: Carmichael (1985), 'Can Unemployment Be Involuntary?'

To explore this idea, use the same model set up as Section 10.2 and the following notation: Let a firm's per period output be $y = y(he)$, where h is the number of hours of labor hired and e is the amount of effort performed by a worker per hour. Assume the price of output is given (and is 1), let w be the wage rate, $t(e)$ is the probability that a worker will be terminated in any given period, z is the fallback position for the worker, $u(w, e)$ is the per period utility of the worker, i is the worker's rate of time preference (and also the rate of interest). Let w^* be the wage rate that maximizes the employer's profit (prior to their selling jobs), and $e^*(w^*)$ the effort level that maximizes the worker's present value of expected utility, given the wage w^*.

1. Assume that the firm is (somehow) constrained to terminate workers for no reason other than insufficient effort. What is the maximum fee b^* that the firm could charge a new employee as a condition of employment if it pays w^*?

2. If such job fees were feasible, what maximization problem would the firm solve in setting the fee, wages, and hiring (b^+, w^+ and h^+)? Give the first order conditions.

3. What are the effects of the opportunity to charge a fee on equilibrium effort and wages? Compare w^+ with w^* and e^+ with e^*.

4. In this new situation, does the labor market clear? Explain your answer.

5. In this new situation, does the employer exercise power over the worker? Explain your answer.

6. Why are such fees uncommon in real economies? (Answer by saying exactly what is missing from the model that is present in the real world which explains why fees are not generally charged.)

Answers.

Note that

$$v = \frac{u - iz}{t} + z$$

thus $v = z$ implies $(u - iz)/t = 0$.

1. If b^* is the maximum fee that the firm could charge, it must satisfy the worker's participation constraint, i.e.,

$$v(e^*, w^* - ib^*) = z \Rightarrow u(e^*, w^* - ib^*) = iz$$

where $w^* - ib^*$ is the net wage, taking account of the opportunity cost to the employee of foregoing returns ib^* on the employee's wealth.

2. The problem for the firm is

$$\max_{b,h,w} \quad \pi = y(he(w)) - wh + ibh$$

$$\text{s.t.} \quad v(e, w - ib) \geq z$$

The associated Lagrangian optimization problem is given by

$$\mathcal{L} = y(he(w)) - hw + ibh + \lambda[v(e(w), w - ib) - z]$$

with the first order conditions:

$$\mathcal{L}_w = y'he' - h + \lambda(v_e e' + v_w) = 0 \tag{10.17a}$$
$$\mathcal{L}_h = y'e - w + ib = 0 \tag{10.17b}$$
$$\mathcal{L}_b = ih - i\lambda v_w = 0 \tag{10.17c}$$
$$\mathcal{L}_\lambda = v - z = 0 \tag{10.17d}$$

Then by (10.17b),

$$y' = \frac{w - ib}{e} \tag{10.18}$$

which equates the marginal product of effort y' with the cost of an hour of labor per unit of effort done per hour, or the cost of a unit of effort $(w - ib)$. From the Lagrangian expression, λ is readily interpreted as the shadow price of the participation constraint, and from (10.17c), we have

$$\lambda = \frac{h}{v_w} \tag{10.19}$$

Substituting $\lambda = h/v_w$ into (10.17a), we have

$$0 = y'he' - h + \frac{hv_e e'}{v_w} + h$$

$$= he'\left(y' + \frac{v_e}{v_w}\right)$$

and thus $y' = -v_e/v_w$.

which gives the effect on profits of a change in the worker's fallback position, namely, the increase in wages necessary to satisfy the worker's participation constraint $(1/v_w)$ times the level of employment h. Substituting λ into (10.17a) gives

$$y' = -\frac{v_e}{v_w}$$

Combining it with (10.18), we have

$$\frac{w - ib}{e} = -\frac{v_e}{v_w} \tag{10.20}$$

which requires that the cost of a unit of effort to the firm (the left side of 10.20) be equal to the (negative of the) marginal rate of substitution between wages and effort in the worker's iso-present-value locus (the right side), as shown in Figure 10.7.

3. The opportunity to charge a fee increases the equilibrium wage and level of effort. This can be seen from Figure 10.7, in which $e^+ > e^*$ (since the participation constraint is "higher" than the best response function) and thus $w^+ > w^*$ as $e(w)$ is increasing.

4. Yes, as the participation constraint binds, the worker is indifferent to taking the job or not. The labor market thus clears; there are no workers "involuntarily unemployed".

5. Paradoxically, in light of the answer to the previous question, yes. While ex ante (before taking the job) rents are zero, ex post rents are actually larger than in the no fee case (for a given z, the equilibrium wage is higher, as it is set not only to induce effort but also to enhance the value of the fee that may be extracted from the prospective worker). Thus the worker receives a rent and hence prefers to be employed rather than terminated. Therefore, the employer does exercise power over the workers.

6. Two likely explanations are a) that nothing would prevent the principal from opportunistically terminating the employee and collecting another fee from a replacement worker (so our assumption that employers could be prevented from opportunistically firing workers is unrealistic) and b) extracting a fee would likely offend the employee's sense of fairness or reciprocity, resulting in a heightened disutility of effort on the job, and a shift downwards of the employee's best response function.

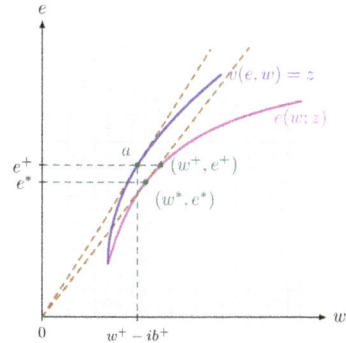

Figure 10.7: Job fees clear the labor market and implement a Pareto-efficient outcome. The employer identifies the blue iso-v locus for which $v = z$ (because they know that the participation constraint will be binding). Along this locus, there is some point a that maximizes the slope of a ray from the origin, thus satisfying

$$\frac{e}{w - ib} = -\frac{v_w}{v_e}$$

To implement this outcome, the employer offers the wage of w^+ (to which the employee responds with e^+) with a fee of b^+. Note that $e^+ > e^*$ and thus $w^+ > w^*$ as the best response curve is upward sloping.

10.7 The no-shirking condition and choice of technique: Efficiency vs. control

Here is a much-simplified one-shot version of the labor discipline model, which, as we will show in Chapter 13, is handy for macroeconomic modeling when applied to the whole economy.

As shown in Figure 10.8, the employer, who as before is the principal and first mover, sets a "no-shirking" level of effort $\underline{e}$, and announces that they will terminate the worker without pay if detected providing less. The employer then figures out what wage is necessary to motivate the worker to work at the no-shirking level and a system of monitoring that results in a probability t that the worker will be terminated if they do not provide $\underline{e}$.

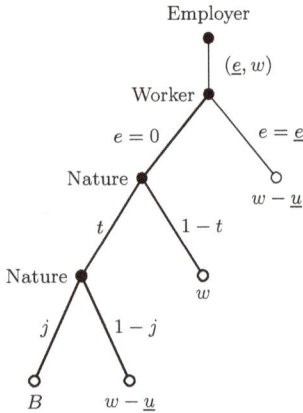

Figure 10.8: The sequence of moves in a one-shot game determining the payoffs to shirking. In response to the employer's statement of the no-shirking level of effort $\underline{e}$, the termination probability t, and the wage w, the worker decides whether to exert $e = 0$ or $e = \underline{e}$. If they exert effort $e = \underline{e}$, they obtain the payoff for working and incurring disutility of effort, $w - \underline{u}$. If they exert no effort, $e = 0$, then nature moves, meaning that there is a probability t they will be terminated and a probability $1 - t$ they will not. If not terminated, they get the wage w (and incur no disutility of effort). If terminated, they will remain jobless (be unemployed) with probability j and receive unemployment benefits, B, or they will be re-employed with probability $1 - j$ and receive the same value of the job that they would have experienced had they not been terminated, $w - \underline{u}$.

The inefficient choice of technology by a profit-maximizing employer is also the subject of Section 10.5.

If the worker provides $\underline{e}$, then with certainty they will not be terminated and will receive the wage w and experience the disutility $\underline{u}$. If the worker provides less than $\underline{e}$, then one of two things may occur: with probability t, the worker is detected and terminated, or with probability $(1 - t)$ they escape detection and are paid w. The worker decides to provide $\underline{e}$ or to not work at all (that is, to provide $e = 0$).

If terminated, one of two things may occur: with probability j they do not find another job and receive the unemployment benefit B; or with probability $1 - j$ they find another job with probability (the job is identical to the job from which the worker was terminated).

1. Write an expression for the least wage consistent with the worker providing effort $\underline{e}$ that is, not shirking. This is termed the no-shirking wage.

2. Use this expression to write an expression for the level of the employment rent that a worker will receive, as a function of j.

Suppose that the value of output is

$$y = fe$$

where $f > 0$ represents the level of labor productivity, and that the probability of detection t differs under different techniques. Denote a technique by (f, t). So techniques differ both in how productive they are and how "transparent" or "opaque" they are (making monitoring, respectively, more or less effective).

3. Assuming that there are no costs other than wages paid at the beginning of the period and that the output is sold at the end of the period, write an expression for the profit rate r with technique (f, t).

4. Suppose that, among different technique, the employer will choose the one with highest profit rate. Is the profitable technique more efficient? Discuss the trade-off between efficiency and control based on your answers above.

Answers.

1. The no-shirking wage should ensure that the expected payoff of providing $\underline{e}$ is not less than that of providing $e = 0$, i.e.

$$w - \underline{u} \geq (1 - t)w + t(1 - j)(w - \underline{u}) + tjB$$

which we assume is satisfied as an equality. This implies

$$w = B + \underline{u} + \frac{1 - t}{t}\frac{\underline{u}}{j} \qquad (10.21)$$

2. The employment rent is the net benefits of the job (wage payment minus disutility of providing effort) in excess of their next best alternative, i.e.

$$\text{Rent} = (w - \underline{u}) - B = \frac{1 - t}{t} \frac{\underline{u}}{j}$$

which is decreasing in j and t.

3. The profit rate is $r = (f\underline{e} - w)/w = (f\underline{e})/w - 1$ under technique (f, t). Given the no-shirking wage (10.21), we have

$$r = \frac{f\underline{e}}{B + \underline{u} + \frac{1-t}{t}\frac{\underline{u}}{j}} - 1$$

4. The iso-r curve in the space of (f, t) with constant profit rate $\bar{r}$ is given by

$$r = \frac{f\underline{e}}{B + \underline{u} + \frac{1-t}{t}\frac{\underline{u}}{j}} - 1 = \bar{r}$$

which could be rewritten as

$$f(t; \bar{r}) = \frac{(1 + \bar{r})}{\underline{e}}w = \frac{(1 + \bar{r})}{\underline{e}}\left(B + \underline{u} + \frac{1-t}{t}\frac{\underline{u}}{j}\right)$$

Since $f(t, \bar{r})$ is decreasing in t, the iso-profit-rate curve is downward-sloping as shown in Figure 10.9. Then technique (f', t') is more profitable than (f^*, t^*) even though $f' < f^*$. That is, the less productive technology is more profitable because it is more transparent, making monitoring more effective.

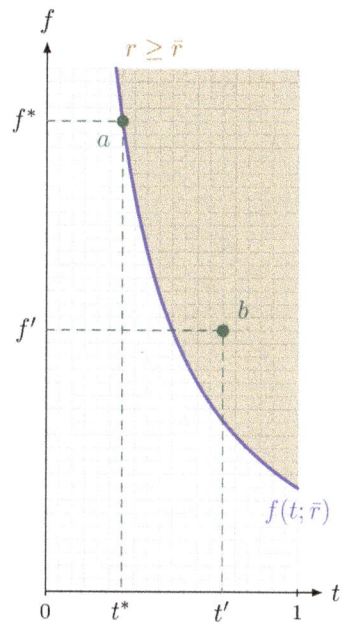

Figure 10.9: Choice of technique. The blue curve represents the iso-r curve $f(t; \bar{r})$ at which the profit rate is $\bar{r}$. The shaded region represents the profitable techniques such that

$$r(f, t) \geq \bar{r}$$

Note that technique b is more profitable than technique a, but it is less efficient as $f' < f^*$.

Credit Markets and Wealth Constraints | 11

Working through the problems in this chapter, you will see that the principal-agent model of lending and borrowing shares with the models in the previous two chapters a conflict over the gains from cooperation stemming from some aspect of an exchange that a contract cannot guarantee. As in the previous principal agent models, in the credit market, too, this results in

- Pareto-efficient Nash equilibria, in which
- the agent receives a rent and
- the principal exercises power over the agent.

But there are also important differences.

Most important is that the credit contract specifies an amount to be repaid (and information about repayment is verifiable), but the contractually specified repayment may not be enforceable. This is because enforcing repayment by a borrower who has limited (or no) wealth is difficult, especially given limited liability laws that effectively cancel the debts of a bankrupt person or business. Another difference is that the conflict of interest between lender and borrower may be mitigated by the lender investing some of their own equity in a project (or putting up collateral).

In this respect, the credit market is more like the market for top managers, whose compensation may include a share of the value of the assets of the firm, more closely aligning the objectives of the manager with those of the owner. Another analogue of equity and collateral in credit markets is profit sharing by employees, which is uncommon except for managerial positions.

Because the ability to borrow funds is often a precondition for a person becoming an employer, the credit and labor markets are linked. Figure 11.2 (on the next page) depicts the key relationships and provides an overview of the role credit markets play in assigning people to the asymmetric positions of principals or agents (or those entirely excluded from these transactions).

Wealthy individuals (for reasons you will explore with the problems that follow) will be able to borrow funds on more favorable terms than the less wealthy and this, along with their wealth, gives them opportunities to become employers, and also principals in other relationships with agents. Working the problems in this chapter, you will see that in the equilibrium of a competitive credit market, compared to those with limited wealth, those with substantial wealth

- pay lower interest rates;
- are able to finance larger projects; and
- finance projects of lower quality.

A result is that wealthy households are advantaged in accumulating more wealth, a positive feedback process that sustains elevated levels of wealth inequality.

Figure 11.1: Knut Wicksell (1851–1926) was known in his native Sweden as a critic of society's institutions, including marriage, religion, and the military, and for advocating the redistribution of wealth and income to the less well-off. Trained in physics and mathematics, he was also among the founders of the neoclassical school of economics. His major contributions include the analysis of credit and interest. In 1911 he wrote that "the mathematical method affords no absolute guarantee against false deductions [...] but [it] has the great advantage [...] that errors committed cannot long be concealed and false opinions cannot be defended long after they have been shown to be wrong." [108, p. xxiii] Source: Album via Alamy

[108]: Wicksell (1934), *Lectures on Political Economy*

©2025 Samuel Bowles and Weikai Chen, CC BY-NC 4.0

https://doi.org/10.11647/OBP.0466.11

Like the models in the previous chapter, our representation here of the lender as principal and the borrower as agent provides a microeconomic analysis of some important features of the macroeconomy.

Most important, the fact that many families are excluded from the credit market or quantity-constrained (limited in how much they can borrow), or are able to borrow only at exceptionally high interest rates means that the consumption smoothing that is the basis of the permanent income hypothesis may not be possible. Without resorting to *ad hoc* cognitive

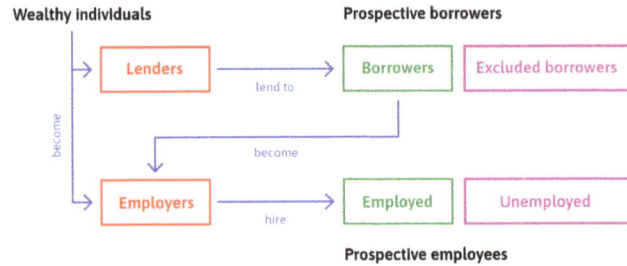

Figure 11.2: The credit and labour markets shape the relationships between groups with different endowments. Horizontal arrows indicate a principal-agent relationship. Lenders and employers are the principals in the figure; their common red color indicates this similarity. Agents — successful borrowers and employees — are colored green to distinguish them from would-be agents (credit market-excluded and unemployed) who are colored purple.

failures (e.g. irrational or "hand to mouth" families), the fact that many families are credit constrained provides a reason why income shocks (e.g. due to a spell of unemployment) entail expenditure shocks, which is the basis of the Keynesian multiplier.

In this chapter, we assume that all actors are risk neutral. We model risk-averse actors in Chapter 12.

To read more about the models on which these problems are based, see Chapter 9 of Bowles [14] and Chapter 12 of Bowles and Halliday [29].

[14]: Bowles (2004), *Microeconomics*

[29]: Bowles and Halliday (2022), *Microeconomics*

11.1 Robinson Crusoe and the Walrasian credit market

This first section describes the economic environment and the next section sets up a basic model (that will also be used in Section 11.6) and explores some of its properties.

Notation alert. We are economizing on notation here, so be careful: f is both the speed of the machine, governing how much will be produced over some given time period, and the probability that the machine will fail, producing no goods at all.

A project (operating a "machine") requires \$1 to carry out, and will fail with probability $f \in [0, 1]$, which is the speed at which the machine is run. The goods produced are available only at the end of the period under the condition that the machine has not failed. The machine will be worth nothing at the end of the period whether it fails or not. If the machine does not fail, the project returns an amount qf net of all costs except interest payments and 0 otherwise, where q is a positive constant, measuring the quality of the project. The actors in this problem are risk-neutral, their interaction is for a single period, and the time period is short enough to ignore their time preference.

To further explore wealth constraints and credit market exclusion, along with policies to overcome the resulting poverty traps, see Section 11.6: When does titling the wealth of the poor not help them? The de Soto effect.

1. *Robinson Crusoe.* To provide a Walrasian benchmark, consider the case in which the machine is owned and operated by a residual claimant (RC). What function will they maximize and what is the first order condition determining the choice of f?

2. *Complete contract on the level of risk.* To explore an alternative (also Walrasian) benchmark, suppose that the operator borrows the funds to operate the machine, promising to repay the lender an interest factor $\delta > 1$. The lender can specify f in the contract (but due to limited liability laws, if the machine fails the borrower is bankrupt and no repayment is made). The operator's income without the project is zero; the lender's is to invest \$1 at the risk-free rate of interest ρ. Give the maximum problem to be solved by the lender and, using the first order condition from this problem, indicate what level of f will be specified in the contract. What will be the lenders' and the borrower's expected income from the project?

3. *Incomplete contract unlimited liability.* Suppose the borrower has some other assets (their house or car) and that they are legally bound to repay the loan irrespective of whether or not the project fails. Show how this case of unlimited liability alters the objective function of both the borrower and lender, with the result that the Nash equilibrium speed of the machine is identical to that under a complete contract. Explain why unlimited liability restores the Walrasian equilibrium even though the speed of the machine is not subject to contract.

Answers.

1. *Robinson Crusoe.* The operator will maximize their expected income

$$y = qf(1-f)$$

and the first order condition determining the choice of f is

$$y_f = q(1-2f) = 0 \Rightarrow f^* = \frac{1}{2}$$

2. *Complete contract on the level of risk.* The operator's expected income is

$$y = (qf - \delta)(1-f)$$

The lender's problem is

$$\max_{f,\delta} \quad Y = \delta(1-f)$$

$$\text{s.t.} \quad y = (qf - \delta)(1-f) \geq 0$$

Note that the participation constraint must be binding. That is

$$\delta = qf$$

> Suppose that the participation constraint is not binding, then the lender could increase δ with the same f which would still satisfy the participation constraint but yield higher expected income.

Then the problem becomes

$$\max_{f} \quad Y = qf(1-f)$$

The first order condition is

$$Y_f = q(1-2f) = 0 \Rightarrow f^* = \frac{1}{2}$$

Then

$$\delta^* = qf^* = \frac{1}{2}q$$

Thus, the lender will offer the contract $(f^*, \delta^*) = (\frac{1}{2}, \frac{1}{2}q)$, as shown in Figure 11.3. The expected income of the operator is 0 as the participation constraint is binding, while that of the lender is $\delta^*(1 - f^*) = q/4$.

3. *Incomplete contract unlimited liability.* The borrower's problem is

$$\max_f \quad y = qf(1 - f) - \delta$$

The first order condition is

$$y_f = q(f - 2f) = 0 \Rightarrow f = \frac{1}{2}$$

which is identical to that under a complete contract. Then the borrower's expected income is

$$y(\delta) = \frac{1}{4}q - \delta$$

The lender's problem is

$$\max_\delta \quad Y = \delta$$

$$\text{s.t.} \quad y(\delta) = \frac{1}{4}q - \delta \geq 0$$

Then the lender would choose

$$\delta^* = \frac{1}{4}q$$

The Nash equilibrium with unlimited liability replicates the Walrasian equilibrium even though the speed of the machine is not subject to contract because if the repayment of the loan can be enforced by contract, then the lender has no interest in f while the borrower internalizes the entire cost of running the machine faster and failing.

11.2 Wealth matters in credit markets: Excluded and quantity-constrained borrowers

This section sets up a basic model based on the economic environment described in Section 11.1 and explores some of its properties. The model here will also be used in Section 11.6.

Incomplete contract, no equity or collateral. The setting remains the same as in Section 11.1 except that the lender has no means to observe the speed at which the machine is run and as a result f is not subject to contract.

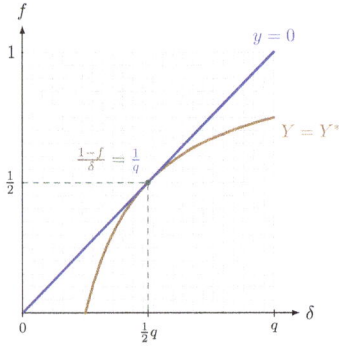

Figure 11.3: Credit market: contractible case. The orange curve is one of the iso-return schedules of the lender

$$Y = \delta(1 - f) = Y^*$$

The slope of the iso-return schedule is $(1 - f)/\delta$. At the solution, the iso-return schedule is tangent to borrower's participation constraint

$$y = (qf - \delta)(1 - f) = 0 \Rightarrow f = \frac{\delta}{q}$$

the slope of which is $1/q$.

An extension of this problem (using the same model) is in Section 11.3: Pareto-improving egalitarian redistribution.

1. Give the borrower's maximization problem and the first order condition for the choice of f.

2. Give the maximization problem to be solved by the lender and the first order condition from this problem, indicate what level of f will be set by the borrower, and find the borrower's and lender's expected incomes from the project.

3. Use the first order conditions of the borrower and lender to show that the resulting allocation is not Pareto-efficient.

4. Why does the borrower operate the machine at a speed faster than that which would maximize the expected income of the project?

Incomplete contract, borrower has some equity. Suppose the operator has an asset $\kappa < 1$ that may be invested in the project or will otherwise earn the risk-free interest rate ρ. If κ is invested in the project, the remainder of the \$1 cost of the project is borrowed by the operator from the lender. Assume that f is not subject to contract. The other assumptions of the problem are unchanged.

5. Give the borrower's first order condition for the choice of f.

6. State the lender's maximization problem and use it to derive the interest factor they will offer and the resulting expected incomes of the two from the project.

7. Find the least level of borrower's wealth, κ^0, such that they would get a loan.

8. Now consider two borrowers with different wealth levels, $\kappa_1 > \kappa_2 \geq \kappa^0$ (κ^0 is the least asset sufficient to secure a loan). If there is a single non-competitive lender, show that the borrower with the larger asset (for projects of the same size and quality) will pay the higher interest factor. Why is this the case?

9. Suppose again that there are two borrowers with different wealth levels, $\kappa_1 > \kappa_2 \geq \kappa^0$. Show that under competitive conditions (zero expected profits for the lender in equilibrium) if both borrowers secure a loan, the one with a lesser asset (smaller κ) will pay a higher interest factor.

10. Suppose that two marginal borrowers of differing wealth levels are just able to finance their projects in competitive equilibrium, and hence both pay the same interest rate δ. Show that the one with a lesser asset (smaller κ) must have a project of higher quality (that is, higher q) than the wealthier borrower.

In his *Equality and Efficiency: The Big Trade-off* Arthur Okun [80] popularized the idea that a society's pursuit of greater equality would come at a cost of reduced economic efficiency. Here is an example of the opposite: a transfer of assets from the wealthy to the less wealthy could allow some of the high-quality projects of the less well-off to be implemented instead of the inferior projects of the rich. The result would be to improve the average quality of projects implemented, raising average incomes.

[80]: Okun (1975), *Equality and Efficiency*

Answers.

1. Given δ, the operator will choose the speed f to maximize their expected income

$$y = (qf - \delta)(1 - f)$$

The first order condition is

$$y_f = q + \delta - 2qf = 0 \Rightarrow f = \frac{1}{2} + \frac{\delta}{2q} \qquad (11.1)$$

2. The lender's problem is

$$\max_{\delta} \quad Y = \delta(1 - f)$$

$$\text{s.t.} \quad f = \frac{1}{2} + \frac{\delta}{2q}$$

That is

$$\max_{\delta} \quad Y = \delta\left(\frac{1}{2} - \frac{\delta}{2q}\right)$$

The first order condition is

$$Y_\delta = \frac{1}{2} - \frac{\delta}{q} = 0 \Rightarrow \delta^* = \frac{1}{2}q$$

and therefore the borrower would set the speed at

$$f^* = \frac{1}{2} + \frac{q/2}{2q} = \frac{3}{4}$$

a higher level of risk than in the complete-contracting or Robinson Crusoe cases. Figure 11.4 illustrates the difference. Note the difference between the participation constraint and the best response function (this explains the difference in the level of risk chosen by the borrower). As a result, the borrower's expected income is positive (because the best response function is above and to the left of the participation constraint), and thus the borrower is receiving a rent. Then the borrower's expected income is

$$y^* = \left(\frac{3}{4}q - \frac{1}{2}q\right)\left(1 - \frac{3}{4}\right) = \frac{1}{16}q$$

and the lender's expected income is

$$Y^* = \frac{1}{2}q\left(1 - \frac{3}{4}\right) = \frac{1}{8}q$$

3. To show that the resulting allocation is not Pareto-efficient, consider a new outcome $(f^* + df, \delta^* + d\delta)$ such that $df < 0$ and

$$2qdf < d\delta < 0 \qquad (11.2)$$

Then we have

$$dy = y_f df + y_\delta d\delta = y_\delta d\delta > 0$$

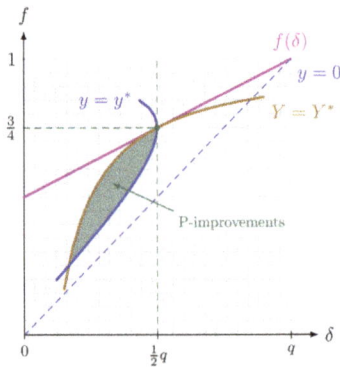

Figure 11.4: Credit market: incomplete contract with no equity or collateral. The dashed blue line is the participation constraint of the borrower. The orange curve is one of the iso-return schedules of the lender

$$Y = \delta(1 - f) = Y^*$$

and the blue curves represent the borrower's iso-expected income locus

$$y = (qf - \delta)(1 - f) = \bar{u}$$

At the solution, the iso-return schedule is tangent to the borrower's best response function

$$f = \frac{1}{2} + \frac{\delta}{2q}$$

which is above the participation constraint

$$y = 0 \Rightarrow f = \frac{\delta}{q}$$

The solution is not Pareto-efficient since any point in the shaded region is a Pareto improvement.

since $y_f = 0$ at the Nash equilibrium and $y_\delta = -(1-f^*) = -1/4 < 0$, and

$$dY = Y_f df + Y_\delta d\delta = -\delta^* df + (1 - f^*)d\delta = -\frac{1}{2}q df + \frac{1}{4}d\delta > 0$$

by (11.2). Therefore, $(f^* + df, \delta^* + d\delta)$ is Pareto-superior to (f^*, δ^*) and thus the latter allocation is not Pareto-efficient as shown in Figure 11.4.

> Note that from (11.2) we have
> $$-\frac{1}{2}q df + \frac{1}{4}d\delta > 0$$
> which is
> $$-\delta^* df + (1 - f^*)d\delta > 0$$

4. Limited liability means that some of the costs of failure will fall on the lender, not the borrower who chooses the level of risk, and this uncompensated external effect of their choice biases them towards risk taking (though, recall, they are risk neutral).

5. For the borrower with wealth sufficient to invest equity κ in the project, the constrained choice problem is

$$\max_{f} \quad y = [qf - (1 - \kappa)\delta](1 - f)$$

then the first order condition is

$$y_f = q - 2qf + (1 - \kappa)\delta = 0 \Rightarrow f^* = \frac{1}{2} + \frac{(1 - \kappa)\delta}{2q}$$

6. The lender's problem is

$$\max_{\delta} \quad \pi = \delta(1 - f)$$

$$\text{s.t.} \quad f = \frac{1}{2} + \frac{(1 - \kappa)\delta}{2q}$$

That is to

$$\max_{\delta} \quad \pi = \delta\left[\frac{1}{2} - \frac{(1 - \kappa)\delta}{2q}\right]$$

The first order condition is

$$\pi_\delta = \frac{1}{2} - \frac{(1 - \kappa)\delta}{q} = 0 \Rightarrow \delta^* = \frac{q}{2(1 - \kappa)} \quad (11.3)$$

Then the borrower would choose

$$f^* = \frac{1}{2} + \frac{(1 - \kappa)}{2q} \frac{q}{2(1 - \kappa)} = \frac{3}{4}$$

and therefore the expected interest factor is

$$\pi^* = \frac{q}{2(1 - \kappa)}\left(1 - \frac{3}{4}\right) = \frac{q}{8(1 - \kappa)}$$

Then the expected income of the two from the project are

$$y^* = \left[\frac{3}{4}q - (1 - \kappa)\frac{q}{2(1 - \kappa)}\right]\left(1 - \frac{3}{4}\right) = \frac{1}{16}q$$

and

$$Y^* = (1 - \kappa)\pi^* = (1 - \kappa) \cdot \frac{q}{8(1 - \kappa)} = \frac{1}{8}q$$

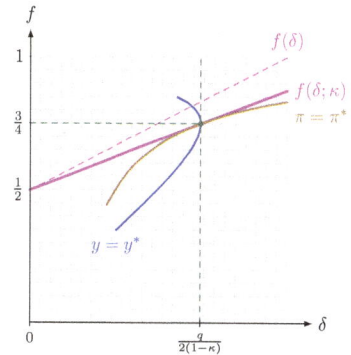

Figure 11.5: Credit market: incomplete contract with some equity. At the solution, the iso-return schedule

$$\pi = \delta(1 - f) = \pi^*$$

is tangent to the borrower's best response function

$$f(\delta; \kappa) = \frac{1}{2} + \frac{(1 - \kappa)\delta}{2q}$$

> Note that $\pi = \delta(1 - f)$ is the expected interest factor actually paid, and the expected income by leading the loan with the size of $(1 - \kappa)$ is $Y = (1 - \kappa)\pi$.

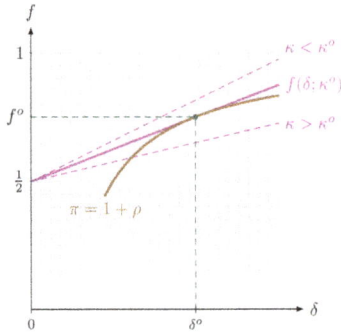

Figure 11.6: Credit market exclusion.
The best response function at the least
level of wealth κ^0 is

$$f(\delta;\kappa) = \frac{1}{2} + \frac{(1-\kappa^0)\delta}{2q}$$

is tangent to the zero profit locus, defined
by

$$\pi = \delta(1-f) = 1 + \rho$$

at (δ^0, f^0). Lesser levels of wealth $\kappa <
\kappa^0$ give a steeper best response function
lying above the zero profit locus.

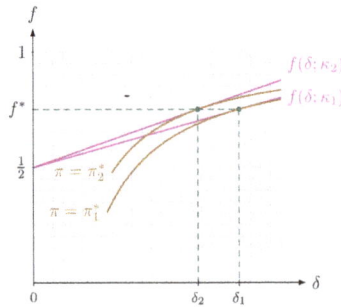

**Figure 11.7: The monopolist lender will
set a higher interest factor when the
borrower is richer.** The tangent points
of the best response functions

$$f(\delta;\kappa_i) = \frac{1}{2} + \frac{(1-\kappa_i)\delta}{2q}, \quad i = 1,2$$

and the iso-return schedule

$$\pi = \delta(1-f) = \pi_i^*, \quad i = 1,2$$

give the equilibrium interest factor δ_1
and δ_2. Given that $\kappa_1 > \kappa_2$, the best
response function with lesser level of
wealth κ_2 is steeper than the one with
κ_1.

7. For the lender to be willing to make a loan to the borrower, the
expected interest factor should be not less than $1 + \rho$; otherwise
the lender would prefer to get the risk-free interest. That is

$$\pi^* = \frac{q}{8(1-\kappa)} \geq (1+\rho) \Rightarrow \kappa \geq 1 - \frac{q}{8(1+\rho)}$$

Therefore, the least level of the borrower's wealth such that they
would get a loan is

$$\kappa^0 = 1 - \frac{q}{8(1+\rho)}$$

As shown in Figure 11.6, lesser levels of wealth give a best response
function lying wholly above the zero profit locus, and hence there is
no offer the lender can make that will generate an expected return
to the leader at least equal to ρ. As a result, borrowers with $\kappa < \kappa^0$
are unable to borrow. They are the credit market-excluded.

8. Given that $\kappa_1 > \kappa_2 \geq \kappa^0$, then the single lender would set different
interest factors according to the first order condition (11.3). Thus,

$$\delta_1 = \frac{q}{2(1-\kappa_1)} > \frac{q}{2(1-\kappa_2)} = \delta_2$$

That is, the borrower with the larger asset will pay the higher
interest factor, as shown in Figure 11.7.

9. In contrast to the monopolistic lender case, with unlimited competition among lenders the zero profit condition (zero expected profits
for the lender) must be satisfied; otherwise additional lenders will
enter the market when expected profits are positive. So the lender's
expected return on the loan to both borrowers must be equal to the
risk-free rate ρ. That is

$$\delta_1(1-f_1) = \pi_1 = 1 + \rho = \pi_2 = \delta_2(1-f_2) \tag{11.4}$$

Therefore, the equilibrium interest rates are determined by the
intersections of the two best response functions and the zero profit
locus. Because the zero profit locus is upward sloping and greater
wealth shifts the best response function downwards, its intersection
with the zero profit locus for the wealthier borrower (κ_1) is to the
left of the corresponding intersection for the less wealthy borrower
(κ_2). As a result, we have the competitive equilibrium interest
factors $\delta_2 > \delta_1$, as shown in Figure 11.8.

10. Suppose that $\kappa_1 > \kappa_2$ and that the both are marginal borrowers
in the sense that, given the different quality of their projects, their
respective levels of wealth are both just sufficient to secure a loan
(like the borrower with κ^0 in Figure 11.8). This means that in
competitive equilibrium they will pay the same interest factor δ,
and then the zero profit condition (11.4) becomes

$$\delta\left[\frac{1}{2} - \frac{(1-\kappa_1)\delta}{2q_1}\right] = (1+\rho) = \delta\left[\frac{1}{2} - \frac{(1-\kappa_2)\delta}{2q_2}\right]$$

and thus

$$\frac{1 - \kappa_1}{q_1} = \frac{1 - \kappa_2}{q_2} \Rightarrow \frac{q_2}{q_1} = \frac{1 - \kappa_2}{1 - \kappa_1} > 1$$

by $\kappa_1 > \kappa_2$. Therefore, $q_2 > q_1$. That is, in order to finance their project, the agent lacking wealth must have a project that is superior to that of the rich agent. The result is that superior projects of the less wealthy will not be financed, while the lower-quality projects of the wealthy will be implemented.

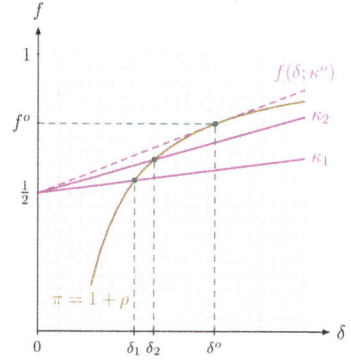

Figure 11.8: Competitive equilibrium interest factor will vary inversely with the wealth of the borrower. The intersections of the best response functions

$$f(\delta; \kappa_i) = \frac{1}{2} + \frac{(1 - \kappa_i)\delta}{2q}, \quad i = 1, 2$$

and the zero profit locus

$$\pi = \delta(1 - f) = 1 + \rho$$

give the equilibrium interest factor δ_1 and δ_2. Given that $\kappa_1 > \kappa_2$, the best response function with lesser level of wealth κ_2 is steeper than the one with κ_1.

11.3 Pareto-improving egalitarian redistribution

Remember where you saw it first: the title of this problem appears to be an oxymoron (an "apparently contradictory pairing of terms"). But you can now show that it is not.

This question is based on the model in Section 11.2 in which a wealthy individual lends \$1 to the operator of a machine whose running speed f and hence the probability of failure of the project is not subject to contract. Now suppose that the government were to confiscate the \$1 of wealth from the lender (that had previously been loaned to the machine operator) and instead transfer it to the operator who would then operate the machine as a residual claimant (the Robinson Crusoe case).

We here assume that all parties are risk neutral. To learn more about how the greater risk aversion of those with less wealth can affect the costs and economic benefits of egalitarian redistribution, have a look at the problems in Chapter 12.

1. Show that the government could impose a tax on the operator (the new owner of the machine), the proceeds of which would be paid to the expropriated wealthy individual such that the Nash equilibrium following the expropriation-tax-transfer policy would be a Pareto improvement over the pre-existing Nash equilibrium.

2. If a Pareto improvement is possible, why could it not be accomplished by (private) Coasean bargaining?

Answers.

1. Recall that, in the case of incomplete contract with no equity or collateral in Section 11.2, the resulting allocation is $f^* = 3/4$, with the joint surplus

$$qf^*(1 - f^*) = \frac{3}{16}q$$

distributed as the expected income of the borrower $y^* = q/16$ and that of the lender $Y^* = q/8$. Now suppose that the government could impose a tax rate τ, with revenue being transferred to the expropriated wealthy individual. The operator's programming problem is

$$\max_f \quad y = (1 - \tau)qf(1 - f)$$

The first order condition is

$$y_f = (1 - \tau)q(1 - 2f) = 0 \Rightarrow f^\tau = 1/2$$

and then the expected income of the operator is

$$y^\tau = (1 - \tau)q/4$$

and that of the lender is

$$Y^\tau = \tau q/4$$

To make the new Nash equilibrium following the expropriation-tax-transfer policy (y^τ, Y^τ) be a Pareto improvement over the pre-existing Nash equilibrium (y^*, Y^*), the government should impose a tax rate such that either the would-be lender or the operator (or both) are strictly better off than before, while not making either worse off. That is

$$\frac{1}{4}(1 - \tau)q \geq \frac{1}{16}q \quad \text{and} \quad \frac{1}{4}\tau q \geq \frac{1}{8}q \Rightarrow \frac{1}{2} \leq \tau \leq \frac{3}{4}$$

If $\tau = 1/2$, then the operator is strictly better off and the would-be lender is no worse off compared to the pre-existing Nash equilibrium; if $\tau = 3/4$, then the would-be lender is strictly better off and the operator is no worse off; and if $1/2 < \tau < 3/4$, then both are strictly better off.

2. The government can accomplish what private Coasean bargaining cannot because the obligation to pay the tax is not subject to limited liability: if the machine fails, the tax must be paid in any case.

11.4 Repeated interactions in the credit market

Many borrowing and lending relationships are ongoing rather than the one-shot (non-repeated) interactions modeled in the previous sections. This section will explain how the lender (the principal) benefits by engaging in a repeated interaction with the borrower (the agent). The model in this section uses the same setup as in Section 11.2, except that the game is repeated.

Notation alert. Recall that f is the speed of the machine and the probability that it will fail, δ is the interest factor and the expected output of the machine is $qf(1-f)$

The fact that the principal confers a rent on the agent in the one-period case (see e.g. Figure 11.4 and the passage above discussing it) raises an interesting question. Could not the principal profit from this fact, by promising to continue lending to the agent as long as the machine did not fail? Would the incentive problems be attenuated if the lender offered the borrower a contingent-renewal contract over an infinite time horizon (as did the employer and employee in the labor market model)?

Suppose the principal uses the failure of the machine as a (noisy) signal of the action taken by the borrower. They then offer a loan (for a single period) with a promise to renew the loan if the project does not fail, and not otherwise. If the present value of the agent's fallback position (the present value of their expected lifetime income if the relationship with the principal is terminated) is z, the rate of time preference is i, and treating the interaction as stationary (time invariant), the present value of agent's income stream, v, is

In equation (11.5) income is received at the end of each period, so $y(\delta, f)$ the first period's income is discounted by $(1 + i)$

$$v = \frac{y(\delta, f) + (1 - f)v + fz}{1 + i} \qquad (11.5)$$

where $y(\delta, f) = (qf - \delta)(1 - f)$.

1. Rearrange equation (11.5) as a closed form expression for v as the sum of the fallback asset z and a rent received by the agent. Explain the terms making up the rent.

2. Give the first order condition for the borrower's choice of f.

3. Assuming $i = z = 0$, derive the resulting best response function of the borrower $f(\delta)$.

4. Using this best response function, show that in the Nash equilibrium of this game (compared to the one-shot variant of the game in Section 11.2)

   a) the interest factor will be lower;

   b) the level of risk chosen by the borrower will be lower; and

   c) the expected payoffs (income and profits respectively) per period will be higher for both borrower and lender.

5. What explains the increased payoffs of the two?

6. Recall the definition of power and explain whether or not the lender exercises power over the borrower.

Answers.

1. From equation (11.5), we have

   $$(1 + i)v = y + (1 - f)v + fz \Rightarrow (i + f)v = y + fz$$

   and thus

   $$v = \frac{y + fz}{i + f} = z + \frac{y - iz}{i + f}$$

   The second term, $(y - iz)/(i + f)$, is the rent received by the agent, where the numerator $y - iz$ is the extra income the agent receives from the project at the end of the period and the denominator is the sum of the rate of time preference and the probability of failure.

2. From equation (11.5), the first order condition $v_f = 0$ implies

   $$v_f = \frac{y_f + (1 - f)v_f - v + z}{1 + i} = \frac{y_f - (v - z)}{1 + i} = 0$$

   Then

   $$y_f = v - z \qquad (11.6)$$

Table 11.1: Credit market results for the case where risk is non-contractible and the borrower has no wealth

Case	Interest factor δ^*	Risk f^*	Expected income per period y^*, Y^*
One-shot game	$\frac{1}{2}q$	$\frac{3}{4}$	$\frac{1}{16}q, \frac{1}{8}q$
Repeated game	$\frac{4}{9}q$	$\frac{2}{3}$	$\frac{2}{27}q, \frac{4}{27}q$

3. Given $i = z = 0$, we have $v = y/f$ and the first order condition (11.6) becomes $y_f = y/f$, or $y - fy_f = 0$. That is

$$(qf - \delta)(1 - f) - f(q + \delta - 2qf) = qf^2 - \delta = 0$$

Then we have the best response function

$$f(\delta) = \left(\frac{\delta}{q}\right)^{1/2} \tag{11.7}$$

4. The lender's problem become

$$\max_{\delta} \quad Y = \delta(1 - f)$$

$$\text{s.t.} \quad f = \left(\frac{\delta}{q}\right)^{1/2}$$

That is

$$\max_{\delta} \quad Y = \delta\left[1 - \left(\frac{\delta}{q}\right)^{1/2}\right]$$

The first order condition is

$$Y_\delta = 1 - \frac{3}{2}\left(\frac{\delta}{q}\right)^{1/2} = 0 \Rightarrow \delta^* = \frac{4}{9}q$$

and therefore the borrower would set the speed at

$$f^* = \left(\frac{4}{9}\right)^{1/2} = \frac{2}{3}$$

Then the borrower's expected income is

$$y^* = \left(\frac{2}{3}q - \frac{4}{9}q\right)\left(1 - \frac{2}{3}\right) = \frac{2}{27}q$$

and the lender's expected income is

$$Y^* = \frac{4}{9}q\left(1 - \frac{2}{3}\right) = \frac{4}{27}q$$

As summarized in Table 11.1, we have a) the interest factor will be lower; b) the level of risk chosen by the borrower will be lower; and the expected payoffs (income and profits respectively) per period will be higher for both borrower and lender.

5. The possibility of repeated interaction with the lender provides an additional incentive for the borrower to operate the machine

prudently, more nearly approximating the expected income maximizing value of $f = 1/2$.

6. The lender exercises power over the borrower because, in response to the possibility that the lender will impose a sanction on the borrower (termination of the ongoing relationship and loss of the rent), the borrower has acted in the interest of the lender (reduced f) which they would not have done in the absence of the sanction (the solution of the one-shot game).

11.5 An alternative (no-shirking type) principal-agent model of the credit market

This model is analogous to the model in Section 10.7 from which we derived the "no-shirking condition" (NSC) in the labor market, where, rather than selecting a continuously varying action, the agent chooses between two discrete choices (work or shirk in the labor market case, here run a machine prudently, or dangerously fast ("speeding")). As with the no-shirking condition for work effort, here we simplify by collapsing the time dimension so that we have a one-shot game.

A borrower seeks a loan of $1 from a lender to finance a machine, which, as in the previous problem, produces an output of goods with a value of qf when it is run at speed f and does not fail; but it fails with probability f, yielding no goods. The lender chooses an interest factor δ.

The borrower's reservation option is zero; the lender's reservation income is $1 + \rho$ where ρ is the risk-free rate of return on an alternative use of the lender's $1. Both lender and borrower are risk neutral. The borrower is protected by limited liability (and so does not repay the loan if the machine has failed); the lender cannot observe the speed at which the machine is run and as a result f is not subject to contract.

We assume that the machine has just two speeds, $f = 0.5$ and $f^+ > 0.5$. The game tree is presented in Figure 11.9. We now seek to determine the credit market analogue to the labor market's "no-shirking condition", also called the NSC (for "no-speeding condition").

1. How does the lender determine the greatest interest factor δ^* such that the borrower's (weak) best response is to set $f = 0.5$? This is the analogy to the NSC for the case of labor effort. Derive an expression for δ^* in terms of the parameters of the problem.

2. What is the borrower's expected income y^* when the NSC is implemented? (Write an expression for y^* in terms of the parameters of the problem.)

3. What is the total surplus when the NSC is implemented, and how it is divided between the lender and borrower?

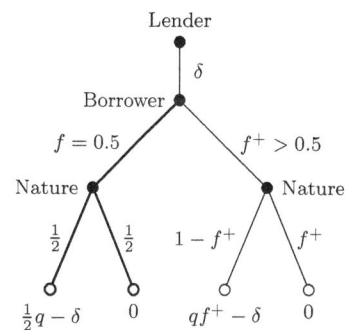

Figure 11.9: The sequence of moves in a one-shot game determining the interest factor. The lender moves first making an offer of the interest factor δ. Then the borrower moves, setting the speed at $f = 0.5$ or $f = f^+$. Then nature moves (meaning that the move is determined by chance). The machine produces an output of goods with a value of qf when it is run at speed f and does not fail; but it fails with probability f yielding no goods. The borrower gets the product net of δ if the machine does not fail, but 0 if it fails.

4. Suppose that $f^+ = 0.8$. Calculate the no-speeding interest factor δ^*, the lender's expected profit, the borrower's expected income, and the amount the lender would be willing to pay to rent a device that would allow information about f to be verifiable.

5. As before, the two possible speeds of the machine are $f = 0.5$ and $f^+ = 0.8$, but now suppose the borrower has some wealth $\kappa < 1$ that they can invest in the project. Write an expression for δ^* (as a function of κ and q). If $\rho = 0.1$ and $q = 5.5$, what is the least κ for which the lender will be given a loan?

Answers.

1. To determine the greatest interest factor δ^* such that the borrower's (weak) best response is to set $f = 0.5$, the lender should choose the interest factor such that the expected income of the borrower when setting $f = 0.5$ is no less than that with f^+. That is

$$y\left(\frac{1}{2}, \delta\right) \geq y(f^+, \delta) \tag{11.8}$$

That is

$$\frac{1}{2}\left(\frac{1}{2}q - \delta\right) \geq (1 - f^+)(qf^+ - \delta) \Rightarrow \left(f^+ - \frac{1}{2}\right)\delta \leq \left(f^+ - \frac{1}{2}\right)^2 q$$

Then

$$\delta \leq q\left(f^+ - \frac{1}{2}\right)$$

Therefore, the greatest interest factor is $\delta^* = q(f^+ - 1/2)$.

2. When the NSC $\delta^* = q(f^+ - 1/2)$ is implemented, the borrower's expected income is

$$y^* = \frac{1}{4}q - \frac{1}{2}\delta^* = \frac{1}{2}q(1 - f^+)$$

3. When the NSC is implemented, we have $f = 0.5$ and the total income from the project to be divided between the borrower and lender is

$$T = qf(1 - f) = \frac{1}{4}q$$

The expected profit of the lender is

$$Y^* = \delta^*(1 - f) = \frac{1}{2}q\left(f^+ - \frac{1}{2}\right)$$

and then T the total surplus is

$$y^* + Y^* = \frac{1}{2}q(1 - f^+) + \frac{1}{2}q(f^+ - \frac{1}{2}) = \frac{1}{4}q = T$$

Therefore, the total surplus is divided between the lender and borrower in the following way: the lender gets half of δ^* and the borrower gets the rest.

4. Given $f^+ = 0.8$, we have the no-speeding interest factor $\delta^* = 0.3q$, the lender's expected profit $Y^* = 0.15q$, and the borrower's expected income $y^* = 0.1q$.

With the device that would allow information about f to be verifiable, the lender's problem is

$$\max_{\delta, f} \quad Y = \delta(1 - f)$$

$$\text{s.t.} \quad y = (qf - \delta)(1 - f) \geq 0$$

With the binding participation constraint, it becomes

$$\max_f \quad Y = qf(1 - f)$$

From the first order condition $Y_f = 0$, we have $f^v = 0.5$ and $\delta^v = 0.5q$. Then, the expected profit of the lender in this case is $Y^v = 0.25q$. Therefore, the lender would pay at most

$$Y^v - Y^* = 0.25q - 0.15q = 0.1q$$

to rent the device.

5. With wealth $\kappa < 1$, the borrower's expected income becomes

$$y(f, \delta) = [qf - (1 - \kappa)\delta](1 - f)$$

The no-speeding condition (11.8) becomes

$$y(0.5; \delta) \geq y(0.8; \delta)$$

That is

$$0.25q - 0.5(1 - \kappa)\delta \geq 0.16q - 0.2(1 - \kappa)\delta \Rightarrow \delta \leq \frac{0.3q}{1 - \kappa}$$

Therefore,

$$\delta^* = \frac{0.3q}{1 - \kappa}$$

The lender would like to make the loan only if the expected profit is no less than what they would receive from the alternative, risk-free investment. That is

$$\delta^*(1 - f) = \frac{0.15q}{1 - \kappa} \geq 1 + \rho \Rightarrow \kappa \geq 1 - \frac{0.15q}{1 + \rho} = 0.25$$

with $\rho = 0.1$ and $q = 5.5$. Therefore, the least κ for which the lender will be given a loan is 0.25.

11.6 When does titling the wealth of the poor not help them? The de Soto effect

The Peruvian economist, Hernando de Soto, proposed to convert the existing non-titled (informally owned) assets of the poor (their home or land, often) to formally titled property so that poor borrowers can commit a greater amount of collateral in their project when seeking to borrow, and so (according to de Soto) can attain a higher standard of living [8, 45].

"Titled" means that the de facto owner of the property has a judicially recognized legal document identifying the property as owned by the owner.

[8]: Besley, Burchardi, and Ghatak (2012), 'Incentives and the de Soto Effect'

[45]: de Soto (2000), *The Mystery of Capital*

To explore how this might work, we suppose the borrower has total assets, K, of two types. The first, untitled wealth (in amount $K - \kappa$), cannot be used as equity or collateral in a loan contract (because the owner is not legally recognized as such), while the second (called κ-wealth) in amount κ may be used as equity or collateral. If the κ-wealth is not invested in the project, it yields a risk-free rate of return of ρ — one unit of κ-wealth used in some other way yields an income of $1 + \rho$ at the end of one period. To simplify the problem, we initially assume that lenders require borrowers to devote all their κ-wealth to the project as equity, if they devote any. By implementing de Soto's plan, the untitled wealth becomes titled and could be used as equity or collateral.

Use the model that you worked with in Section 11.2: the "machine" costing \$1 is operated at speed f (which is also the probability that the machine will fail) and yields expected income of $qf(1 - f)$. Limited competition among lenders is common in many of the loan markets used by the world's poor; to illustrate this case we assume that there is a single monopolistic lender offering a loan with interest factor δ.

1. What further assumptions about the problem (not mentioned above) are sufficient to make this a principal-agent problem?

2. For a borrower with titled wealth $\kappa < 1$ sufficient to secure a loan prior to the implementation of de Soto's plan, write down the borrower's expected income and give the first order condition for their choice of the level of f to maximize this expected income from the project.

3. Given the borrower's best response function, write down the lender's maximization problem. Give the first order condition for their choice of δ to maximize their expected rate of profit and determine the Nash equilibrium values of f^* and δ^*.

4. Using what you have shown so far, give the effect of a small increase in the borrower's titled property κ on

   a) the borrower's expected income, and

   b) the lender's expected rate of profit.

5. Does the borrower benefit from de Soto's plan? Explain why or why not.

6. Can you think of any institutional change (excluding redistributing assets or somehow making information on f verifiable) in this problem's setup that would reverse your answer to the previous question?

7. What is the minimum level of the borrower's titled wealth to secure a loan, κ_0?

8. Could an excluded borrower benefit from de Soto's plan? If so, how? If not, why not?

9. Now, relaxing the assumption that the lender can require the borrower to invest their entire titled wealth in the project, if a previously excluded borrower with $K > \kappa_0$ but no titled wealth could choose the amount of untitled wealth that they would title, how much would they title? How much of their titled wealth would they invest in the project ($\kappa \leq K$)? Explain your answer.

Answers.

1. The assumptions are: 1. *Limited liability*: the borrower repays nothing if the project fails. It reflects the common institution of limited liability; if the project fails, the lender may not take the borrower's assets. 2. *Non-verifiable information* about an action of the agent about which the lender and borrower have conflicting interests (the speed of the machine f is non-verifiable, so contracts cannot be written in f).

2. The borrower's expected income is

$$y = [qf - \delta(1 - \kappa)](1 - f)$$

The first order condition for their choice of f to maximize y is

$$y_f = q + \delta(1 - \kappa) - 2qf = 0$$

which gives the borrower's best response function

$$f^* = \frac{1}{2} + \frac{\delta(1 - \kappa)}{2q} \qquad (11.9)$$

3. Given this best response function, the lender finds the value of δ that maximizes the expected rate of profit:

$$\max_{\delta} \quad \pi = \delta(1 - f)$$

$$= \delta \left[\frac{1}{2} - \frac{\delta(1 - \kappa)}{2q} \right]$$

The first order condition for the choice of δ is

$$\pi_\delta = \frac{1}{2} - \frac{\delta(1 - \kappa)}{q} = 0$$

and then

$$\delta^* = \frac{q}{2(1 - \kappa)}$$

Substituting this expression for δ^* into (11.9), we have

$$f^* = \frac{1}{2} + \frac{1}{4} = \frac{3}{4}$$

4. Given δ^* and f^*, we calculate the expected income of the borrower:

$$y^* = \frac{q}{16} \tag{11.10}$$

and the lender's expected rate of profit

$$\pi^* = \frac{q}{8(1 - \kappa)} \tag{11.11}$$

   a) From (11.10) we see that the borrower's expected income is independent of their titled wealth κ, or

$$\frac{dy^*}{d\kappa} = 0$$

   b) From (11.11) we have that the effect of variations in κ on π^* is

$$\frac{d\pi^*}{d\kappa} = \frac{q}{8(1 - \kappa)^2} > 0$$

5. An increase in titled wealth does not increase the borrower's expected income. This happens because the borrowers are required to devote all their titled wealth to the project as equity and any increases in their own equity in the project are nullified by higher interest rates (as $d\delta^*/d\kappa > 0$) so that the expected income from borrowing is independent of κ. Therefore the borrower does not benefit from de Soto's plan.

6. If the credit market had been competitive (so that a zero expected profit condition held) then de Soto's plan would benefit the poor both (i) by allowing some excluded borrowers to secure a loan (as is the case also in the monopolistic credit market, shown in the answer to the next question) and also (ii) by securing a loan at a lower rate of interest, or a larger loan, or a loan for a lower quality (lower q) project.

7. The borrower can secure a loan when the lender's expected return is

$$\pi^* \geq 1 + \rho \Rightarrow \kappa \geq 1 - \frac{q}{8(1 + \rho)} \equiv \kappa_0$$

   where κ_0 denotes the minimum level of a borrower's titled wealth to to secure a loan.

8. Let κ_e be the titled wealth of the excluded borrower. Then we have

$$\kappa_e < \kappa_0 = 1 - \frac{q}{8(1 + \rho)} \tag{11.12}$$

The income (without borrowing) of an excluded borrower is $y_{EB} = \kappa_e(1 + \rho)$ when they invest all their titled wealth κ_e in the alternate investment opportunity. If de Soto's plan was instituted, their expected income would be $y_{DS} = q/16$ which is the same as expected income in equation (11.10). Thus, the excluded borrower could benefit from de Soto's plan if

$$y_{DS} > y_{EB} \Leftrightarrow \kappa_e < \frac{q}{16(1 + \rho)} \qquad (11.13)$$

Therefore, an excluded borrower could benefit from de Soto's plan if their titled wealth is sufficiently small. Moreover, when the quality of the project is high enough such that

$$q > \frac{16(1 + \rho)}{3}$$

then the inequality (11.12) implies (11.13). In this case, all excluded borrowers could be better off if de Soto's plan is implemented.

9. They would title all wealth K since untitled wealth gives no return at all. They would at most invest $\kappa = \kappa_0$ in the project and borrow the rest $(1 - \kappa_0)$ from the leader, since the κ has no effect on the borrower's expected income (shown above).

11.7 Wealth constraints: Why the poor face a limited set of contractual opportunities

The previous problems in this chapter have addressed cases in which an agent who has borrowed funds from the principal selects a level of risk that is not subject to contract. Here we have a case where the agent does not choose some explicit level of risk (like the speed of the machine in previous questions), but instead a level of effort, which will affect the probability that the project will succeed or will fail. So the agent is indirectly choosing a risk level.

This problem also differs from the previous ones in that the agent is exposed to the risk of losing their pre-existing asset. The liability of the agent — that is, the loss incurred if the project fails — is limited only by the wealth of the agent.

The idea for this problem came from Karla Hoff [62].

[62]: Hoff (1996), 'Market Failures and the Distribution of Wealth'

The output of a project depends on the agent's effort because it influences whether a "good" or "bad" state occurs. For example, the crop may fail or it may grow, and this is influenced (but not uniquely determined) by the agent's actions. The agent selects an (onerous and unobserved) effort level $e \in [0, 1]$, which influences whether the good or bad state occurs, the former happening with probability $g(e)$ with $g' > 0$. Total revenues of the project in the good and bad state respectively are Y and y with

$$0 < Y - y \le 2$$

The disutility of effort is e^2, and to simplify things by a harmless normalization, let's say that $g(e) = e$. Because the agent is risk neutral, they maximize expected income minus the disutility of effort.

1. If the person we are calling the "agent" were instead the owner of the output of the project (meaning they owned the revenues y or Y, whichever occurred), how would they select the level of effort? Give the first order condition and the level of effort they would choose (write e in terms of Y and y, and call this e^r).

Suppose, instead, that a principal owns the project (and hence receives the income Y or y) and seeks to maximize expected profits by devising a payment scheme whereby the agent gets w (which could be negative, that is, a penalty rather than a conventional wage) in the bad state and W in the good state. The agent starts the interaction with wealth z. The wage offered in the bad outcome cannot be less than $-z$ (in the bad outcome, the most the principal can take from the agent is everything the agent has). It may help to think of the agent's wealth as the maximum collateral the agent can put up: by transacting with the principal, the agent stands to receive W and stands to lose some amount not to exceed z. The agent's fallback utility is z and the utility from transacting with the principal is the agent's initial wealth plus their expected income minus the disutility of effort, i.e.,

$$u = z + We + w(1 - e) - e^2$$

2. The agent varies e to maximize expected utility. What is their best response function?

3. Knowing the agent's best response function, the principal varies W and w to maximize their expected profits (assuming that the participation constraint is satisfied). Write down the programming problem and show that $w = -z$.

4. Given that we now know that $w = -z$, what is the relevant first order condition for the principal's choice of W and indicate what value of W the principal will choose?

5. If the principal implements their optimal pay scheme (w^N, W^N), what level of e (call it e^N) will the agent choose?

6. Why does e^N differ from e^r, the level of effort that occurs when the agent is residual claimant?

7. Find the threshold level of wealth z_0 such that the agent would participate.

8. Suppose an amount of wealth Δz were transferred to the agent. Assuming that Δz is small enough that the agent would still participate in the interaction, what effect does this have on the agent's effort level e^N, the agent's utility u^N, and the principal's profits π^N?

9. Why would the principal prefer to transact with wealthier agents (assuming wealthier agents have the same fallback positions as the less wealthy, namely, zero)?

Answers.

1. The utility of the agent is

$$u = Yg(e) + y[1 - g(e)] - e^2 = Ye + y(1 - e) - e^2$$

The first order condition is

$$u_e = Y - y - 2e = 0 \Rightarrow e^r = \frac{1}{2}(Y - y)$$

2. The agent varies e to maximize their utility:

$$u = z + We + w(1 - e) - e^2 = z + w + (W - w)e - e^2$$

The first order condition is

$$u_e = W - w - 2e = 0 \Rightarrow e = \frac{1}{2}(W - w)$$

which defines their best response function.

3. The principal's expected profit is

$$\pi = y - w + [(Y - y) - (W - w)]e$$

and the problem is

$$\max_{W,w} \quad \pi = y - w + [(Y - y) - (W - w)]e$$

$$\text{s.t.} \quad e = \frac{1}{2}(W - w)$$

$$w \geq -z$$

Next, we show that $w = -z$ via proof by contradiction. Suppose that (W^*, w^*, e^*) is the solution such that $e^* = (W^* - w^*)/2$ and $w^* > -z$, then a lower $w' = w^* - \varepsilon \geq -z$ together with $W' = W^* - \varepsilon$ and the same e^* satisfies both constraints but yield higher profit $\pi' > \pi^*$, which is contradiction. Therefore, we have $w = -z$ at the solution.

4. Knowing the agent's best response function $e = (W - w)/2$ and $w = -z$, the principal's profit becomes

$$\pi = y + z + \frac{1}{2}(Y - W - y - z)(W + z)$$

To maximize π by varying W, the first order condition is

$$\pi_W = \frac{1}{2}(Y - y - 2z - 2W) = 0 \Rightarrow W^N = \frac{1}{2}(Y - y) - z$$

The expected return to the principal is

$$\pi = g(e)(Y - W) + [1 - g(e)](y - w)$$

Letting $g(e) = e$ and rearranging terms, this may be written as a linear function of e:

$$\pi = y - w + [(Y - y) - (W - w)]e$$

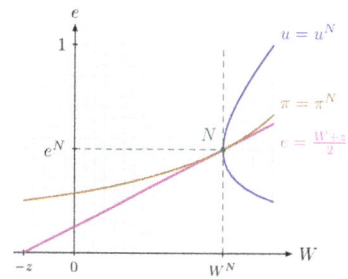

Figure 11.10: The equilibrium wage and the effort level. Given $w = -z$, the principal would choose the wage W^N at the tangent point of the agent's best response function

$$e = \frac{W - w}{2} = \frac{W + z}{2}$$

and one of the principal's iso-profit curves

$$\pi = (Y - W)e + (y + z)(1 - e) = \pi^N$$

In this figure, we assume $Y = 2.5$, $y = 0.5$, $z = 0.5$, and therefore we have $e^N = 0.5$ and $W^N = 0.75$.

5. Given $W^N = (Y - y)/2 - z$, we have

$$e^N = \frac{1}{2}(W^N + z) = \frac{1}{4}(Y - y)$$

6. The marginal benefit of exerting more effort is $Y - y$ when the agent is the residual claimant, and $W^N + z = (Y - y)/2$ when they are not. So e^N differs from e^r because, when the agent is not residual claimant, their incentives are diluted.

7. Given that $w^N = -z$, $W^N = (Y - y)/2 - z$, and $e^N = (Y - y)/4$, the agent's utility at equilibrium is

$$u^N = z + W^N e^N + w^N (1 - e^N) - (e^N)^2 = \frac{1}{16}(Y - y)^2 \quad (11.14)$$

The agent will participate only when their utility at the Nash equilibrium is no less than the fallback utility z, i.e., $u^N \geq z$. That is

$$z \leq \frac{1}{16}(Y - y)^2$$

Therefore, we have the threshold level of wealth $z_0 = (Y - y)^2/16$.

8. From (11.14) we know that u^N does not depend on z, and thus the agent's utility remains the same when agent's wealth becomes $z' = z + \Delta z$. Given $w = -z$ and $W - w = 2e$, the principal's profit is

$$\pi = y - w + [(Y - y) - (W - w)]e$$
$$= y + z + (Y - y)e - 2e^2$$

at the solution. Note that e does not depend on z, so when z becomes $z' = z + \Delta z$, the principal's profit is

$$\pi' = \pi^N + \Delta z$$

Figure 11.11: Interaction with the wealthier agent yields higher expected profit. Having greater wealth and thus a higher fallback position $z' > z$ shifts the agent's best response function upward from

$$e = \frac{W + z}{2}$$

to

$$e = \frac{W + z'}{2}$$

The effort level at the solution remains the same at e^N, while the principal's expected profit increases, $\pi' > \pi^N$. In this figure, we assume that $Y = 2.5$, $y = 0.5$, $z = 0.25$, $z' = 0.5$, so $W^N = 0.75$ and $e^N = e' = W' = 0.5$.

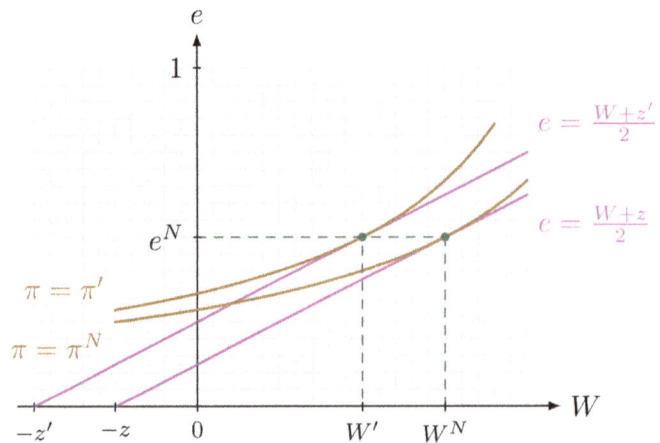

9. The principal would prefer to transact with wealthier agents because they will get higher expected profits by taking more from

the agent if the project fails, with the same effort level provided by the agents, as illustrated by

$$\frac{d\pi^N}{dz} = 1 > 0$$

Risk and Inequality: Redistribution as Insurance | 12

In the problems and notes introduced thus far, we have assumed that, in cases involving risk, the decision makers are risk neutral, so that their maximizing expected payoffs is equivalent to maximizing expected utility. Here we introduce risk aversion. We model this by representing expected payoffs as a "good" and risk exposure as a "bad."

A more restricted interpretation commonly used in economics is that risk aversion derives from the fact that utility is an increasing and concave function of income (or wealth), $u(y)$. In this formulation, the degree of risk aversion, called the Arrow-Pratt measure, is $-u''/u'$ or (roughly) "how concave" the utility function is. Our formulation (derived from the work of Sinn [93] and Meyer [76]) is more general as it includes psychological characteristics such as anxiety about unknown outcomes and other reasons for risk aversion, instead of being restricted to diminishing marginal utility of wealth. It is also less cumbersome mathematically.

In these problems, we adopt the simplification that the degree of risk is simply the difference between the "good" and the "bad" state, the two states occurring with equal probability. Results are readily extended to have the variance of the distribution of outcomes be the measure of risk. Another important simplification is that we do not analyze the problem of uncertainty in which — in contrast to risk — the distribution of unknown future events is not known and cannot be estimated. Many of the important problems facing humanity today — climate change, for example — concern substantial uncertainty and not just risk.

In the problems below, you will see that we consider insurance broadly to be any costly action or policy that reduces the level of risk to which one is exposed. By this standard, a linear tax proportional to realized income, the proceeds of which are paid out equally to all members of society, is a form of insurance.

Some background for the problems in this chapter is found in Chapter 13 of Bowles and Halliday [29]. Unless you are already familiar with this way of modeling risk, you may want to begin with Section 12.1 which lays out a simple version of the approach.

12.1 Taking risks: Basics

Like every farmer, Anil faces risks. One of them is that, depending when the rainy season arrives, his harvest may either be abundant (the good state) or meager (the bad state), the difference in value to Anil between the two being Δ, which is his degree of risk exposure. The date at which he plants his seeds determines the value of Δ. The two states are equally likely, so the expected value of his crop ($\hat{y}$) is just the mean of the good and bad state. We can write his realized income — what he actually will get — as

$$y = \hat{y}(\Delta) \pm \frac{1}{2}\Delta$$

[93]: Sinn (1983), *Economic Decisions under Uncertainty*

[76]: Meyer (1987), 'Two-Moment Decision Models and Expected Utility Maximization'

Risk

The term risk is conventionally used in economics to describe situations in which payoffs depend on contingencies and the probabilities of each contingency occurring are known. Risk may be compared to uncertainty, which describes situations where the decision maker does not know and cannot learn the probabilities of future events affecting their payoffs.

"It is not certain that nothing is certain." — Blaise Pascal, *Pensées (Thoughts)* (1670)

Risk aversion

A risk-averse person will choose a certain outcome valued at x over a lottery whose expected value is greater than x.

[29]: Bowles and Halliday (2022), *Microeconomics*

There is a cost to limiting his risk exposure. The expected value of his crop $\hat{y}$ — the mean of the good and bad state — depends on Δ according to the following risk return schedule

$$\hat{y}(\Delta) = \alpha\Delta - \frac{\beta}{2}\Delta^2$$

with values of α and β (both positive) such that the function is increasing for low values of Δ. Were he risk neutral, Anil would just select the value of Δ that maximizes $\hat{y}$. But he is risk averse, as his expected utility function with expected income as a good and risk exposure as a bad indicates:

$$u(\hat{y}, \Delta) = \hat{y}(\Delta) - \frac{\mu}{2}\Delta^2$$

where $\mu > 0$, so Anil faces a tradeoff.

1. Represent the risk-return schedule and Anil's utility function by two or more indifference loci (with Δ on the x-axis) along with an indifference locus of a risk-neutral person.

2. If Anil selects Δ to maximize his expected utility, give the first order condition and show that he will

   a) equate the marginal rate of transformation of risk exposure into expected income to the marginal rate of substitution between risk exposure and expected income

   b) and as a result take less risk (a) the greater is his risk aversion and (b) the greater is the degree of diminishing returns to risk taking.

3. What is the *certainty equivalent* level of expected income y^c associated with Anil's choice of Δ?

4. Explain why in this setting the actor selected a level of risk less than the level that maximizes expected income while in the similar setting of the credit market (e.g. Section 11.2) the borrower selected a level of risk (f, the speed of the machine) in excess of the expected income maximizing level.

Certainty equivalent

The certainty equivalent level of income (or wealth) is the level of certain income that would be valued equally to some other outcome in which realized income is subject to risk.

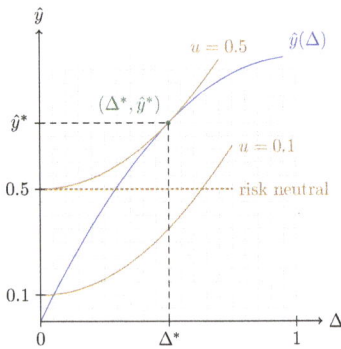

Figure 12.1: The risk return schedule and indifference loci. The blue curve represents the risk return schedule

$$\hat{y}(\Delta) = \alpha\Delta - \frac{\beta}{2}\Delta^2$$

and the orange curves are two indifference loci

$$u(\hat{y}, \Delta) = \hat{y}(\Delta) - \frac{\mu}{2}\Delta^2 = \bar{u}$$

or

$$\hat{y} = \bar{u} + \frac{\mu}{2}\Delta^2$$

The orange dotted line represents an indifference locus of a risk neutral person. This figure is constructed assuming $\alpha = \beta = \mu = 2$.

Answers.

1. See Figure 12.1.

2. Anil's programming problem is

$$\max_{\hat{y}, \Delta} \quad u(\hat{y}, \Delta) = \hat{y}(\Delta) - \frac{\mu}{2}\Delta^2$$

$$\text{s.t.} \quad \hat{y}(\Delta) = \alpha\Delta - \frac{\beta}{2}\Delta^2$$

That is,

$$\max_{\Delta} \quad u = \alpha\Delta - \frac{1}{2}(\beta + \mu)\Delta^2$$

Then the first order condition of his choice of Δ is

$$u_\Delta = \alpha - (\beta + \mu)\Delta = 0 \qquad (12.1)$$

a) From the first order condition 12.1 we have

$$MRT = \hat{y}_\Delta = \alpha - \beta\Delta = \mu\Delta = -\frac{\bar{u}_\Delta}{\bar{u}_{\hat{y}}} = MRS$$

b) From the first order condition 12.1 we have expected utility-maximizing level of risk is

$$\Delta^* = \frac{\alpha}{\beta + \mu} \qquad (12.2)$$

which is decreasing in both μ (his risk aversion) and β (the degree of diminishing returns to risk taking).

3. Given the expected utility-maximizing level of risk (12.2) we have

$$u^* = \alpha\Delta^* - \frac{1}{2}(\beta + \mu)(\Delta^*)^2 = \frac{\alpha^2}{2(\beta + \mu)}$$

then the certainly equivalent level of expected income is

$$y^c = u^* = \frac{\alpha^2}{2(\beta + \mu)}$$

> Note that, given a risk-free level of income $\hat{y} = y^c$ (so $\Delta = 0$), Anil's utility is
>
> $$u(y^c, 0) = y^c$$

4. There are two reasons why less than the expected income maximizing level of risk is selected. First, here the actor is risk averse, while the borrower was assumed to be risk neutral. Second, here the actor is residual claimant on the consequences of the risk level he selects, while due to the limited liability in the credit market, the downside of the borrower's risk choice (that is, the cost of failure) is shared with the lender. This is an uncompensated external effect of the borrowers risk choice that occurs as the result of the unintentional but also unavoidable de facto insurance that is extended to the borrower as part of the loan with an unenforceable repayment contract. (See also Section 11.2.)

12.2 Free tuition: Can it be fair to those who will not continue their education?

The funding of university education raises difficult economic and ethical questions. This problem uses a model of risky choices to explore some of the alternatives through the situation faced by Gloria, a prospective university student.

After completing her 2-year community college degree, Gloria is considering whether she should take a job she has been offered as a medical technician or instead go on to a 4-year college for 2 more years, get a B.A., and try her luck on the job market later. The job she has been offered will pay her 2, 3000 dollars annually with a possible extra 3, 000 dollars if she passes a qualification test 2 years later (she thinks she has a 50-50 chance of passing).

If she completes her B.A. she knows that her job prospects will improve but she is unsure about

> ► how good at doing university-level classwork she will be, and
> ► whether the major field of study she chooses will be in high demand or not if and when she graduates.

Taking these into account, she thinks that, if she decides to continue her education, she is equally likely to be offered a job for 71, 500 or 82, 500 dollars annually. Calling the former the "bad state" and the latter the "good state" then the risk she faces if she continues her studies — the difference Δ between the good state and the bad state — is 11, 000 dollars. By the same reasoning, the risk she faces if she does not continue is 3, 000 dollars.

These risks are not the only problem: there is also the cost. If she does not continue her education, she has 140, 000 dollars in savings that she can use to buy a Treasury bill that with no risk will earn her 5, 500 dollars a year.

The outcomes of the two options are presented in Table 12.1.

Table 12.1: The outcomes of the two options

	Living Style & Wealth	Income & Interest
Option 1	Less education + $140K saving	$23K + $5.5K (interest) + ($3K or 0)
Option 2	More education	$71.5K or $82.5K

For simplicity, assume that she is indifferent between living and working as a medical technician on the one hand and attending two additional years of education on the other, and between holding a B.A. degree per se and having 140, 000 dollars saving, regardless of the income or interest generated from them. In other words, she will only compare the last column in Table 12.1. Assume that Gloria values the possible outcomes that she may experience according to the utility function

$$u(\hat{y}, \Delta) = \hat{y}^{\alpha}(15 - \Delta)^{\beta} \tag{12.3}$$

where $\hat{y}$ is her expected income level (in thousand dollars, annually), $0 \le \Delta < 15$, and $\alpha, \beta \ge 0$.

1. What are the expected income levels and level of risk facing Gloria if she continues (use the superscript 1) and if she does not (superscript 0)?

2. Assuming that $\alpha = \beta = 1$, show that Gloria will not continue her education.

But many students and others are protesting the high cost of higher education and demand the elimination of tuition. Others oppose this idea as it would mean replacing the funds once paid by students and their families with tax revenues collected from the population. This would mean conferring advantages on the relatively better off — those completing higher education — at a tax cost of the less well-off average tax payer. An economist, seeking to resolve the dispute, points out that the government could through its tax system finance higher education in a fair way that would not discourage people like Gloria from continuing their education.

Here is the idea: eliminate tuition and then, for those who choose more higher education, impose a tax that (i) is sufficient to fund higher education now that no fees are collected, but (ii) the tax paid by each graduate is a given fraction of their income so that those who end with lower incomes — elementary school teachers, or poets, for example — pay much less than their education costs, while those who landed high paying jobs — in, say, real estate or finance — pay more than their education cost.

The plan might make pursuing more education an attractive option without imposing taxes on those not attending higher education to provide these advantages for others. It works because the tax system in this proposal is effectively providing insurance so that the bad state is not as bad as it would otherwise be.

3. What tax rate, denoted by τ^*, would the government set to ensure that the cost of education can be covered by the expected tax collected, assuming that people will work 10 years before retirement?

4. Given the tax rate τ^*, what are the expected income levels and level of risk facing Gloria if she continues (use the superscript τ)?

5. Will Gloria decide to continue her education or not, again assuming $\alpha = \beta = 1$? Assume that, under the new tax scheme, Gloria chooses not to invest her savings even if she does not continue her education.

Answers.

1. If she continues her education (shown by point B in Figure 12.2), the expected income level and level of risk facing Gloria are

$$\hat{y}^1 = \frac{1}{2}(82.5 + 71.5) = 77$$
$$\Delta^1 = 82.5 - 71.5 = 11$$

and if she does not (point A) , they become

$$\hat{y}^0 = 23 + 5.5 + \frac{1}{2} \cdot 3 = 30$$
$$\Delta^0 = 3$$

2. Given the utility function (12.3) and $\alpha = \beta = 1$, we have

$$u(\hat{y}^1, \Delta^1) = 77 \cdot (15 - 11) = 308$$
$$u(\hat{y}^0, \Delta^0) = 30 \cdot (15 - 3) = 360$$

therefore, Gloria will not continue her education, as shown in Figure 12.2.

Figure 12.2: The education choice with tuition. Given the utility function

$$u = \hat{y}^{\alpha}(15 - \Delta)^{\beta}$$

with $\alpha = \beta = 1$, the expected income level and risk facing Gloria if she does not continue her education, given by point A, is

$$A = (\Delta^0, \hat{y}^0) = (3, 30)$$

and that if she does, given by point B, is

$$B = (\Delta^1, \hat{y}^1) = (11, 77)$$

Gloria will not continue her education since

$$u^A = 360 > u^B = 308$$

With the tax $\tau^* = 2/11$, the expected income level and risk facing Gloria if she continues her education, given by point C, becomes

$$C = (\Delta^\tau, y^\tau) = (9, 63)$$

and thus

$$u^C = 378 > u^A = 360$$

In this case, Gloria will continue her education.

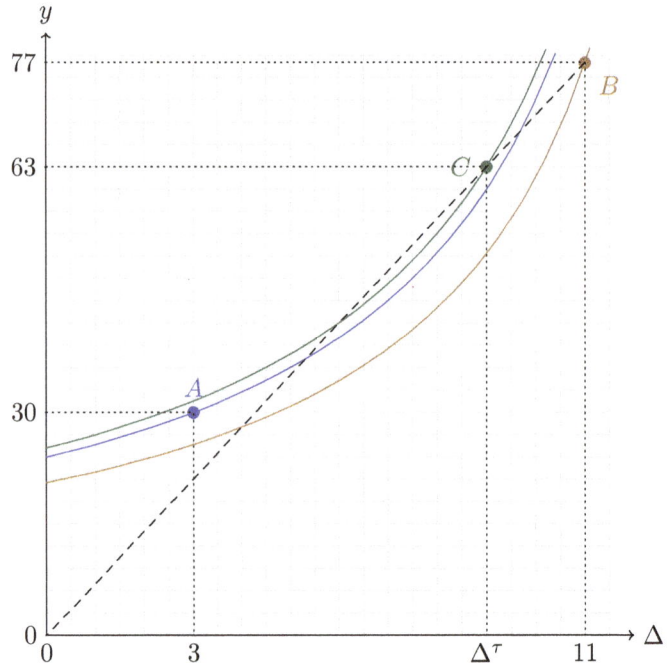

3. To understand the effect of the tax, notice that after-tax risk exposure and income are affected in the same way by the tax: both are reduced by the same factor:

$$\hat{y}^\tau = (1 - \tau)\hat{y}^1$$
$$\Delta^\tau = (1 - \tau)\Delta^1$$

This means that the combination of expected income and risk exposure that she will experience with the free tuition plus a graduates' tax program will lie on a ray from the origin through point B, with the distance toward the origin from B along this ray depending on the cost of education that the tax must cover.

With free tuition, the expected income before tax if Gloria continues her education is $\hat{y}^1 = 77$. Then the expected tax collected in ten years is given by

$$T = 10\hat{y}^1\tau = 770\tau$$

To ensure that the cost of education is covered by the expected tax collected, we have

$$T = 140 \Rightarrow \tau^* = \frac{140}{770} = \frac{2}{11}$$

4. Given $\tau^* = 2/11$, the expected income level after tax and level of risk facing Gloria if she continues are

$$\hat{y}^\tau = (1 - \tau)\hat{y}^1 = 63$$
$$\Delta^\tau = (1 - \tau)\Delta^1 = 9$$

as shown in Figure 12.2.

5. If Gloria does not continue her education, the utility is again

$$u(\hat{y}^0, \Delta^0) = 360$$

If she does, it becomes

$$u(\hat{y}^\tau, \Delta^\tau) = 63 \cdot (15 - 9) = 378 > u(\hat{y}^0, \Delta^0)$$

therefore, she will continue her education.

.

12.3 Is equality the enemy of innovation?

High marginal tax rates are said to reduce risk taking. But among the most innovative countries in the world are Sweden, Finland, Germany and Denmark,[1] all countries in which high marginal tax rates result in substantial egalitarian redistribution. The following model of risk and expected income will demonstrate that a linear tax and lump-sum transfer can decrease inequality and increase risk taking a) with constant absolute risk aversion and b) with decreasing absolute risk aversion.

Risk exposure — the income difference between the good state and the bad state, occurring with equal probability — is Δ.

A linear tax is levied on realized income, reducing both after-tax income and risk exposure by the factor $(1 - t)$. Average per person tax revenue is the tax rate times mean income, $t\bar{y}$, and this is distributed in equal lump sums to the entire population. We assume for simplicity that there is no "leaky bucket" problem (some tax revenue being used up in the process of distribution), so the person with mean before-tax expected income, $\bar{y}$, receives a lump-sum transfer equal to their expected tax payment so that their expected disposable income is unaffected. Therefore, for this individual whose after-tax disposable income is not affected by the tax and transfer, the after-tax expected income and risk exposure are

$$y^T = (1 - t)\bar{y} + t\bar{y} = \bar{y}$$
$$\Delta^T = (1 - t)\Delta$$

Suppose that for this person, the expected income before tax

$$\bar{y} = \alpha + \beta \ln(\Delta)$$

is increasing and concave in risk (Δ) over the relevant range.

An individual chooses a level of risk with expected total income (taking account of the tax and transfer) to maximize the utility

$$u(\bar{y}^T, \Delta^T) = \bar{y}^T - \frac{1}{2}(\Delta^T)^2$$

1. Find the marginal rate of substitution between risk and expected income. How does it change with constant risk and increasing expected income?

> **Decreasing absolute risk aversion**
>
> The tendency of a person to be less risk averse if they have more income (or wealth).

1: See the Bloomberg's index, for 2022, here.

The idea here is not new, see, e.g. Domar and Musgrave [47].

[47]: Domar and Musgrave (1944), 'Proportional Income Taxation and Risk-Taking'

> **Linear tax and lump-sum transfer**
>
> A tax that is proportional to income (a linear tax), the proceeds of which are divided equally and transferred to citizens (a lump sum).

2. What is the marginal rate of transformation of experienced risk into after-tax income? Is it unaffected by the level of the tax?

3. Show that the linear tax and lump-sum transfer can increase risk taking.

Suppose that the individual utility function exhibits decreasing absolute risk aversion, i.e., the marginal rate of substitution between risk and income (the indifference curve slope) declines with an increase in $\bar{y}^T$ given Δ^T.

4. Does the above demonstration hold for (poorer) individuals whose disposable income is increased by the tax and transfer?

5. How about those whose disposable income falls as a result of the tax and transfer?

Answers.

1. The marginal rate of substitution between risk and expected income is
$$MRS = -\frac{u_{\Delta^T}}{u_{\bar{y}^T}} = \Delta^T$$

which remains constant with constant risk and increasing expected income. That is, the utility function exhibits a constant absolute risk aversion (CARA).

2. The marginal rate of transformation of experienced risk into after-tax income is
$$MRT = \frac{d\bar{y}^T}{d\Delta^T} = \frac{d\bar{y}^T}{d\Delta} \cdot \frac{d\Delta}{d\Delta^T} = (1-t)\frac{d\bar{y}}{d\Delta} \cdot \frac{1}{(1-t)} = \frac{d\bar{y}}{d\Delta} = \frac{\beta}{\Delta}$$

which is unaffected by the level of tax t, as shown in Figure 12.3.

3. The utility function can be written as
$$u = (1-t)\bar{y} + t\bar{y} - \frac{1}{2}(1-t)^2\Delta^2 = \bar{y}(\Delta) - \frac{1}{2}(1-t)^2\Delta^2$$

The first order condition of the utility maximization problem is

$$u_\Delta = \frac{\beta}{\Delta} - (1-t)\Delta = 0 \Rightarrow \Delta = \left(\frac{\beta}{1-t}\right)^{1/2} \tag{12.4}$$

which can also be derived by setting $MRS = MRT$, i.e., $\Delta^T = (1-t)\Delta = \beta/\Delta$. Then we have

$$\frac{d\Delta}{dt} > 0$$

so a higher tax rate incentivizes risk taking.

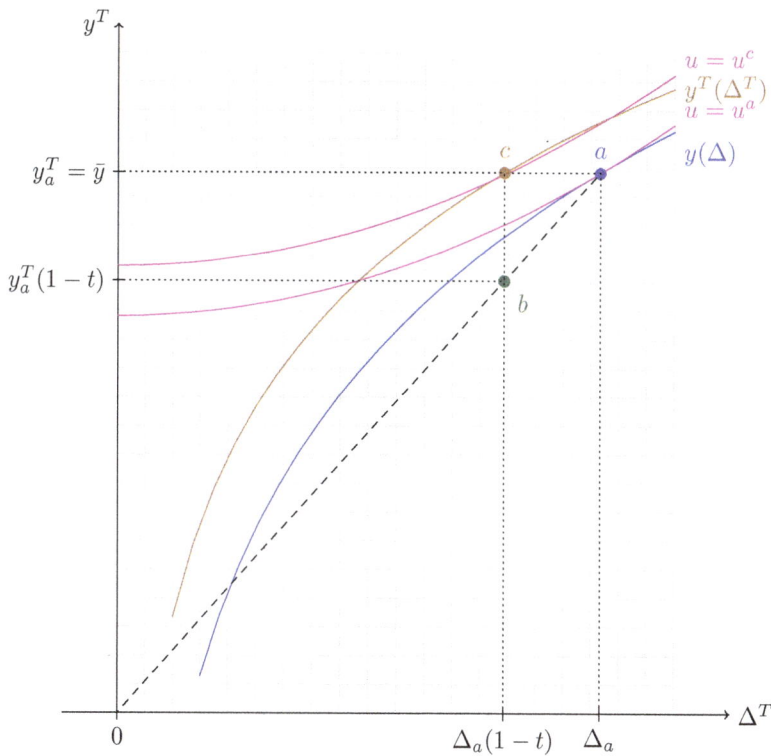

Figure 12.3: Taxation and risk taking.
Given the risk return schedule without tax

$$\bar{y}(\Delta) = \alpha + \beta \ln(\Delta)$$

and the utility function

$$u = \bar{y}^T - \frac{1}{2}(\Delta^T)^2$$

the individual will maximize their utility at point a, which is the tangency between the indifference curve $u = u^a$ and the risk return schedule. Because the tax proportionally reduces both expected after-tax-before-transfer income and risk exposure, the implementable levels of both $y^T(1-t)$ and $\Delta(1-t)$ are given by the dashed ray from the origin through a, points closer to the origin representing higher tax rates. Suppose that the tax implemented is that illustrated by point b, at which the individual having selected risk level Δ_a now experiences a reduced risk level $\Delta_a(1-t)$. Assume that the person in this figure is the mean income person such that $y_a^T = \bar{y}$. The lump-sum transfer restores expected income to the before-tax level, shown by point c, with the associated risk return schedule $y^T(\Delta^T)$. Since

$$MRT_a = MRT_c$$

the slope of the after-tax-before-transfer risk return schedule associated with the choice of risk level Δ_a is invariant in the tax rate.

4. Yes. With decreasing absolute risk aversion the demonstration holds a fortiori for (poorer) individuals whose disposable income is increased by the tax and transfer: for them, experienced risk aversion (the slope of the indifference curve) will be reduced not only due to mitigated risk exposure, but also to declining absolute risk aversion along with their increase in disposable income.

5. No. For those whose disposable income falls as a result of the tax and transfer, there will be some level of income (above the mean) such that the increased absolute risk aversion associated with their reduction in income more than offsets the reduction in risk exposure, so an individual at that income level would choose some level of risk less than before.

Inequality: Institutions, Market Structure, and Policy | 13

In this chapter, we consider policies to affect the distribution of income or wealth using the models introduced in the previous chapters and extending them to apply to an entire national economy.

The principal-agent model of the labor market and the firm along with a model of the process of competition in product markets provide a model of aggregate employment, unemployment, the real wage, and the profit share. This information can then be used to derive a Lorenz curve for income in the economy (along with the Gini coefficient).

The model identifies a set of parameters that can be the target of policy interventions — the degree of competition in product markets, the productivity of labor, the unemployment benefit, the disutility of the worker providing effort up to the standard set by the employer, and the ease of detecting and firing a worker who fails to do so (shirks).

The equilibrium of what we call the "whole economy model" provides a set of outcomes towards which the realized state of the economy would tend in the long run given the structural characteristics we have built into the model. These include the conflict among firm owners for market shares and profits and between the owners and their employees over real wages and on the job effort.

Though it represents the entire economy, we do not call it a macroeconomic model, because that term would suggest an analysis of aggregate demand in the spirit of Keynes. Exogenous fluctuations in aggregate demand could be represented as displacements from the structural equilibrium that would either be temporary or might lead to changes in the underlying structure, altering the long-run equilibrium of the model.

Nor do we call it a general equilibrium model, as that would suggest an interest in relative prices in the spirit of Arrow and Debreu in a setting in which (as Arrow stressed) the distribution of income is determined exogenously, that is, by the distribution of initial endowments. The only relative price in our model is the real wage (nominal wage relative to the price of the single product). Because the model takes account of the interplay of both labor and product markets, we could call it general equilibrium for economists more interested in income distribution than relative prices.

The original ideas in the model are closest to the analysis of varying degrees of competition in markets with homogeneous goods of Augustin Cournot, and the models of the multi-dimensional conflicts between workers and their employers of Michal Kalecki and how these make it difficult to eliminate structural unemployment.

Some background for the problems in this chapter is found in Chapters 11 and 15 (and especially sections 11.10 and 11.11) of Bowles and Halliday [29]. This work is available as a free pdf from the authors' webpages.

The whole economy model developed there is based on two equations:

Figure 13.1: Antoine Augustin Cournot (1801–1877), developed the first mathematical models of the process of competition among firms ranging from two (duopoly), to a few (oligopoly), to many. He studied mathematics as an undergraduate and later received advanced degrees in the fields of astronomy, mechanics, and law. He is credited with having had a hand in persuading Léon Walras — a founder of the school of neoclassical economics — to take up the subject. Wikimedia Commons, public domain, https://commons.wikimedia.org/wiki/File:Antoine_Augustin_Cournot.jpg

[29]: Bowles and Halliday (2022), *Microeconomics*

©2025 Samuel Bowles and Weikai Chen, CC BY-NC 4.0

https://doi.org/10.11647/OBP.0466.13

▶ an economy-wide adaptation of the no-shirking condition, called the *wage curve*, to represent the conditions under which employees will supply effort to the production process; and

▶ what we call the *competition condition*, that gives the real wage that results from the degree of price markup over the cost of production consistent with the degree of competition among sellers in product markets.

To apply the no-shirking wage (modeled for a single firm in Section 10.7) to an entire economy, we borrow from our modeling of the monopsonist employer in a local labor market (Section 13.6), whose average cost of hiring an hour of (non-shirking) labor was increasing in the level of hiring. Following that logic, we use the unemployment rate in the economy as a whole to endogenize j, the probability of remaining unemployed if fired. We use the following notation: H is the fraction of the labor force that is employed, we let

$$j = j(H) = 1 - H$$

and use the no-shirking wage equation (from Section 11.10 of Bowles and Halliday [29]) with the following notation: B is the unemployment benefit (a lump sum), w^N is the no-shirking wage, t is the probability that a shirking worker will be detected and fired, and $\underline{u}$ is the disutility to the worker of supplying the required level of effort. The no-shirking wage is:

$$w^N = B + \underline{u} + \frac{1-t}{t(1-H)}\underline{u}$$

This is called the *wage curve* (see Figure 13.3).

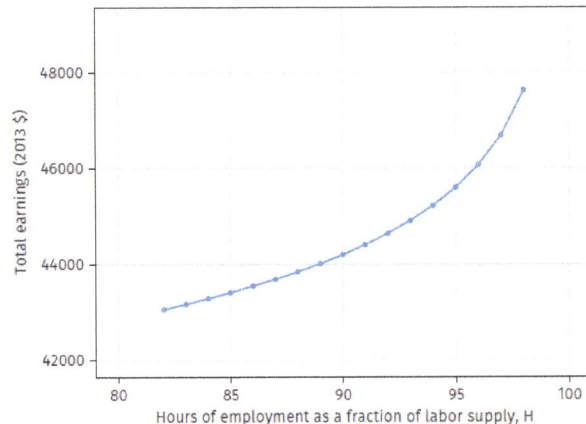

Figure 13.2: Michal Kalecki (1899–1970), initially trained as an engineer, was a Polish macroeconomist whose writings anticipated the later work of Keynes. He was distinctive, however, in the central role that class conflict between owners and workers plays in his models. In his book *The Political Aspects of Full Employment*, he showed that even if the elimination of unemployment were possible due to government spending, it would not be sustainable. He reasoned that owners of firms would oppose full employment because it would lead to a reduction of their political power vis-à-vis their employees and squeeze their profits. His theory of income distribution was based on the market power of owners of firms as sellers of the goods that workers as consumers would purchase. Album via Alamy

[29]: Bowles and Halliday (2022), *Microeconomics*

Figure 13.3: The wage curve. The sample of 2.34 million workers are males aged 26–64 over the years 1979–2013. Earnings are in 2013 dollars. Source: *CORE. The Economy.*

The real wage consistent with the competition condition, w^c, implements a price markup over cost and an expected rate of economic profits such that (given the opportunity cost of capital) there is no net entry or exit of firms from the market, given the level of barriers to entry (defined as the probability b that a firm attempting entry will fail). Section 13.4 below develops an explicit expression of the competition condition, showing that the real wage consistent with the competition condition will be higher:

▶ the more competitive the economy is, that is, the lesser are the barriers to entry (b);

▶ the greater is the productivity of labor (γ); and

▶ the lower is the opportunity cost of capital (ρ).

Economic profits

Economic profit is revenues minus costs including the opportunity cost of capital goods used in production.

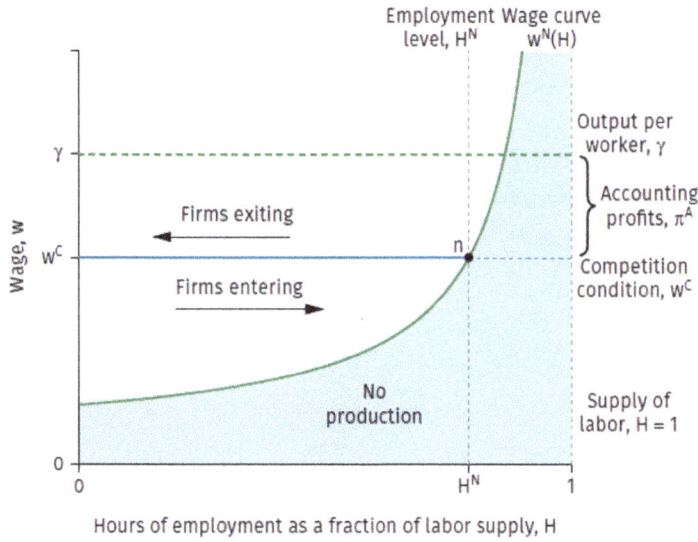

Figure 13.4: Equilibrium in the product and labor markets of the whole economy. This figure shows the wage curve and the competition condition, the two equations making up the whole economy model. If you are unfamiliar with this model, you might want to read sections 11.10 and 11.11 of Bowles and Halliday [29].

If there are no barriers to entry — unlimited competition — this equation becomes a zero (economic) profit condition.

[29]: Bowles and Halliday (2022), *Microeconomics*

Here we begin with a set of problems on the Gini coefficient as a measure of inequality; working these problems will clarify how the nature of property rights and contracts affects the degree of inequality of continuously varying measures like wealth and income.

13.1 A summary of economic differences among people: The Gini coefficient

The Gini coefficient is a measure of inequality of some quantity (e.g. income or wealth), defined as one-half the mean absolute difference in that quantity between all unique pairs of individuals in a population, relative to the average value of the quantity. For example, consider a distribution of a total income of 15 among the population of three household as given in Figure 13.5. Then the Gini coefficient is

Gini coefficient

The Gini coefficient is a measure of inequality of some quantity (e.g. income or wealth), defined as one-half the mean absolute difference in that quantity between all unique pairs of individuals in a population relative to the average value of the quantity. It takes the value of 1 if a single person owns all of the wealth, and a value of zero if wealth is equally distributed.

$$g = \frac{1}{2}\left(\frac{7+8+1}{3}\right) \Big/ \left(\frac{10+2+3}{3}\right) = \frac{8}{15} \approx 0.53$$

1. For the case illustrated in Figure 13.5, consider the following two extreme cases and find the Gini coefficients: (i) the richest household has all of the income; and (ii) the total income is equally shared among all of the three households.

2. Suppose that there is a total wealth of Y, which is evenly split among the r members of the total population of $n > r$. The rest of the population have no wealth. For this population:

   a) Write down an expression g in terms of n and r. (Hint: To answer the questions below it may help to recall that the

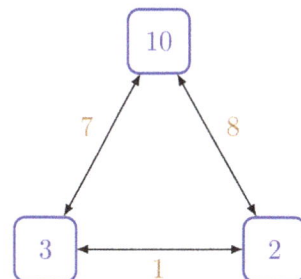

Figure 13.5: Income distribution among three households (I). Each node represents a household with their income levels indicated by the number inside the nodes. Each edge represents a comparison of the incomes of the two households. On each edge is the absolute difference in income between the pair being compared.

total number of edges in a complete graph with n nodes is $n(n-1)/2$.)

b) Show that for $r > 1$, g increases as the number of members in class without wealth increases (holding constant the size of the wealthy class).

Suppose that $n = 2r$, so half of the population is rich and half is without wealth, and define δ as the fraction of all pairs in which the two have different levels of wealth. Show that for this population:

c) $\delta = g$, meaning that the Gini coefficient equals the fraction of all pairs in the population for which wealth differs; and

d) $g \to 0.5$ when the population is large, i.e., $r \to \infty$.

Background on the Gini coefficient (including some ideas about how to approach the problems below) can be found in Bowles and Carlin [19] and Bowles and Carlin [16].

[19]: Bowles and Carlin (2023), 'Axioms and Intuitions about Societal Inequality'

[16]: Bowles and Carlin (2020), 'Inequality as Experienced Difference'

Answers.

1. The income distribution in the two cases is presented in Figure 13.6a and Figure 13.6b. The Gini coefficient when the richest household has all the income is

$$g = \frac{1}{2}\left(\frac{15+15+0}{3}\right) \Big/ \left(\frac{15+0+0}{3}\right) = 1$$

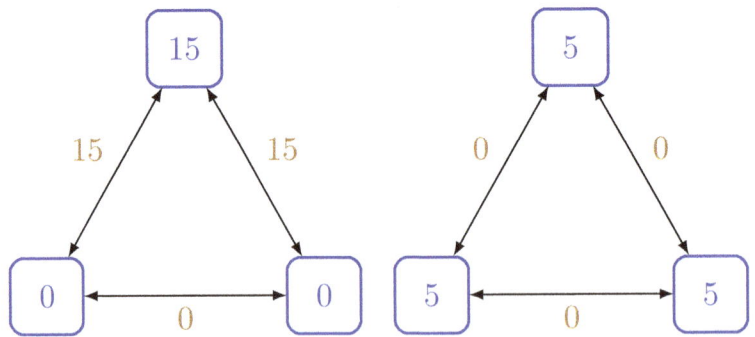

Figure 13.6: Income distribution among three households (II).

(a) The richest household has all the income 15 while the rest 0.

(b) The total income is equally shared among the three households.

When the total income is equally shared, it becomes

$$g = \frac{1}{2}\left(\frac{0+0+0}{3}\right) \Big/ \left(\frac{5+5+5}{3}\right) = 0$$

2. a) The number of unique pairs in a population of size n is

$$T = \frac{n(n-1)}{2}$$

Note that the only unequal pairs in the population are the r wealth holders interacting with the $n - r$ wealthless individuals, with both members of the pair experiencing a wealth difference of Y/r. By definition,

$$g = \frac{1}{2}\left(\frac{\frac{Y}{r} \cdot (n - r)r + 0}{T}\right) \bigg/ \left(\frac{Y}{n}\right) = \frac{n - r}{n - 1}$$

b) Since

$$\frac{dg}{dn} = \frac{(n - 1) - (n - r)}{(n - 1)^2} = \frac{r - 1}{(n - 1)^2} > 0, \quad \forall r > 1$$

we have that g is increasing in n holding r constant.

c) Given $n = 2r$, we have

$$g = \frac{2r - r}{2r - 1} = \frac{r}{2r - 1}$$

Note that, of all the $(2r - 1)r$ unique pairs in this population, there are r^2 pairs that are between a wealth-holding individual and an individual with no wealth, and therefore

$$\delta = \frac{r^2}{(2r - 1)r} = \frac{r}{2r - 1} = g$$

This result is illustrated in Figure 13.7.

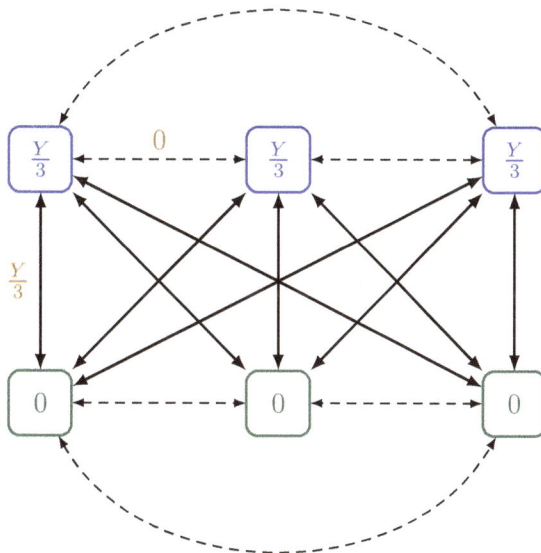

Figure 13.7: **Wealth distribution in the an economy of "haves" and "have nots."** The population consists of two classes with equal size $r = 3$. The blue nodes represent the individual in the rich class with equal share of wealth within the group. The green nodes represent the poor class with no wealth. Each edge represents a comparison of the incomes of the two persons. The dashed edge means that the difference in wealth is zero. There are $r^2 = 9$ solid edges with positive wealth differences. In this case, the Gini coefficient is

$$g = \frac{1}{2}\left(\frac{\frac{Y}{3} \cdot 9}{15}\right) \bigg/ \left(\frac{Y}{6}\right) = 0.6$$

which equals the number of solid edges as a fraction of all edges.

It is quite intuitive to imagine the two extreme cases in which $g = 1$ and $g = 0$ respectively, but it may not be easy to think of what an economy with $g = 0.5$ would be like. The case of an economy with a class of owners and those without property here gives us an example.

d) Note that

$$g = \frac{r}{2r - 1} = \frac{1}{2 - 1/r} \rightarrow \frac{1}{2} \text{ as } r \rightarrow \infty$$

the Gini coefficient is close to 0.5 when the population is large. This gives one example of a case intermediate between $g = 1$

(one person has all of the wealth) and $g = 0$ (wealth is equally distributed).

13.2 Inequality and average income

Inequality with coerced labor: A benchmark case. Suppose that a single person owns many units of land, one of which they cultivate themselves, and, further, that they are able to require (through physical threats, at no cost to themself) the three farmers who cultivate their other plots to provide a level of effort $e = 1$, the same as they devote to their own unit of land. Output resulting from cultivation is proportional to effort, with $e = 1$ producing one unit of output. The landowner provides an amount s to each of his workforce for their subsistence, so, as a result, the landowner receives an surplus of $1 - s$ from each of the workers.

1. Draw a figure similar to Figure 13.5 for this case and calculate the Gini coefficient.

2. Now suppose the landowner can engage another worker on the same terms. Calculate the new Gini coefficient.

3. Show that for this case, the Gini coefficient is independent of the number of coerced workers engaged by the landowner and explain why this is so.

Inequality in a sharecropping economy. Consider a case of sharecropping as in the previous set of questions, except the landowner may no longer coerce the sharecroppers into providing $e = 1$. The landowner owns all of the land and farms one unit of the land themselves, while making the other units available to three sharecroppers for cultivation in return for the landlord receiving a share $1 - s$ of the crop. (The sharecropper's share of the crop they produce is s.) Remembering that the level of output is equal to the amount of effort devoted to cultivation, where E and e are the amount of effort the landowner and the sharecropper allocates to cultivating their crops, respectively. The utility function of the landowner is

$$U = E + 3(1 - s)e - \frac{1}{2}E^2$$

and the utility function of the sharecropper is

$$u = se - \frac{1}{2}e^2$$

4. Show that the landlord will set $E = 1$. What is the effort level that the farmers will select, given s?

5. Based on the income of the four people, draw a figure representing the income distribution for the case where $s = 1/2$ and calculate the Gini coefficient.

6. Draw a figure representing the income distribution, but (assuming that utility like income is comparable across individuals) calculate the Gini coefficient in terms of individuals' *utility* instead of income. How does it compare to the Gini coefficient in terms of income?

The relationship between inequality and average income. Continuing with the sharecropping economy with share *s* and the Gini coefficient in terms of income above:

7. Find the landlord's income (as a function of *s*). What is the value of *s* that maximizes the landowner's income? Why is the landlord's income not monotonically decreasing in *s*?

8. Calculate the average income. Why is it increasing in *s*?

9. Calculate the Gini coefficient, and discuss the relationship between inequality and average income.

Answers.

1. In this arrangement, the landowner's income is the sum of output from his own cultivation (which is 1, given that he devotes $E = 1$) and an amount $1 - s$ from each of the 3 workers, i.e., $4 - 3s$, while each worker receives income s. The income distribution is represented in Figure 13.8. The difference between the landowner and any of the workers is

$$(4 - 3s) - s = 4(1 - s)$$

and since the workers receive the same income, the difference between any pair of them is just 0. There are a total of 6 unique pairs. Hence, the Gini coefficient is

$$g = \frac{1}{2}\left(\frac{4(1 - s) \cdot 3}{6}\right) \Big/ \left(\frac{3s + (4 - 3s)}{4}\right) = 1 - s$$

This is another case in which a redistribution of wealth to the less wealthy prospective borrowers could increase total output, contrary to the idea that egalitarian programs come at a cost of reduced average incomes. The opposite of this putative "efficiency-equality trade-off" is often the case when one takes account of the incomplete nature of contracts: an egalitarian redistribution of wealth, for example, can transform employees or sharecroppers into landowners working their own land and residual claimants on their choices about how hard to work, implementing efficient allocations.

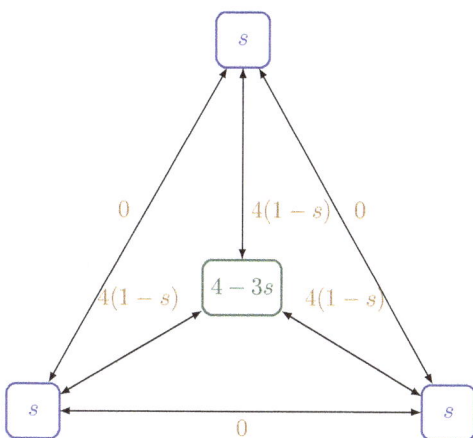

Figure 13.8: The income distribution in the economy with coerced labor. The green node at the center represents the landowner, and the blue ones the workers. The number along the edge is the absolute difference in income between the individuals.

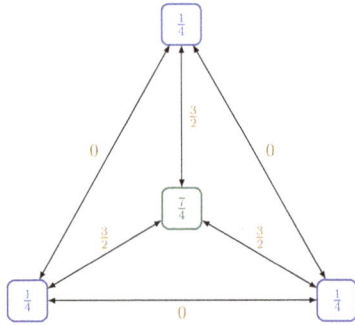

Figure 13.9: The income distribution in the sharecropping economy. The green node represents the landowner, and blue ones represent the sharecroppers. The number along the edge is the absolute difference in income between the two individuals.

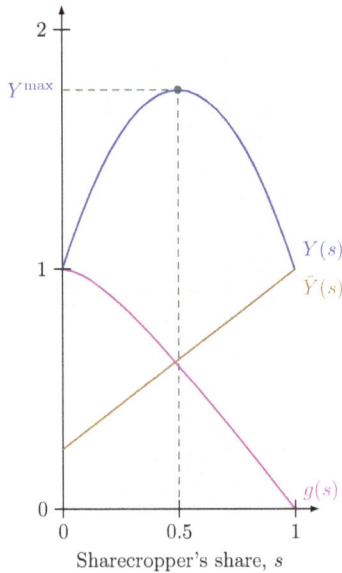

Sharecropper's share, s

Figure 13.10: The landowner's income, average income and Gini coefficient as functions of the share. The landowner's income

$$Y(s) = 1 + 3(1 - s)s$$

achieves its maximum at $s = 0.5$. The average income

$$\bar{Y}(s) = \frac{1 + 3s}{4}$$

is increasing in s, while the Gini coefficient for income

$$g(s) = \frac{(1 - s)(1 + 4s)}{1 + 3s}$$

is decreasing in s.

2. Suppose the landowner engages another worker on the same terms. This adds four additional pairs (the new worker compared with the landowner and three other workers) into our calculation of the Gini coefficient. The income of the landowner becomes $5 - 4s$ due to the additional amount $1 - s$ from the new worker, and landowner-worker difference becomes $(5 - 4s) - s = 5(1 - s)$. Hence, the Gini coefficient becomes

$$g = \frac{1}{2}\left(\frac{5(1 - s)\cdot 4}{10}\right) \Big/ \left(\frac{4s + (5 - 4s)}{4}\right) = 1 - s$$

3. To show that the Gini coefficient is independent of the number of coerced workers engaged by the landowner, let $n - 1$ be the total number of coerced workers engaged, and, thus, there are a total of n individuals including the landowner. Then the landowner's income is $n - (n-1)s$. The landowner-worker difference is $n - (n-1)s - s = n(1 - s)$. There are $n - 1$ such pairs between the landowner and the coerced workers. Note that the total number of edges in a graph with n nodes is $n(n - 1)/2$, which is the total number of unique pairs between n individuals. Since the workers have the same income, the differences in income among them are all 0. Therefore, the Gini coefficient is

$$g = \frac{1}{2}\left(\frac{n(1 - s)\cdot(n - 1)}{n(n - 1)/2}\right) \Big/ \left(\frac{(n - 1)s + [n - (n - 1)s]}{n}\right) = 1 - s$$

4. For the landowner, the first order condition of E to maximize U is

$$U_E = 1 - E = 0 \Rightarrow E = 1 \tag{13.1}$$

For the sharecropper the first order condition of e to maximize u is

$$u_e = s - e = 0 \Rightarrow e = s \tag{13.2}$$

5. Given $s = 1/2$, the sharecropper would choose $e = s = 1/2$ and receive an income of $1/2 \cdot 1/2 = 1/4$, and the landowner, who selects $E = 1$, would receive an income of $1 + 3 \cdot 1/2 \cdot 1/2 = 7/4$. The difference in income between the landowner and each sharecropper is $7/4 - 1/4 = 3/2$. Landowner's and sharecropper' income and the differences between all unique pairs are represented in Figure 13.9. The Gini coefficient for income is

$$g_i = \frac{1}{2}\left(\frac{3/2\cdot 3}{6}\right) \Big/ \left(\frac{1/4 \cdot 3 + 7/4}{4}\right) = \frac{3}{5}$$

6. Given $s = 1/2$, $E = 1$ and $e = 1/2$, the utility of the landowner is

$$U = 1 + 3 \cdot \frac{1}{2} \cdot \frac{1}{2} - \frac{1}{2} = \frac{7}{4} - \frac{1}{2} = \frac{5}{4}$$

and the utility of the sharecropper is

$$u = \frac{1}{2} \cdot \frac{1}{2} - \frac{1}{2} \cdot \frac{1}{4} = \frac{1}{8}$$

The difference in utility between the landowner and each share-cropper is $5/4 - 1/8 = 9/8$. Hence, the Gini coefficient in terms of utility is

$$g_u = \frac{1}{2}\left(\frac{9/8 \cdot 3}{6}\right) \bigg/ \left(\frac{1/8 \cdot 3 + 5/4}{4}\right) = \frac{9}{13} > \frac{9}{15} = \frac{3}{5} = G_i$$

The distribution of income is more equal than the distribution of utility.

7. From equations (13.1) and (13.2), we have $E = 1$ and $e = s$ and thus the income of the landowner is

$$Y(s) = E + 3(1-s)e = 1 + 3(1-s)s$$

which achieves its maximum at $s^* = 0.5$ as shown in Figure 13.10. The landowner's income is not monotonically decreasing in s because the increase in landowner's income from taking a greater share of the sharecropper's output is outweighed by the decrease in sharecroppers' output as a result of the sharecropper choosing a lower level of effort when maximizing their utility.

8. Given $e = s$, the income of the sharecropper is

$$y = se = s^2$$

and thus the average income is

$$\bar{Y}(s) = \frac{Y + 3y}{4} = \frac{1 + 3s(1-s) + 3s^2}{4} = \frac{1 + 3s}{4}$$

which is increasing in s because the total output from the three sharecroppers $3s$ is increasing in s, which is due to the effort level that each sharecropper selects to maximize their utility increases in s, as shown in Figure 13.10.

9. The Gini coefficient is

$$g(s) = \frac{1}{2}\left(\frac{3(Y-y)}{6}\right) \bigg/ \bar{Y} = \frac{(1-s)(1+4s)}{1+3s}$$

which is decreasing in s for $s \in [0, 1]$, as shown in Figure 13.10. It follows that the average income is decreasing in the Gini coefficient, as shown in Figure 13.11.

Where contracts are incomplete — in this case, there being no enforceable contractual specification of the level of effort provided by the less well-off members of the population — the "big trade-off" between economic efficiency and equality disappears, and is replaced by the possibility of egalitarian redistributions of income that increase average income, as illustrated by this question. See also Section 11.3 in which you are asked to design a *Pareto-improving egalitarian redistribution of wealth*.

Note that

$$g'(s) = -\frac{4s(2+3s)}{(1+3s)^2} < 0$$

for $s < 1$ and thus $g(s)$ is decreasing in s.

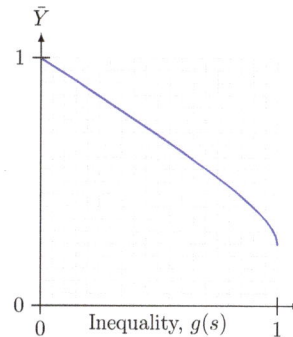

Figure 13.11: The relationship between inequality and average income. Given the average income

$$\bar{Y}(s) = \frac{1+3s}{4}$$

and the Gini coefficient

$$g(s) = \frac{(1-s)(1+4s)}{1+3s}$$

this figure shows the graph of the average income as a decreasing function of Gini coefficient.

13.3 Network structure, bargaining, and inequality

[10]: Borgerhoff Mulder, Bowles, et al. (2009), 'Intergenerational Wealth Transmission and the Dynamics of Inequality in Small-Scale Societies'
[23]: Bowles and Fochesato (2024), 'The Origins of Enduring Economic Inequality'

Prior to the development of farming (producing food rather than hunting or gathering it) 11 thousand years ago, most early human societies were strikingly egalitarian, with limited differences in wealth, at least by comparison to modern levels of inequality [10, 23]. Is it possible that part of the explanation of their more equal societies could be based on the fact that the network structures of hunters and gatherers differed from the network structures of farming (and later industrial) societies?

Suppose that n people can participate in a mutual assistance social network G. Members of the network benefit from the links they have to other members and, typically, a direct link is more valuable than an indirect one, and the further the indirect link is, the less value it is for the member.

For network-based models, see the discussion on collective action in an Indian village (Palanpur) in Section 2.4 and segregation in Section 2.5. An excellent text on networks is Jackson [64].

Let $N_i(k)$ be the set of members that are at distance k from i, meaning the shortest path between i and any person in the set $N_i(k)$ is exactly k. Denote the number of elements in $N_i(k)$ by $n_i(k)$, which is the number of links with distance k. Let $\delta \in (0, 1)$ be the rate of decay such that the value of one indirect link with distance k is equivalent to a fraction δ^{k-1} of the value of a direct link.

[64]: Jackson (2008), *Social and Economic Networks*

The parameter δ is exogenously determined by social and ecological conditions. For example, if the goods transacted in the economic network are perishable or the services exchanged required face-to-face interaction, then indirect links are less valuable and δ is small, indicating rapid decay for more distant links. Define the total number of links weighted by distances by

$$q_i(\delta) = \sum_{k=1}^{\infty} \delta^{k-1} n_i(k)$$

For each person i, the benefit of the economic network is a increasing function of q_i. But maintaining a direct link costs the person something, such as time spent together or the duty to help others. Taking both the benefits and costs into account, we can define the value of the network to a member i over some given period of time as

$$v_i(G) = f(q_i(\delta)) - cd_i \qquad (13.3)$$

where f is a increasing function with $f(0) = 0$, $d_i = n_i(1)$ is the degree of node i (the number of direct links), and c is the cost of maintaining a direct link over the same period of time. The value to a person who is not in the network (a singleton) is zero, a fact that will become relevant once we introduce bargaining over the distribution of income on the network.

Pairwise stable network

A *pairwise stable* network is a stationary state of the given network formation process, which means that no member would be better off by cutting any existing link, nor would both members of any pair of members benefit from forming a new link.

Star

A *star* over n nodes is a network where one node is connected to all other $n - 1$ nodes, which are not connected among themselves.

Consider the following rules of network formation: any pair of members can form a link if both agree, and any member can sever its link unilaterally.

A *pairwise stable* network is a stationary state of the given network formation process, which means that no member would be better off by cutting any existing link, nor would both members of any pair of members benefit from forming a new link. We consider a concrete case in which $n = 4$ and $f = q^2$.

1. Suppose that, in a society of hunters and gatherers, the food (meat) that is shared among the network is perishable (and movement of the food from node to node is slow). The value of indirect links is therefore low, with $\delta_h = 0.2$. In contrast, in an agricultural society, food (cereals) can be stored for a longer time, making indirect links more valuable with $\delta_a = 0.8$. Assume the cost of maintaining a direct link $c = 2$ in both societies. Show that a complete network is pairwise stable in the society of hunters and gatherers, and the *star* is pairwise stable in the agricultural society. Which one is more unequal given the value function in (13.3)?

2. Under what conditions of δ and c is complete network pairwise stable? When is the star network pairwise stable?

3. Can both the complete network and star be (strictly) pairwise stable for the same parameter (δ, c)?

Anthropological evidence shows the co-existence of both dense, nearly complete networks and star-like networks in some herding societies [9].

4. Assume that $c = 2.5$ and $\delta = 0.5$ from here onward. Suppose that the central node in a star, acting as an essential intermediary, has some bargaining power, as they can commit to a take-it-or-leave-it offer to the peripheral nodes, asking for a transfer from each of them in exchange for not severing their link. Peripheral nodes can either accept the transfer demand, receiving the value given by (13.3) minus the transfer, or refuse the offer, receiving zero (the value of not being in the network after severing the link). What is the largest transfer that the central node can ask from the peripheral nodes? Provide the resulting distribution of value received by each node and give the Gini coefficient (see Section 13.1) representing the degree of inequality in this population.

[9]: Bollig (2006), *Risk Management in a Hazardous Environment*

5. Suppose a member in the complete network has take-it-or-leave-it power similar to the center of the star above. Determine the largest transfer this member can demand, give the incomes of the members of the network and the associated Gini coefficient, and compare the resulting distribution of values with your answer to the previous question.

Answers.

1.   a) In the society of hunters and gatherers, the value of the complete network to any member is

$$f(n-1) - c(n-1) = 9 - 6 = 3$$

If one member were to cut a link with another member, the value of the remaining network to that member, as shown in Figure 13.12, is

$$f((n-2) + \delta_h) - c(n-2) = (2 + 0.2)^2 - 4 = 0.84$$

which is smaller than the value of the complete network. Therefore, there is no incentive for any member to cut any existing link and thus the complete network is pairwise stable.

Figure 13.12: The complete network and the remaining network after cutting one link. Each agent, such as the orange node labeled 2 in the complete network on the left, has three direct connections, so $q_2 = 3$ and $d_2 = 3$. If agent 2 cuts the connection with agent 3 (the edge highlighted in green), the resulting network is shown on the right. In this new network, agent 2 has 2 direct connections (with agents 1 and 4) and 1 indirect connection to agent 3 at a distance of $k = 2$, so $q_2 = 2 + \delta$ and $d_2 = 2$.

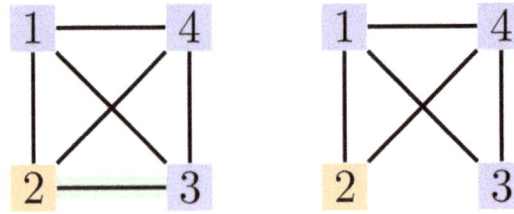

b) In the agricultural society, the central member has no incentive to cut any link with a peripheral node since

$$f(3) - 3c = 3 > f(2) - 2c = 0$$

For the peripheral nodes, they have no incentive to cut the link with the center since

$$f(1 + 2\delta_a) - c = (1 + 1.6)^2 - 2 = 4.67 > f(0) = 0$$

nor to form a new link since

$$f(1 + 2\delta_a) - c = 4.67 > f(2 + \delta_a) - 2c = (2 + 0.8)^2 - 4 = 3.84$$

Therefore, the star network is pairwise stable in the agricultural society.

c) All the members in a complete network receive the same value, while in a star network with n nodes there are going to be $n - 1$ unequal pairs, each composed by the central node and a peripheral node. Therefore, the star in the agricultural society is more unequal than the egalitarian complete network in the society of hunters and gatherers.

2. For the complete network to be pairwise stable, no one should be better off by cutting any links:

$$f(3) - 3c > f(2 + \delta) - 2c \Rightarrow c \leq 9 - (2 + \delta)^2$$

For a star network to be pairwise stable, the following conditions must be met:

a) The center has no incentive to cut any link:

$$f(3) - 3c \geq f(2) - 2c \Rightarrow c \leq 5$$

b) The peripheral nodes have no incentive to cut the link with the center:

$$f(1 + 2\delta) - c \geq 0 \Rightarrow c \leq (1 + 2\delta)^2$$

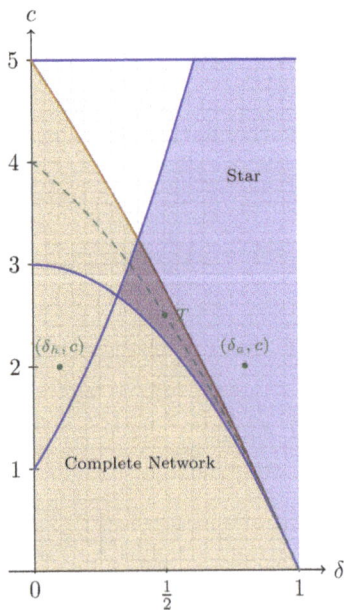

Figure 13.13: The conditions of stable network. The orange shaded region represents the combinations of decay rate δ and cost c for which the complete network is pairwise stable

$$c \leq 9 - (2 + \delta)^2$$

while the blue shaded region represents those for which the star network is pairwise stable

$$3(1 - \delta^2) \leq c \leq \min\{5, (1 + 2\delta)^2\}$$

The overlap indicates the combinations for which both the complete network and the star network are pairwise stable.

c) The peripheral nodes have no incentive to form a new link:

$$f(1 + 2\delta) - c \geq f(2 + \delta) - 2c \Rightarrow c \geq 3(1 - \delta^2)$$

Therefore, star is pairwise stable if and only if

$$3(1 - \delta^2) \leq c \leq \min\{5, (1 + 2\delta)^2\}$$

as shown in Figure 13.13.

3. Yes, both the complete network and the star network are pairwise stable if

$$3(1 - \delta^2) \leq c \leq \min\{9 - (2 + \delta)^2, (1 + 2\delta)^2\}$$

as shown in Figure 13.13.

4. For a peripheral node, the value of the star network is

$$f(1 + 2\delta) - c = (1 + 2 \cdot 0.5)^2 - 2.5 = 1.5$$

and their fallback position is zero. Thus, the largest transfer the central node can ask from each of the peripheral nodes is 1.5. Thus, the outcome of the bargaining is:

- the central node receives the value of the star $f(3) - 3c = 9 - 7.5 = 1.5$, plus the transfers $1.5 \cdot 3 = 7.5$, which equals to the total surplus (the sum of the individual values of the network) of the star, 6.
- all the peripheral nodes get zero.

The Gini coefficient is $g_s = 1$.

5. For any node in the complete network, the value is

$$f(3) - 3c = 9 - 3 \cdot 2.5 = 1.5$$

The fallback positions of those members without take-it-or-leave-it power are

$$f(2 + \delta) - 2c = (2 + 0.5)^2 - 2 \cdot 2.5 = 1.25$$

Then the largest transfer is

$$1.5 - 1.25 = 0.25$$

and thus the outcome of the bargaining is

- the member with take-it-or-leave-it power receives

$$1.5 + 3 \cdot 0.25 = 2.25$$

and
- all the others get

$$1.5 - 0.25 = 1.25$$

The Gini coefficient in this case is

$$g_c = \frac{1}{2}\left(\frac{3\cdot(2.25-1.25)}{4\cdot(4-1)/2}\right)\Big/\left(\frac{2.25+1.25\cdot 3}{4}\right) = \frac{1}{6}$$

The outcome here is more equal than the previous one on the star as $g_c < g_s$.

13.4 Product market structure and the distribution of income

Consider an economy with

- many firms producing a single homogeneous good
- using only a homogeneous labor input
- which is hired and paid a nominal wage of w^n at the beginning of a period,
- with a resulting output of γ per hour of labor hired
- being sold at the price per unit of p at the end of the period.

Firms will enter from the rest of the world if their expected profits from entry exceed the opportunity cost of capital ρ; with a small probability a firm will exit for exogenous reasons (e.g. firm death) and firms also exit if the profit of incumbent firms falls short of the opportunity cost of capital.

Suppose that a firm entering the economy pays the cost of producing the product but, due to barriers to entry, will fail to sell the goods with probability b (for "barriers").

Competition condition

The *competition condition* is an expression for the real wage in terms of the level of barriers to entry, the productivity of labor, and the opportunity cost of capital such that the number of firms in the economy is stationary.

1. Write down what we term the *competition condition*, namely an expression for the real wage $w^c = w^n/p$ in terms of b, γ, and ρ, such that the number of firms in the economy is stationary. (Hint: model the decision of a prospective entering firm.)

2. Use the competition condition to derive expressions for

   a) the labor share of total income (σ_w)

   b) the accounting profit share (σ_A); and

   c) the economic profit share (σ_E).

Lorenz curve

The *Lorenz curve* plots the relationship between the percentage of the population whose income is less than or equal to a certain amount and the percentage of total income received by them. The Gini coefficient is the area between the Lorenz curve and the line of perfect equality divided by the total area below the line of perfect equality.

3. Use the competition condition you have just derived along with the rest of the whole economy model (specifically, the wage curve) to show that a competition policy that reduced barriers to entry would result in an increase in total income, more equally distributed.

Answers.

1. A prospective firm will attempt entry if the expected price is greater than the opportunity cost of attempted entry, i.e.,

$$p(1 - b) > (1 + \rho)\frac{w^n}{\gamma} \qquad (13.4)$$

Note that (by definition) the inverse of the productivity of labor, $1/\gamma$, is the labor time it takes to produce one unit of output.

while a incumbent firm will exit if the inequality is reversed. Therefore, in order for the number of firms in the economy to be stationary, equation (13.4) must be satisfied as an equality. Then the real wage determined by the competition condition is

$$w^c = \frac{w^n}{p} = \frac{1 - b}{1 + \rho}\gamma \qquad (13.5)$$

2. a) The labor share of total income is the ratio of the hourly real wage to the value of output produced by a worker in an hour, and therefore,

$$\sigma_w = \frac{w^c}{\gamma} = \frac{1 - b}{1 + \rho}$$

   b) The profit share is one minus the wage share,

$$\sigma_A = 1 - \sigma_w = 1 - \frac{1 - b}{1 + \rho} = \frac{\rho + b}{1 + \rho}$$

   c) The economic profit share is the fraction of total income received by the owners of the capital goods used in production in excess of the opportunity cost of capital, i.e.

$$\sigma_E = \frac{\gamma - (1 + \rho)w^c}{\gamma} = 1 - (1 + \rho)\sigma_w = b$$

3. From the expression for w^n in equation (13.5) (the competition condition), we have that

$$\frac{dw^n}{db} = -\frac{p\gamma}{1 + \rho} < 0$$

Thus, reducing b shifts w^n upwards, raising wages and (by the positive slope of the wage function) employing some of the previously unemployed, which necessarily will reduce the Gini coefficient. (You can experiment with numerical values for this exercise in the next question.)

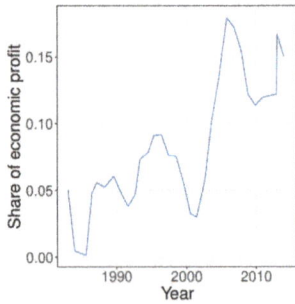

Figure 13.14: The share of economic profits in total income for the U.S. over the period 1984–2014. The other shares are wages and the difference between economic profits and accounting profits, namely the profits corresponding to the opportunity cost of the capital goods used in production. Source: Barkai [5]

[5]: Barkai (2020), 'Declining Labor and Capital Shares'

Figure 13.15: The markup ratio and the Gini coefficient in the United States. Gini coefficient data from 1979 to 2015 are for market income (income before taxes and government transfers) and for 1967 to 1978 are for money income (income after government cash transfers but before taxes) adjusted upwards so as to be comparable to market income inequality. The mark-up ratio, that is $(p - c)/c$, is for all firms in the U.S. weighted by firm size. The fact that the mark-up ratio and the Gini coefficient tend to move together over time is consistent with the theory of inequality conveyed by our whole economy model, but we cannot conclude that changes in the mark-up ratio are causing the changes in the Gini coefficient without taking account of other possible influences on the two series. Source: De Loecker, Eeckhout, and Unger [44], US Census Bureau, Historical Income Tables: Income Inequality and Congressional Budget Office.

[44]: De Loecker, Eeckhout, and Unger (2020), 'The Rise of Market Power and the Macroeconomic Implications'

13.5 Experimenting with history: Market structure, the wage curve, and rising inequality in the U.S.

This section introduces you to a model of the whole economy along with the Lorenz curve and Gini coefficient calibrated to it. The income of the three sets of economic actors in the whole economy model — employers, employees, and the unemployed — and the distribution of the population across these sets allows us to define a Lorenz curve (and associated Gini coefficient) corresponding to any state realized in the whole economy model.

As an example, you could experiment with parameter values to see if you can come up with a consistent explanation of the substantial increase in income inequality in the U.S. between the 1980s and the 2020s (Figure 13.15).

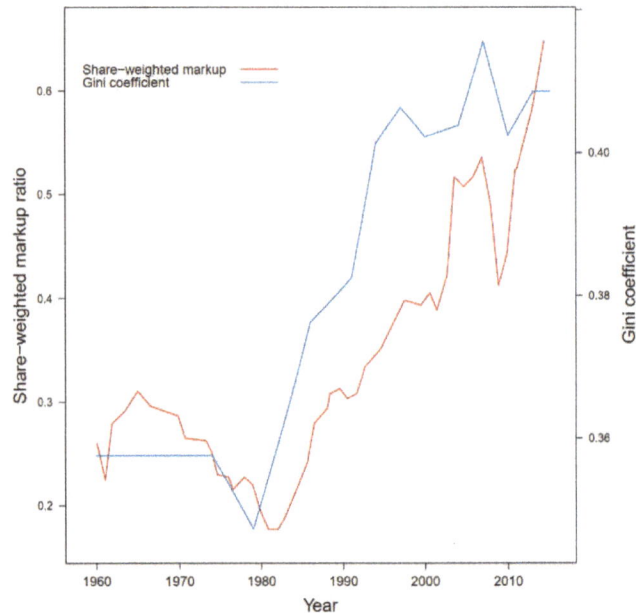

Using the whole economy model as described in the introduction to Chapter 13 and summarized in Figure 13.16, refer to the following interactive app: https://bowles-halliday.github.io/bh-textbook//graphs/fig15-15.html

The meaning of the parameters are given below:

- B: unemployment benefits
- ρ: opportunity cost of capital
- γ: Output per hour (which equals the inverse of the labor time required to produce one unit)
- b: barriers to entry
- t: termination probability
- u: disutility of effort

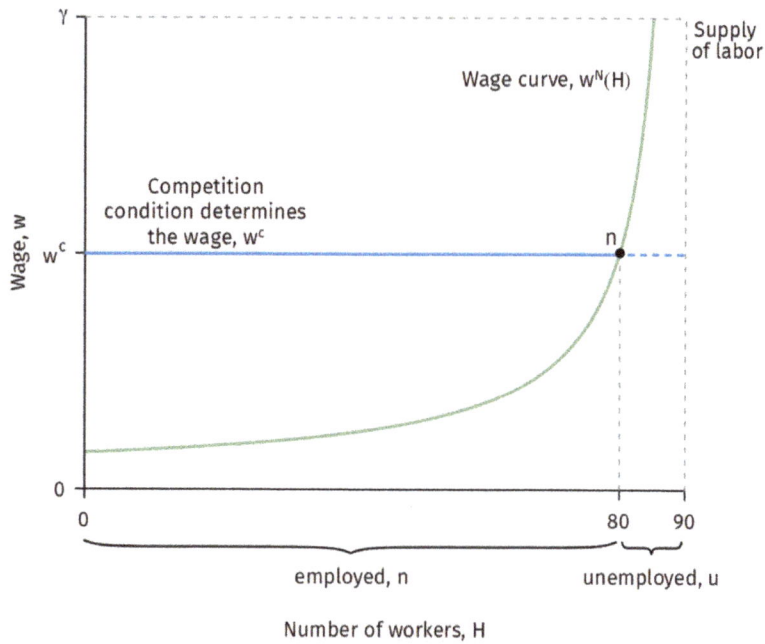

(a) The whole economy model: wage curve and competition condition curve.

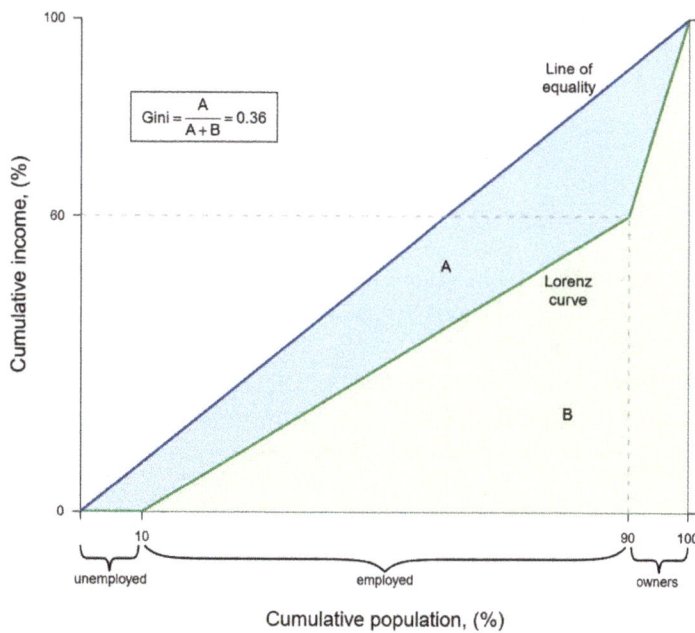

(b) The Lorenz curve associated with the whole economy.

Figure 13.16: The whole economy model and the Lorenz curve. In panel (a) we show the wage curve and the wage determined by the competition condition for an economy in which there are 90 workers of whom 80 are employed, receiving 60 percent of total income (that is, the wage share), and 10 are unemployed, receiving no income. There are also 10 employers who are owners of 10 firms each of which employs 8 of the workers ($8 \times 10 = 80$). Together, these 100 people form an economy and have access to income from work that can be depicted using a Lorenz curve (panel (b)) with its corresponding Gini coefficient. The Gini coefficient for the model economy shown is 0.36.

You can use sliders for the parameters below to explore the impacts of policy interventions on the Nash equilibrium states of the model.

1. Identify a set of parameter values that will roughly satisfy the conditions present in the 1980s (higher unemployment, lower Gini coefficient). Roughly here means do not attempt to reproduce the exact levels; this is a model, not the real world itself. Describe what you find.

2. Identify a set of parameter values that will roughly satisfy the conditions present in the 2010s-2020s (lower unemployment, higher Gini). Describe what you find.

3. Do you think that in this model there are plausible alternative parameter values to the ones you found above that will also satisfy the conditions described above? Say what they might be, or if you think not, then why not?

13.6 Monopsony and the minimum wage

Using the no-shirking condition derived in Section 10.7, consider the case of a single firm in a local labor market that hires a substantial fraction h of the relevant labor supply for this particular kind of employment in the location. Suppose that the probability that a worker will remain unemployed is a function of the firm's own level of employment in the local labor market, $j(h) = 1 - h$, and specify a reduced form expression of the no-shirking wage as a function of h, $w(h)$.

Suppose that firm's revenue function is

$$f(\underline{e}h) = 4\ln(\underline{e}h)$$

The game between the employer in each of the (identical) workers is as described in Figure 10.8, and assume that the unemployment benefit $B = 0$, the no-shirking effort level $\underline{e} = 1$, the disutility of performing the no-shirking level of effort $\underline{u} = 1$, and the probability that a worker performing less than the no-shirking level will be detected and fired $t = 0.5$. The cost of hiring labor $w(h)h$ is the variable cost.

1. Find the level of hiring that a profit-maximizing firm will do (a figure showing the firm's average and marginal cost of hiring hours of labor and the marginal revenue product of an hour of labor may help here, and in the questions that follow).

Suppose that a legal minimum wage is imposed (the firm may not pay less than w^m).

2. Find the employment level when the minimum wage is set to be $w^m = 5$.

3. Explain how the imposition of the minimum wage could increase the level of employment.

Other counties
■ Contiguous border county pairs (with minimum wage difference)

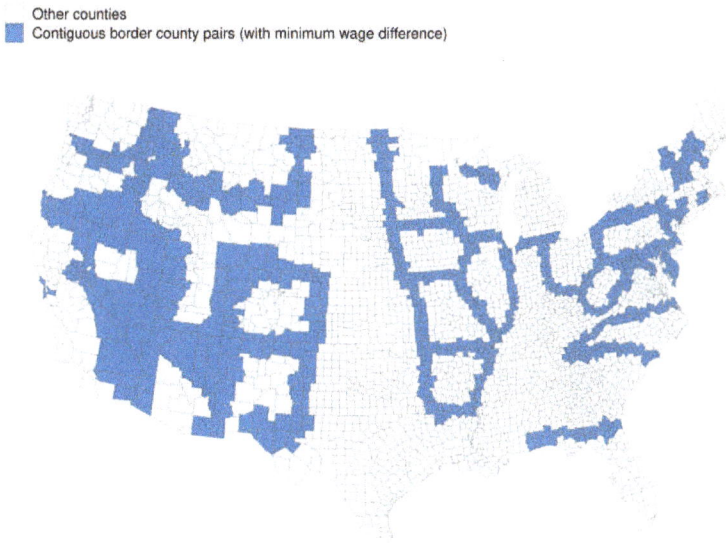

Figure 13.17: A research design to determine the employment effects of the minimum wage. This map of the U.S. shows (in blue) the paired counties that were compared in one study, in most cases those located on the boundary of two states with different levels and changes in the levels of the minimum wage. Source: Dube, Lester, and Reich [48].

4. Give the range of minimum wage levels for which the employment effect of the imposition of a minimum wage is positive. What minimum wage would maximize the level of employment by the firm?

[48]: Dube, Lester, and Reich (2016), 'Minimum Wage Shocks, Employment Flows, and Labor Market Frictions'

5. Suppose that all of the workers who might be employed in this firm (those currently employed and those not) were members of a labor union that has the power (by credibly threatening to strike) to set the wage. If they would like to maximize the total wage income paid by the firm (which could be shared among the members, including those not employed), what wage would the trade union impose?

Answers.

1. To maximize profit

$$\pi(h) = f(\underline{e}h) - w(h)h$$

the first order condition is

$$\frac{d\pi}{dh} = f'\underline{e} - (w_h h + w(h)) = 0 \Rightarrow f' = w_h h + w$$

That is, the marginal revenue product ($mrp = f'$) of hiring more equals the marginal cost of hiring more ($mc = w_h h + w$).

Given the parameters, we have marginal revenue product

$$mrp = f' = \frac{4}{h}$$

the average cost of labor is just the no-shirking condition which is

$$ac = w(h) = 1 + \frac{1}{1-h}$$

Recall, from Section 10.7, that the no-shirking condition is:

$$w = B + \underline{u} + \frac{1-t}{t}\frac{\underline{u}}{j}$$

$$= 1 + \frac{1}{1-h}$$

given that $B = 0$, $\underline{u} = 1$, $t = 0.5$, and $j = 1 - h$.

and the marginal cost

$$mc = w_h h + w = \frac{h}{(1-h)^2} + 1 + \frac{1}{1-h} = 1 + \frac{1}{(1-h)^2}$$

Then letting h^a represent the profit-maximizing level of employment, $mrp = mc$ gives us

$$\frac{4}{h^a} = 1 + \frac{1}{(1-h^a)^2} \implies (h^a - 2)(h^{a2} - 4h^a + 2) = 0$$

which implies $h^a = 2 - \sqrt{2} \approx 0.586$. The wage is determined by the least wage required to hire h^a non-shirking workers, or $w^b = w(h^a) \approx 3.4$, as shown in Figure 13.18.

2. Suppose the minimum wage $w^m = 5$. Let h^m be the solution to $w(h) = w^m$, i.e.

$$h^m = w^{-1}(w^m) = 1 - \frac{1}{w^m - 1} = 0.75$$

then the average cost function becomes

$$ac(h) = \max\{w^m, w(h)\} \cdot h = \begin{cases} w^m h & h \leq h^m \\ w(h)h & h > h^m \end{cases}$$

As shown in Figure 13.19, the marginal cost function is not differentiable at $h = h^m$,

$$mc(h) = w^m < mrp(h) \text{ for } h < h^m$$

and

$$mc(h) = 1 + \frac{1}{(1-h)^2} > mrp(h) \text{ for all } h > h^m$$

Therefore, to maximize profit the employment level would be $h^m = 0.75$ when the minimum wage is $w^m = 5$.

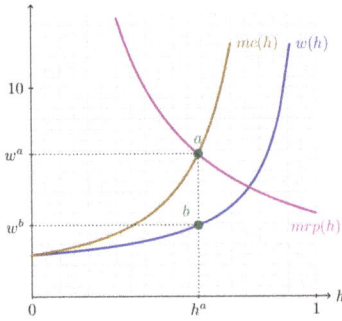

Figure 13.18: The monopsonist's profit-maximizing level of hiring and wage. Given that

$$mrp = f_h = \frac{4}{h}$$

$$ac = w(h) = 1 + \frac{1}{1-h}$$

and

$$mc = 1 + \frac{1}{(1-h)^2}$$

the condition for profit maximization ($mrp = mc$) is satisfied at point a with a profit-maximizing level of hiring of h^a. The employer pays a wage given by the point on the average cost curve that corresponds to the level of hiring h^a, shown at the intersection at point b with the wage $w^b = w(h^a)$.

Figure 13.19: Monopsony hiring level with a minimum wage. With minimum wage $w^m \in (w^b, w^c)$, the marginal cost becomes

$$mc(h) = w^m < mrp(h) \quad \forall h < h^m$$

and

$$mc(h) = 1 + \frac{1}{(1-h)^2} > mrp(h) \quad \forall h > h^m$$

so that profit is increasing when $h < h^m$ and decreasing when $h > h^m$. Therefore the condition for profit maximization (though mc is not defined) is satisfied at point m with a profit-maximizing level of hiring of h^m.

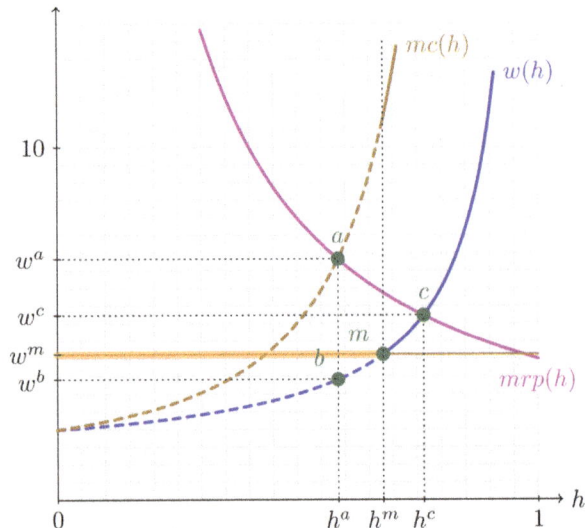

3. The imposition of the minimum wage increases the profit-maximizing employment level in this case because at employment levels such that the (fixed) minimum wage exceeds the (rising) average cost of labor (the no-shirking condition) the marginal cost of hiring more non-shirking labor is just the minimum wage itself, and this is less than the marginal cost implied by the no-shirking condition. So the firm hires more because, while raising the average cost of labor, the minimum wage reduces the marginal cost (over this range of hiring).

4. An increase in the minimum wage will increase the profit-maximizing level of employment in the firm $h^m(w^m)$ as long as the marginal revenue product of labor at $h^m(w^m)$ exceeds the average cost of labor $w(h^m)$ at that level of employment. So h^m is increasing for w^m in (w^b, w^c) and decreasing when $w^m > w^c$. Therefore, to ensure $h^m > h^a = h^b$ (where h^b is the employment level at w^b), the minimum wage w^m must be in the range (w^b, w^a), i.e., $3.4 < w^m < 6.8$, and $w^m = w^c \approx 5.2$ is the wage that will implement the maximum employment level, $h^c \approx 0.764$, as shown in Figure 13.20.

So the minimum wage that would maximize employment is the greatest value of w^m such that at the employment level $h^m(w^m)$ we have $mrp(h^m) = w(h^m)$. Letting h^c be the level of employment satisfying this condition, we have

$$\frac{4}{h^c} = 1 + \frac{1}{1 - h^c} \Rightarrow (h^c)^2 - 6h^c + 4 = 0$$

which implies $h^c = 3 - \sqrt{5} \approx 0.764$. The wage rate satisfying the no-shirking condition ($w(h)$) at this level of employment is $w^c = w(h^c) \approx 5.2$, which is the minimum wage that will maximize the level of employment. Increases in w^m above 5.2 will induce the firm to hire less.

5. For continuity of notation, let the wage set by the trade union be w^m. For $w^m \in [w^b, w^c]$, the level of employment $h^m(w^m)$ will be determined by the inverse of the average cost of labor function $w(h)$ and for $w^m > w^c$ by the inverse of the marginal revenue product function $mrp(h)$. Thus we have

$$h^m = \begin{cases} w^{-1}(w^m) = 1 - \frac{1}{w^m - 1} & w^b < w^m \le w^c \\ mrp^{-1}(w^m) = \frac{4}{w^m} & w^m > w^c \end{cases} \qquad (13.6)$$

Therefore,

$$ti(w^m) = w^m h^m(w^m) = \begin{cases} w^m \left(1 - \frac{1}{w^m - 1}\right) & w^b < w^m \le w^c \\ w^m \cdot \frac{4}{w^m} = 4 & w^m > w^c \end{cases}$$

Then the total wage income is increasing in (w^b, w^c) since h^m is increasing. It remains constant for $w \ge w^c$, which is due to the logarithmic form of the revenue function f. Between (w^b, w^c) the total wage income ranges approximately between (2,4) therefore, the union would choose any $w^m \ge w^c \approx 5.2$ to maximize their total income.

At h^a the maximum level of wage such that the firm can hire h^a workers and make non-negative profits is $w^a = mrp(h^a) = 4/(2 - \sqrt{2}) \approx 6.8$.

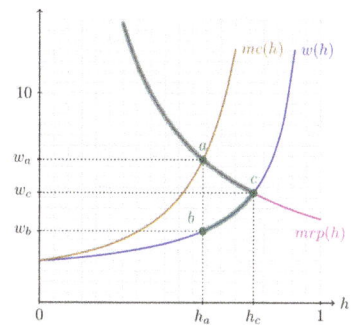

Figure 13.20: The monopsonist's profit-maximizing level of hiring with minimum wage (or a trade union set wage), w^m. For $w^m > w_b$, the employment level is

$$h^m = \begin{cases} w^{-1}(w^m) & w_b < w^m \le w_c \\ mrp^{-1}(w^m) & w^m > w_c \end{cases}$$

The monopsonist's solutions lie between **b** and **c** along the wage curve $w(h)$ and above point **c** along the curve $mrp(h)$.

The inverse cost of labor function gives the level of hiring as a function of the no-shirking wage

$$w = 1 + \frac{1}{1 - h} \Rightarrow 1 - h = \frac{1}{w - 1}$$

then

$$h = 1 - \frac{1}{w - 1}$$

The inverse of the mrp function gives the level of hiring as a function of the mrp

$$w = \frac{4}{h} \Rightarrow h = \frac{4}{w}$$

13.7 A rent-seeking state: Politics as *who gets what, when, and how*

In most of the problems that we have introduced so far, the "policy maker" is a hypothetical mechanism designer proposing rules of the game intended to implement improved outcomes for society.

[70]: Lasswell (1936), *Politics*

A less idealized view of the policy maker is suggested by the title of Harold Lasswell's *Politics: Who gets What, When, and How*, written when Adolf Hitler had just come to power in Germany.

Consistent with Lasswell's view that politics is about the distribution of wealth and income, we present a model in which the state is a self-regarding player and its exercise of power (possibly limited by citizens) determines who gets what. In this model, a governing elite extracts rents from citizens by taxation in excess of the cost of the public goods provided to the citizens. A key idea in the model is that, while the citizens in a democratic society have some power over the state (due to the possibility that they might be able to dismiss the elite), they cannot bind the elite to any particular policy.

One way to model this is as a game against nature where the elite is the sole player and there is some probability of removal of the elite from power (by means of election) represented by a draw (by "nature") from a distribution that depends on the level of provision of the public good. The state elite (considered as a single actor) selects a level of public goods to provide per period, g, that maximizes its expected rent, R. The elite is assumed to know the likelihood that their rule will be terminated for each level of g. We take the level of taxation per citizen t to be exogenously determined.

In decision theory, a "game against nature" is a setting with a single actor choosing an action, the payoffs of which are contingent on the subsequent realization of some state that will be chosen by "nature" (there may be other players, but with no actions to choose). An example is the Dictator Game. Strictly speaking, a game against nature is not a game, as there is no strategic interaction.

The key variables of interest are:

- $\rho \in [0, 1]$, the extent of the *rule of law*, so $1 - \rho$ is the probability that the elite will be removed independently of the level of provision of public goods (for example by a military *coup d'etat*).
- $\Gamma(1 - g/t) \in [0, 1]$, the extent of *citizens' opposition* to the government due to its taking rents rather than providing public goods (as might vary with the degree of freedom of the press and other sources of information). The function $\Gamma(\cdot)$ is increasing and convex in its argument.
- $\delta \in [0, 1]$ is the degree of *democratic accountability*, meaning the extent to which citizens' opposition to the government will result in the elite being removed.

Thus, taking a sufficiently short time period so that we can ignore the possibility that both reasons that a regime might be terminated (weakness of rule of law or insufficient public goods) would occur in a single period, the probability that the elite will be removed can be defined as

$$\lambda = (1 - \rho) + \rho \delta \Gamma \left(1 - \frac{g}{t}\right)$$

Now we give the function $\Gamma(\cdot)$ an explicit representation so that

$$\Gamma\left(1 - \frac{g}{t}\right) = \frac{\gamma}{2}\left(1 - \frac{g}{t}\right)^2$$

where γ is just a constant such that $\gamma \in [0, 2]$, so the per period probability of regime termination is

$$\lambda = (1 - \rho) + \frac{1}{2}\rho\delta\gamma\left(1 - \frac{g}{t}\right)^2 \qquad (13.7)$$

In the first period, the regime receives a per period rent $t - g$ and then the elite is displaced or not; in the latter case, another period is played with the elite's strategy unchanged (the game is time invariant), this process continuing until the regime is terminated, after which the elite receives nothing forever, and the game ends. The elite does not discount future rents (the termination probability plays a role analogous to a discount rate, and for simplicity we just abstract from time preference).

1. Give the elite's constrained choice problem.

2. How will the elite determine the level of public good provision? Show the first order condition and explain its economic meaning.

3. Show the effect on the regime's choice of public goods provision of changes in ρ, δ, and γ. Explain your results.

4. Using the regime's first order condition derived from equation (13.7), show that they will choose to capture some rents even when the citizens' opposition to rent-seeking and democratic accountability are at their maximum values. What is it about the model setup that explains this?

5. Given the parameter values $\rho = 5/6$, $\delta = 8/9$, and $\gamma = 1.8$, what level of public goods will be provided?

Answers.

1. The elite's problem is to

$$\max_{g} \quad R = (t - g) + R(1 - \lambda) = \frac{t - g}{\lambda}$$

Therefore, the elite's expected rent R is per period rent (taxes t minus expenditures on public goods g) times the expected duration of the regime, which the inverse of the probability of regime termination λ.

2. The first order condition of the choice of g is

$$R_g = \frac{1}{\lambda^2}[-\lambda - \lambda_g(t - g)] = 0 \Rightarrow \lambda = -\lambda_g(t - g)$$

which can be expressed as the marginal cost of public goods provision equal to the marginal benefit public goods provision:

By $R = (t - g) + R(1 - \lambda)$, the first order condition (13.8) can also be derived from

$$R_g = -1 + R_g(1 - \lambda) - R\lambda_g = 0$$

$$1 = -\lambda_g R \qquad (13.8)$$

The marginal cost term on the left is rent lost by providing more public goods. The marginal benefit term on the right is the marginal effect of providing more public goods in reducing the likelihood of a termination $(-\lambda_g)$ times the total expected rent R. From (13.7), we have

$$\lambda_g = -\frac{\rho \delta \gamma}{t}\left(1 - \frac{g}{t}\right) \qquad (13.9)$$

Substituting into the first order condition $\lambda = -\lambda_g(t - g)$ yields

$$(1 - \rho) + \frac{1}{2}\rho\delta\gamma\left(1 - \frac{g}{t}\right)^2 = \frac{\rho\delta\gamma}{t}\left(1 - \frac{g}{t}\right)(t - g)$$

That is

$$1 - \rho = \frac{1}{2}\rho\delta\gamma\left(1 - \frac{g}{t}\right)^2$$

then

$$\left(1 - \frac{g}{t}\right)^2 = \frac{2(1 - \rho)}{\rho\delta\gamma}$$

Noting that $g \leq t$, the choice of g is

$$g(t) = t\left[1 - \sqrt{\frac{2}{\delta\gamma}\left(\frac{1}{\rho} - 1\right)}\right] \qquad (13.10)$$

3. From (13.10) we have

   a) $g_\rho > 0$: an increase in the extent of the rule of law would induce a higher level of public good provision.

   b) $g_\delta > 0$: an increase in the extent of the citizen's opposition to the government's rents-taking would induce a higher level of public good provision.

   c) $g_\gamma > 0$: an increase in the degree of democratic accountability would induce a higher level of public good provision.

4. Given $\delta = 1$ and $\gamma = 2$, equation (13.10) gives

$$g = t\left(1 - \sqrt{\frac{1}{\rho} - 1}\right) < t$$

when $\rho < 1$. Therefore, the elite will choose to capture some rents $g - t > 0$. This is because, in the setup, the probability of regime termination given by (13.7) implies that $\lambda_g = 0$ at $g = t$ as shown in (13.9), so there is no cost to taking some small rent (reducing g by a small amount). To see this, return to equation (13.8), the first order condition for the elite's choice of g, and think about the benefits and costs to the elite of providing fewer public goods. The marginal cost (the right-hand side) in terms of its effect on the likelihood that the regime is terminated is zero when $g = t$, and of course the elite benefits directly by simply appropriating the reduced expenditure on public goods for themselves (the left-hand side).

5. Given the following parameter values $\rho = 5/6$, $\delta = 8/9$ and $\gamma = 1.8$, we have

$$g = t\left[1 - \sqrt{\frac{2}{8/9 \cdot 1.8}\left(\frac{1}{5/6} - 1\right)}\right] = \frac{1}{2}t$$

Endogenous Preferences: The Evolution of Cooperation | 14

Evolutionary game theory allows us to explore how institutions and preferences change over time. It also addresses some of the shortcomings of simple comparative static analysis by making explicit the process of change itself. Evolutionary modeling differs from the standard Walrasian paradigm in that

▶ the object analysed is the process of change in a space of possible states, rather than the properties of a stationary state (usually thought to be unique);

▶ modeling the process of change requires taking account of who interacts with whom, to engage in what game or games, and the conditions, including chance events, under which players will change their strategy choices;

▶ changing strategies is not based on expected utility maximization but instead on empirically grounded social learning mechanisms such as copying the successful, conforming to the majority, and changing your strategy if things are not going well;

▶ knowledge is typically assumed to be scarce and local so that actors' beliefs are based on limited information (for example, concerning the past play of a sample of other players);

▶ the resulting dynamics often involve strategic complementarities, conformist learning, and other sources of positive feedbacks, resulting in a multiplicity of stationary states;

▶ in order to make predictions about the likelihood that each of these multiple equilibria will be observed, evolutionary modeling must include a method of equilibrium selection, which, necessarily, will be probabilistic.

Evolutionary models in economics have strong affinities with the field of population biology, where natural selection is represented as a process in which alleles that are copied more frequently (through greater reproductive success of the individuals bearing them) proliferate in a population. In economics, the field of cultural evolution studies the dynamics of individual behaviors and preferences in which the process of change is based not on mutation, genetic inheritance, and differential reproduction, but instead on experimentation (including mistakes) and learning.

The problems in this and the next chapter will give you practice with some of the modeling tools used by evolutionary economists and others. In this chapter, we work with models of the evolution of cooperation and of preferences (for example altruism) supporting cooperative outcomes. In the next chapter, we study the evolution of conflicts affecting the distribution of gains to cooperation.

To learn more about evolutionary game theory have a look at Young [113] and Weibull [107]. These problems are based on models developed in Chapters 11-14 of Bowles [14] and Bowles and Gintis [27].

Figure 14.1: Charles Darwin (1809–1882). In his *On the Origin of Species*, published in 1859, Darwin proposed that species evolve over time through a process of natural selection. He later explained that the key concept — "the struggle for existence" — actually came from economics: "the doctrine of Malthus applied [. . .] to the whole animal and vegetable kingdoms." While Darwin's work focused primarily on the biological realm, his ideas have had a profound impact in all of the sciences, including the study of cooperation. Evolutionary game theory formalizes many Darwinian ideas — especially the importance of differential copying — and explores how cooperation can emerge and persist even among self-interested individuals, highlighting the role of social structure in shaping social behavior. Photo by Julia Margaret Cameron (1869), Wikimedia Commons, public domain, https://commons.wikimedia.org/wiki/File:Charles_Darwin_01.jpg

[113]: Young (1998), *Individual Strategy and Social Structure*

[107]: Weibull (1995), *Evolutionary Game Theory*

[14]: Bowles (2004), *Microeconomics*

[27]: Bowles and Gintis (2011), *A Cooperative Species*

"In the language of biology, one might say that history is realized through the natural selection of accidents." — Trotsky [103, pp. 494–495]

[103]: Trotsky (1970), *My Life*

Cultural evolution

The change over time in behaviors and preferences that are learned from parents, other elders, and peers rather than being genetically inherited from parents.

Conformist learning

When updating their type, conformist learners favor adopting traits that are more common in a population.

14.1 Conformist learning and altruistic preferences

A major controversy in the social and biological sciences concerns the evolution of altruistic behaviors (toward non-kin) in humans and other animals. Conformist cultural transmission may have contributed to the evolutionary success of altruism.

Consider a large population in which individuals may be of two types (or norms): altruistic or not. One's type dictates one's behavior when interacting with others. Altruists pay a cost c and confer a benefit b on another person, while Non-Altruists confer no benefits and pay no costs.

Suppose individuals are randomly paired to interact in a game in which their payoffs depend on their own type and the type of the player with whom they are paired. They occasionally update their type in light of two pieces of information, their payoffs relative to others' and the frequency of the two traits in the population.

Define the degree of conformism, $\lambda \in [0, 1)$, as the importance of the conformist aspect of the learning process relative to the payoff-based influences on updating, with $1 - \lambda$ therefore being the relative importance of payoffs, and let k be the population frequency of Altruists for which conformist learning exerts no effect (possibly one-half). So if the fraction of Altruists in the population $p > k$, the prevalence of altruistic types favors Altruism in the updating process, independently of the (also frequency-dependent) expected payoffs to the two norms. We define the cultural fitness of Altruism and Non-Altruism,

$$
\begin{aligned}
r_a &= \frac{1}{2}[\lambda(p - k) + (1 - \lambda)(b_a(p) - b_n(p))] \\
r_n &= \frac{1}{2}[\lambda(k - p) + (1 - \lambda)(b_n(p) - b_a(p))]
\end{aligned}
\tag{14.1}
$$

where $b_a(p)$ and $b_n(p)$ are the expected payoff to Altruists and Non-Altruists, respectively.

A derivation of the replicator equation 14.2 from the setup summarized in equation 14.1 is in Bowles [14]

[14]: Bowles (2004), *Microeconomics*

To study the evolution of the frequency of Altruists in the population, we derive the following expression, termed a replicator equation (because it tracks how the two traits are replicated (copied) over time):

$$
\frac{dp}{dt} = p' - p = p(1 - p)\beta(r_a - r_n)
\tag{14.2}
$$

Here the adoption coefficient β is a positive constant reflecting the greater effect on switching of relatively large differences in replication propensities (appropriately scaled so that the probability of switching varies over the unit interval). So $\beta(r_a - r_n)$ determines the direction of change in p while $p(1 - p)$, the frequency with which unlike types are paired, affects the speed of change.

An evolutionary equilibrium is a value of p such that the population distribution is stationary (so that the value given by equation (14.2) is zero).

Let k in equation (14.1) be $1/2$. Pairing is random.

1. Given b and c, find the expected payoff $b_a(p)$ and $b_n(p)$.

2. Is there some value of λ, the "degree of conformism", such that both Altruism and Non-Altruism are *evolutionary stable strategies* (ESSs)? If so, give the range of values of λ for which this is true.

3. Identify all of the equilibria.

4. Is the interior equilibrium stable?

5. Show that an increase in the degree of conformism enlarges the basin of attraction of the all-Altruism equilibrium.

Evolutionary stable strategy

An *evolutionary stable strategy* (ESS) is one such that in a population consisting entirely of one type, an alternative strategy, if introduced, will not proliferate.

Answers.

1. The payoff matrix is given in Table 14.1. Then, given the population fraction of the Altruists p, the expected payoff

$$b_a(p) = p(b - c) + (1 - p)(-c) = pb - c$$
$$b_n(p) = pb$$

	Altruism	Non-Altruism
Altruism	$b - c$	$-c$
Non-Altruism	b	0

Table 14.1: **The Game of Altruism**. Row player's payoff in the symmetric game

2. For it to be an ESS in this replication dynamics, Altruism, when it is the incumbent strategy, must produce more replicas than the alternative ("invading") strategy (Non-Altruism), thus eliminating it from the population. This requires $r_a(1) > r_n(1)$ which is equivalent to

$$b_n(1) - b_a(1) = c < \frac{\lambda}{1 - \lambda}(1 - k)$$

Recalling that $k = 1/2$, this becomes

$$c < \frac{\lambda}{2(1 - \lambda)} \implies \lambda > \frac{2c}{2c + 1}$$

So if conformist learning is sufficiently important, Altruism may be evolutionarily stable even though Altruists are always at a payoff disadvantage irrespective of p.

By similar reasoning, it can be shown that $r_n(0) > r_a(0)$ for any $\lambda \in [0, 1)$, and thus Non-Altruism is also an ESS. Therefore, when

$$\frac{2c}{2c + 1} < \lambda < 1$$

both Altruism and Non-Altruism are ESSs.

Figure 14.2: Cultural equilibrium with Altruism. The stationary value of p requires that, at $p = p^*$, the conformist pressures favoring the copying of Altruist are offset by payoff advantages of Non-Altruist. The payoff effect is

$$b_n(p) - b_a(p) = c$$

and the conformism effect is

$$\frac{\lambda(p - k)}{1 - \lambda}$$

assuming $c = 0.5$, $k = 0.5$ and $\lambda = 0.6$.

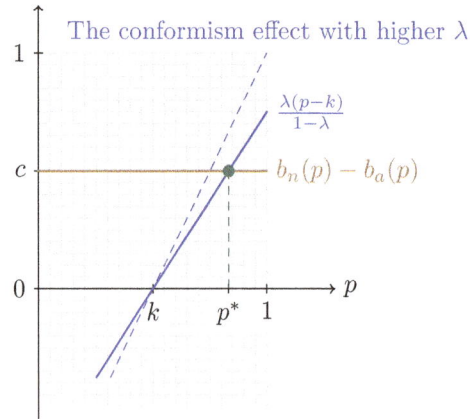

The conformism effect with higher λ

$\frac{\lambda(p-k)}{1-\lambda}$

$b_n(p) - b_a(p)$

3. To find all the equilibria, we look for all values of p such that $dp/dt = 0$. From equation (14.1), it is clear that $dp/dt = 0$ if p is either 0 or 1, or if $r_a - r_n = 0$ which requires

$$b_n(p) - b_a(p) = \frac{\lambda}{1 - \lambda}(p - k)$$

That is

$$c = \frac{\lambda}{1 - \lambda}(p - k)$$

and therefore

$$p^* = k + \frac{1 - \lambda}{\lambda}c = \frac{1}{2} + \frac{1 - \lambda}{\lambda}c$$

To ensure that $p^* \in (0, 1)$, we have

$$\lambda > \frac{2c}{1 + 2c}$$

From $p^* < 1$ we have

$$\frac{1}{2} + \frac{1 - \lambda}{\lambda}c < 1 \Rightarrow \frac{1}{\lambda} - 1 < \frac{1}{2c}$$

and thus

$$\lambda > \frac{2c}{1 + 2c}$$

4. To check whether the interior equilibrium p^* is stable or not, we calculate the derivative of dp/dt with respect to p at p^*.

$$\frac{d(dp/dt)}{dp} = (1 - 2p^*)\beta[r_a(p^*) - r_n(p^*)]$$
$$+ p^*(1 - p^*)\beta\left[\lambda + (1 - \lambda)\left(\frac{db_a}{dp} - \frac{db_n}{dp}\right)\right]$$
$$= p^*(1 - p^*)\beta\lambda > 0$$

since $r_a(p^*) = r_n(p^*)$ and $db_a/dp - db_n/dp = 0$. This means that a small displacement of p above p^* will lead to a further increase, that is, away from p^*. Therefore, the interior equilibrium p^* is unstable.

5. The basin of attraction of the all-Altruism equilibrium is the range of values of p between 1 and p^*. Since

$$1 - p^* = \frac{1}{2} - \frac{1 - \lambda}{\lambda}c$$

is increasing in λ, an increase in the degree of conformism λ enlarges the basin of attraction.

14.2 The evolution of cooperation: Repeated interactions, segmentation, and punishment of free riders

This section explores ways that cooperation may be sustained even in a population of self-regarding people.

In a large population, individuals interact in pairs, the strategy sets and payoffs being given by the standard Prisoner's Dilemma Game as shown in Table 14.2.

	Cooperation	Defect
Cooperate	b	d
Defect	a	c

Table 14.2: The Prisoner's Dilemma Game. Row player's payoff in the symmetric game with $a > b > c > d$ and $2b > a + d$

Figure 14.3: Herbert Gintis (1940–2023) Having left mathematics (and shoemaking) to study economics, Herbert Gintis pioneered the study of endogenous preferences. A portion of his doctoral dissertation titled 'A Radical Analysis of Welfare Economics and Individual Development' was published in the *Quarterly Journal of Economics* in 1972. It begins with: "[...] welfare depends not only on what an individual has but on what he/she is." He went on to explain how "changes in the structure of economic institutions produce changes in [...] paths of individual development." In later work (some of it with Sam Bowles), he drew on anthropology, evolutionary biology, and experimental economics to model and measure econometrically how we come to be the people we are, including ethical behavior, generosity towards others, and our capacity to cooperate. Photo courtesy of Marci Gintis

Individuals update their types occasionally, taking account of the average payoffs of the two types in recent interactions and adopting the trait with the higher expected payoff. The updating process is as in Section 14.1 but with $\lambda = 0$, so conformist transmission is absent and the updating process is simply payoff-dependent.

1. Explain why, when the interactions are one-shot games (played once and not repeated), cooperation will not persist in the population (here and below you may find it useful to present a graph of the problem).

Now consider the following modification of the game.

Retaliation. In each period the interaction takes place and with probability q this period will be the last (otherwise it continues for at least one more period). Agents may adopt Nice Tit for Tat strategies. As the repetition takes place over a very short time period, you may ignore the time preference of the actors.

2. Show the payoff matrix for this game where the strategies are Nice Tit for Tat (T) and Unconditional Defect (D).

3. Give the condition necessary for Nice Tit for Tat (T) to be an ESS.

Segmentation. Think of the population as living in homogeneous "villages" as well as a "cosmopolitan city," where the distribution of inhabitants is representative of the entire population. The interaction is one-shot and the fraction of the population that are x-types is p. The pairing of individuals to interact is non-random: a type will be paired with their own type under two conditions: they play locally in a village where they will meet only their own type, or they play in the city where, depending on the distribution of types in the city, they may be randomly paired with their own type.

> **Nice tit for tat**
>
> *Nice tit for tat* is the following strategy in a repeated Prisoners' Dilemma Game: cooperate in the first period (hence "nice") and in successive periods play what the other player did in the previous period.

Then an x will be paired with an x not p percent of the time, but $\mu_{xx} = s + (1-s)p > p$ percent of the time. Correspondingly, y-types will be paired with x-types $\mu_{yx} = (1-s)p < p$ percent of the time.

Segmentation

In evolutionary modeling, a *seg-mented* population is one in which the likelihood of any two individuals interacting is affected by the structure of the population into sub-populations within which interactions are more likely than would occur by chance (and between which, less likely). Also termed *assortation*.

Segmentation is also modeled in Sections 14.3 and 14.4 .

The punishers in this setup are based on ethnographic evidence on how order is maintained in small scale societies before the emergence of states. A model of this process can be found in Bowles and Choi [21] and Boyd, Gintis, and Bowles [34].

[21]: Bowles and Choi (2013), 'Coevolution of Farming and Private Property During the Early Holocene'
[34]: Boyd, Gintis, and Bowles (2010), 'Coordinated Punishment of Defectors Sustains Cooperation and Can Proliferate When Rare'

The difference between these two conditional probabilities, s, is the degree of segmentation. Suppose two available strategies are Unconditional Cooperate (C) and Unconditional Defect (D). Let p be the fraction of cooperators in the population.

4. Write the expected payoffs if the degree of segmentation is s.

5. If $a = 5$, $b = 4$, $c = 3$, and $d = 0$, indicate the smallest value of s such that some positive level of cooperation can be sustained in the population.

Punishment of defectors. There is no segregation and the interaction is non-repeated (it is one-shot), but when a defector meets a cooperator, the defector may receive a punishment which reduces their benefits by $\delta(a - b)$, the probability that this punishment will be inflicted being p, the fraction of cooperators (those adopting the strategy Cooperate and Punish) in the population. You may imagine that when a cooperator is defected upon, all the fellow cooperators join forces and attempt to punish (at no cost for the cooperators) the defector, the probability that they will succeed depending on how prevalent they are in the population.

6. Write equations giving the payoffs of the two strategies: Defect (D) and Cooperate and Punish (P).

7. Indicate the values of δ for which Cooperate and Punish is an ESS.

Answers.

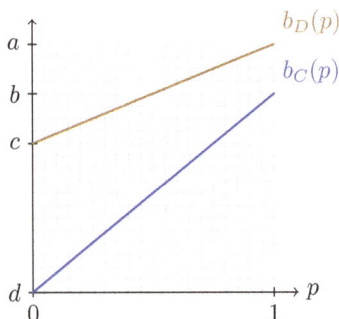

Figure 14.4: Frequency-dependent payoffs in the Prisoner's Dilemma Game. The expected payoff to being a Cooperator is

$$b_C(p) = pb + (1-p)d$$

and that to being a Defector is

$$b_D(p) = pa + (1-p)c$$

with $a > b > c > d$ and $2b > a + d$.

1. Let the fraction of cooperators in the population be p. Then the expected payoff to being a cooperator and defector are

$$b_C(p) = pb + (1-p)d$$
$$b_D(p) = pa + (1-p)c$$

respectively. As shown in Figure 14.4, for any $p \in [0,1]$, $b_D(p) > b_C(p)$ since $a > b > c > d$. Therefore, should cooperation occur in the population, it will not persist, given the updating process.

2. The payoff matrix is shown in Table 14.3. For instance, using the notation $\pi(T, D)$ to mean the expected payoff to playing Tit for Tat against a Defector, we have

$$\pi(T, T) = b + b(1-q) + b(1-q)^2 + \cdots = b/q$$
$$\pi(T, D) = d + c(1-q) + c(1-q)^2 + \cdots = c/q + d - c$$

The expression for $\pi(T, T)$ is just the payoff of b per period, lasting for the expected duration of the game, which is the inverse of the probability of termination or $1/q$. The expression for $\pi(T, D)$ is the mutual defect payoff for as many periods as the game continues except for the first period in which the T-player cooperates with a defector and as a result gets d rather than c.

3. For the strategy T to be an ESS, either

$$\pi(T,T) > \pi(D,T)$$

or

$$\pi(T,T) = \pi(D,T) \text{ and } \pi(T,D) > \pi(D,D)$$

holds. Since

$$\pi(T,D) = \frac{c}{q} + d - c < \frac{c}{q} = \pi(D,D)$$

the necessary condition is

$$\pi(T,T) > \pi(D,T)$$

That is,

$$\frac{b}{q} > \frac{c}{q} + a - c$$

which requires

$$\frac{b-c}{a-c} > q$$

In other words, the payoff advantage of mutual cooperation over mutual defection $(b-c)$ relative to the payoff advantage of defecting on a cooperator over mutual defection $(a - c)$ is greater than the termination probability.

4. The expected payoff to being a cooperator is

$$b_C^s(p) = [s + (1 - s)p]b + (1 - s)(1 - p)d$$
$$= d + (b - d)[s + (1 - s)p]$$

and that to being a defector is

$$b_D^s(p) = [s + (1 - s)(1 - p)]c + (1 - s)pa$$
$$= c + (a - c)(1 - s)p$$

as shown in Figure 14.5.

5. Given $a = 5$, $b = 4$, $c = 3$, and $d = 0$, the expected payoffs become

$$b_C^s(p) = 4s + 4(1 - s)p$$
$$b_D^s(p) = 3 + 2(1 - s)p$$

For some small positive level of cooperation to be sustained, it requires

$$b_C^s(p) \geq b_D^s(p)$$

for some small p. Since $b_C^s(p) - b_D^s(p) = 4s - 3 + 2(1 - s)p$ is continuous and increasing in p, it is sufficient that

$$b_C^s(0) \geq b_D^s(0) \Rightarrow 4s \geq 3$$

Therefore, the smallest value of s is 0.75, as shown in Figure 14.5.

Recall that the sum S of an infinite geometric series $\sum_{n=0}^{\infty} ar^n$ with $|r| < 1$ is given by $S = a/(1 - r)$, hence $\sum_{n=0}^{\infty} b(1 - q)^n = b/q$.

Table 14.3: The payoff matrix for the game with strategies Nice Tit for Tat (T) and Unconditional Defect (D). Shown are row player's payoff in the symmetric game.

	T	D
T	b/q	$c/q + d - c$
D	$c/q + a - c$	c/q

Figure 14.5: Frequency-dependent payoffs in the Prisoner's Dilemma Game with segregation. The expected payoff to being a Cooperator is

$$b_C^s(p) = d + (b - d)[s + (1 - s)p]$$

and that to being a Defector is

$$b_D^s(p) = c + (a - c)(1 - s)p$$

Assuming $a = 5, b = 4, c = 3$ and $d = 0$, the solid lines represent the payoffs with $s = 0.25$. For some small positive level of cooperation to be sustained, it must be that $b_C^s(0) \geq b_D^s(0)$, as represented in the dashed line. Thus

$$d + (b - d)s \geq c \Rightarrow s \geq \frac{c - d}{b - d} = \frac{3}{4}$$

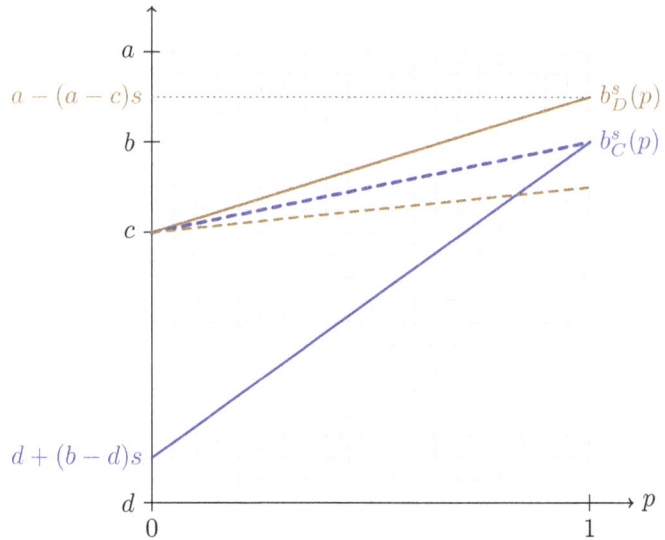

6. The payoff matrix is shown in Table 14.4. Note that

$$\pi(D, P) = (1 - p)a + p[a - \delta(a - b)] = a - p\delta(a - b)$$

The expected payoffs to P and D are, respectively,

$$b_P^\delta(p) = pb + (1 - p)d$$
$$b_D^\delta(p) = p[a - p\delta(a - b)] + (1 - p)d$$

Table 14.4: The payoff matrix for the game with strategies Cooperate and Punish (P) and Defect (D). Shown are row player's payoff in the symmetric game.

	P	D
P	b	d
D	$a - p\delta(a - b)$	d

7. For Cooperate and Punish (P) to be ESS, the incumbent P-players in an all-P population ($p = 1$) must produce more replicas than D and hence will eliminate the entrant strategy D, which requires

$$b_P^\delta(1) > b_D^\delta(1)$$

That is,

$$b > a - \delta(a - b) \Rightarrow \delta > 1$$

If $\delta > 1$, then the expected punishment of a player who defects on a cooperator (a P-player), that is, $\delta(a - b)$, exceeds the benefit to the defector of defecting rather than cooperating with a cooperator, that is $(a - b)$.

14.3 Learning, imitation, and segmentation

Sometimes it makes sense to just copy what most others are doing (conformist learning, a form of social learning). And sometimes studying the current situation and making one's own decision (individual learning) is a better strategy. This problem explores the intuition that copying others may be a good strategy if most people in the population have adopted the individual learning strategy and if the environment is not changing too much from period to period.

Consider a changing environment in which each member of a population with n members (a large even number) may adopt one of two strategies in which members are randomly matched with other members. The *individual learning strategy* (L) is to research the environment at a cost of c and, on the basis of the resulting knowledge, to select an action, which yields benefits of b. The *imitation strategy* (I) costs nothing, and yields benefits of b if the imitator is matched with a learner and $b - \sigma$ if the imitator is matched with another imitator, where $\sigma > c$ is a suitably normalized measure of the environmental variability.

Let p be the fraction of the population who are learners. Suppose that individuals periodically change their strategy when paired with an individual using the other strategy and if the other strategy on the average yielded higher payoffs in the previous period. Otherwise, they retain their strategy (they do not change).

1. Find the interior stationary value p^* in this dynamic.

2. Show that average payoffs among the population are not maximized in the outcome of this game.

3. Explain why this is so. What accounts for the coordination failure?

4. What are the equilibria of this game (stationary values of p) and which, if any, are asymptotically stable? Explain why.

5. Say which, if either, strategy is an ESS.

Suppose, now, that pairing is non-random and that pairings are made according to a degree of segmentation coefficient $s \in (0, 1)$. That is, if the fraction of the population that are x-types is p, then x-types will be paired with their own type on average not p percent of the time but $\mu_{xx} = s + (1 - s)p > p$ percent of the time. Correspondingly, y-types will be paired with x-types $\mu_{yx} = (1 - s)p < p$ percent of the time.

> **Asymptotically stable**
>
> If some stationary state, call it p^*, is *asymptotically stable*, then a sufficiently small displacement of the state away from p^* will result in a movement back towards p^*. *Neutral stability* (also termed *Lyapunov stability*) is a weaker concept, dropping the "self correcting" characteristic of asymptotic stability and requiring only that the dynamic in question does not induce a movement further away from p^*.

6. Write down the expected payoffs of the two strategies under this non-random pairing.

> Segmentation is also explored in Section 14.2.

7. What is the equilibrium fraction of individual learners under this matching rule $p^*(s)$? Is it greater than $p^*(0)$, the stationary fraction without segmentation?

In this setup, imagine that you were a planner (social engineer) with the power to dictate both the strategies adopted by each member of the population and also who should be matched with whom. The pairings need not be one-to-one; you may pair the same individual with multiple other individuals. You wish to maximize average payoffs of the entire population.

8. What pairing rule (network structure) will maximize average payoffs for a given $p \in (0, 1)$?

9. What are the average payoffs under your plan for a given $p \in (0, 1)$?

10. With the pairing rule you chose, what distribution of strategies would you implement?

11. Explain why the planner's pairing rule could be implemented as a Nash equilibrium among expected payoff-maximizing individuals with complete information about the distribution of types in the population and the structure of the network.

12. Explain why it cannot be a stationary state under the updating process explained above, that is, copying the strategy of those who attained higher payoffs in the previous period.

Answers.

1. The expected payoffs to L and I are, respectively,

$$b_L(p) = b - c$$
$$b_I(p) = pb + (1-p)(b-\sigma) = b - \sigma + p\sigma$$

At the stationary value p^* in this dynamic, it must be the case that

$$b_L(p^*) = b_I(p^*) \Rightarrow p^* = 1 - \frac{c}{\sigma} \qquad (14.3)$$

2. The average payoff of the population is

$$pb_L(p) + (1-p)b_I(p) = b - \sigma + (2\sigma - c)p - \sigma p^2$$

The first order condition for maximizing average payoffs is

$$2\sigma - c - 2\sigma p^{\max} = 0 \Rightarrow p^{\max} = 1 - \frac{c}{2\sigma}$$

which is different from p^*.

3. The coordination failure occurs because learners generate social benefits in excess of their private benefit as they convey information to imitators when they are copied. Thus, the equilibrium level of learners is less than the socially optimal level.

4. Given the dynamic

$$\frac{dp}{dt} = \beta p(1-p)(b_L - b_I)$$

the stationary values of p are $p = 0$, $p = 1$, and $p = p^*$. Since

$$\frac{d(dp/dt)}{dp}(p) = \beta[(1-2p)(b_L - b_I) - p(1-p)(b_L' - b_I')]$$

we have that both $p = 0$ and $p = 1$ are unstable because

$$\frac{d(dp/dt)}{dp}(0) = \beta[b_L(0) - b_I(0)] = \beta(\sigma - c) > 0$$
$$\frac{d(dp/dt)}{dp}(1) = -\beta[b_L(1) - b_I(1)] = \beta c > 0$$

while the interior stationary value p^* is asymptotically stable because

$$\frac{d(dp/dt)}{dp}(p^*) = -\beta p^*(1 - p^*)[b'_L(p^*) - b'_I(p^*)] = -\beta p^*(1 - p^*)\sigma < 0$$

5. Consider the learning strategy; it is not an ESS since

$$b_L(1) = b - c < b = b_I(1)$$

For the imitation strategy,

$$b_I(0) = b - \sigma < b - c = b_L(0)$$

Therefore, it is not an ESS, either.

6. Under non-random pairing with the degree of segmentation s, the expected payoff to L remains the same, i.e., $b^s_L(p) = b - c$. The expected payoff to I becomes

$$b^s_I(p) = (1 - s)pb + [1 - (1 - s)p](b - \sigma) = b - \sigma + (1 - s)p\sigma$$

7. The equilibrium $p^*(s)$ requires $b^s_L = b^s_I$. That is

$$b - c = b - \sigma + (1 - s)p\sigma$$

Then,

$$p^*(s) = \frac{\sigma - c}{\sigma(1 - s)} = \frac{1}{1 - s}\left(1 - \frac{c}{\sigma}\right) = \frac{1}{1 - s}p^*$$

where $p^* = 1 - c/\sigma$ is the stationary value when there is no segmentation as shown in (14.3). Therefore, $p^*(s) > p^*(0)$ for $s > 0$. In other words, the stationary value with segmentation $p^*(s)$ is greater than that without segmentation. This is because the imitators are more likely to interact with each other with segmentation, which will lead them to have low payoffs so that some of them adopt the individual learning strategy.

8. To maximize the average payoff, an imitator must be always matched with a learner for any $p \in (0, 1)$.

9. Under this pairing rule, the payoff to a learner is $b - c$, and that to a imitator is b. Therefore, the average payoff is

$$p(b - c) + (1 - p)b = b - pc$$

10. To maximize the average payoff, p must be positive but as small as possible (so that there is at least one learner to pair imitators to). Therefore, $p = 1/n$, i.e., one member of the population adopts the learning strategy and the rest imitation.

11. Under the pairing rule, the above outcome can be implemented as a Nash equilibrium. Note that the only individual learner has no incentive to deviate since their payoff would as a result fall from

Endogenous Preferences: The Evolution of Cooperation

$b - c$ to $b - \sigma$ (recall that $\sigma > c$). The imitators, who benefit from free riding on the sole learner, would not deviate either.

12. It cannot be a stationary state in the above copy-the-successful updating process. Under this rule, the individual learner would switch to imitation since the payoff to imitation under the planner's assignment is b, higher than that to learning $b - c$. Your answers to this and the previous question show that the Nash equilibrium concept may give a different prediction from an alternative empirically plausible model of learning and imitating.

Note that the Nash equilibrium and the copy-the-successful updating rule can be seen at the two extremes in terms of the sophistication of players. Consider an intermediate case: when n is large such that the individual learner cannot observe the entire network, so they are uncertain about p. They know p is very small, but they don't know for sure they are the only learner in the population. Then, even as an expected payoff-maximizer, they might decide to imitate instead of learn: as long as they believe that it is likely that there is at least one other learner among the $n - 1$ people they are matched with. In this case, the planner's average payoff maximizing allocation ($n - 1$ imitators all matched with 1 learner) could not be implemented as a Nash equilibrium.

14.4 Community, cooperation, and the gains from trade

Where contracts are incomplete, exchange is sometimes sustained by trading only with those of known reputation, for example by trading repeatedly with a limited number of exchange partners or by a process of segmentation that ensures that trustworthy people interact with each other more than would happen by chance.

These community-based trading practices may facilitate trade by altering the process of cultural evolution so as to support a higher fraction of trusting and cooperative members of the population. But the practices also restrict exchange. In each of the three examples just given, the effect is to limit the selection of exchange partners in some way, and this imposes costs which may take the form of foregone exchange opportunities, failure to find a partner with whom a mutually beneficial trade can be made, foregone economies of scale, and the like.

Let's consider a particular case — segmentation — and represent a dyadic exchange as a prisoners' dilemma in which Cooperate means trust the other and offer to exchange goods at some mutually beneficial price, while Defect means steal or otherwise cheat one's exchange partner.

Suppose people live in villages that are homogeneous by type and a fraction s of their interactions takes place in their village, the rest occurring in the city where the types are mixed. Define the degree of segmentation as follows: if the fraction of the population who are cooperators is α, the probability that a cooperator will be paired with a

A related problem about civil society as a distinctive form of governance is Section 6.4. For background on civil society, have a look at Bowles and Carlin [17, 20].

[17]: Bowles and Carlin (2020), 'Shrinking Capitalism'
[20]: Bowles and Carlin (2025), 'Civil Society'

Some background for this problem is found in Bowles and Gintis [25, 26].

[25]: Bowles and Gintis (2002), 'Social Capital and Community Governance'
[26]: Bowles and Gintis (2004), 'Persistent Parochialism'

fellow cooperator is no longer α but $s + (1 - s)\alpha$, where s is the *degree of segmentation* of the population. Correspondingly, the probability of a defector meeting a fellow defector is now $s + (1 - s)(1 - \alpha)$. If $s = 1$, likes are paired with likes whatever the population composition, and if $s = 0$, pairing is random. Homogeneous sub-groups are not necessary for segmentation to occur; the "village" and "city" example is just a particularly transparent case. We take the pairing rule implied by the degree of segmentation as an exogenously given characteristic of the clustering of types supported by residence patterns, ethnic boundaries, or any other structural characteristic giving rise to non-random matching.

Furthermore, suppose that the more segmented the economy (a greater value of s as defined above), the less is the likelihood (λ) that one will be paired with a person with whom there are beneficial trades potentially to be made (conditional on the exchange being executed without theft, cheating, and so on). To formalize this, we say that with probability $1 - \lambda$ the interaction yields zero for both parties: they have nothing to exchange that would benefit the two.

To summarize the relevant trade-offs, let $\lambda = 1 - s^3$ so that, if segmentation is complete, one never makes a trade, and if segmentation is absent, one always makes a trade. Assume that the payoff matrix is given by Table 14.5 and updating is as modeled in Section 14.1 but is based on expected payoffs alone (conformist learning is absent).

	Cooperation	Defect
Cooperate	3	1
Defect	5	2

Table 14.5: The Prisoner's Dilemma Game. Row player's payoff in the symmetric game

1. Show that if $s = 0$, then the equilibrium fraction of trusting and cooperative members of the population is $\alpha^* = 0$.

2. What is the minimal value of s such that $\alpha^* > 0$? If $s = 0.6$, what is α^*? For what values of s is $\alpha^* = 1$?

3. Suppose for the moment that $\lambda = 1$ and is exogenous (i.e., it does not depend on s, contrary to the above account). Write an expression for the average payoff in equilibrium (π^*) and show that $d\pi^*/ds > 0$ for those values of s which support an equilibrium value of $\alpha^* \in (0, 1)$. This means that average payoffs are increasing with the degree of segmentation conditional on being sure of finding a trading partner with whom a mutually beneficial trade is possible.

The key to answering the next question is the following trade off: segmentation by type may support the evolution of cooperative norms that facilitate trade when contracts are incomplete but also reduce the likelihood of finding a partner with whom to trade in mutually beneficial ways. Increases in s attenuate the payoff disadvantage of cooperators and also decrease the likelihood that matching will result in the potential for mutually beneficial trades (affecting both types adversely).

4. Now take account of the endogeneity of the likelihood of a mutually beneficial transaction: $\lambda = \lambda(s)$. Write the expected profits in equilibrium: $\pi^e = \lambda(s)\pi^*(s)$. Is there a level of s that maximizes π^e? Explain how profits in equilibrium vary with s.

Answers.

Let $\pi^C(\alpha, s)$ and $\pi^D(\alpha, s)$ be the expected payoffs to cooperators and defectors, respectively, in a population. Then we have

$$\pi^C(\alpha, s) = \lambda(s)[3s + (1 - s)(1 + 2\alpha)] \qquad (14.4)$$

and

$$\pi^D(\alpha, s) = \lambda(s)[2s + (1 - s)(2 + 3\alpha)] \qquad (14.5)$$

1. If $s = 0$, then $\lambda(s) = 1$. The expected payoffs to cooperators and defectors are respectively

$$\pi^C(\alpha, 0) = 1 + 2\alpha$$

and

$$\pi^D(\alpha, 0) = 2 + 3\alpha$$

Then for any $\alpha \in [0, 1]$ we have

$$\pi^C(\alpha) < \pi^D(\alpha)$$

which means that Defect is the dominant strategy. Therefore, the equilibrium fraction of trusting and cooperative members of the population is $\alpha^* = 0$.

2. For a positive level of α^* to be an equilibrium, it must be the value of α equating the two above expected payoffs:

$$\pi^C(\alpha^*, s) = \pi^D(\alpha^*, s)$$

or

$$\alpha^*(s) = \frac{s}{1 - s} - 1$$

Then

 a) For there to be an $\alpha^*(s) > 0$, we must have $s > 0.5$.

 b) If $s = 0.6$, then $\alpha^* = 0.5$.

 c) Let $\alpha^*(s) = 1$, we have

$$\frac{s}{1 - s} - 1 \geq 1 \Rightarrow s \geq \frac{2}{3}$$

3. From the discussion above, we have

$$\alpha^*(s) = \begin{cases} 0 & 0 \leq s \leq \frac{1}{2} \\ \frac{s}{1-s} - 1 & \frac{1}{2} < s < \frac{2}{3} \\ 1 & \frac{2}{3} \leq s \leq 1 \end{cases} \qquad (14.6)$$

Since $\lambda = 1$, the average payoff in equilibrium (π^*) is given by

▶ when $\alpha^* = 0$,

$$\pi^* = \pi^D(0, s) = 2s + 2(1 - s) = 2$$

▶ when $\alpha^* = 1$,

$$\pi^* = \pi^C(1, s) = 3s + 3(1 - s) = 3$$

▶ for any $\alpha^* \in (0, 1)$, we have

$$\pi^* = \pi^C(\alpha^*(s), s) = \pi^D(\alpha^*(s), s) = 6s - 1$$

Therefore, we have

$$\pi^*(s) = \begin{cases} 2 & 0 \leq s \leq \frac{1}{2} \\ 6s - 1 & \frac{1}{2} < s < \frac{2}{3} \\ 3 & \frac{2}{3} \leq s \leq 1 \end{cases} \tag{14.7}$$

and thus we have $d\pi^*/ds = 6 > 0$ for $1/2 < s < 2/3$ which supports an equilibrium value of $\alpha^* \in (0, 1)$.

4. For $\lambda(s) = 1 - s^3$, the expected profits in equilibrium is

$$\pi^e = \lambda(s)\pi^*(s) = \begin{cases} 2(1 - s^3) & 0 \leq s \leq \frac{1}{2} \\ (6s - 1)(1 - s^3) & \frac{1}{2} < s < \frac{2}{3} \\ 3(1 - s^3) & \frac{2}{3} \leq s \leq 1 \end{cases} \tag{14.8}$$

Over the first range ($s \leq 1/2$), you know from the answer to the previous sub section that everyone is defecting, and they receive the mutual defect payoff (2) in those cases for which a mutually beneficial exchange is possible, the frequency of which is declining in s. This explains the first, declining, portion of the average payoffs function in the figure.

For $1/2 < s < 2/3$, the fraction of those cooperating increases and the higher payoffs when two cooperators meet more than offsets the reduced likelihood of a potentially mutually beneficial trade entailed by an increase in the degree of segmentation. So profits increase with s over this range.

For values of $s \geq 2/3$ everyone is cooperating so further increases in s just reduce the frequency of beneficial trades (which, when they occur, result in the payoff of mutual cooperation, 3). So profits decline with increases in s.

To find the maximum of π^e, we have

▶ for $s \in [0, 1/2]$, $\pi^e(s)$ is decreasing with $\pi^e(0) = 2$ and $\pi^e(1/2) = 1.75$
▶ for $s \in (1/2, 2/3)$, $\pi^e(s)$ is increasing since

$$\frac{d\pi^e}{ds} = 6 + 3s^2 - 24s^3 > 0 \quad \forall s \in \left(\frac{1}{2}, \frac{2}{3}\right)$$

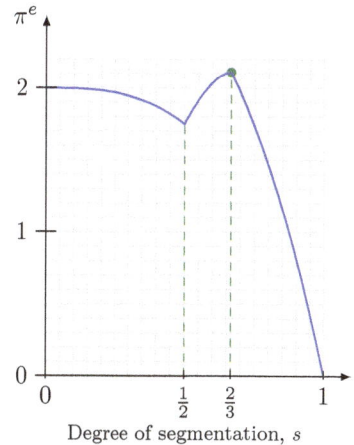

Figure 14.6: The expected profit in equilibrium with $\lambda(s) = 1 - s^3$. The expected profit in equilibrium as a function of the degree of segmentation s

$$\pi^e = \begin{cases} 2(1 - s^3) & 0 \leq s \leq \frac{1}{2} \\ (6s - 1)(1 - s^3) & \frac{1}{2} < s < \frac{2}{3} \\ 3(1 - s^3) & \frac{2}{3} \leq s \leq 1 \end{cases}$$

achieves its maximum at $s = 2/3$.

▶ for $s \in [2/3, 1]$, $\pi^e(s)$ is decreasing, and at $s = 2/3$ it exceeds the previous maximum at $s = 0$:

$$\pi^e(2/3) = \frac{19}{9} > 2 = \pi^e(0)$$

Therefore, $s = 2/3$ maximizes the expected payoff in equilibrium, as shown in Figure 14.6. This example demonstrates that, even though segmentation limits trade, there can still be some level of $s > 0$ such that it supports higher average payoffs than in the case without segmentation.

The Evolution of Conflict over the Distribution of Gains from Cooperation

15

Some social institutions — private property, markets, states, worship of supernatural beings, social ranking, and sharing the necessities of life among non-kin, for example — have emerged independently and been ubiquitous over long periods of the human experience. Others — polyandry or central economic planning, for example — have been of passing importance, and generally have occupied limited ecological niches. Talcott Parsons, an important sociologist of the mid-20th century, termed the former "evolutionary universals," by which he meant those ways of ordering society that crop up, persist, and are adopted with sufficient frequency in a variety of circumstances to suggest their general evolutionary viability [83].

Parsons offered the convergent evolution of vision in many species as a biological analogy; another would be flight. For society, Parsons identified (among others) money, markets, bureaucracy, social stratification, and liberal democracy as a set of modern social arrangements toward which independent societal trajectories would tend (he predicted the demise of Communist Party rule and central planning in the Soviet Union). Friedrich Hayek referred to the nexus of markets and private property — his "extended order" — in a similar vein [59].

Is economic inequality an example of Parsons' evolutionary universals? Can the study of evolutionary processes contribute to our understanding of the conditions under which a population will experience substantial levels of inequality of wealth (or some other economic measure)?

Evolutionary models have been used to explain the remarkably common fifty-fifty division of crop shares between farmers and landowners around the world, including in the U.S. state of Illinois. Similar models have been the basis of an explanation of both the very long-term persistence of highly egalitarian hunting and gathering populations in which most material wealth was held in common and the subsequent prehistoric emergence of very unequally held private property in stored foods and animals during the late Neolithic period in western Eurasia.

The latter study used a variant of the Hawk-Dove-Bourgeois Game from biology. This game is the basis of three of the problems below. Though the game is non-cooperative (binding agreements among the players are not feasible), the players are contesting over a "prize" which is possible due to their interacting (like the farmer and the landlord). This is why we refer to conflicts over the division of the gains from cooperation.

These models are described in Young and Burke [114] and Bowles and Choi [22]. The models on which the problems in this chapter are based are presented in Chapters 2, 11 – 13 in Bowles [14].

[83]: Parsons (1964), 'Evolutionary Universals in Society'

[59]: Hayek (1988), *Fatal Conceit*

Figure 15.1: John Maynard Smith (1920–2004) was trained as an engineer (he designed military aircraft during World War II) but later took up mathematics and genetics (airplanes were too "noisy and old fashioned"). He developed his Hawk Dove Game to understand conflicts among non-human animals, including spiders battling over their webs, which he recognized in his model by adding a property-owning strategy, Bourgeois. (The term — not commonplace among biologists — probably came from his political orientation: he had been a member of the Communist Party of Great Britain until resigning in protest of the brutal repression of the Hungarian revolution by the Soviet Union in 1956.) Along with George Price and others, he introduced game theory to biology and is credited with contributing to the creation of the new field of evolutionary game theory. Source: Corbin O'Grady Studio / Science Photo Library.

[114]: Young and Burke (2001), 'Competition and Custom in Economic Contracts'

[22]: Bowles and Choi (2019), 'The Neolithic Agricultural Revolution and the Origins of Private Property'

[14]: Bowles (2004), *Microeconomics*

©2025 Samuel Bowles and Weikai Chen, CC BY-NC 4.0

https://doi.org/10.11647/OBP.0466.15

15.1 Conspiracy of doves, bourgeois invasion

This question explores the costly nature of conflict over the distribution of wealth or income and how recognition of ownership may reduce conflicts, but only if the relevant property rights are sufficiently well defined and mutually recognized.

Consider the Hawk-Dove Game. Doves, when they meet, share a prize, while when Hawks meet, they fight over the prize, inflicting costs on one another; and when a Hawk meets a Dove, the Hawk takes the prize without a fight. The prize to be divided is v, the cost of losing a fight is $c > v$, and the probability of a Hawk winning a contest against another Hawk (they are identical) is $1/2$. When they meet, Doves divide the prize equally and without cost.

Thus, the payoff matrix is as shown in Table 15.1. Members of this population are randomly paired to play the Hawk-Dove Game, and we let $b_H(p)$ and $b_D(p)$ be the expected payoff to being a Hawk and a Dove, respectively, in a population in which the fraction of Hawks is p.

> If p is the fraction of a large (infinite) population that are Hawks, then the probability of being paired with a Hawk (for both Hawks and Doves) is p.

We will see that this population may be rife with conflicts (among the Hawks), so we will call the land they inhabit Hobbes Island, honoring the 17th-century philosopher who posited that life without government would be "a war of all against all."

Assume that, at the end of every period, each member of the population produces a number of exact replicas (excluding mutations) equal to ϕ plus the payoff to the game, so the payoffs are in units of offspring surviving to reproductive age, that is, fitness (ϕ is called the "baseline fitness").

Normalizing the total population to unity, we can write next year's population frequency of Hawks, p' as

$$p' = \frac{p(b_H + \phi)}{pb_H + (1-p)b_D + \phi} \tag{15.1}$$

Table 15.1: Hawk-Dove Game (row player's payoffs). Note that the fitness (number of offspring surviving to reproductive age) is equal to ϕ plus the game payoffs.

	Hawk	Dove
Hawk	$(v-c)/2$	v
Dove	0	$v/2$

1. From equation (15.1), derive the replicator equation

$$\Delta p = \frac{1}{\underline{b}}p(1-p)(b_H - b_D)$$

where $\underline{b} = pb_H + (1-p)b_D + \phi$, that is, mean fitness.

2. Find the stationary interior value of p (the population fraction of Hawks) for the Hawk-Dove Game, show that it is not Pareto-efficient, and explain what accounts for this coordination failure.

> An interior value of p is one for which both Hawks and Doves are present in the population, that is, $0 < p < 1$. Think of Pareto efficiency in fitness terms: no member of the population could have higher fitness without some other member having less fitness.

3. Human capacities for collective action often allow us to overrule evolutionary tendencies that predominate in other animals. Imagine that in a human population playing the Hawk-Dove Game, a law was proposed outlawing playing Hawk, its approval being dependent on majority vote (and its cost of implementation assumed to be zero). Assume that player voters are initially distributed according to the equilibrium frequency of Hawks. Would a majority

	Hawk	Dove	Bourgeois
Hawk	$(v-c)/2$	v	$v/2 + (v-c)/4$
Dove	0	$v/2$	$v/4$
Bourgeois	$(v-c)/4$	$v/2+v/4$	$v/2$

Table 15.2: Hawk-Dove-Bourgeois Game (row player's payoffs)

of the population support the proposed law? Explain why or why not. If passage required unanimity, would the law pass?

Now suppose that in any interaction the members of the pair have an equal probability of being the "owner" of the prize and consider the type of strategy called "Bourgeois"[95] according to which a player's action is conditioned on their ownership status (either owner or not, the latter called "intruder"), i.e., "if owner play Hawk, if intruder, play Dove". Then the payoff matrix of this Hawk-Dove-Bourgeois Game is as shown in Table 15.2.

[95]: Smith (1974), 'The Theory of Games and the Evolution of Animal Conflicts'

4. Suppose a yacht with a few Bourgeois types was wrecked on the shores of Hobbes Island whose (large) population of Hawks and Doves was distributed according to the equilibrium fractions you just found above. Can the shipwrecked Bourgeois types invade the mixed population of Hobbes Island?

Now consider the case in which some fraction of the time $\mu \in [0,1)$ intruding Bourgeois players mistakenly believe they are owners (when they are not), or in any case act that way, playing Hawk, while in the role of owner they always play Hawk as before. This strategy, called Contested Bourgeois, is denoted by $B(\mu)$. We restrict $\mu < 1$ because if $\mu = 1$, then Contested Bourgeois is just a Hawk claiming the prize irrespective of its ownership.

5. Find the expected payoffs to this strategy, when played against itself $\pi(B(\mu), B(\mu))$, and the expected payoff to an invading Hawk in a large population made up entirely of Contested Bourgeois players $\pi(H, B(\mu))$. Can the Hawk invade successfully?

6. What is the least value of μ such that a few Contested Bourgeois can invade an equilibrium population of Hawks and Doves?

Answers.

1. By equation (15.1) and $\underline{b} = pb_H + (1-p)b_D + \phi$, we have

$$\Delta p = p' - p = \frac{p(b_H + \phi)}{pb_H + (1-p)b_D + \phi} - p$$

$$= \frac{p(b_H + \phi) - p[pb_H + (1-p)b_D + \phi]}{pb_H + (1-p)b_D + \phi}$$

$$= \frac{p(1-p)b_H - p(1-p)b_D}{\underline{b}}$$

$$= \frac{1}{\underline{b}}p(1-p)(b_H - b_D)$$

2. To find a stationary value of p, set $\Delta p = 0$. Then the interior stationary value of the population fraction of Hawks is $p^* \in (0, 1)$ such that $b_H(p^*) = b_D(p^*)$. That is,

$$b_H(p^*) = p^* \cdot \frac{v - c}{2} + (1 - p^*)v = 0 + (1 - p^*) \cdot \frac{v}{2} = b_D(p^*)$$

Therefore, $p^* = v/c$.

Since

$$\frac{db_H(p)}{dp} = \frac{v - c}{2} - v = -\frac{v + c}{2} < 0$$

and

$$\frac{db_D(p)}{dp} = -\frac{v}{2} < 0$$

a decrease in the population fraction of Hawks will make both Hawks and Doves better off, as shown in Figure 15.2. Thus, the equilibrium in this population is Pareto-inferior to any $p < p^*$, and so any interior stationary state is not Pareto-efficient.

This coordination failure occurs because the dynamics of the population are determined by reproductive success of the members of each type — their own fitness — which does not take into account the effect that a change in p has on the expected fitness of all members of the population. If the fraction of Hawks in the population is less than v/c, Hawks will produce more offspring than Doves, increasing p and reducing the expected fitness of all members of the population (including the Hawks).

3. As shown above, the payoff to both Hawks and Doves is declining in the fraction of Hawks, so both are better off the fewer Hawks there are. For any interior stationary value p^*,

$$b_H(p^*) = b_D(p^*) < b_D(0) = \frac{v}{2}$$

Therefore, the law will pass under both majority vote and unanimity rules.

4. At $p^* = v/c$, both the expected payoff of being a Hawk and that of being a Dove are equal to

$$b_H(p^*) = b_D(p^*) = \left(1 - \frac{v}{c}\right) \cdot \frac{v}{2}$$

The expected payoff to the Bourgeois interacting with the original population is

$$b_B^* = p^* \cdot \frac{v - c}{4} + (1 - p^*)\left(\frac{v}{2} + \frac{v}{4}\right) = \left(1 - \frac{v}{c}\right) \cdot \frac{v}{2}$$

which is the same as the expected payoff of being a Hawk or a Dove. Moreover, the payoff to the Bourgeois when interacting with the same type is $v/2$, which is larger than b_B^*. Thus the expected payoff of being a Bourgeois is larger than that of being a Hawk or a Dove, and therefore the Bourgeois types can invade the mixed population of Hobbes Island.

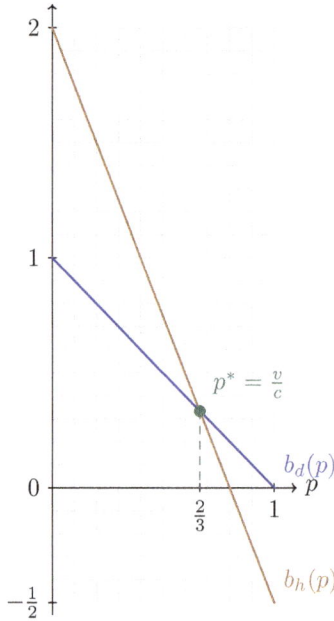

Figure 15.2: Frequency-dependent payoffs in the Hawk-Dove Game ($v = 2$, $c = 3$). The expected payoff to being a Hawk is

$$b_H(p^*) = p^* \cdot \frac{v - c}{2} + (1 - p^*)v$$

and that to being a Dove is

$$b_D(p^*) = \frac{v}{2}(1 - p)$$

and the stationary interior value of p given by $b_H(p^*) = b_D(p^*)$ is $p^* = v/c$.

5. With probability one-half the Contested Bourgeois individual is a possessor, playing Hawk, facing an intruder who as a contested Bourgeois correctly plays Dove $(1 - \mu)$ of the time, granting v to the possessor, but with probability μ mistakenly plays Hawk, leading to the conflict payoff $(v - c)/2$. With probability one-half the Contested Bourgeois individual is an intruder who correctly plays Dove with probability $(1 - \mu)$, receiving 0, and with probability μ mistakenly plays Hawk, repeating the mistaken conflict payoff $(v - c)/2$. Therefore,

$$
\pi(B(\mu), B(\mu)) = \frac{1}{2}\left[(1 - \mu)v + \mu \cdot \frac{v - c}{2}\right] + \frac{1}{2}\left[0 + \mu \cdot \frac{v - c}{2}\right]
$$
$$
= \frac{1}{2}(v - \mu c)
$$

Similarly, the expected payoffs to an invading Hawk is

$$
\pi(H, B(\mu)) = \frac{1}{2}\left[(1 - \mu)v + \mu \cdot \frac{v - c}{2}\right] + \frac{1}{2} \cdot \frac{1}{2}(v - c)
$$
$$
= \frac{1}{2}(1 - \mu)v + \frac{1}{4}(1 + \mu)(v - c)
$$

and then

$$
\pi(B(\mu), B(\mu)) - \pi(H, B(\mu)) = -\frac{1}{4}(1 - \mu)(v - c) > 0
$$

for $\mu < 1$. Therefore, the Hawk invasion will fail. Note that if $\mu = 1$ (the intruding Contested Bourgeois always mistakes another's possession as their own), then there is no payoff advantage for the Contested Bourgeois type because, when not in possession, its play is identical to the Hawk.

6. Since the Contested Bourgeois plays either Hawk or Dove, when an invading Contested Bourgeois interacts with the population at $p^* = v/c$, they get $b_H(p^*)$ when playing Hawk or $b_D(p^*)$ when playing Dove. Thus the expected payoff is just some weighted average of $b_H(p^*)$ and $b_D(p^*)$.

Furthermore, as shown above at the equilibrium $p^* = v/c$, we have

$$
b_H(p^*) = b_D(p^*) = (1 - \frac{v}{c})\frac{v}{2}
$$

so any weighted average of $b_H(p^*)$ and $b_D(p^*)$ is constant. Then the expected payoff to an invading Contested Bourgeois interacting with the population at p^* is just $b_H(p^*) = b_D(p^*)$.

Therefore, for the few Contested Bourgeois types to successfully invade the equilibrium population, it requires that their payoff when they (rarely) interact with each other be superior to the payoffs of Hawks and Doves:

$$
\pi(B(\mu), B(\mu)) \geq p_H(p^*) = p_D(p^*)
$$

That is

$$
\frac{1}{2}(v - \mu c) \geq \left(1 - \frac{v}{c}\right) \cdot \frac{v}{2} \Rightarrow \mu \leq \frac{v^2}{c^2}
$$

Therefore, the least value of μ such that Contested Bourgeois can invade an equilibrium population of Hawks and Doves is $(v/c)^2$.

15.2 Conformist Hawks and Doves

Though introduced as a model of natural selection on genetically transmitted traits, the Hawk-Dove model has also been used to study cultural evolution, where individual behaviors are learned (literally, copied from parents, other adults, peers) rather than being genetically inherited. Cultural change occurs in this framework when a person of one cultural type switches to a different type (or the children of a person of one type adopt a type different from their parents). To recognize the role of conformism as well as of payoffs in the process by which people update their types, we introduce the idea of cultural fitness below.

Individuals are randomly paired to play a Hawk-Dove Game in which the prize $v = 2$ and the cost of fighting $c = 3.5$, and they periodically update their type by consulting both the expected payoffs of the two types (b_H and b_D respectively) in the previous period and the fraction of the population that are Hawks (p), giving a weight α to the prevalence of Hawks (p) and $(1 - \alpha)$ to payoff differences in the updating process. Conformist learning effects are present if the likelihood of copying a trait (either Hawk or Dove) is greater the more common that type is in the population, regardless of payoff differences.

Table 15.3: Hawk Dove Game (row player's payoffs)

	Hawk	Dove
Hawk	−0.75	2
Dove	0	1

Assume that conformist effects are absent if $p = 1/2$. Thus, the conformist effect on updating is $\alpha(p - 1/2)$ and the payoff-based effect is $(1 - \alpha)(b_H - b_D)$. You may benefit by drawing a figure of both the Hawk-Dove payoffs, and of the updating equilibrium with conformism.

1. Let $p^*(\alpha)$ denote the stationary value of p given the indicated value of α. Suppose $\alpha = 0$ so that conformism is absent. Assuming the both Hawks and Doves are in the population, what is the stationary population frequency of Hawks, $p^*(0)$?

2. Now assume that conformism is present such that $\alpha = 1/3$. Write down the condition for an interior value of p to be stationary and explain it in words.

3. What is this stationary population frequency of Hawks, $p^*(1/3)$?

4. Why is $p^*(1/3)$ greater than $p^*(0)$, the stationary population in absence of conformism?

5. Show that, under the parameter values above, $p^*(1/3)$ is asymptotically stable.

6. What is the least value of α such that $p^*(\alpha) = 1$?

Answers.

1. When conformism is absent and both Hawks and Doves are in the population, the stationary population frequency of Hawks, $p^*(0)$, requires the equality of the expected payoffs.

$$b_H = -0.75p + 2(1-p) = 1 - p = b_D$$

Thus $p^*(0) = 4/7$, which is just v/c as expected from your answer the second part of Section 15.1.

2. With conformism, the cultural fitness of a type, designated r_H and r_D, is a weighted average of the conformism effect and payoff-based effect.

$$r_H = \alpha \left(p - \frac{1}{2} \right) + (1 - \alpha) \left[b_H(p) - b_D(p) \right]$$

$$r_D = \alpha \left(\frac{1}{2} - p \right) + (1 - \alpha) \left[b_D(p) - b_H(p) \right]$$

The condition for an interior value of p to be stationary is $r_H(p) = r_D(p)$, which requires

$$b_D(p) - b_H(p) = \frac{\alpha}{1 - \alpha} \cdot \left(p - \frac{1}{2} \right) \tag{15.2}$$

In words, in a stationary state the effect of differential payoff favoring Doves (the left-hand side) offsets the effect of conformism favoring Hawks because $p > 1/2$ (the right-hand side).

3. From equation (15.2) and $\alpha = 1/3$, we have

$$\frac{7}{4}p - 1 = \frac{1}{2}p - \frac{1}{4}$$

and thus $p^*(1/3) = 3/5$, which, using generic values for payoffs, is just $3v/(4c - 2v)$.

4. In the absence of conformism, the payoff difference must be zero at stationary state, whereas with conformism and with the fraction of Hawks greater than one-half, the payoff to Doves must exceed the payoff to Hawks to offset the positive effect of conformism on the cultural fitness of Hawks. Moreover, the payoff difference $b_D(p) - b_H(p) = 7p/4 - 1$ is increasing in p, as shown in Figure 15.3. Therefore, we could expect that $p^*(1/3) > p^*(0)$.

5. It is sufficient to show that the derivative of dp/dt with respect to p at p^* is negative:

$$\frac{d(dp/dt)}{dp} = p^*(1 - p^*) \left[\alpha + (1 - \alpha) \left(\frac{db_H}{dp} - \frac{db_D}{dp} \right) \right] < 0$$

As $b_H(p) - b_D(p) = 1 - 7p/4$, we have

$$\frac{db_H}{dp} - \frac{db_D}{dp} = -\frac{7}{4}$$

Figure 15.3: The stationary value of p requires that at $p = p^*$ the conformist pressures favoring the copying of Hawk be offset by payoff advantages of Doves. The payoff effect is

$$b_D(p) - b_H(p) = \frac{7}{4}p - 1$$

In absence of conformism, the stationary value

$$p^*(0) = \frac{4}{7}$$

is determined by p-intercept of the payoff effect. When $\alpha = 1/3$, the conformism effect is

$$\frac{\alpha}{1-\alpha} \cdot (p - k) = \frac{1}{2}p - \frac{1}{4}$$

Its intersection with the payoff effect determines the stationary value of p,

$$p^*\left(\frac{1}{3}\right) = \frac{3v}{4c - 2v} = \frac{3}{5}$$

The dashed blue line shows the conformism effect when $\alpha = 3/5$. In this case, the stationary value of p is

$$p^*\left(\frac{3}{5}\right) = 1$$

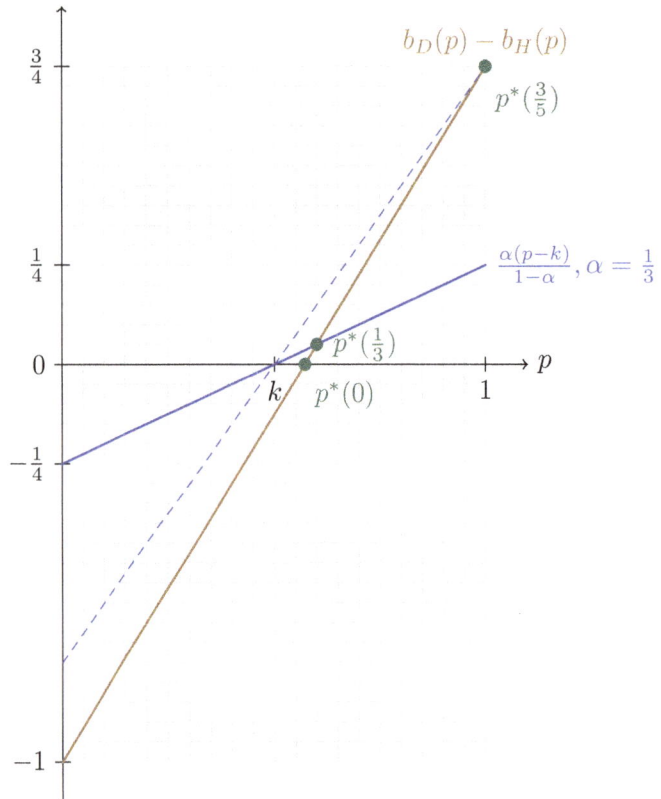

then

$$\alpha + (1 - \alpha)\left(\frac{db_H}{dp} - \frac{db_D}{dp}\right) = \alpha - \frac{7}{4}(1 - \alpha) = -\frac{5}{6} < 0$$

when $\alpha = 1/3$. Therefore, the inequality holds.

6. From equation (15.2), we have

$$\frac{7}{4}p - 1 = \frac{\alpha}{1 - \alpha} \cdot \left(p - \frac{1}{2}\right)$$

and thus $p^*(\alpha) = (4 - 6\alpha)/(7 - 11\alpha)$. Then $p^*(\alpha) = 1$ requires

$$4 - 6\alpha = 7 - 11\alpha$$

and therefore $\alpha = 3/5$ is the least value of α such that $p^*(\alpha) = 1$.

15.3 Risk dominance and evolutionary stable distributional conventions

Interested in conventions? Read Young [112].

[112]: Young (1996), 'The Economics of Convention'

Landlords and the farmers who work their land as sharecroppers play a Nash Demand Game in which the landlords may claim either 1/2 or 3/4 of the crop, while farmers may claim either 1/2 or 1/4 of the crop. When claims add up to 1 (that is, the entire crop) or less, each gets their claim, each getting zero otherwise. Farmers and landlords are randomly paired to play a one-shot non-cooperative game and they adopt strategies that are best responses to the previous period's distribution of strategies in the larger population of which they are a part.

Let p be the fraction of farmers who claim $1/2$, and q the fraction of landlords who claim $1/2$. Then we characterize an outcome of the game as a couplet (p, q), of which there are a large number. We say that an outcome of the game is plausible if you would expect to see this frequently if you observed the outcomes of many such games.

1. Identify any outcomes of this game that you would consider plausible and explain your answer.

2. Is every Nash equilibrium of this game a plausible outcome? If so, explain why. If not, give an example of an implausible Nash equilibrium and explain why it is not plausible.

Suppose that the total amount of output produced by the farmer depends on how the crop will be distributed. So in the $(1, 1)$ outcome (all landlords and all farmers claim half) the total crop to be divided is 1, while in the $(0, 0)$ outcome it is $1 + \alpha$ where $\alpha > -1$.

3. Which Nash equilibrium is risk dominant if $\alpha \le 0$?

4. For what values of α is the $(0, 0)$ outcome risk dominant?

5. In actual sharecropping contracts whether in India or the U.S. state of Illinois or elsewhere, the 50-50 division is the most widely observed contract [114]. Provide an explanation based on your answers to the above questions.

> **Convention**
>
> A convention is one of two or more possible patterns of behavior in an interaction that may persist over time because conforming to the convention is a best response for all of those participating as long as most others also conform to it. Driving on the right or on the left are two conventions.

For example, if there are just two landlords and three farmers, then $p \in \{0, 1/3, 2/3, 1\}$ and $q \in \{0, 1/2, 1\}$ and thus there are $3 \times 4 = 12$ possible combinations of (p, q).

Section 13.2 provides one microeconomic model of why the total output produced by the farmer may vary inversely with the fraction of the crop that they have to transfer to the landlord: the less effort devoted to cultivation by the farmer, the smaller is the share of the crop that the farmer can keep.

[114]: Young and Burke (2001), 'Competition and Custom in Economic Contracts'

Answers.

1. An outcome that is not a Nash equilibrium is not plausible because, not being a mutual best response, players would have an incentive to change their strategy. The two Nash equilibria that are plausible are $(p, q) = (1, 1)$ or $(p, q) = (0, 0)$; both are conventions.

2. The Nash equilibrium $(p, q) = (1/3, 1/2)$ is not plausible since it is not stable, i.e., a small change in either p or q would lead to larger deviations from it. For example, an increase in p (the fraction of farmers who claim $1/2$) would induce more landlords to claim $1/2$ and thus increase q, which would in turn cause p to increase further.

3. Using the expression $b_{1/2}^L(p)$ to mean the landlord's expected payoff to playing $1/2$ when p is the fraction of farmers playing $1/2$ in the last period (and the rest of the notation below analogously defined), the expected payoff of the landlords are

$$b_{1/2}^L(p) = \frac{1}{2}$$

$$b_{3/4}^L(p) = \frac{3}{4}(1 - p)(1 + \alpha)$$

The expected payoff of the farmers are

$$b^F_{1/2}(q) = \frac{1}{2}q$$

$$b^F_{1/4}(q) = \frac{1}{4}(1 + \alpha)$$

If $\alpha \leq 0$, $1/2$ is the landlord's risk-dominant strategy since

$$b^L_{1/2}\left(\frac{1}{2}\right) > b^L_{3/4}\left(\frac{1}{2}\right)$$

while the strategy $1/2$ is the farmer's (weakly) risk-dominant strategy since

$$b^F_{1/2}\left(\frac{1}{2}\right) = b^F_{1/4}\left(\frac{1}{2}\right)$$

Therefore, $(1, 1)$ is risk dominant.

4. To make $(0, 0)$ a risk-dominant outcome, both $1/4$ and $3/4$ must be risk-dominant strategies for the farmers and the landlords, respectively, which requires

$$\begin{cases} b^L_{1/2}(\frac{1}{2}) < b^L_{3/4}(\frac{1}{2}) \\ b^F_{1/2}(\frac{1}{2}) < b^F_{1/4}(\frac{1}{2}) \end{cases} \Rightarrow \begin{cases} \frac{1}{2} < \frac{3}{8}(1 + \alpha) \\ \frac{1}{4} < \frac{1}{4}(1 + \alpha) \end{cases} \Rightarrow \alpha > \frac{1}{3}$$

Therefore, for $\alpha > 1/3$, the outcome $(0, 0)$ is risk dominant.

5. A possible explanation consists of the following statements.

   a) Even if people are risk neutral, a convention is more likely to be widely observed if it is risk dominant.

   b) In order for the (0,0) outcome to be risk dominant, the farmer would have to be more than a third more productive i.e., $\alpha > 1/3$ under the unequal contract than when receiving a 50-50 share, which seems unlikely.

15.4 Lords and Merchants

This question was inspired by Brenner [35] and Dobb [46]. See also Acemoglu, Johnson, and Robinson [1].

[35]: Brenner (2003), *Merchants and Revolution*

[46]: Dobb (1947), *Studies in the Development of Capitalism*

[1]: Acemoglu, Johnson, and Robinson (2005), 'The Rise of Europe: Atlantic Trade, Institutional Change, and Economic Growth'

The emergence of sustained economic growth under capitalist institutions required that private economic transactions be protected from predatory confiscations of property or extractions by political authorities. In many parts of Europe in the 17th and 18th centuries, cities became centers of commerce and nascent manufacturing in part because urban areas — for example the "free cities" of southern Germany — developed new social norms and legal structures protecting private economic actors from arbitrary political impediments. This problem — making use of the Hawk Dove Games in Sections 15.1 and 15.2 — illustrates this dynamic.

Members of two classes — Lords and Merchants — are paired to interact in the following one-shot game: when a Merchant interacts with a

Merchant, they exchange goods, dividing an income in excess of their next best alternatives of s equally; when a Lord interacts with a Merchant, the Lord simply confiscates the entire surplus; and when Lords meet each other, they engage in competitive displays of wealth and power (tournaments, feasts) costing each Lord an amount c. There are no other costs or types of income. The payoff matrix for this game is presented in Table 15.4.

Suppose that there is mobility between the two classes (the children of Lords may become Merchants, and the children of Merchants may become Lords, say, by intermarriage). Some children, upon becoming adults, switch classes if the *other* class had a higher payoff on average in the previous generation.

1. If the Merchants and the Lords are paired randomly to play the game, write down the expected payoffs of the members of the two classes (let p be the fraction of the population that are Lords).

2. Given these payoffs, what is p^*, the equilibrium fraction of the population that are Lords?

3. Say whether either all are Lords ($p = 1$) or all are Merchants ($p = 0$) is an evolutionarily stable strategy (ESS).

4. Say whether p^* is asymptotically stable.

Suppose, now, that urban areas have grown up, so with probability u, Merchants interact in the city, where there are only Merchants, and with probability $(1-u)$, Merchants are randomly paired with either Merchants or Lords, meeting a Lord with probability p. Similarly, because the society is partially segregated by class, Lords are also automatically paired with a Lord with probability u, while being paired randomly with the whole population with probability $(1 - u)$.

5. Write down the expected payoff functions of the Merchants and the Lords given the new pairing rule.

6. What is the equilibrium value of $p^*(u)$ under the new pairing rule?

7. Is $p^*(u)$ larger or smaller than p^* under random pairing? Explain why.

Answers.

1. The expected payoff of Lords is

$$b_L(p) = -pc + (1 - p)s = s - p(c + s)$$

and that of Merchant is

$$b_M(p) = 0 + (1 - p) \cdot \frac{s}{2} = \frac{1}{2}(1 - p)s$$

Table 15.4: The Game of Lords and Merchants (row player's payoffs)

	Lord	Merchant
Lord	$-c$	s
Merchant	0	$s/2$

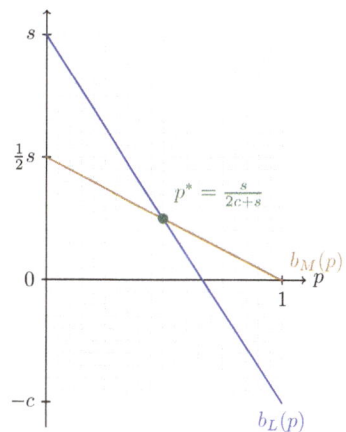

Figure 15.4: Frequency-dependent payoffs in the Game of Lords and Merchants. The expected payoff to being a Lord is

$$b_L(p) = -pc + (1 - p)s$$

and that to being a Merchant is

$$b_M(p) = \frac{1}{2}(1 - p)s$$

and the stationary interior value of p given by $b_L(p^*) = b_M(p^*)$ is

$$p^* = \frac{s}{2c + s}$$

In this figure, $s = 1$ and $c = 0.5$.

2. At the equilibrium p^*, we have

$$b_L(p^*) = b_M(p^*) \Rightarrow p^* = \frac{s/2}{c + s/2} = \frac{s}{2c + s} \qquad (15.3)$$

as shown in Figure 15.4.

3. Neither all are Lords ($p = 1$) nor all are Merchants ($p = 0$) is an ESS since

$$b_L(0) = s > \frac{s}{2} = b_M(0)$$

so Lords can invade an all-Merchant society, and

$$b_M(1) = 0 > -c = b_L(1)$$

so Merchants can invade an all-Lord society.

4. Yes, p^* is asymptotically stable since

$$\frac{d(b_L - b_M)}{dp} = -c - \frac{s}{2} < 0$$

so at p^* (where the expected payoffs of the two types are equal), a small increase in the fraction of the population that are Lords will result in a payoff advantage for the Merchants, resulting in a reduction in p.

5. The expected payoff function of the Merchants is now

$$\pi_M(p;u) = u \cdot \frac{s}{2} + (1-u)b_M(p) = \frac{s}{2}[u + (1-u)(1-p)]$$

and that of the Lords is

$$\pi_L(p;u) = u \cdot (-c) + (1-u)b_L(p) = -uc + (1-u)[s - p(c+s)]$$

6. By $\pi_M(p;u) = \pi_L(p;u)$ we have

$$p^*(u) = \frac{s}{2c+s} - \frac{u}{1-u} \qquad (15.4)$$

under the new pairing rule as shown in Figure 15.5.

7. From (15.3) and (15.4), we have $p^*(0) = p^*$, and for any $u \in (0,1)$

$$p^*(u) = p^* - \frac{u}{1-u} < p^*$$

Therefore, the equilibrium value of Merchants under the new pairing rule is smaller than that under random pairing. Moreover, if u is sufficient large that $u/(1-u) \geq s/(2c+s)$, then $p^* = 0$. In other words, Lords go extinct when being a Lord is strictly dominated, i.e., $\pi_L(p;u) < \pi_M(p;u)$.

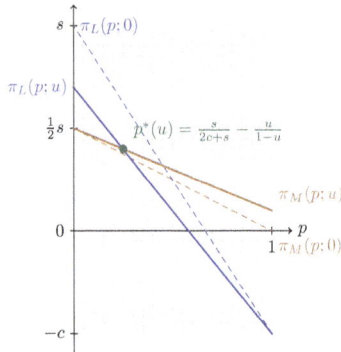

Figure 15.5: Frequency-dependent payoffs in the Game of Lords and Merchants under the new pairing rule. The expected payoff to being a Lord is

$$\pi_L(p;u) = -uc + (1-u)[s - p(c+s)]$$

and that to being a Merchant is

$$\pi_M(p;u) = \frac{1}{2}s[u - (1-u)p]$$

and the stationary interior value given by $\pi_L(p;u) = \pi_M(p;u)$ is

$$p^*(u) = \frac{s}{2c+s} - \frac{u}{1-u}$$

In this figure, $s = 1$, $c = 0.5$ and $u = 0.2$. The dashed lines represent the expected payoffs when $u = 0$.

15.5 Collective action: Payoffs and conformism

Competition and other forms of social interaction may give rise to convergent or divergent dynamic trajectories. We know a lot about convergence-inducing processes; divergence is less well studied but apparently important empirically.

Here is an example: in the latter part of the 20th century, union density (the fraction of labor force belonging to unions) rose in those countries in which density was initially high and fell in those countries in which density was low. Figure 15.6 shows the density for the countries on which comparable data are available. The evident divergence in union density could be the result of positive feedbacks such that a larger union density makes union membership more attractive. Suppose the costs of being a

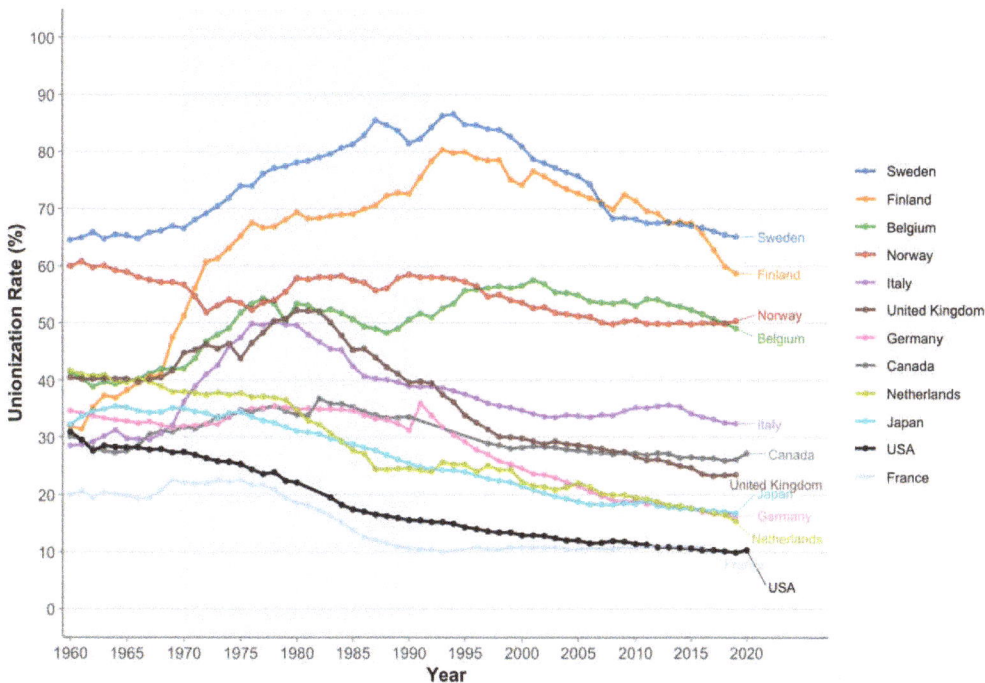

Figure 15.6: Divergent Development of Union Densities, 1960–2024 (shaded area = 1970–1992). Since 2000, there has been little change in unionization rate in any of the countries (neither convergence nor divergence). Source: OECD, Trade Union Density.

union member are c and the material benefits (e.g., the result of more worker-friendly governmental policies) are b, a public good enjoyed by all workers (whether members or not) in proportion to union density $d \equiv n/N$ and $b = \beta d$, where n is the number of members and N the labor force and $\beta > c > \beta/N > 0$.

Feelings of solidarity (or conformism) are strong, however, so being a union member among nonmembers is uncomfortable, as is not joining when most have joined. Thus, the utility of a member is

$$u^m = b - c + \gamma \left(d - \frac{1}{2} \right) \tag{15.5}$$

while the utility of a nonmember is

$$u^n = b + \gamma \left(\frac{1}{2} - d \right) \tag{15.6}$$

with the strength of conformist feeling $\gamma > 0$. Assume that members of the population switch their status (member to nonmember or vice versa) in response to the utilities associated with each.

1. Find the interior stationary values of d, that is, $d^* \in (0, 1)$.

2. Give the parameter values for which union membership is an ESS, and for which non-membership is an ESS.

3. What aspect of the setup of the problem accounts for the possibility of multiple stable equilibria?

Answers.

1. At the interior stationary value d^*, we have $u^m(d^*) = u^n(d^*)$. That is

$$u^m(d^*) = \beta d^* - c + \gamma(d^* - \frac{1}{2}) = \beta d^* + \gamma(\frac{1}{2} - d^*) = u^n(d^*)$$

which implies

$$d^* = \frac{1}{2} + \frac{c}{2\gamma}$$

as shown in Figure 15.7.

Figure 15.7: The utilities of the union member and the nonmember. The utility of a member is

$$u^m(d) = \beta d - c + \gamma(d - \frac{1}{2})$$

and that to being a nonmember is

$$u^n(d) = \beta d + \gamma(\frac{1}{2} - d)$$

and the interior stationary value of d given by $u^m(d^*) = u^n(d^*)$ is

$$d^* = \frac{1}{2} + \frac{c}{2\gamma}$$

In this figure, we assume $\beta = 1.5$, $\gamma = 2$ and $c = 0.5$.

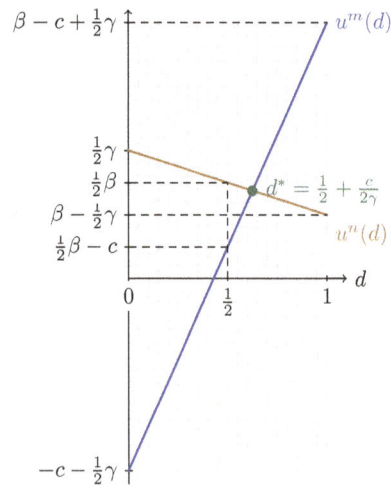

2. For non-membership to be an ESS, we must have

$$u^n(0) > u^m(0) \Leftrightarrow \gamma > -c$$

which holds since $\gamma > 0$ and $c > 0$. For membership to be an ESS, we must have

$$u^m(1) > u^n(1) \Leftrightarrow \gamma > c$$

That is, the conformist feeling should be strong enough to outweigh the cost of being a union member.

3. The two stable stationary states (the two ESSs) occur because the cost of membership discourages people joining a union if nobody else has joined, along with the positive feedbacks due to the fact that one person's union membership is complementary with others' membership, the associated benefits increasing in the fraction of the population that are members sufficiently to offset the membership cost if most have become members.

Projects: From Learning Economics to Doing Economics | **16**

Most of the problems we have presented in the previous chapters have given you practice in working with one or more models that we have provided. Much of the hard work of doing economics, however, goes beyond solving well defined applied mathematics problems and involves choosing among models, possibly extending a well known set up in some way to address a new question, or even developing entirely new models. The problems in this chapter are more of this second kind, requiring considerable thought in the choice of model and its application to a specific problem in the world.

The questions in this chapter work well as a group project with responses explained in a short presentation or paper. In our teaching experience, students have been very engaged in working these problems towards the end of the semester, and have often been surprised and pleased at how the concepts and skills they have learned can illuminate real-world problems. As the questions we ask below are somewhat open-ended, we do not provide answers.

16.1 An employment subsidy (or wage subsidy)

Employment subsidies are a widely discussed means of increasing employment in labor-surplus economies, or among less skilled workers in advanced countries. Suppose that n identical firms each hire h hours of identical labor, varying both h and w, the hourly wage, to maximize profits, which depend on total labor effort, which is the product of hours hired and effort per hour, e.

Consider two types of subsidy paid to owners of each firm:

- an *employment subsidy*: the subsidy is a fixed amount s per hour of labor hired by the firm, or
- a *wage subsidy*: the subsidy is a fixed fraction σ of the total wages paid by the firm.

Using the model of the individual firm's choice of a labor discipline strategy and level of hiring in Section 10.2 and taking the zero-subsidy case as a benchmark

1. Indicate the effects of the two types of subsidy on the equilibrium wage, effort, and employment levels of a single firm that does not have monopsony power in the labor market so that z, the fallback position of each worker, is exogenous. (You may assume that the taxes supporting this subsidy have no effects on this problem.)

2. Using the whole economy model (so as to be able to study the effects on aggregate employment and wages), explain how the subsidy (of either type) affects a) the competition condition, b) the wage curve, and c) the resulting Nash equilibrium level of employment.

This question arose during a very active debate on economic policy in the late 1990s on how to address newly democratic South Africa's massive unemployment problem. One of the authors (Bowles) had been asked by President Nelson Mandela to participate in his Labour Market Commission (a group of business leaders and trade union officials) and to devise policies (as he put it) "to eradicate the footprints of apartheid in South African labour markets." Bowles devised a wage subsidy policy (to be financed by a tax on the assets of firms). But he did not persuade his colleagues on the Commission or President Mandela to support it. Trade unionists in the capital intensive sectors of the economy — mining and metal working — joined their employers in opposing the plan.

©2025 Samuel Bowles and Weikai Chen, CC BY-NC 4.0
https://doi.org/10.11647/OBP.0466.16

3. Why would a subsidy of either type be likely to have a larger effect on equilibrium employment if the level of unemployment was substantial? (Hint: what do you know about the shape of the wage curve?)

16.2 The private exercise of power

Using the set up of the labor discipline model in Section 10.2

1. Propose one or more cardinal measures of the amount of power that the principal wields over the agent in the Nash equilibrium of the game, sufficient to support a statement such as "employers have more power over their workers in firm A (or country A) than in firm B (or country B);"

2. Contrast your use of the term "power" in answering the first part of this question with the terms market power, purchasing power, and bargaining power.

16.3 Domestic "labor discipline": Can the principal agent model be "exported"?

Sometimes, models developed to address a particular set of problems can provide insights in entirely different applications. One of the early principal-agent models of the relationship between an employer and an employee under incomplete contracts, for example, was inspired (the author tells us) by Gary Becker's model of crime deterrence (the "incomplete contract" relationship between law enforcement and citizens) [6, 38]. Can the employer-employee principal-agent model, suitably modified, be "exported" to a seemingly very different field to provide insights about the division of labor in the home?

[6]: Becker (1968), 'Crime and Punishment'
[38]: Calvo (1979), 'Quasi-Walrasian Theories of Unemployment'

Consider the determination of domestic work and the sharing of income by a couple, one of whom works for a given wage outside the home (we'll call him the "husband", with apologies for being so conventional and out of date) and the other (we'll call her the "wife") who cares for the home. Domestic work produces a public good for the two (a clean house, for example). Representing this as a principal-agent model,

If you worked the problems in Section 4.5, you will already be familiar with the idea of domestic labor producing a public good.

1. For the Nash equilibrium of this problem, provide an expression for the share of the paid worker's income received by the home worker (w) and the amount of domestic work done (e).

Short side of a market

The short side of a non-clearing market is the side (either demand or supply) on which the number of desired transactions is least.

Some things to think about:

2. Does the marriage market clear? Explain what this would mean. If not, which of the two is on the short side of the market?

3. Assuming that there are no barriers to divorce, so either of the two could "walk away" from the relationship should they wish, explain how the "husband" can nonetheless exercise power over the "wife." To see how the term power can be used in this setting, return to Section 10.2 on the power of employers over workers in the labor discipline model.

4. Could this model explain the practice of wealth transfers at marriage from the bride's family to the groom's or vice versa, termed dowry or bride price, respectively? Hint: for an analogy that you might develop into an answer, return to "Buy this job" (Section 10.6)

Extension:

5. Contrast your "domestic labor discipline" model with a transaction costs approach to this problem. (Bargaining with transaction costs is the subject of Section 7.3.) What are the relevant transaction-specific investments made by the two members of the couple? Are they likely in your culture (or some other culture with which you are familiar) to differ by gender? What are the similarities and key differences between this approach and the principal-agent approach?

16.4 The BIG idea: An incentive-compatible revenue-neutral guaranteed income

Philippe van Parijs, Robert van der Veen, and others have proposed a universal unconditional basic income grant (BIG). This question explores the idea of an incentive-compatible BIG, namely one whose implementation would sustain incentives to invest, employ labor, and provide effort on the job. We ask, specifically, what is the largest incentive-compatible BIG [13, 105].

[13]: Bowles (1992), 'Is Income Security Possible in a Capitalist Economy?'
[105]: Veen and Parijs (1986), 'A Capitalist Road to Communism'

Assume all employed workers work for an hour. Under the BIG, a linear tax (meaning with a flat rate, τ) is levied on every employed worker, the proceeds being distributed unconditionally to all members of the population. Assume that half of those in the population are employed, a quarter are unemployed, and a quarter are not in the labor force. The maximal size of the grant is constrained by the requirement that it cannot reduce after tax profits (so that the level of investment is sustained) or diminish workers' motivation to provide effort (so the productivity of an our of labor is sustained).

Because, as a result of these constraints, profits are not taxed and because all workers (including those not working) are identical, we assume this proposal has no effect on the demand for labor, so the expected duration of a spell of unemployment is unaffected. You may also abstract from any changes in labor supply. Assume that the implementation of the BIG is accompanied by the elimination of unemployment insurance (define this as B, the replacement income a worker receives if unemployed) and that the net effect of the tax, the BIG, and the elimination of unemployment insurance on the government budget is zero. (The policy package is revenue neutral.)

Figure 16.1: Beatrice Webb (1858–1943), was an English economist who invented the term "collective bargaining." She and her husband Sidney were leaders of the Fabian Society, advocating democratic socialism. She was one of four co-founders of the London School of Economics. Wikimedia Commons, CC BY-SA 4.0, https://commons.wikimedia.org/wiki/File:Beatrice_Webb,_1943.jpg

If $B = w/2$ where w is the equilibrium wage prior to the introduction of the BIG,

1. Taking into account the fact that we now have $B = 0$, what is the maximum tax that can be levied on employed workers without reducing the equilibrium level of aggregate employment?

2. What is the resulting per-person grant if the policy is to be revenue neutral (the tax and the elimination of the unemployment benefit are sufficient to fund the grant to all members of the population)?

3. Show that under this tax and grant a family composed of two employed workers, one unemployed person and one out of the labor force, experiences no change in family income or total effort provided, while those with relatively more non-employed members gain income.

4. What effect if any would you expect this BIG to have on relationships among the members of a family whose income is unaffected.

5. What is the effect of the maximal BIG on the Gini coefficient for the income of private sector workers (including the unemployed, but abstracting from the income received by employers and public officials).

16.5 The dual economy and history's hockey sticks

The term "history's hockey sticks" is sometimes used to describe the data on the level of per capita income from the year 1000 to the present in Great Britain, China, India, Italy, and Japan , as shown in Figure 16.3.

The kink in the time series is associated with two developments:

▶ rapid increases in the productivity of labor in an emerging capitalist sector of the economy, and
▶ a shift of labor out of other lower productivity forms of employment into the capitalist sector, working for wages in firms competing for profit with other firms.

This account makes it clear that the name we have used for "the whole economy model" (in the introduction to Chapter 13) is not really correct. What the model includes is the part of the economy that is made up of private firms — their owners, customers, and workers — and the unemployed, that is, a capitalist sector of the economy. The model leaves out those working for governments or non-profit organizations, independent producers who are neither employers nor workers and unpaid care work (raising children, caring for the elderly for example).

In many lower-income economies, a substantial fraction of all the work done is not employment by a private firm or a government but instead working for oneself or as part of a family. Examples of those working in the informal economy are farming families, small shopkeepers, and

Figure 16.2: Arthur Lewis (1915–1991) won a Nobel Prize (and also knighthood from the British Queen) for his work in economics, but economics was not his field of choice. Born in the Caribbean island (and then British colony) of Saint Lucia, Lewis finished secondary school at age 14. As a young boy required to remain at home for a couple of months due to illness, he learned so much studying by himself and being taught by his father that, when he returned to school, he was transferred from grade 4 to grade 6. "I wanted to be an engineer," he wrote, "but this seemed pointless since neither the government nor the white firms would employ a black engineer." At the London School of Economics he was the student of Friedrich Hayek. With his 1954 paper introducing a dual economy with a modern "capitalist" sector and a "subsistence" sector Lewis sought to return economic thinking to its roots. He wrote in the opening paragraph of his most famous paper: "The classics, from Smith to Marx enquired how production grows through time [and] determined simultaneously income distribution and income growth, with the relative prices of commodities as a minor by-product.". Keystone Press via Alamy

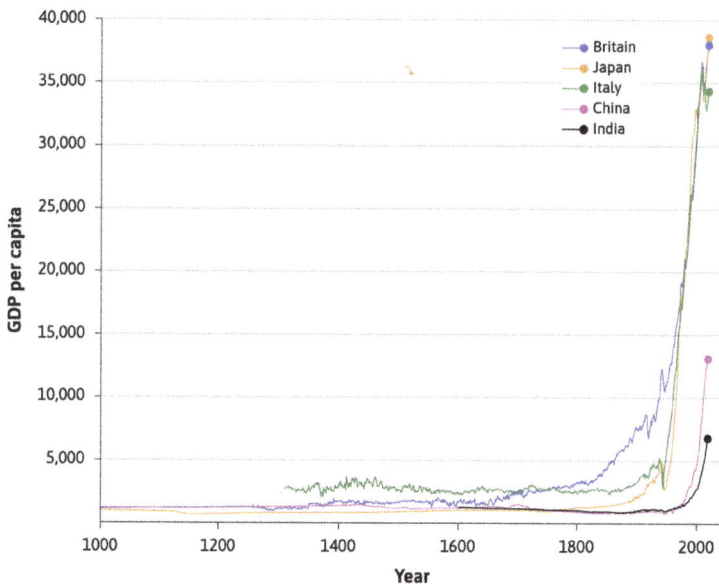

Figure 16.3: History's hockey stick: Gross domestic product per capita in five countries (1000–2018). Source: CORE Econ.

other small businesses relying on unpaid family members for work but not regularly paying wages to employees.

The institutions of the informal economy share with the capitalist economy two aspects of the rules of the game:

► *Markets*: people buy and sell goods and services on markets
► *Private property*: what they buy and sell, and the tools, land, and other capital goods they use in production are privately owned.

But the informal economy differs from the rest of the economy in an important way:

► *Self-employment*: Those working in the informal sector are neither employers nor workers, and they are not compensated by wages or salaries.

In the informal sector, incomes take forms other than wages and salaries. Included are revenues above costs of production from producing crops, profits associated with buying goods at wholesale prices and selling them at a profit, or paying for some service provided.

The informal sector in India makes up something like half the entire economy (measured by people engaged). But informal sectors exist in all economies: much of what is termed gig work is part of the informal economy, for example driving for Uber or Lyft, those finding work through platforms such as Taskrabbit, and others paid by the task completed rather than by the hour.

In low-income economies, people working in the informal sector are for the most part poor due to the relatively low productivity of the technologies, limited use of capital goods, and inability to exploit economies of scale.

We can repurpose and extend the whole economy model to include an informal sector and the capitalist sector. The new element in the model is the informal sector itself. In this setup, there is no unemployment.

In the higher income countries, governments employ between roughly 15 and 30 percent of the workforce. In the U.S., time spent on work done in the home — "housework" and "care work" — is a substantial fraction of total working time. More than a third of the working time of women — work at home plus paid work — is at home.

Informal sector

The informal sector is comprised of the economic activities of family farmers, small shopkeepers, and others who work outside the home and independently of an employer — whether a private firm or a government — and without hiring workers.

Dual economy

The dual economy is one in which employment outside the home and not for government is of two kinds: work compensated by incomes other than wages or salaries in the informal sector and employment for wages and salaries in what is termed the capitalist sector.

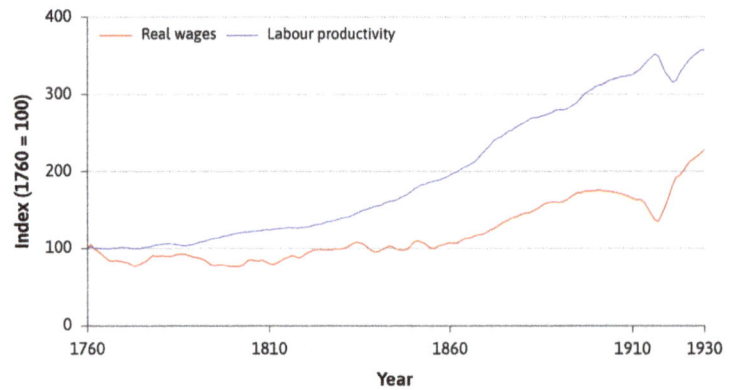

Figure 16.4: Labour productivity and real wages of Britain using five-year centred moving averages

Everyone engaged in the economy is working in either the capitalist or the informal sector.

For employed workers in the capitalist sector, receiving the average income in the informal sector is the fallback option. A worker in the capitalist sector who loses their job returns to working with their family in the informal sector receiving, like the other family members, the average income.

1. Adapt the whole economy model as described in the introduction to Chapter 13 to represent the dual economy so that the labor force works in both a capitalist sector and an informal sector. What is the new wage curve?

2. Beginning from a state in which the informal economy employs more than half of the labor force, explain a process by which the capitalist sector would grow (measured by employment for wages as a fraction of the labor force) along with increases in both wages (in the capitalist sector) and incomes in the informal sector.

3. Innovation in the capitalist sector could have effects quite different from this optimistic scenario (rising workers' incomes in both sectors). Figure 16.4 shows that during the industrial revolution in the 18th and 19th centuries, wages did not increase despite substantial increases in productivity. Using the whole economy model repurposed as your dual economy model, reconstruct your response to the previous question with a somewhat different narrative given by the alternatives below (consider them singly, not jointly)

   ▶ *Change in the degree of competition*: the productivity increase was made possible by a new technology with strong economies of scale, so that the process of competition became a winner-take-all game and barriers to entry rose.
   ▶ *A capitalist sector technology that competes with informal sector goods*: the new technology in the capitalist sector requires very little labor to produce large quantities of a good, the production of which was initially a major source of income in the informal sector (during the industrial revolution in

Britain the capitalist sector produced textiles by power looms, competing with hand loom production in the informal sector).

16.6 After NAFTA: The distribution of the gains from trade in a dual economy

A country (South) with a large traditional grain growing sector protected by tariffs and subsidies shares a border with another country (North) with ideal grain growing conditions and a highly productive agricultural sector. In both countries, there is also an industrial sector organized on capitalist principles, namely private firms hiring wage workers to produce goods intended to be sold for a profit. The reservation position for wage workers in the South is to return to working on their family's farm in the traditional agricultural sector (as in the Lewis model of growth in a dual economy).

An international trade economist proposes a free trade area for the two countries, removing tariffs and subsidies, showing that substantial gains from trade will result for both countries and claiming that employees in the South will enjoy higher (real) wages as a result. A worker asks you if the claim is correct. The trade economist is certainly right about the gains from trade; but what about the wage increases?

1. How would the trade agreement (removing tariffs and subsidies in the South) affect the wage curve?

2. How would this affect real wages in the short run (meaning prior to the South economy moving to the new Nash equilibrium?)

3. Use the competition condition (assumed for the moment to be unaffected by the trade agreement) to consider the long-run impact on wages in the South and on the distribution there of workers between farming and the industrial sector.

4. How might the trade agreement affect the parameters of the competition condition in ways that would (as the trade economist said) raise the real wage in the South in the very long run?

16.7 Apartheid because of or in spite of capitalism

Prior to 1994, the apartheid system in South Africa restricted non-white workers' access to the labor market of the modern (capitalist) sector of the economy. According to the infamous pass laws, those working in the urban areas required a pass, which was revoked if they were fired, requiring them to return to close-to-subsistence living in one of the territories called Bantustans. South African scholars have debated whether this system lowered profits in the white-owned modern economy (by restricting the supply of labor) or raised profits (at least initially by providing businesses with a favorable labor discipline environment).

Before responding to this problem you may want to review the whole economy model as described in the introduction to Chapter 13 and the dual economy model described in Section 16.5.

This scenario is not hypothetical. While teaching a crash course in economics for trade unionists in 1990, just before the implementation of the North American Free Trade Agreement (NAFTA) a textile worker from the U.S. state of North Carolina told one of the authors (Bowles) that she believed that "the trade agreement would lower wages on both sides of the Rio Grande" meaning, both in Mexico and the U.S. He objected, explaining the trade economist's logic for why wages in Mexico would rise. But thinking more about the no-shirking condition, he began to suspect that she had been right. Here is the opinion-editorial he and Mehrene Larudee wrote in the *New York Times* (1993), explaining why the textile worker from North Carolina may have been right.

Before responding to this problem you may want to review the whole economy model as described in the introduction to Chapter 13 and the dual economy model described in Section 16.5. Though not required to answer this question, you may be interested in some of the historical background, which you'll find in Part Two of Wood [109].

[109]: Wood (2000), *Forging Democracy From Below*

Use the labor discipline model (the no-shirking condition) to develop the latter argument. What additional information would you need to determine which position is more nearly correct? Can the no-shirking condition help explain why many (white) employers eventually came to oppose apartheid? (Hint: Think about how their mistreatment in a system of racial exclusion may have affected the workers' disutility of providing the work effort on which their employers' profits depended, and how this in turn may have altered the no-shirking condition).

16.8 How gig work will affect the whole economy

The gig economy — working by means of platforms like Uber, Lyft, TaskRabbit, DoorDash, Handy, Upwork, and MTurk — is made up of independent producers selling completed tasks rather than renting their labor time to an employer. Adapt the models in previous chapters to represent both the relationship between the platform owner and the gigster (gig worker) and a "whole economy" made up of a capitalist sector and a gig sector (see the model described in the introduction to Chapter 13). For the latter, you may want to illustrate your model using the tool at https://bowles-halliday.github.io/bh-textbook/graphs/fig15-15.html.

16.9 The whole economy effect of AI and robotics

Adapt the whole economy model (described in the introduction to Chapter 13) to study the possible effects of AI and robotics on the levels of wages, employment, and inequality. This should include explaining which parameters of the model might be affected, and how these changes would alter the long-term equilibrium of the model. You may want to illustrate your model using the tool at https://bowles-halliday.github.io/bh-textbook/fig15-15.html. Note that in the model there is just one type of labor, so you are not asked to take account of the fact that AI or robotics may be complements to one type of labor and substitutes for another.

Bibliography

[1] Daron Acemoglu, Simon Johnson, and James Robinson. 'The Rise of Europe: Atlantic Trade, Institutional Change, and Economic Growth'. In: *American Economic Review* 95.3 (2005), pp. 546–579. https://doi.org/10.1257/0002828054201305 (cited on page 246).

[2] George A. Akerlof. 'Labor Contracts as Partial Gift Exchange'. In: *The Quarterly Journal of Economics* 97.4 (1982), pp. 543–569 (cited on page 150).

[3] George A. Akerlof and Janet L. Yellen. 'The Fair Wage-Effort Hypothesis and Unemployment'. In: *The Quarterly Journal of Economics* 105.2 (1990), pp. 255–283. https://doi.org/10.2307/2937787 (cited on page 150).

[4] W. Brian Arthur. 'Complexity and the Economy'. In: *Science* 284.5411 (1999), pp. 107–109. https://doi.org/10.1126/science.284.5411.107 (cited on page 6).

[5] Simcha Barkai. 'Declining Labor and Capital Shares'. In: *The Journal of Finance* 75.5 (2020), pp. 2421–2463. https://doi.org/10.1111/jofi.12909 (cited on page 210).

[6] Gary S. Becker. 'Crime and Punishment: An Economic Approach'. In: *Journal of Political Economy* 76.2 (1968), pp. 169–217 (cited on page 254).

[7] Gary S. Becker. *Accounting for Tastes*. Cambridge, MA and London, England: Harvard University Press, 1996 (cited on page 26).

[8] T. J. Besley, K. B. Burchardi, and M. Ghatak. 'Incentives and the de Soto Effect'. In: *The Quarterly Journal of Economics* 127.1 (2012), pp. 237–282 (cited on page 176).

[9] Michael Bollig. *Risk Management in a Hazardous Environment: A Comparative Study of Two Pastoral Societies*. Vol. 2. Cham: Springer, 2006 (cited on page 205).

[10] Monique Borgerhoff Mulder et al. 'Intergenerational Wealth Transmission and the Dynamics of Inequality in Small-Scale Societies'. In: *Science* 326.5953 (2009), pp. 682–688. https://doi.org/10.1126/science.1178336 (cited on page 204).

[11] Samuel Bowles. 'The Production Process in a Competitive Economy: Walrasian, Neo-Hobbesian, and Marxian Models'. In: *The American Economic Review* 75.1 (1985), pp. 16–36 (cited on page 142).

[12] Samuel Bowles. *Capitalist Technology: Endogenous Claim Enforcement and the Choice of Technique*. Economics Working Papers 8878. University of California at Berkeley, 1988 (cited on page 152).

[13] Samuel Bowles. 'Is Income Security Possible in a Capitalist Economy?: An Agency-Theoretic Analysis of an Unconditional Income Grant'. In: *European Journal of Political Economy* 8.4 (1992), pp. 557–578. https://doi.org/10.1016/0176-2680(92)90041-E (cited on page 255).

[14] Samuel Bowles. *Microeconomics: Behavior, Institutions, and Evolution*. Princeton, N.J.: Princeton University Press, 2004 (cited on pages 1, 2, 9, 15, 23, 33, 51, 69, 80, 95, 109, 122, 127, 140, 142, 162, 221, 222, 237).

[15] Samuel Bowles. *The Moral Economy: Why Good Incentives Are No Substitute for Good Citizens*. New Haven, CT: Yale University Press, 2016 (cited on pages 29, 80).

[16] Samuel Bowles and Wendy Carlin. 'Inequality as Experienced Difference: A Reformulation of the Gini Coefficient'. In: *Economics Letters* 186 (2020), p. 108789. https://doi.org/10.1016/j.econlet.2019.108789 (cited on page 198).

[17] Samuel Bowles and Wendy Carlin. 'Shrinking Capitalism'. In: *AEA Papers and Proceedings* 110 (2020), pp. 372–377. https://doi.org/10.1257/pandp.20201001 (cited on pages 79, 232).

[18] Samuel Bowles and Wendy Carlin. 'What Students Learn in Economics 101: Time for a Change'. In: *Journal of Economic Literature* 58.1 (2020), pp. 176–214. https://doi.org/10.1257/jel.20191585 (cited on page 3).

[19]   Samuel Bowles and Wendy Carlin. 'Axioms and Intuitions about Societal Inequality: What Does the Gini Coefficient Measure?' In: *Journal of Income Distribution* 32.3-4 (2023), pp. 45–53. https://doi.org/10.25071/1874-6322.40591 (cited on page 198).

[20]   Samuel Bowles and Wendy Carlin. 'Civil Society: Governance Beyond Markets and States'. In: *Annual Review of Economics* (2025) (cited on page 232).

[21]   Samuel Bowles and Jung-Kyoo Choi. 'Coevolution of Farming and Private Property During the Early Holocene'. In: *Proceedings of the National Academy of Sciences* 110.22 (2013), pp. 8830–8835. https://doi.org/10.1073/pnas.1212149110 (cited on page 226).

[22]   Samuel Bowles and Jung-Kyoo Choi. 'The Neolithic Agricultural Revolution and the Origins of Private Property'. In: *Journal of Political Economy* 127.5 (2019), pp. 2186–2228. https://doi.org/10.1086/701789 (cited on page 237).

[23]   Samuel Bowles and Mattia Fochesato. 'The Origins of Enduring Economic Inequality'. In: *Journal of Economic Literature* 62.4 (2024), pp. 1475–1537. https://doi.org/10.1257/jel.20241718 (cited on page 204).

[24]   Samuel Bowles and Herbert Gintis. 'Walrasian Economics In Retrospect'. In: *The Quarterly Journal of Economics* 115.4 (2000), pp. 1411–1439. https://doi.org/10.1162/003355300555006 (cited on page 3).

[25]   Samuel Bowles and Herbert Gintis. 'Social Capital and Community Governance'. In: *Economic Journal* 112.483 (2002), pp. 419–436 (cited on page 232).

[26]   Samuel Bowles and Herbert Gintis. 'Persistent Parochialism: Trust and Exclusion in Ethnic Networks'. In: *Journal of Economic Behavior & Organization* 55.1 (2004), pp. 1–23 (cited on page 232).

[27]   Samuel Bowles and Herbert Gintis. *A Cooperative Species: Human Reciprocity and Its Evolution*. Princeton, NJ; Oxford: Princeton University Press, 2011 (cited on page 221).

[28]   Samuel Bowles, Herbert Gintis, and Melissa Osborne. 'The Determinants of Earnings: A Behavioral Approach'. In: *Journal of Economic Literature* 39.4 (2001), pp. 1137–1176. https://doi.org/10.1257/jel.39.4.1137 (cited on page 150).

[29]   Samuel Bowles and Simon D. Halliday. *Microeconomics: Competition, Conflict, and Coordination*. Oxford: Oxford University Press, 2022 (cited on pages 1, 2, 9, 18, 23, 33, 51, 69, 80, 95, 109, 140, 162, 185, 195–197).

[30]   Samuel Bowles and Sung-Ha Hwang. 'Social Preferences and Public Economics: Mechanism Design when Social Preferences Depend on Incentives'. In: *Journal of Public Economics* 92.8 (2008), pp. 1811–1820. https://doi.org/10.1016/j.jpubeco.2008.03.006 (cited on page 34).

[31]   Samuel Bowles and D. Kendrick. *Notes and Problems in Microeconomic Theory*. Chicago, IL: Markham Publishing, 1970 (cited on pages 1, 2).

[32]   Samuel Bowles and Yongjin Park. 'Emulation, Inequality, and Work Hours: Was Thorsten Veblen Right?' In: *The Economic Journal* 115.507 (2005), F397–F412. https://doi.org/10.1111/j.1468-0297.2005.01042.x (cited on page 62).

[33]   Samuel Bowles and Sandra Polania-Reyes. 'Economic Incentives and Social Preferences: Substitutes or Complements?' In: *Journal of Economic Literature* 50.2 (2012), pp. 368–425 (cited on page 29).

[34]   Robert Boyd, Herbert Gintis, and Samuel Bowles. 'Coordinated Punishment of Defectors Sustains Cooperation and Can Proliferate When Rare'. In: *Science* 328.5978 (2010), pp. 617–620. https://doi.org/10.1126/science.1183665 (cited on page 226).

[35]   Robert Brenner. *Merchants and Revolution: Commercial Change, Political Conflict, and London's Overseas Traders, 1550-1653*. London; New York: Verso, 2003 (cited on page 246).

[36]   Martin Brown and Peter Philips. 'The Historical Origin of Job Ladders in the US Canning Industry and Their Effects on the Gender Division of Labour'. In: *Cambridge Journal of Economics* 10.2 (1986), pp. 129–145 (cited on page 152).

[37]   Edmund Burke. 'Reflections on the Revolution in France'. In: *Democracy: A Reader*. Chicago, IL: Chicago University Press, 1955, p. 86 (cited on page 1).

[38]   Guillermo Calvo. 'Quasi-Walrasian Theories of Unemployment'. In: *The American Economic Review* 69.2 (1979), pp. 102–107 (cited on page 254).

[39]   Lorne Carmichael. 'Can Unemployment Be Involuntary? Comment [Equilibrium Unemployment as a Worker Discipline Device]'. In: *American Economic Review* 75.5 (1985), pp. 1213–1214 (cited on page 155).

[40]   R. H. Coase. 'The Nature of the Firm'. In: *Economica* 4.16 (1937), pp. 386–405. https://doi.org/10.1111/j.1468-0335.1937.tb00002.x (cited on pages 139, 140).

[41]   R. H. Coase. 'The Problem of Social Cost'. In: *The Journal of Law & Economics* 3 (1960), pp. 1–44 (cited on page 96).

[42]   CORE. *The Economy 2.0: Microeconomics*. Oxford: Oxford University Press, 2023 (cited on page 2).

[43]   Robert A. Dahl. 'On Removing Certain Impediments to Democracy in the United States'. In: *Political Science Quarterly* 92.1 (1977), pp. 1–20 (cited on page 6).

[44]   Jan De Loecker, Jan Eeckhout, and Gabriel Unger. 'The Rise of Market Power and the Macroeconomic Implications'. In: *The Quarterly Journal of Economics* 135.2 (2020), pp. 561–644. https://doi.org/10.1093/qje/qjz041 (cited on page 210).

[45]   Hernando de Soto. *The Mystery of Capital: Why Capitalism Triumphs in the West and Fails Everywhere Else*. New York: Basic Books, 2000 (cited on page 176).

[46]   M. Dobb. *Studies in the Development of Capitalism*. New York: International Publishers, 1947 (cited on page 246).

[47]   Evsey D. Domar and Richard A. Musgrave. 'Proportional Income Taxation and Risk-Taking'. In: *The Quarterly Journal of Economics* 58.3 (1944), pp. 388–422. https://doi.org/10.2307/1882847 (cited on page 191).

[48]   Arindrajit Dube, T. William Lester, and Michael Reich. 'Minimum Wage Shocks, Employment Flows, and Labor Market Frictions'. In: *Journal of Labor Economics* 34.3 (2016), pp. 663–704 (cited on page 213).

[49]   Armin Falk and Michael Kosfeld. 'The Hidden Costs of Control'. In: *American Economic Review* 96.5 (2006), pp. 1611–1630. https://doi.org/10.1257/aer.96.5.1611 (cited on page 31).

[50]   Joseph Farrell. 'Information and the Coase Theorem'. In: *Journal of Economic Perspectives* 1.2 (1987), pp. 113–129. https://doi.org/10.1257/jep.1.2.113 (cited on page 96).

[51]   Ernst Fehr and Klaus M. Schmidt. 'A Theory of Fairness, Competition, and Cooperation'. In: *The Quarterly Journal of Economics* 114.3 (1999), pp. 817–868. https://doi.org/10.1162/003355399556151 (cited on page 24).

[52]   Roberto Galbiati and Giulio Zanella. 'The Tax Evasion Social Multiplier: Evidence from Italy'. In: *Journal of Public Economics* 96.5 (2012), pp. 485–494 (cited on page 34).

[53]   Mauro Gallegati et al. 'What's That Got to Do with the Price of Fish? Buyers Behavior on the Ancona Fish Market'. In: *Journal of Economic Behavior & Organization*. Special Section: Fish Markets 80.1 (2011), pp. 20–33. https://doi.org/10.1016/j.jebo.2011.01.011 (cited on page 80).

[54]   Herbert Gintis. 'A Radical Analysis of Welfare Economics and Individual Development'. In: *The Quarterly Journal of Economics* 86.4 (1972), pp. 572–599. https://doi.org/10.2307/1882043 (cited on page 225).

[55]   Edward L. Glaeser, Bruce I. Sacerdote, and Jose A. Scheinkman. 'The Social Multiplier'. In: *Journal of the European Economic Association* 1.2-3 (2003), pp. 345–353. https://doi.org/10.1162/154247603322390982 (cited on page 34).

[56]   Kathryn Graddy. 'Markets: The Fulton Fish Market'. In: *Journal of Economic Perspectives* 20.2 (2006), pp. 207–220. https://doi.org/10.1257/jep.20.2.207 (cited on page 80).

[57]   John Harte. *Consider a Spherical Cow: A Course in Environmental Problem Solving*. Mill Valley, CA: University Science Books, 1988 (cited on page 1).

[58]   Friedrich A. Hayek. 'The Use of Knowledge in Society'. In: *American Economic Review* 35 (1945), pp. 519–530 (cited on page 3).

[59] Friedrich A. Hayek. *Fatal Conceit: Errors of Socialism*. Ed. by W. W. Bartley. Collected Works of F. A. Hayek Series. Chicago, IL: University of Chicago Press, 1988 (cited on page 237).

[60] Himanshu, Peter Lanjouw, and Nicholas Stern. *How Lives Change: Palanpur, India, and Development Economics*. Oxford: Oxford University Press, 2018 (cited on page 15).

[61] Jack Hirshleifer. 'The Dark Side of the Force: Western Economic Association International 1993 Presidential Address'. In: *Economic Inquiry* 32.1 (1994), pp. 1–10 (cited on pages 11, 106).

[62] Karla Hoff. 'Market Failures and the Distribution of Wealth: A Perspective from the Economics of Information'. In: *Politics & Society* 24.4 (1996), pp. 411–432 (cited on page 179).

[63] David Hume. *The Philosophical Works*. Ed. by T. H. Green and T. H. Grose. Darmstadt: Scientia Verlag, 1964 (cited on page 9).

[64] Matthew O. Jackson. *Social and Economic Networks*. Princeton, NJ: Princeton University Press, 2008 (cited on pages 15, 204).

[65] Daniel Kahneman. 'New Challenges to the Rationality Assumption'. In: *Journal of Institutional and Theoretical Economics* 150.1 (1994), pp. 18–36 (cited on page 23).

[66] Daniel Kahneman, Peter P. Wakker, and Rakesh Sarin. 'Back to Bentham? Explorations of Experienced Utility'. In: *The Quarterly Journal of Economics* 112.2 (1997). In Memory of Amos Tversky (1937-1996), pp. 375–405 (cited on page 23).

[67] Willemien Kets et al. 'Inequality and Network Structure'. In: *Games and Economic Behavior* 73.1 (2011), pp. 215–226 (cited on pages 15, 16).

[68] Alan Kirman. *Complex Economics: Individual and Collective Rationality*. The Graz Schumpeter Lectures. New York: Routledge, 2010 (cited on page 6).

[69] Peter Lanjouw and Nicholas Stern. *Economic Development in Palanpur over Five Decades*. Oxford: Clarendon Press, 1998 (cited on page 15).

[70] Harold D. Lasswell. *Politics: Who Gets What, When, How*. New York: Whittlesey House, 1936 (cited on page 216).

[71] A. P. Lerner. *The Economics of Control: Principles of Welfare Economics*. New York: Macmillan, 1944 (cited on page 3).

[72] David K. Levine. 'Modeling Altruism and Spitefulness in Experiments'. In: *Review of Economic Dynamics* 1.3 (1998), pp. 593–622. https://doi.org/10.1006/redy.1998.0023 (cited on page 25).

[73] Karl Marx. *Grundrisse: Foundations of the Critique of Political Economy*. New York: Vintage Books, 1973 (cited on page 139).

[74] Andreu Mas-Colell et al. *Microeconomic Theory*. Oxford: Oxford University Press, 1995 (cited on page 2).

[75] Gioia de Melo. *Peer Effects Identified Through Social Networks: Evidence from Uruguayan Schools*. Working Papers 2014-05. Mexico City: Banco de México, 2014 (cited on page 34).

[76] Jack Meyer. 'Two-Moment Decision Models and Expected Utility Maximization'. In: *American Economic Review* 77.3 (1987), pp. 421–30 (cited on page 185).

[77] John H. Miller. *A Crude Look at the Whole: The Science of Complex Systems in Business, Life, and Society*. New York: Basic Books, 2016 (cited on page 6).

[78] Suresh Naidu. *Terms of Service: Free and Unfree labor from American Slavery to Artificial Intelligence*. Harvard University Press, 2026 (cited on page 122).

[79] Seung-Yun Oh, Yongjin Park, and Samuel Bowles. 'Veblen Effects, Political Representation, and the Reduction in Working Time over the 20th Century'. In: *Journal of Economic Behavior & Organization* 83.2 (2012), pp. 218–242. https://doi.org/10.1016/j.jebo.2012.05.006 (cited on page 62).

[80] A.M. Okun. *Equality and Efficiency: The Big Tradeoff*. Godkin Lectures at Harvard University. Brookings Institution, 1975 (cited on page 165).

[81] Elinor Ostrom. *Governing the Commons: The Evolution of Institutions for Collective Action*. First Edition. Cambridge: Cambridge University Press, 1990 (cited on page 87).

[82] Vilfredo Pareto. *Manual of Political Economy*. New York: A.M. Kelley, 1971 (cited on page 95).

[83] Talcott Parsons. 'Evolutionary Universals in Society'. In: *American Sociological Review* 29 (1964), p. 339. https://doi.org/10.2307/2091479 (cited on page 237).

[84] Matthew Rabin. 'Incorporating Fairness into Game Theory and Economics'. In: *American Economic Review* 83.5 (1993), pp. 1281–1302 (cited on page 25).

[85] William H. Sandholm. *Population Games and Evolutionary Dynamics*. Cambridge, MA: MIT Press, 2010 (cited on page 70).

[86] Thomas C. Schelling. *The Strategy of Conflict*. Cambridge, MA: Harvard University Press, 1980 (cited on page 51).

[87] Katrin Schmelz. 'Enforcement May Crowd Out Voluntary Support for COVID-19 Policies, Especially Where Trust in Government Is Weak and in a Liberal Society'. In: *Proceedings of the National Academy of Sciences* 118.1 (2021), e2016385118. https://doi.org/10.1073/pnas.2016385118 (cited on page 31).

[88] Juliet Schor. *The Overworked American: The Unexpected Decline of Leisure*. New York: Basic Books, 1992 (cited on page 62).

[89] Rajiv Sethi and Rohini Somanathan. 'Racial Inequality and Segregation Measures: Some Evidence from the 2000 Census'. In: *The Review of Black Political Economy* 36.2 (2009), pp. 79–91. https://doi.org/10.1007/s12114-009-9042-6 (cited on page 18).

[90] Carl Shapiro and Joseph E. Stiglitz. 'Equilibrium Unemployment as a Worker Discipline Device'. In: *The American Economic Review* 74.3 (1984), pp. 433–444 (cited on page 142).

[91] Herbert A. Simon. 'A Formal Theory of the Employment Relationship'. In: *Econometrica* 19.3 (1951), pp. 293–305 (cited on pages 6, 109).

[92] Herbert A. Simon. *The Sciences of the Artificial*. Third Edition. Cambridge, MA: The MIT Press, 1996 (cited on page 6).

[93] Hans-Werner Sinn. *Economic Decisions under Uncertainty*. Second English Edition. Amsterdam: North-Holland Publishing Company, 1983 (cited on page 185).

[94] Hans-Werner Sinn. 'The Selection Principle and Market Failure in Systems Competition'. In: *Journal of Public Economics* 66.2 (1997), pp. 247–274. https://doi.org/10.1016/S0047-2727(97)00043-1 (cited on page 57).

[95] John Maynard Smith. 'The Theory of Games and the Evolution of Animal Conflicts'. In: *Journal of Theoretical Biology* 47.1 (1974), pp. 209–221 (cited on pages 105, 239).

[96] A. Spence. 'Job Market Signaling'. In: *The Quarterly Journal of Economics* 87.3 (1973), pp. 355–374 (cited on page 62).

[97] Alexandra Stevenson and Jack Ewing. 'U.S. Tax Bill May Inspire Cuts Globally, While Fueling Trade Tensions'. In: *The New York Times* (2017) (cited on page 56).

[98] G.J. Stigler. *The Theory of Price*. New York: Macmillan, 1987 (cited on page 3).

[99] George J. Stigler and Gary S. Becker. 'De Gustibus Non Est Disputandum'. In: *The American Economic Review* 67.2 (1977), pp. 76–90.

[100] Robert Sugden. 'Spontaneous Order'. In: *Journal of Economic Perspectives* 3.4 (1989), pp. 85–97. https://doi.org/10.1257/jep.3.4.85 (cited on page 6).

[101] Michael Taylor. *The Possibility of Cooperation*. Cambridge: Cambridge University Press, 1987 (cited on page 10).

[102] John Tierney. 'A Tale of Two Fisheries'. In: *The New York Times* (2000) (cited on page 52).

[103] Leon Trotsky. *My Life: An Attempt at an Autobiography*. New York: Pathfinder Press, 1970 (cited on page 222).

[104] Thorstein Veblen. *The Theory of the Leisure Class. An Economic Study of Institutions*. New Delhi: Aakar Books, 2005 (cited on page 62).

[105]   Robert J. van der Veen and Philippe van Parijs. 'A Capitalist Road to Communism'. In: *Theory and Society* 15.5 (1986), pp. 635–655 (cited on page 255).

[106]   Leon Walras. *Elements of Pure Economics*. London: George Allen and Unwin, 1954 (cited on page 139).

[107]   Jorgen W. Weibull. *Evolutionary Game Theory*. Cambridge, MA: Mit Press, 1995 (cited on page 221).

[108]   Johan Gustaf Knut Wicksell. *Lectures on Political Economy*. Ed. by Lionel Robbins. London: Routledge and Sons, 1934 (cited on page 161).

[109]   Elisabeth Jean Wood. *Forging Democracy From Below: Insurgent Transitions in South Africa and El Salvador*. Cambridge University Press, 2000 (cited on page 259).

[110]   Erik Olin Wright. *Class Counts*. Cambridge University Press, 2000 (cited on page 122).

[111]   Evgeny Yakovlev. 'Demand for Alcohol Consumption in Russia and Its Implication for Mortality'. In: *American Economic Journal: Applied Economics* 10.1 (2018), pp. 106–49. https://doi.org/10.1257/app.20130170 (cited on page 34).

[112]   H. Peyton Young. 'The Economics of Convention'. In: *Journal of Economic Perspectives* 10.2 (1996), pp. 105–122. https://doi.org/10.1257/jep.10.2.105 (cited on page 244).

[113]   H. Peyton Young. *Individual Strategy and Social Structure: An Evolutionary Theory of Institutions*. Princeton, NJ: Princeton University Press, 1998 (cited on page 221).

[114]   H. Peyton Young and Mary A Burke. 'Competition and Custom in Economic Contracts: A Case Study of Illinois Agriculture'. In: *The American Economic Review* 91.3 (2001), pp. 559–573. https://doi.org/10.1257/aer.91.3.559 (cited on pages 237, 245).

[115]   Amotz Zahavi. 'Mate Selection—A Selection for a Handicap. Mate Selection'. In: *Journal of Theoretical Biology* 53.1 (1975), pp. 205–214. https://doi.org/10.1016/0022-5193(75)90111-3 (cited on page 62).

[116]   Chengxiang Zhuge et al. 'The Role of the License Plate Lottery Policy in the Adoption of Electric Vehicles: A Case Study of Beijing'. In: *Energy Policy* 139 (2020), p. 111328. https://doi.org/10.1016/j.enpol.2020.111328 (cited on page 91).

Glossary

A

Altruistic preferences Altruistic preferences motivate a person to help others even at a cost to themselves. 26

Assurance Game An Assurance Game is a 2-person, symmetric, strategic interaction with two strict Nash equilibria, one of which is Pareto-superior to the other. 10

Asymptotically stable If some stationary state, call it p^*, is *asymptotically stable*, then a sufficiently small displacement of the state away from p^* will result in a movement back towards p^*. *Neutral stability* (also termed *Lyapunov stability*) is a weaker concept, dropping the "self correcting" characteristic of asymptotic stability and requiring only that the dynamic in question does not induce a movement further away from p^*. 229

B

Bargaining power In the Nash bargaining model the share of the total rents gained by one of the two bargainers is termed their *bargaining power*. The term is something of a misnomer as it appears to refer to an explanation of the share of the surplus that a bargainer gets, but is really just a description of the outcome of the bargain. 101

Bayesian Nash equilibrium A Bayesian Nash equilibrium is a strategy profile that is a mutual best response among all players given their beliefs about the other players' types. 25

Best response A strategy is a player's best response (also termed best reply) to the strategies adopted by others if no other strategy available would result in higher expected payoffs. A weak best response is a strategy for which there exists at least one other strategy with equal payoffs (so it is not a strict best response). 11

C

Certainty equivalent The certainty equivalent level of income (or wealth) is the level of certain income that would be valued equally to some other outcome in which realized income is subject to risk. 186

Common property resource A common property resource is rival and non-excludable. 36

Competition condition The *competition condition* is an expression for the real wage in terms of the level of barriers to entry, the productivity of labor, and the opportunity cost of capital such that the number of firms in the economy is stationary. 208

Complete contract A contract is complete if it (a) covers all of the aspects of the exchange in which anyone affected by the exchange has an interest, and (b) is enforceable (by the courts) at close to zero cost to the parties. 5

Conformist learning When updating their type, conformist learners favor adopting traits that are more common in a population. 222

Convention A convention is one of two or more possible patterns of behavior in an interaction that may persist over time because conforming to the convention is a best response for all of those participating as long as most others also conform to it. Driving on the right or on the left are two conventions. 245

Coordination failure A coordination failure occurs when the non-cooperative interaction of two or more people results in an outcome that is worse for at least one of those involved and not better for any. 36

Cultural evolution The change over time in behaviors and preferences that are learned from parents, other elders, and peers rather than being genetically inherited from parents. 222

D

Decreasing absolute risk aversion The tendency of a person to be less risk averse if they have more income (or wealth). 191

Degree The degree of a node is the number of edges that are connected to that node. 15

Distance The distance between two nodes in a network is the number of edges on the shortest path between the two nodes. 16

Dominant strategy A strategy is dominant if it yields the highest payoff for a player for any strategy chosen by the other players. Weak dominance refers to the case where there are one or more other strategies yielding the same payoff. 12

Dominant strategy equilibrium A dominant strategy equilibrium is a strategy profile in which all players play a dominant strategy. 53

Dual economy The dual economy is one in which employment outside the home and not for government is of two kinds: work compensated by incomes other than wages or salaries in the informal sector and employment for wages and salaries in what is termed the capitalist sector. 257

E

Economic class An economic class is a set of people who engage in similar contracts with members of other classes. 121

Economic profits Economic profit is revenues minus costs including the opportunity cost of capital goods used in production. 196

Enforcement rent In a principal–agent relationship, an enforcement rent is the excess of the value of the transaction to the agent over the agent's fallback option. The prospect of losing the enforcement rent if the principal terminates the transaction induces the agent to act in the principal's interest. 110

Evolutionary stable strategy An *evolutionary stable strategy* (ESS) is one such that in a population consisting entirely of one type, an alternative strategy, if introduced, will not proliferate. 223

Excludable A good is excludable if a would-be user may be denied access to the good at a low or zero cost. 36

F

Fallback position A player's fallback position (or reservation option) is the payoff they receive in their next best alternative. 52

First mover A player who can commit to a strategy in a game before other players have acted is a first mover. 27

G

Game theory Game theory is a branch of applied mathematics that studies strategic interactions with important applications in economics, the other social sciences, biology, and computer science. 2

Gini coefficient The Gini coefficient is a measure of inequality of some quantity (e.g. income or wealth), defined as one-half the mean absolute difference in that quantity between all unique pairs of individuals in a population relative to the average value of the quantity. It takes the value of 1 if a single person owns all of the wealth, and a value of zero if wealth is equally distributed. 197

H

Hawk Dove Game In a 2 × 2 Hawk Dove Game neither Hawk nor Dove is a best response to itself and the two asymmetrical strategy profiles are Nash equilibria in which the Hawk player's payoffs exceed the Dove's. 10

I

Incentive compatibility constraint The incentive compatibility constraint, ICC, describes the limits on the outcomes that a first mover may implement, showing how a second mover will respond to each of the actions (or strategies) that the first mover might take (including incentives designed to alter the second mover's behavior), also known as the second mover's best response function. 110

Inequality aversion A preference for more equal outcomes and a dislike for both disadvantageous inequality that occurs when others have more than the actor and advantageous inequality that occurs when the actor has more than others. 24

Informal sector The informal sector is comprised of the economic activities of family farmers, small shopkeepers, and others who work outside the home and independently of an employer — whether a private firm or a government — and without hiring workers. 257

Institutions Institutions are the laws, informal rules, and mutual expectations which regulate social interactions among people and between people and the biosphere. 5

L

Linear tax and lump-sum transfer A tax that is proportional to income (a linear tax), the proceeds of which are divided equally and transferred to citizens (a lump sum). 191

Lorenz curve The *Lorenz curve* plots the relationship between the percentage of the population whose income is less than or equal to a certain amount and the percentage of total income received by them. The Gini coefficient is the area between the Lorenz curve and the line of perfect equality divided by the total area below the line of perfect equality. 208

M

Mixed-strategy Nash equilibrium A mixed strategy is a probability distribution over the set of actions. A mixed-strategy Nash equilibrium is a mixed-strategy action profile in which all players maximize their expected payoff given others' mixed strategy. 12

N

Nash equilibrium A Nash equilibrium is a profile of strategies — one strategy for each player — each of which is a best response to the strategies of the other players. 11

Nice tit for tat *Nice tit for tat* is the following strategy in a repeated Prisoners' Dilemma Game: cooperate in the first period (hence "nice") and in successive periods play what the other player did in the previous period. 225

Non-cooperative game A non-cooperative game is a strategic interaction in which the players' choice of a strategy is not subject to a binding (enforceable) agreement. 9

O

Optimal contract A contract is said to be optimal if the one or more Nash equilibria of a game played non-cooperatively under this contract are Pareto-efficient. 48

Other-regarding preferences In choosing which action to take, a person with other-regarding preferences (including altruism and inequality aversion as well as envy, spite, and hostility towards others) takes account of the effect of their choice on the states experienced by others as well as themselves. 26

P

Pairwise stable network A *pairwise stable* network is a stationary state of the given network formation process, which means that no member would be better off by cutting any existing link, nor would both members of any pair of members benefit from forming a new link. 204

Pareto-improving lens The set of allocations that are (at least weakly) Pareto-superior to the fallback options of the players is the Pareto-improving lens. 50

Participation constraint A participation constraint is an expression giving the minimal conditions under which an actor will voluntarily participate in an exchange or other economic interaction. 83

Path A path is a sequence of edges that connect a sequence of nodes, such that all nodes are distinct. 16

Power Agent B has power over A if, by imposing or threatening to impose sanctions on A, B is capable of affecting A's actions in ways that advance B's interests, while A lacks this capacity with respect to B. 143

Preferences Preferences are evaluations of outcomes of one's actions that provide reasons for taking one course of action over another. 24

Prisoner's Dilemma Game A Prisoners' Dilemma is a 2×2 social interaction in which there is a unique Nash equilibrium (that is also a dominant strategy equilibrium), but there is another outcome that gives a higher payoff to both players (and also a higher total sum of payoffs than any other outcome), so that the Nash equilibrium is not Pareto-efficient. 10

Public good A public good generates benefits that are non-rival and non-excludable. 36

R

Reciprocal preferences A person with reciprocal preferences places a positive value on the payoffs of others who they believe to be generous or to have upheld other social norms, and a negative value on the payoffs of those who they believe to have treated others badly. A person with reciprocal preferences, as a result, may help others who uphold social norms and punish those who violate norms, even at a cost to themselves. 25

Risk The term risk is conventionally used in economics to describe situations in which payoffs depend on contingencies and the probabilities of each contingency occurring are known. Risk may be compared to uncertainty, which describes situations where the decision maker does not know and cannot learn the probabilities of future events affecting their payoffs. 185

Risk aversion A risk-averse person will choose a certain outcome valued at x over a lottery whose expected value is greater than x. 185

Risk neutrality A risk neutral person is indifferent between receiving x dollars with certainty and playing an uncertain lottery with the same expected value. A risk neutral person is not risk averse. 118

Risk-dominant strategy The risk-dominant strategy in a 2×2 game is the strategy that would maximize the player's expected payoffs if the other's strategy choices were equally likely. 11

Rival A good is rival if one person's use of the good reduces the availability of the good to others. 36

S

Segmentation In evolutionary modeling, a *segmented* population is one in which the likelihood of any two individuals interacting is affected by the structure of the population into sub-populations within which interactions are more likely than would occur by chance (and between which, less likely). Also termed *assortation*. 226

Short side of a market The short side of a non-clearing market is the side (either demand or supply) on which the number of desired transactions is least. 254

Social multiplier The social multiplier measures the indirect effects of some exogenous change, in which an individual's action ($a_i(s)$) is affected not only by the exogenous variations in some parameter (s) but also by the actions taken by others ($a_{-i}(s)$) in response to variations in s. 34

Social planner The social planner is a fictive individual who designs incentives, constraints, and other ways of affecting people's behavior such that their non-cooperative interactions will result in some socially desirable property, such as an allocation that is Pareto-efficient or that maximizes the sum of individuals' welfare. 28

Star A *star* over n nodes is a network where one node is connected to all other $n - 1$ nodes, which are not connected among themselves. 204

State- (or situation-)dependent preferences If a person's valuation of states (outcomes) depends on the state or situation which the person is currently experiencing, we say that their preferences are state-dependent (or situation-dependent; this latter expression is closer to the way psychologists use the term). 31

Strategy sets A list for each player of every course of action available to them at each point where they must make a choice (including actions that depend on the actions taken by other players, or on chance events). The strategies selected by each of the players — the outcome of the game — is called the strategy profile. 10

Strict Nash equilibrium A Nash equilibrium is strict if a player deviating from it would have strictly lower payoffs, thereby excluding a weak mutual best response as a non-strict Nash equilibrium. 13

T

Take-it-or-leave-it power A player with take-it-or-leave-it (TIOLI) power in a two-person bargaining game can specify the entire terms of the exchange — for example, both the quantity to be exchanged and the price — in an offer, to which the other player responds by choosing to accept ("take it") or reject ("leave it" and as a result receive their fallback option). 52

Technical efficiency An allocation is technically efficient if there is no alternative allocation in which the same output is produced with less of one input and not more of any. 143

Tragedy of the commons The tragedy of the commons is a term used to describe a coordination problem in which self-interested individuals acting non-cooperatively and adopting their dominant strategies deplete a common property resource, lowering the payoffs of all. 52

Transaction specificity An asset is *transaction-specific* to the extent that its value in its current use exceeds the value in its next best alternative. 103

U

Uncompensated external effects Uncompensated external effects (also called externalities, external economies and dis-economies, or simply external effects) are benefit or costs experienced by others as the result of an action taken by some individual. 60

V

Verifiable information Information that can be used in legal proceedings to enforce a contract or other agreement is termed verifiable information. 123

Index

An italic page number indicates the location of the definition of the term in the text (see also the glossary).

About the Team

Alessandra Tosi was the managing editor for this book.

Sophia Bursey and Adèle Kreager proof-read this manuscript.

Jeevanjot Kaur Nagpal designed the cover. The cover was produced in InDesign using the Fontin font.

The author typeset the book in LaTeX and compiled the index.

Jeremy Bowman produced the PDF, paperback and hardback editions.

Hannah Shakespeare was in charge of marketing.

This book was peer-reviewed by Sofia Izquierdo Sanchez, and an anonymous referee. Experts in their field, these readers give their time freely to help ensure the academic rigour of our books. We are grateful for their generous and invaluable contributions.

www.ingramcontent.com/pod-product-compliance
Lightning Source LLC
Chambersburg PA
CBHW042022230326
41598CB00085B/7432